PATERNOSTER BIBLICAL MONOGRAPHS

Paul and Conflict Resolution

An Exegetical Study of Paul's Apostolic Paradigm

in 1 Corinthians 9

PATERNOSTER BIBLICAL MONOGRAPHS

A complete listing of all titles in this series and Paternoster Theological Monograph
will be found at the close of this book.

PATERNOSTER BIBLICAL MONOGRAPHS

Paul and Conflict Resolution

An Exegetical Study of Paul's Apostolic Paradigm in 1 Corinthians 9

Robinson Butarbutar

Wipf & Stock
PUBLISHERS
Eugene, Oregon

Wipf and Stock Publishers
199 W 8th Ave, Suite 3
Eugene, OR 97401

Paul and Conflict Resolution
An Exegetical Study of Paul's Apostolic Paradigm in 1 Corinthians 9
By Butarbutar, Robinson
Copyright©2007 Paternoster
ISBN 13: 978-1-55635-479-3
ISBN 10: 1-55635-479-7
Publication date 5/18/2007
Previously published by Paternoster, 2007

This Edition Published by Wipf and Stock Publishers by arrangement with Paternoster

Paternoster
9 Holdom Avenue
Bletchley
Milton Keyes, MK1 1QR
Great Britain

PATERNOSTER BIBLICAL MONOGRAPHS

Series Preface

One of the major objectives of Paternoster is to serve biblical scholarship by providing a channel for the publication of theses and other monographs of high quality at affordable prices. Paternoster stands within the broad evangelical tradition of Christianity. Our authors would describe themselves as Christians who recognise the authority of the Bible, maintain the centrality of the gospel message and assent to the classical credal statements of Christian belief. There is diversity within this constituency; advances in scholarship are possible only if there is freedom for frank debate on controversial issues and for the publication of new and sometimes provocative proposals. What is offered in this series is the best of writing by committed Christians who are concerned to develop well-founded biblical scholarship in a spirit of loyalty to the historic faith.

Series Editors

I. Howard Marshall, Honorary Research Professor of New Testament, University of Aberdeen, Scotland, UK

Richard J. Bauckham, Professor of New Testament Studies and Bishop Wardlaw Professor, University of St Andrews, Scotland, UK

Craig Blomberg, Distinguished Professor of New Testament, Denver Seminary, Colorado, USA

Robert P. Gordon, Regius Professor of Hebrew, University of Cambridge, UK

Tremper Longman III, Robert H. Gundry Professor and Chair of the Department of Biblical Studies, Westmont College, Santa Barbara, California, USA

I dedicate this work to my late father, J. Butarbutar, my mother, Mrs. Butarbutar, my wife, Ms Srimiaty Rayani Simatupang, my children, Martin and Melanchthon Bonifacio, and my spiritual mother and benefactor, Margery Batterbee.

Contents

Preface	xiii
Acknowledgements	xv
Abbreviations	xvii

Chapter 1

Introduction — 1

1.1 Objectives and Procedures — 1
1.2 Preliminary Statements — 2
1.2.1 *What is Paul Doing in 1 Corinthians 8:1-11:1? Mediating in a Dispute* — 2
1.2.2 *On the Nature of 1 Corinthians 9: A Defended Paradigm* — 9
1.3 Methodology — 10

Chapter 2

The Interpretative Context of 1 Corinthians 9 — 12

2.1 What Triggered the Emergence of the Corinthian Dispute over εἰδωλοθύτων? — 12
2.1.1 *Is Paul to be Blamed?* — 15
2.1.2 *Are Foreign Teachings to be Blamed?* — 22
    a. The Influence of Judaism — 22
    b. The Influence of Gnosticism — 32
    c. The Influence of the 'Over-Realized Eschatology' — 34
    d. The Influence of Epicureanism — 35
2.1.3 *Internal Dispute* — 37
    a. Between the Rich and the Poor (?) — 37
    b. Drawing Boundary Lines: A Proposal — 53

2.2	The Location of εἰδωλοθύτων: Determining the Historical Context	61
2.3	Literary Context: Paul's Unified Arguments	84
2.3.1	*The Unity of 1 Corinthians 8:1-11:1*	84
2.3.2	*The Overall Interpretation of 1 Corinthians 8:1-11:1*	88
2.4	Some Concluding Remarks	103

Chapter 3
Understanding Paul's Apostolic Paradigm
(1 Corinthians 9) — **105**

3.1	Defending the Ground for the Paradigm: 1 Corinthians 9:1-3	105
3.1.1	*Introductory Remarks*	105
3.1.2	*The Enigma of 1 Corinthians 9:3: What Is Examined?*	107
3.1.3	*The Use of the Defended Apostolic Practice as a Paradigm*	110
3.1.4	*Identifying Paul's Examiners: An Intractable Task*	112
3.2	The First Paradigm: Forgoing ἐξουσία (1 Corinthians 9:4-18)	117
3.2.1	*Introductory Remarks*	117
3.2.2	*The Importance of Corinthians' ἐξουσία in Paul's Eyes*	117
3.2.3	*The Meaning of ἐξουσία in 1 Corinthians 8:9-9:18*	121
3.2.4	*The Historical Context of Corinthians' ἐξουσία*	124
3.2.5	*Paul's Renunciation of his ἐξουσία (1 Corinthians 9:4-18): The Paradigm*	128
3.3	The Second Paradigm: Self-enslavement (1 Corinthians 9:19-23)	167
3.3.1	*Review of Scholarship*	167
3.3.2	*The Historical Context of Paul's Readers in Relation to 1 Corinthians 9:19*	172
3.3.3	*The Purpose of Paul's Discourse*	176

3.3.4	*Paul's Elaboration of His Self-enslavement: A Historical Narration*	178
3.3.5	*Historical Reconstruction of Paul's Accommodation in Corinth*	189
3.4	The Third Paradigm: The Importance of Self-control (1 Corinthians 9:24-27)	192
3.5	Concluding Remarks	196

Chapter 4
Some Implications — 200

4.1	On the Emergence of the Dispute over εἰδωλοθύτων and the Unity of Paul's Discourse in 1 Corinthians 8:1-11:1	200
4.2	On the Question of Paul's Defence	204
4.3	On the Use of Paul's Refusal to Live off the Gospel as a Paradigm	206

Chapter 5
1 Corinthians 9 and the Solution of the Crisis of the HKBP: A Case Study — 214

5.1	Introductory Remarks	214
5.2	Sustained Attempts to Oust the Top Leadership of the Church	215
5.3	Dispute Over the Intervention of the Military Decree	218
5.3.1	*The Justification for the Support of the Military Decree*	218
5.3.2	*The Justification for the Opposition of the Military Decree*	222
5.4	The Effect of the Disagreement over the Military Decree	226
5.5	Efforts of Reconciliation: The Relevance of 1 Corinthians 9	227
5.5.1	*Failure after Failure*	228
5.5.2	*Re-united at Last: A Joint Synod*	230

5.6	Concluding Remarks	233
	Dramatis Personae	234

Chapter 6
Conclusions — **236**

Bibliography — **241**

Author Index — **264**

Scripture Index — **270**

Preface

In 1996 I was commissioned by the leadership of my church, the Batak Christian Protestant Church (Huria Kristen Batak Protestant), to undertake doctoral studies at Trinity Theological College, Singapore with a scholarship from the United Evangelical Mission (UEM). At that time the church was experiencing a crisis caused by military/state intervention into the internal affairs of the church. This crisis, which began in 1993 and came to an end in 1998, may be said to be the most serious crisis experienced by church members and workers of the HKBP, who had to make a personal and faith decision on whether to accept or to resist the intervention of the state into the internal affairs of the church. In making the decision one had to consider the consequences that would follow. The state did not tolerate any opposition to its intervention through a military decree which appointed new leadership for the church. Immediately after this decree was issued, the church was divided into three factions: one opposing the decree, another accepting it, and still another remaining neutral. The effect of the division was such that even now, long after the end of the crisis, efforts for reconcilition within the church aimed at healing wounds and restoring relationships have not been very successful.

I therefore began my doctoral studies with the question of how the earliest Christians in the New Testament, especially as shown in communication and correspondence with their leaders, dealt with the tendency towards and the reality of divisions caused by their pluralistic backgrounds. In my research I focused on the correspondence between Paul and his Corinthian converts which, to me, is an attempt on the part of Paul to help the Corinthian Christians deal with their differences in various matters, including the question of whether or not food offered to idols can be eaten (1 Corinthians 8-10). Since I submitted my dissertation in March 1999 I have updated it with reference to recent publications on the issue, by undertaking further research at Tyndale House, Cambridge in 2003 and at Trinity Theological College, Singapore in 2005. My research shows that the issue of food offered to idols was the most divisive for the Corinthian Christians.

This book is the result of my research into 1 Corinthians 9 in particular. It argues that 1 Corinthians 8-10 show an art of conflict resolution on the part of Paul. He encourages those who want to eat food offered to idols to refrain from doing so, without negating their sound theological arguments concerning their right to eat, yet without justifying the views of those who refuse to eat. What Paul writes in 1 Corinthians 9 is crucial in this regard because he uses his own example of renouncing his apostolic right to financial support to convince one party in the dispute not to eat food offered to idols. He has to do so because those who want to eat food offered to idols justify their desire on the basis of theological arguments and civic rights.

Thus 1 Corinthians 9 has a clear message for conflict resolution today in the church and also in society. What is most important is not solid theological and civic arguments, but the willingness to renounce one's rights for the sake of others. This, according to Paul, is based on the example of Christ. It is this renouncement of rights that Paul asked the Corinthian Christians to imitate in their dispute. Further, the present book shows that, without the willingess of the parties in the HKBP crisis to forgo their arguments for the sake of others, the crisis would not have been solved in 1998.

Dispute and conflict within a church is nothing new in the history of the church. The nature, intensity and effect of the conflict vary from place to place and era to era. But dispute and conflict within a church have more often than not led to disunity because of the unwillingness of the parties involved to prioritize the welfare of others. It is high time for churches today to imitate the example of Christ, who put first the welfare of those he loved. It is only by so doing that the church in our time will be in a position to help others in society resolve numerous conflicts that have taken many lives.

October 2006
Medan, North Sumatra
Indonesia.

Acknowledgements

This book, which is the result of my doctoral studies in 1996-1999 under South East Asia Graduate School of Theology, would not have come into existence without the support of many. It is therefore my privilege to give thanks to the following: Prof. Dr. W.J. Dumbrell, my Chief-Supervisor, for his prompt response to my written work and for his perceptive advice in my research from the early stage until the completion of my dissertation. Dr. Tan Kim-Huat, my Co-Supervisor and the Registrar of Postgraduate School of Trinity Theological College, whose meticulous criticisms and numerous constructive comments on my work from the time when I was doing my course-work until the completion of my dissertation, helped me to articulate my thought clearer than might have been otherwise. Dr. Yeow Choo Lak, the Area Director of the South East Asia Graduate School of Theology, for making sure that I would get proper supervision at the Trinity Theological College even before I started my studies. The Librarian of Trinity Theological College, Ms. Lau Jen Sin, and her staff for giving me the privilege of occupying one desk at the Trinity Theological College Library and, sometimes without my knowledge, for ordering books related to my area of research. Dr. Bruce W. Winter, the Warden of Tyndale House, Cambridge, for not only granting me the privilege of using the facilities of this excellent library in the period of January-June 1998 and May-July 2003, but also for his willingness, amidst his hectic schedule, to spend time with me in his study room and at a breakfast table discussing my research interest. Canon Dr. John Chew, former Principal of Trinity Theological College and now Archbishop of Anglican Church in South East Asia, who always supported my research. In fact, it was the conversation I had with him at the OMF-Mission House, Jakarta, in 1994, that made me decide to do my research at Trinity Theological College, Singapore. Ms. Kay Maria Jones, the Secretary of St. Peter's Hall Trinity College where I stayed for more than two years, who was always willing to offer her proofreading assistance. The Warden of St. Peter's Hall, Rev. Soon Soo Kee, his wife and my fellow residents of this hall who were always supportive of my research. The Batak Christian Protestant Church (HKBP) which, under the leadership of the Rt. Rev. D. Dr. S.A.E. Nababan LLD (1987-1998), granted me a study leave since July 1996. Rev. Dr. S. Zollner who, as the Director of the Department of Recruitment and Scholarship of the United Evangelical Mission (UEM) based in Wuppertal, Germany, faithfully provided all the funds needed for my studies. Friends at St. Martin's Church, Cambridge, in particular Ms. Margery Batterbee whose additional financial support enabled me to carry out my research in Cambridge in February-July 1998 and then in May-July 2003 with the presence of my family. Dr. D.L. Baker, my teacher during my undergraduate studies at the HKBP-Theological Seminary, Pematangsiantar, who motivated me to undertake my research for the benefit of the church in Indonesia in the future, and to publish its result for wider usage. My pastor colleagues (Gomar Gultom, Saut H. Sirait, Ramlan Hutahaean, Ladestam Sinaga and others) who encouraged me to pursue my studies even at a time when the church was in need of my ministry. My wife, Srimiaty Rayani Simatupang who, despite her heavy task of bringing up our children, Martin Butarbutar and Melanchthon Butarbutar, was always willing to become a listening ear to my research questions and discoveries. She deserves more than any thanks I could possibly offer here. My parents, especially my late father, J. Butarbutar, who in his retiring age could not enjoy the privilege of receiving support from his son because of my study, and who passed away while I was doing my course-work. I dedicate this work to them.

Since 2003 I have made many promises to Paternoster Press to submit the final text, but this has been delayed due to my hectic work schedule as the Asia Regional Coordinator of the United Evangelical Mission. Therefore I would like to thank Mr. Jeremy Mudditt and Dr. Anthony Cross for their assistance in helping me to conform to the Paternoster Press format for publication, and for their patience in waiting for the final manuscript. I would like also to express my gratitude to Dr. Tan Kim-Huat, Prof. Anthony Thiselton, and Dr. David L. Baker for their commendation of this book.

Abbreviations

ABSA	*Annual of the British School at Athens.*
AJA	*American Journal of Archaeology.*
ANRW	*Aufstieg und Niedergang der römischen Welt.*
AS	*Ancient Society.*
ATR	*Anglican Theological Review.*
Bib	*Biblica.*
BA	*Biblical Archaeologist.*
BAR	*Biblical Archaeology Review.*
BICS	*Bulletin of the Institute of Classical Studies .*
BJRL	*Bulletin of the John Rylands Library.*
BMCR	*Bryn Mawr Classical Review.*
BR	*Biblical Review.*
BT	*The Bible Translator.*
BZ	*Biblische Zeitschrift.*
CBQ	*Catholic Biblical Quarterly.*
CBR	*Current in Biblical Research.*
CQ	*Classical Quarterly.*
CP	*Classical Philology.*
CR	*The Classical Review.*
CSCA	*California Studies in Classical Antiquity.*
EA	*Ex Auditu.*
Ev.Q	*Evangelical Quarterly.*
Exp.Tim	*Expository Times.*
ET	*English Translation*
FF	*Food and Foodways.*
GRBS	*Greek, Roman and Byzantine Studies.*
GTJ	*Grace Theological Journal.*
HBT	*Horizons in Biblical Theology.*
HTR	*Harvard Theological Review.*
Int	*Interchange.*
JAAR	*Journal of the American Academy of Religion.*
JAC	*Jahrbuch für Antike und Christentum.*
JECS	*Journal of Early Christian Studies.*
JBL	*Journal of Biblical Literature.*
JD	*Jian Diao.*
JETS	*Journal of the Evangelical Theological Society.*
JRA	*Journal of Roman Archaeology.*
JRH	*Journal of Religious History.*
JSNT	*Journal for the Study of the New Testament.*
JRS	*Journal of Roman Studies.*
JTS	*Journal of Theological Studies.*

NovT	*Novum Testamentum.*
NTS	*New Testament Studies.*
Phil	*Philologus.*
R	*Religion.*
RB	*Revue Biblique.*
RE	*Review and Expositor.*
ST	*Studia Theologica.*
TAPA	*Transactions of the American Philological Association.*
TJ	*Trinity Journal.*
TynBul	*Tyndale Bulletin.*
Phil	*Philologus.*
VC	*Vigiliae Christianae*
ZNW	*Zeitschrift für die Neutestamentliche Wissenschaft.*

Chapter 1

Introduction

1.1 Objectives and Procedures

The objectives of this book are two-fold. First, by interpreting 1 Corinthians 9 in its proper context, it aims to establish the reason Paul insists on making his apostolic practice, being examined though it is by some people (1 Cor. 9:3), an example to be imitated by some Corinthian Christians in their internal dispute over the issue of food offered to idols. It will be argued that Paul uses his apostolic practice of renouncing his right to financial support for the sake of the gospel in order to discourage some Corinthian Christians from insisting on using their right (ἐξουσία, 8:9) to eat food offered to idols (8:9-13). As we look closely at Paul's discourse in 1 Corinthians 9, we will discover that Paul's forgoing of his right to financial support in his missionary work was not caused by his negative view of the practice of receiving support by other missionaries, nor by his attempt to be different from the paid philosophers of the day, nor by his desire not to be put within the possible various framework of giving culture of his converts, as has been proposed by a number of scholars – significant though they are for understanding Paul's contemporaries and the world of his readers - but purely because of how he saw the gospel of Jesus Christ, namely he saw it as being free of charge. This is the determining factor.

Such a usage is in the present context very significant mainly because some Corinthian Christians justify their right to eat food offered to idols with various strong reasons, namely (a) a theological knowledge of the monotheistic God and non-existence of idols (8:4-6) and its impact on the neutrality of food before God (8:8); (b) their freedom status and (c) their belief in the aphoristic saying that 'everything is permitted' (10:23 cf. 6:12). Paul does it not because he is in conflict with them or disagrees with the legality of their right and the reasons used to strengthen it. Rather, it is because of his motivation to protect their counterparts in the dispute over the issue, the weak, and to prevent them from destroying themselves. 1 Corinthians 9 shows Paul's art of conflict resolution.

Secondly, this book seeks to emphasize that Paul's insistence on using his defended apostolic example of renouncing his right to financial support must be seen as a ground for establishing the legacy of such an example in addressing the dispute over food offered to idols, then in the first century AD and now in our attempt to bring to an end any dispute, even of a different kind or nature, within the church today.

To achieve those objectives, this book conducts the following procedures. After presenting preliminary statements on the nature of Paul's discourse (1 Cor 8:1 - 11:1) and the function of 1 Corinthians 9 therein in section 1.2, and discussing the methodology of our interpretation in section 1.3, it establishes the interpretative historical and literary context of 1 Corinthians 9 in chapter 2. The interpretation of 1 Corinthians 9 will then be carried out in chapter 3.

It will be made clear in chapter 2 that Paul is facing a church which was in dispute over the question of food offered to idols. Their dispute over the issue, which was otherwise a normal issue for Christians turning from pagan religions, was occasioned by the desire of their contemporaries to propagate the Imperial cult aimed at securing the favour of the Roman authorities toward the city. Those who wanted to participate in the cult justified their position with their right, and this right was supported by some arguments. However, others refused to participate for fear of having contact with idols. Since the former were likely to influence the latter, we argue that Paul's discourse in 1 Corinthians 8:1 - 11:1 is aimed at discouraging them from insisting on using their right to eat food offered to idols without negating their arguments nor validating their counterparts' views.

It is for this purpose that 1 Corinthians 9 has an important function, as we will make clear in chapter 3. By reading 1 Corinthians 9 in this way, we will be able to draw some major implications in chapter 4 on various unresolved issues in Corinthian studies, such as the coherence of Paul's response in 1 Corinthians 8:1 - 11:1, the connection between 1 Corinthians 9 and 1 Corinthians 1-4, and the reason why the issue of financial support reappears in 2 Corinthians. Moreover, what Paul proposes in 1 Corinthians 9 and how he does it has major implications not only for missionary work, but also and more importantly, on how we may solve any dispute within the church today. Along this line, we will present in chapter 5 the solution of the crisis of the Batak Christian Protestant Church in Indonesia as an example of the importance of following Paul's paradigm as described in 1 Corinthians 9 in solving various issues that have rocked the church worldwide. A general conclusion will be drawn in chapter 6.

1.2 Preliminary Statements

1.2.1 What is Paul Doing in 1 Corinthians 8:1 - 11:1? Mediating in a Dispute

The main question that one must ask when reading 1 Corinthians 8:1 - 11:1 is the following: Is Paul trying to defend himself against his readers, or rather, is he trying to mediate in a dispute among his readers over the issue of food offered to idols? Some have argued that the former is the case. Various attempts have therefore been made to explain the reasons why the whole Corinthian Church opposed him on the issue. Under the quest for Paul's opponents in 1 Corinthians, the influence of foreign teachings such as Judaizing activity, Gnosticism, Philonic Wisdom, realized eschatology and Epicureanism[1] has been blamed for the opposition. Some scholars have even argued that it was Paul himself who caused their opposition. Either his previous letter (5:9-13), which is thought to have prohibited his converts from eating food offered to idols in order to obtain a legitimation of his Gentile mission from the leadership of the Jerusalem church,[2] or his own constant rejection of food offered to idols,[3] have been proposed to be the reasons for their opposition. Those who argue for the emergence of the issue of food offered to idols as being occasioned by the previous letter will conclude that Paul is criticized by Corinthian Christians for being inconsistent on the matter of food offered to idols. They argue that when he was in Corinth Paul ate it, but later prohibited his converts from eating it. Consequently, the mentioning of the weak in 1 Corinthians 8:7 is said to be Paul's hypothetical creation.[4] Those unwilling to accept the view that Paul changed his attitude towards food offered to idols but still regard him as the cause of the problem propose a different explanation for the conflict. P.D. Gooch, for instance, argues that Paul never ate food offered to idols and that the cause of the Corinthian Christians' opposition was Paul's own constant conscious rejection of it. The reason he did not prohibit them from eating it while he was in Corinth was because he did not want to confuse his prospective converts. Paul prohibited them only after their entrance into the community.[5] Furthermore, it is argued that those who accused Paul of being inconsistent with regard to food offered to idols were the same as those who criticized his apostolic status and practice (9:3).[6] In other words, they are those who examined him for rejecting their offer of monetary gift and for limiting their freedom (6:12).[7] As a corollary, they are thought to be the same people as those who aligned with the leading figures other than

---

1 See section 2.1 below for a detailed presentation of these foreign teachings.
2 J.C. Hurd, *The Origin of 1 Corinthians* (New York: Seabury, 1965) 225-26; G.D. Fee, "II Corinthians VI. 14-VII.1 and Food Offered to Idols" in *NTS* 23 (1977) 140-61, esp. 150-51; Pandang Yamsat, "The Ekklesia as Partnership: Paul and Threats to Koinonia in 1 Corinthians." Unpublished PhD. Thesis (Sheffield University, December 1992) 204-06, 211, 227-229.
3 P.D. Gooch, *Dangerous Food. 1 Corinthians 8-10 in its Context* (Waterloo: WLUP, 1993) 86, 94-95, 97, 140-143.
4 Hurd, *The Origin*, 225-26; Yamsat, "Partnership," 227-28.
5 Gooch, *Dangerous Food,* 72, 142-143.
6 G.D. Fee, *The First Epistle to the Corinthians.* NIC (Grand Rapids: Eerdmans, 1987) 393; C.K. Barrett, *The First Epistle to the Corinthians* (New York/Evanston: Harper and Row, 1968) 200.
7 P. Marshall, *Enmity in Corinth: Social Conventions in Paul's Relations with the Corinthians* (Tübingen: J.C.B. Mohr, 1987) 215-16, 284.

Paul (1:12, 3:4,22), those who judge him (4:3-4), who make a big fuss about his failure to come to Corinth (4:18-19) and, therefore, want Apollos to revisit the city (16:12).

However, the view that Paul is facing a united view on the part of his readers begs the question, simply because 1 Corinthians itself does not lend support to this picture. Their leadership alignment itself (1:12 - 4:21) indicates the existence of divisions among themselves. It is therefore unlikely that within such a divided community all members would oppose Paul on individual issues such as food offered to idols. There is reason to suggest that their divisions were not unrelated to the fact that, as they clustered around the patronage of different households (such as Stephanas, Titius Justus, Gaius, Prisca and Aquila and Phoebe, 1 Cor. 1:11,14-16, 16:15-18; Rom. 16:1-2,23), they met as a whole for the special purpose such as the celebration of the Lord's Supper *only* occasionally (11:18a). Apart from this occasional meeting, each household had its own regular meeting.[8] In such an atmosphere, local loyalties and rivalries were bound to happen.[9] The existence of division among Corinthian Christians must be taken into account in our reconstruction of the emergence of the issue of food offered to idols, even though the extent of their division is as yet to be determined. Is it just "a matter of diverse tendencies" which wrongly makes use of the names of the apostles, as proposed by R.P. Martin?[10] Or is it like the political sphere in which factions exist, as suggested by L.L. Welborn[11]

---

8 Cf. F.V. Filson, "The Significance of the Early House Churches" in *JBL* 58 (1939) 105-12, esp. 110: "The existence of several house churches in one city goes far to explain the tendency to party strife." Also E.A. Judge, *The Social Pattern of the Christian Groups in the First Century. Some Prolegomena to the Study of New Testament Ideas of Social Obligation* (London: TP, 1960) 37.

9 See G.W. Clarke, "The Origins and Spread of Christianity" in A.K. Bowmann et al., (eds.), *The Cambridge Ancient History*. 2nd ed. Vol. X, *The Augustan Empire 43 BC-AD 69* (Cambridge: CUP, 1996) 848-72, esp. 861.

10 R.P. Martin, *New Testament Foundations: A Guide for Christian Students* (Exeter: Paternoster, 1978) 186.

11 L.L. Welborn, "On the Discord in Corinth: 1 Corinthians 1-4 and Ancient Politics" in *JBL* 106 (1987) 85-111, esp. 88, 98-100, 107-08, argues that since Paul's language in 1 Corinthians 1-4 is similar to the language of political topoi used to characterise conflicts within the city-states by Graeco-Roman historians to prevent *stasis* (= strife), what is faced by Paul is one of parties struggling for power in the community rather than a theological controversy. The condition described in 1 Corinthians 1 - 4 is similar in nature with how the Greco-Roman historians and rhetors characterised conflicts within the city states. The instigators of the factions were the rich who were trying to exert their influence on the new community by the use of wealth, patron-client system and religious knowledge.

and M.M. Mitchell?[12] Or is it just "divisions, cliques, bickerings" among themselves over wisdom, teachers of wisdom and themselves being wise, as argued by J. Munck,[13] or more serious than that?[14] Or is Paul addressing both factionalism and "a deeper problem of which divisions are a manifestation, 'a far reaching failure in the community members' own-estimation, with [their] exaggerated pretensions to knowledge (3:18-19) and faulty regard or denigration of others (4:6-7)," as suggested by B. Fiore?[15]

In fact, it may be argued that the Corinthian Christians were also divided along issue lines (1 Cor. 7-16). This can clearly be seen not only on the issue of marriage, sex, circumcision, slavery (1 Cor. 7), food offered to idols (1 Cor. 8:1 - 11:1), head-covering (1 Cor. 11:2-16), the gifts of the Spirit (1 Cor. 12-14), but probably also on the resurrection of the dead. While some questioned the rationality of the bodily resurrection of the dead (1 Cor. 15:12), others practiced baptism on behalf of the dead (15:29). In fact, the extent of their unity was such that two of their members were involved in litigation on small matter (1 Cor. 6:1-11)[16] and that even in the

---

12 M.M. Mitchell, *Paul and the Rhetoric of Reconciliation: An Exegetical Investigation of the Language and Composition of 1 Corinthians* (Louisville: Westminster/John Knox Press, 1991) 302. Developing Welborn's view, Mitchell examines the whole letter of 1 Corinthians from the perspective of a deliberative rhetorical language of a political topoi. She has come to the conclusion that Paul's argument is not to preserve but create unity among the factious Corinthians. Paul is not siding with or confronting a particular party but against factionalism itself.

13 J. Munck, "The Church Without Factions. Studies in 1 Corinthians 1-4" in *Paul and the Salvation of Mankind* (London: SCM, 1959) 135-167.

14 N.A. Dahl, "Paulus apostel og menigheten i Korinth (1 Kor. 1-4)" in Norsk Teologist Tidsskrit (1953) 1-23, (ET) "Paul and the Church at Corinth according to 1 Corinthians 1-4" in W.R. Farmer et al., (eds.), *Christian History and Interpretation. Studies Presented to John Knox* (Cambridge: CUP, 1967) 313-35, See N. Hyldahl, "The Corinthian 'Parties' and the Corinthian Crisis" in *ST* 45 (1991) 19-32, esp. 21-26, here 19. Similarly, J.D.G Dunn, *1 Corinthians* (Sheffield: SAP, 1995) 32-33; also W. Baird, "One Against Another: Intra-Church Conflict in 1 Corinthians" in ET. Fortna and Beverly R. Gaventa (eds.), *The Conversation Continues. Studies in Paul and John in honor of J. Louis Martyn* (Nashville: AP, 1990) 116-36, esp. 116 whose review of the study of the Corinthian opponents has come up with the same conclusion, namely that the Corinthians were having an internal-conflict and Paul is against factionalism and the arrogance of the Corinthians which fostered it; also Rollin Ramsaran, *Liberating Words: Paul's Use of Rhetorical Maxims in 1 Corinthians 1-10* (Pennsylvania: TPI, 1996) 30.

15 B. Fiore, "'Covert Allusion' in 1 Corinthians 1-4" in *CBQ* 47 (1985) 85-102, esp. 86-87, 101.

16 If it is true that, as argued by Helen Parkins, "The 'consumer city' domesticated? The Roman city in élite economic strategies" in Helen M. Parkins (ed.), *Roman Urbanism Beyond the Consumer City* (London, New York: Routledge, 1997) 82-111 esp. 88-89, the urban economy of Roman city was "inextricably bound up with the

celebration of the Lord's Supper they had divisions (1 Cor. 11:17-34).[17] It is small wonder that they failed to collect the money for the saints in Jerusalem (1 Cor. 16:14). The extent of their division was such that Paul considered recommending Stephanas and his people to be their local leaders as one preferable practical solution to their immediate need for local leadership to prevent further disunity of the church (1 Cor. 16:15-18). The policy of sending delegates such as Timothy to remind the Corinthians of his ways (4:17; 16:10), which was meant to maintain communication,[18] was no longer adequate.

Scholars coming from the perspective of the view that Corinthian Christians were socially stratified would argue for the existence of conflicting views among Corinthian Christians on the issue of food offered to idols. They argue that the dispute is between the strong and the weak, the rich and the poor. This has been initiated by G. Theissen[19] and developed by some scholars such as D.B. Martin[20] and D.G. Horrell, to mention just a few.[21] In this light, Paul is seen to be in favour of the poor by giving his renunciation as an example.

However, the view that the issue in 1 Corinthians 8:1 - 11:1 is between the rich and the poor is not supported by the text. Even if we follow Theissen's thesis, it is still implausible to argue that the poor are therefore

---

households of élite families...comprising many mini-economies: the economies of individual households" (90-92), the litigation of civic case involving two Roman Corinthian Christians was not surprising. For such an atmosphere provided a fertile ground for competition between the households in terms of status.

17 The phrase ἀκούω σχίσματα ἐν ὑμῖν ὑπάρχειν καὶ μέρος τι πιστεύω in 11:18, which has always been rendered as "I hear that there are divisions among you and 'I partly believe it,'" seems to contradict what Paul has strongly combated in 1 Cor 1:10-4:21. Hence, J. Munck "The Church" argues there were no factions in the church. There were only divisions, cliques and bickerings. More serious impact of such a rendering is the view that 1 Corinthians 11:17-34 belongs to a different time (see W. Schmithals, *Gnosticism in Corinth. An Investigation of the Letters to the Corinthians* [Nashville: AP, 1971] 90). However, B.W. Winter, "Appendix. 'I Partly Believe It' or 'I Believe a Certain Report' in *After Paul Left Corinth: The Influence of Secular Ethics and Social Change* (Grand Rapids: Eerdmans, 2001) 159-63, refutes such a translation of 11:18. He instead translates the phrase 'καὶ μέρος τι πιστεύω' as 'I believe certain report,' thus arguing for the confirmation of the preceding phrase 'I hear that there are divisions among you.'

18 W.A. Meeks, *The First Urban Christians: The Social World of the Apostle Paul* (New Haven and London: YUP, 1983) 76.

19 G. Theissen, *The Social Setting of Pauline Christianity* (Edinburgh: T and T Clark, 1982) 126-128.

20 D.B. Martin, *The Corinthian Body* (New Haven and London: YUP, 1995) 56, 58.

21 D.G. Horrell, *The Social Ethos of Pauline Christians: Interests and Ideology in the Corinthian Correspondence from 1 Corinthians to 1 Clement* (Edinburgh: T and T Clark, 1996) 120-23, 199-235, esp. 234.

the only ones who support Paul's apostolic status and practice of renouncing his right to financial support, given the likelihood that, as recognized by Theissen himself, the factionalism addressed by Paul in 1 Corinthians 1:12 - 4:21 is between the high status struggling for power by using the support of their clients.[22] It is not totally unlikely that among those who align themselves with Paul there are some who come from a wealthy background. They might agree with Paul's not accepting financial support. Stephanas, for instance, whom Paul recommends to be one of the local leaders (1 Cor. 15:15-18), might be of this background. Indeed, those baptized by Paul (i.e., Crispus and Gaius and Stephanas) are likely to be of high status (1 Cor. 1:14). Since Paul speaks against even those who align themselves with him on the basis of baptism (1:13-18), it is likely also that on issues of dispute in 1 Corinthians 7-16 he may address those who might embrace the view which they thought would find support in Paul's teaching.

Therefore, as we shall show in chapter 2, the interpretation of 1 Corinthians 9 will be carried out with the understanding that the dispute among Corinthian Christians over the issue of food offered to idols emerged not because of Paul himself (his past behaviour or teaching), nor by the influence of foreign teachings, nor the socio-economic differences existing between his Corinthian converts. Rather, it was caused by the Corinthian Christians' attempts to draw boundary lines amongst themselves and the people from outside their Christian community. While some wanted to have a totally open relationship with the society, others wanted to have a total disengagement with their contemporaries. In particular, it is also suggested in this book that although the issue of boundary lines was common among first century Christians turning from pagan religions and that the Corinthian case of food offered to idols was quite ordinary (hence the contexts cover also the market and the invitation of an unbeliever, most probably in his house [1 Cor. 10:25 and 28-29]), what made the Corinthian case unique was that their task of drawing the boundary lines coincided with the enthusiasm prevalent among the populace to attend the Isthmian games in which the worship of the imperial cult was practiced.

This suggestion will be supported by a study on the importance of the patron-client relationship in the Corinthian celebration of the Isthmian games and worship of the imperial cult. The Corinthian Christians had to decide whether or not they should go along with the popular mood of the people in attending the games and the imperial cult at which food offered to idols was consumed. As a result, any food associated with idolatry became the subject of contention among Corinthian Christians.

The heart of the matter, therefore, does not seem to be on the food itself or the location of the act of eating or even their theological knowledge of

---

22 Theissen, *Social Setting*, 55-57.

God's existence, idol's non-existence and of the neutrality of food before God. Rather, *it is the grounds on which they eat or not, and on their fears of acting against those grounds.* Some were afraid of acting against their right, their freedom status and their belief in the aphoristic saying that 'everything is permitted.' Others, however, feared idolatry and all its forms. The former justified their fear with theological and popular arguments to insist on exercising their ἐξουσία (right, 1 Cor. 8:9) to eat food offered to idols. We will see that the issue of right was very central among those who wanted to eat food offered to idols. This right was closely related to the nature of the city as a Roman colony where the question of citizenship and privileges therein was very much alive amongst its populace.

It is therefore argued further in chapter 2 that Paul is not defending himself against the whole Corinthian church. Rather, he is trying to unite a church which is in dispute over the issue of food offered to idols.[23] It is within this unifying purpose that Paul's discourse in 1 Corinthians 8:1 - 11:1 must be seen. How he safeguards the unity of the church without ignoring the legitimate view or fear of those involved in the dispute is worthy of investigation. In this light, Paul's answers in 1 Corinthians 8:1 - 11:1 are seen as a unified argument within which 1 Corinthians 9 must be seen. This is against those who have divided 1 Corinthians 8:1 - 11:1 and those who have made too much a distinction between 1 Corinthians 8:1-9:27 and 10:23 - 11:1 on the one hand, and 10:1-22 on the other by emphasizing the difference in places where the act of eating is carried out, as though the ancient people made a sharp distinction between the place and the eating of food that was related to idols or idolatry.

We will argue that, being aware of the intensity of their dispute and the legality of their arguments but, at the same time, being anxious about the danger of idolatry, throughout 1 Corinthians 8:1 - 11:1 Paul employs a very tactful method whereby he attempts to prevent some Corinthian Christians from eating food offered to idols and thereby being involved in idolatry, without negating their right and its justifications. He prevents those who argue that idols do not exist from eating food offered to idols without negating their views, yet in a way that would not encourage those associated with or fearful of idols to think that idols do exist. It is toward

---

23 J. Murphy-O'Connor, "Freedom from the Ghetto (1 Corinthians 8:1-13; 10:23-11:1)" in *RB* 85 (1978) 543-74, here 544, is very certain of the existence of two viewpoints among Paul's readers. He writes: "no evidence contradicts the traditional opinion that there were two groups within the Corinthian church." cf. B.W. Winter, *After Paul Left Corinth: The Influence of Secular Ethics and Social Change* (Grand Rapids: Eerdmans 2001) 1-4, who argues that although having problems over their former teachers, Paul's converts have a consensus about asking Paul over difficult matter because they do not have any apostolic guidance on the issue as yet. At least they are not clear about whether what some of them do is appropriate.

this purpose that we can see the contribution 1 Corinthians 9 within the overall discourse of Paul. In it we see Paul using his apostolic paradigm to support his exhortation already described in 8:9-13. It is only by connecting this chapter with chapter 8 that we can see the coherence of 1 Corinthians 8:1-13 with 10:1-22.

1.2.2 On the Nature of 1 Corinthians 9: A Defended Paradigm

Our thesis on the existence of dispute among Paul's readers and on the unity of 1 Corinthians 8:1 - 11:1 will also enable us to address the question of the function of 1 Corinthians 9, one that has divided scholars. The dispute has been caused by 1 Corinthians 9:3 where the existence of some people who examine Paul is self evident. Some see it as an example, but others regard it as a defence. The former see this chapter in relation to chapter 8.[24] Accordingly, the ἀνακρίνουσίν of 9:3 has not been translated in the present tense but in the future, indicating that the examination is to be seen in the future. However, those who argue that there were some opponents of Paul in Corinth want to see it as a defence. To do so, they tend to separate chapter 9 from its present position, regarding it as a separate defence of his apostleship in a certain context unrelated and tagged to the present context either by Paul himself or by a later interpolator.[25] Various terms are used to describe it. As we shall see, even those who do not want to eject chapter 9 from its present position have difficulties in answering the question of why Paul included it in his discourse of food offered to idols.

I submit the view that within the context of his discourse 1 Corinthians 9 functions primarily as an example. However, due to the existence of some people who have criticized Paul's apostolic status because of his practice of renouncing the right to financial support, which he now uses as an example, and in order to make it credible in the eyes of those whom he asks to forgo their right to eat food offered to idols, 1 Corinthians 9:1-3 reveals that Paul has to defend his apostolic status. This is undoubtedly because there is no reason for Paul to go on explaining his apostolic example to be followed by those who want to exercise their right (8:9) if this example and, correspondingly, his apostolic status are being examined. Indeed, it may be argued that such apostolic example would not have been brought by Paul to his discourse were it not for addressing those who insisted on eating food offered to idols on the basis of their right. Paul would not have had any reason to

---

24 W. Willis, "An Apostolic Apologia? The Form and Function of 1 Cor 9" in *JSNT* 24 (1985) 33-48, esp. 33-38; D.B. Martin, *Slavery As Salvation: The Metaphor of Slavery in Pauline Christianity* (New Haven: YUP, 1990) 77-79.

25 See chapter 2 section 2.3 for various proposals made by scholars regarding the seemingly awkward position of 1 Corinthians 9.

defend it here had there not been any need for him to use it for addressing those who wanted to use their right to eat food offered to idols.

1.3. Methodology

As in all other New Testament studies, the question of method is increasingly very dominant, and in terms of achieving the goal of interpretation of the text, is in fact very determinative. This is particularly so in establishing the nature of the problems addressed by Paul in 1 Corinthians. One's interpretation of 1 Cor 8:1 - 11:1 is determined by his or her understanding of the nature of the problem being addressed. In turn, one's perception of the nature of the problem is determined by his or her methodology. Without neglecting the methodologies current in the studies of 1 Corinthians 9, the author takes the text as the primary consideration in establishing the nature of the problem. The suggestions made by scholars about the nature of the problem will be examined by the text itself which we consider as our primary source. Yet, a socio-historical study of Corinth as a Roman city will also be used to shed some light on what the text indicates. We will employ these two methods not only in investigating the emergence and intensification of the dispute over food offered to idols, but also on our interpretation of 1 Corinthians 8:1 - 11:1, particularly 1 Corinthians 9. We will not follow the two extreme methodologies used so far by scholars in interpreting 1 Corinthians 8:1 - 11:1, namely that of theological/ideological method and sociological one, for both have some pitfalls. Nor will we return to the old methodology, that of etymological study, for it also has some pitfalls.

For instance, in constructing what might be the case with regard to the issue of food offered to idols – whether it was caused by religious or social issues - it is better to be sensitive as much as possible to Paul's own words. If he is silent about the economic notion of the case, we should not try to read it in an economic sense, whatever our view on the economic condition of Corinthian Christians may be. If he does use terms which can be read in an economic sense, we can try to see it in that way, although with great care.

In determining the sociological and religious backgrounds of the participants of the dispute over food offered to idols, for instance, the absence of any economic or social elements in Paul's description of the case and in his solution to it must warn us against reading our presumed conception of the socio-economic composition of the Corinthian Christians into our text, even if in other passages of 1 Corinthians such a conception may still be possible (e.g. 1 Cor. 1:26). Apparently, in our text Paul does not discuss the issue in sociological terms. Instead, he indicates the presence of a religious element in the case by the use of phrases such as "those who are accustomed to idols" (8:7). This must be seen as an indication that the passage reveals more of a religious or theological matter than a social one. Although it is still possible to say that one's theological conception might have a bearing on his or her social behaviour,[26] there is no strong reason to generalize that such is the case in all issues.

A further instance is the use of 'strong' and 'weak' by scholars, initiated by Theissen. The absence of the term 'strong' throughout 8:1 - 11:1 must warn us against reading our subject matter as a conflict between the 'strong' and the 'weak,' much less in an economic sense, even though in other passages there is reason to see Paul as describing his readers in terms which may be related to economic status (such as 1:26-29 and 11:17-34, especially 11:22). Meggitt rightly points out that in 1:26-29 Paul contrasts δυνατός, ἰσχυρός, κρατός with the τὰ ἀσθενῆ in terms of 'this world.' But in 8:11-12 he uses it in terms of συνείδησις.[27] Even in 8:1 - 11:1 the context of the use of the term 'weak' in 8:9-10 and 9:22a differs. In the former, the term 'weak' is not seen in an economic sense, even though in 1:26 there is an indication of the strong and weak in economic sense. Whereas its meaning in 8:9 and 10 is determined by the use of 'συνείδησις,' which cannot be confined to the low status or the less stable person, Paul's expression in 9:22a that he became 'weak' cannot automatically be equated with the 'weak' of 8:9 (cf. 10:27-28) not only because of the use of κερδαίνειν but also because Paul does not use συνείδησις in 9:22a. He uses a general term which, if seen in Paul's past experience among them, relates more to social and physical meaning (cf. 1 Cor. 2:3; 4:10b) than to conscience (8:7-12). Therefore, the meaning must be referred to the historical context upon which Paul's use of the weak in our text is based.

Our exegetical study of 1 Corinthians 9 depends on an understanding of its literary context which is substantiated by our studies of the historical background not only of the origin and complexity of the issue of food offered to idols among Corinthian Christians, but also of the materials used by Paul in his discourse. It will be made clear that the role of 1 Corinthians 9 in the overall discourse of Paul (1 Cor. 8:1 - 11:1) is best appreciated when we see it in its own textual and historical context.

---

26   Horrell, *Social Ethos,* 7,184-95, 235.
27   J.J. Meggitt, *Paul, Poverty and Survival* (Edinburgh: T and T Clark, 1998) 108. C.K. Barrett, "Eidolothyta Once More" in *On Paul. Aspects of His Life, Work and Influence in the Early Church* (London: T and T Clark, 2003) 29-30, states that the use of the term 'strong' and 'weak' streches the text too far.

CHAPTER 2

The Interpretative Context of 1 Corinthians 9

Since 1 Corinthians 9 is placed in between 1 Corinthians 8 and 10:1 - 11:1, that is to say, in the middle of Paul's response to the Corinthian Christians' question of εἰδωλοθύτων, it is reasonable to see this issue as the context within which we must read 1 Corinthians 9. Accordingly, we need to establish the origin of the issue, its intensity, its historical contexts, and Paul's overall response in 1 Corinthians 8:1 - 11:1, for only by so doing can we see the role of 1 Corinthians 9 in the whole discourse of Paul on the issue of food offered to idols.

2.1 What Triggered the Emergence of the Corinthian Dispute over εἰδωλοθύτων?

How the issue of εἰδωλοθύτων arose among the Corinthian Christians is still debated by scholars. In this section, I will present some suggestions that have been proposed regarding the cause of the dispute, after which I will propose my own reconstruction through which the interpretation of 1 Corinthians 9 is best carried out. We will first of all see how the advocates of the quest for Paul's opponents in first Corinthians have explained the origin of the issue. Among the proponents of this quest two reasons have been given to explain the existence of Paul's opponents on the matter of food offered to idols. One sees Paul himself as the cause, the other regards the presence of foreign teachings in Corinth as the reason for their disagreement with him. One of those foreign teachings is said to be that propagated by Judaizers. It was F.C. Baur in 1831[1] who first expressed this view. It has been followed up by many such as Lütgert,[2] Schlatter,[3] Mary E.

---

1 F.C. Baur, "Die Christuspartei in der korinthischen gemeinde" in *Tübinger Zeitschrift für Theologie* 5 (1831) 61-206, and "Die Christuspartei in der korinthischen Gemeinde, der Gegensatz des paulinischen und petrinischen Christentums in der ältesten Kirche, der Apostel Petrus in Rom" in Klaus Scholder (ed.), *Ausgewhälte Werke in Einzelausgaben* I (Stuttgart and Bad Canstatt: Ffrommann, 1963) 1-146. See Munck, "The Church," 135, Hyldahl, "The Corinthian "Parties," 19.
2 W. Lütgert, *Freiheitspredigt und Schwärmgeister in Korinth: ein Beitrag zur Charakteristik der Christus Partei* (Gütersloh: C. Bertelsmann, 1908) 59, 86, 96, 99, who argued that, even though the Judaizers and wisdom-lovers were present in

Andrews,[4] T.W. Manson,[5] C.K. Barrett,[6] P. Vielhauer,[7] N.A. Dahl,[8] M.D. Goulder,[9] Timothy L. Carter[10] and J. Murphy-O'Connor.[11] Almost along the

> Corinth, the chief opponents were the Christ party, namely those who had distorted Paul's doctrine of freedom, and as a result embraced sexual licence and inflated the value of visions and revelations. They possessed God's Spirit which led them to have access to knowledge which in turn gave them a freedom of action even beyond what Paul taught and imagined. This possession caused them to question the resurrection of the dead, emancipate women and slaves, and led them to speak in tongues, abused the Lord's Supper and promoted licentiousness and asceticism. See Will Deming, *Paul on Marriage and Celibacy: the Hellenistic Background of 1 Corinthians 7* (Cambridge: CUP, 1995) 21-22.

3 A. Schlatter, *Die Korinthische Theologia*. BFCT 18 (Gütersloh: C. Bertelsmann, 1914) 28-29, 35-36, improved Lütgert's work and argued that the Corinthians were influenced by Jewish Christians from Palestine who went beyond Scripture in some ways such as a consciousness of present fulfilment, a perfectionism visible in 1 Corinthians 4:8 and 1 Corinthians 15. See David W. Kuck, *Judgement and Community Conflict. Paul's Use of Apocalyptic Judgment Language in 1 Corinthians 3:5-4:5* (Leiden: E.J. Brill, 1992) 19.

4 Mary E. Andrews, "The Party of Christ in Corinth" in *ATR* 19 (1937) 17-29. Mary argued that there are four parties, but Christ party was the most important; also A.E. Chapple, "Local Leadership in the Pauline Churches: Theological and Social Factors in its Development. A Study Based on 1 Thessalonians, 1 Corinthians and Philippians." Ph.D Thesis (Durham University, 1984) 308-17, argues that Christ party is the trouble maker and source of many problems. People of this group disregard ethical norms taught by Paul, Apollos and Cephas. Their pneumatic status enables them to claim that they have ἐξουσία and liberty expressed in the slogan that 'everything is permitted,' resulting in libertine conduct (5:1, 6:12-20; 8:1; 10:23ff.).

5 T.W. Manson, "The Corinthian Correspondence (1)" in *Studies in the Gospels and Epistles* (Manchester: UP, 1962) esp. 194.

6 In his commentary, *A Commentary on the Epistle to the Corinthians* (London: A and C Black, 1968) and his later essay, "Cephas and Corinth" in *Essays on Paul* (London: SPCK, 1982) 28-39, esp. 37.

7 P. Vielhauer, "Paulus und die Kephaspartei in Korinth" in *NTS* 21 (1975) 341-52, explores the importance of Cephas.

8 Dahl, "Paul and the Church at Corinth," 313-335.

9 M.D. Goulder, "Σοφία in 1 Corinthians" in *NTS* 37 (1991) 516-34, argues for it on the basis of the use of *sophia* which he sees in relation to *torah* not in the sense of general *Torah*, but in that of *halakha*. *Sophia* is seen as, under the inspiration of the Spirit, "words of wisdom" interpreted from the gospel. The Jewish Christians were those appealing to charismatic phenomenon such as visions, glossolalia and others. Paul is said to have addressed them in chapters 1, 4, 7 and 12-15, but his own group are addressed in chapters 5-6, 8-10 and 11. See the critique of his thesis by Christoper Tuckett, "Jewish Christian Wisdom in 1 Corinthians?" in Stanley E. Porter et al. (eds.) *Crossing the Boundaries. Essays in Biblical Interpretation in Honour of Michael D. Goulder* (Leiden: E.J. Brill, 1994) 201-219, here 218-19. In his recent book, *Paul and the Competing Mission in Corinth* (Massachusetts:

same line, another view is that which argues for Jewish Hellenistic Philonic esoteric teaching as the cause. It is believed to have been introduced in Corinth by Apollos. This view has been championed by R.A. Horsley in 1976-1980,[12] who refines Reitzenstein's and Birger Pearson's works.[13] Others refer to Gnosticism[14] or proto-Gnosticism.[15] Other scholars look into the over-enthusiastic appreciation of Christian gospel, the so-called realized eschatology. This is argued by E. Käsemann (1969),[16] F.F. Bruce (1971),[17]

Hendriksen, 2001) 2, 14-15, Goulder revives Baur's work, although on a slightly different basis, namely seeing them not as the nomics unindependent of Peter and the Jerusalem apostles, but those pneumatics amongst Jewish Christians whose view on food offered to idols, namely to eat it on the basis of their gnosis gained through visions, was not shared by the Jerusalem apostle, nor by Paul. They nevertheless label themselves as belonging to Peter.

10 Timothy L. Carter, "'Big Men' in Corinth" in *JSNT* 66 (1997) 45-67, esp. 61-64, who sees Cephas party as the rich who were critical of Paul's unwillingness to be supported by them in exchange for his service.

11 J. Murphy-O'Connor, *Paul: A Critical Life* (Oxford: Clarendon Press, 1996) 283-90, 293-95, 302-04, who argues that the Judaizers were not those who came from James to Antioch (Gal. 2:11ff.), as suggested by D. Catchpole, "Paul, James, and the Apostolic Decree" in *NTS* 23 (1977) 428-44. Rather, they were representatives of the Antiochian Judaizers who managed to make an alignment with the spirit people of Corinthian church whose position was attacked by Paul in 1 Corinthians. In fact, Murphy-O'Connor argues that the pain endured by Paul in his painful visit was provoked not by the incestuous man or one of the litigants, but by an intruder, a spokesman of the Judaizers. They intended to destroy Paul's authority in the churches he founded. The intruders' campaign was to propagate the idea that Paul "was a dishonest representative of the church which had sent him out to proclaim the common faith. A traitor to his commission, Paul preached his own ideas, not the common gospel." (295).

12 R.A. Horsley, "Pneumatikos vs. Psychikos: Distinctions of Spiritual Status among the Corinthians" in *HTR* 69 (1976) 169-288; "Wisdom of Word, Words of Wisdom" in *CBQ* 39 (1977) 224-239; "The Background of the Confessional Formula in 1 Cor. 8.6" in *ZNW* 69 (1978) 130-35; "How Can Some of You Say That There Is No Resurrection of the Dead?: Spiritual Elitism in Corinth" in *NovT.* 20 (1978) 203-31; "Consciousness and Freedom among the Corinthians: 1 Corinthians 8-10" in *CBQ* 40 (1978) 574-89; "Spiritual Marriage with Sophia" in *VC* 33 (1979) 30-45; "Gnosis in Corinth: 1 Corinthians 8;1-6" in *NTS* 27 (1980) 32-51.

13 R. Reitzenstein, *Hellenistic Mystery Religions: Their Basic Ideas and Significance* (Pittsburgh: Pickwick Press, 1978); B.A. Pearson, *The Pneumatikos-Psychikos Terminology in 1 Corinthians* (SBLDS, 12; Missoula, MT: Scholars Press, 1973).

14 Schmithals, *Gnosticism,* 226.

15 K.K. Yeo, *Rhetorical Interaction in 1 Corinthians 8 and 10. A Formal Analysis with Preliminary Suggestions for a Chinese Cross-Cultural Hermeneutics* (Leiden: E.J. Brill, 1995) 130.

16 E. Käsemann, *New Testament Questions of Today* (Philadelphia: Fortress, 1969) see 72-73, 78-81, 120-131.

A.C. Thiselton (1978),[18] and G.D. Fee (1987).[19] Indeed, from a philosophical point of view, Epicurean teaching[20] and first century Platonism which influenced persons of high status especially on the aphoristic saying that 'everything is permitted'[21] are also thought to have caused the emergence of the issue.

In the following we will first describe in detail the above said influences. Thereafter we will see how other scholars utilizing socio-historical approach explain the reason for the emergence of the issue. Then we will present our view that the existence of disagreement among Corinthian Christians themselves was the reason for the emergence of the issue.

2.1.1 Is Paul to be Blamed?

It has been suggested that the issue of food offered to idols is Paul's own problem. He is thought to have been a missionary, that is to say an outsider, who in his previous letter (1 Cor. 5:9-13) introduced the Jerusalem decree[22] or imposed his constant rejection of idolatry on his converts even though the latter had no qualms about the issue.[23] This imposition is said to have been rejected by his converts because it was thought to be contradictory to his teaching of freedom or inconsistent with his behaviour while in Corinth when he also ate food offered to idols.

It is J.C. Hurd who strongly argues that it was Paul's previous letter (1 Cor. 5:9-13), which is believed to have contained the command and

---

17 F.F. Bruce, *1 and 2 Corinthians* (Grand Rapids: Eerdmans, 1971) 49-50.
18 A.C. Thiselton, "Realized Eschatology at Corinth" in *NTS* 24 (1978) 510-26, esp. 515-16, here 523, has been the strongest proponent. He says that "in every single section from the beginning of the epistle to xiv. 40 there occurs evidence of both a realized eschatology and an enthusiastic theology of the Spirit on the part of the Corinthians." On 1 Corinthians 7, Thiselton is followed by G.J. Laughery, "Paul: Anti-marriage? Anti-sex? Ascetic? A Dialogue with 1 Corinthians 7:1-40" in *Ev.Q* 69 (1997) 109-28, esp. 112-14. According to Kuck, *Judgement,* 19-20, it was Karl Barth, *The Resurrection of the Dead* (New York: Fleming H. Revell, 1933. German original in 1925) 5-6, who first argued that the denial of the resurrection was behind all the church's problems. The critique of the realized eschatological view is surveyed by Kuck, *Judgement,* 27-31.
19 Fee, *The First Epistle,* 389, prefers the term 'spiritual eschatology': their outlook was that of having arrived (see 4:8) - not in eschatological sense, but in a 'spiritual' sense.
20 Graham Tomlin, "Christians and Epicureans in 1 Corinthians" in *JSNT* 68 (1997) 51-72.
21 Winter, *After Paul left,* 77-80.
22 Hurd, *The Origin,* 240-70, esp. 260; Fee, *The First Epistle,* 362-63; Ralf Bruce Terry, *A Discourse Analysis of First Corinthians* (Dallas: Summer Institute of Linguistics, 1996) 47.
23 Yamsat, "Partnership," 204-206, 211, 227-29; Gooch, *Dangerous Food,* 136.

enforcement of the Apostolic Decree,[24] that triggered the dispute between Paul and the whole church because it condemned the idolatrous practices and forbade the Corinthians to eat food sacrificed to idols. In this letter Paul is thought to have compromised his position in order to seek legitimization of his Gentile mission from the leadership of the church in Jerusalem. Part of the previous letter is thought to have been preserved in 2 Corinthians 6:14 - 7:1. In their letter to Paul the Corinthian Christians questioned his advice which they saw as being inconsistent with his teaching previously taught when he was in Corinth, and correspondingly, his apostolic authority. Hurd believes that Paul had initially taught his converts that because of the gospel of freedom everything was lawful and those who possessed knowledge should not be afraid of eating idol meat or of the temptation to immorality. Therefore, Hurd argues that it was because of their letter that Paul presented in 1 Corinthians 8-10 his modification of his original hard line on idol-meat. Paul's appeal for the Corinthians to care for the weak (8:7-13) is said to be hypothetical in character.[25] In other words, their opposition was not caused by any outside religious aspirations prevalent in their environment. Rather, it was motivated by their desire to defend what they had learned from Paul himself.

Even though there is no strong evidence in 1 Corinthians 5:9-13 or in 1 Corinthians 8-10 for suggesting that Paul had previously asked his readers to act according to the Jerusalem decree,[26] Hurd's view has been developed by some scholars. G.D. Fee, for instance, argues that Paul's previous letter was originally intended to address the return of the Corinthian converts to their former practice of attending cult meals.[27] In his letter Paul forbade

---

24 Gooch, *Dangerous Food*, 140 n. 21, notes that the view that the Apostolic Council decisions might have been related to Paul's position in our text was first expressed by J. Weiss, *Der erste Korintbrief* (Göttingen: Vandenhoeck/ Ruprecht, 1910) 213, and by A. Ehrhardt, "Social Problems in the Early Church. 1. The Sunday Joint of the Christian Housewife", chap. 12 of *The Framework of the New Testament Stories* (Manchester: MUP, 1964) 275-290.

25 Hurd, *The Origin*, 117-25, 225-226.

26 Gooch, *Dangerous Food*, 141, rightly refutes Hurd's hypothesis. He writes: "The farther one moves from the letter itself into the stages of dialogue preceding it, the more the reconstruction depends on inference rather than evidence, and thus becomes more tenous." Cf. also Peder Borgen, "Catalogues of Vices: The Apostolic Decree and the Jerusalem Meeting" in J. Neusner et.al., (eds.), *The Social World of Formative Christianity and Judaism* (Philadelphia: FP, 1988) 126-41, esp. 138, who argues that the Jerusalem council had not taken any decision on dietary matters. It became an issue at Antioch, Corinth, and elsewhere.

27 Fee, "II Corinthians VI. 14-VII.1," 140-61, esp. 150-51. Cf. W.H. Lawson, *First Corinthians 9:24-10:22 in Its Contextual Framework*. Ph.D. Diss. The Southern Baptist Theological Seminary (Ann Arbor: UMI, 1984) 46-47, 82, 99, 101-02, who argues that Paul's previous letter disciplined some Corinthian Christians for

them (1 Cor. 5:9-13). Moreover, Fee argues that while in Corinth Paul exercised his principle of becoming 'all things to all men' (1 Cor 9:19) in matters of idol meat in general, he was seen to indulge in such food in one context but in another to refrain from it. Later, this changeable conduct caused some to question his apostolic status and authority. The place of 1 Corinthians 9 in between 1 Corinthians 8 and 10 is not unrelated to the Corinthians' letter in which they defend their position with their monotheistic knowledge of God. To them it is a matter of indifference not only *whether* but also *where* to eat idol food. Their question to Paul "is not simply 'may we' or 'why can't we'" eat food offered to idols, but ["w]hy can't we accept the invitation to join our unbelieving friends at table in the temple of Apollo or Serapis?"[28] Their question is antagonistic in nature, arguing "for the right to continue to join pagan friends in the feast at the temple."[29] Hence 1 Corinthians 8-10 is seen as Paul's response to their defensive slogans (1 Cor. 8:1,4,8,10 and in 9:1 and 10:1-4).[30]

One who accepts Hurd's view on the conflict between Paul and his converts, but refuses to see the imposition of the Jerusalem Decree as its trigger and rejects the view that Paul ate food offered to idols while in Corinth, is P.D. Gooch[31] who, instead, argues that Paul is responsible for the emergence of the problem between himself and his readers. He argues that the matter of food offered to idols has always been a problem to Paul himself.[32] Hence the claims that: "The only player (actual and not hypothetical!) to admit any problem with idol food, then, is Paul."[33] Again

---

maintaining their relationship with pagan friends to the extent that they were involved in eating meat sacrificed to idols. In response, they questioned Paul's position and, in fact, "argued for their right to participate in every form of what they considered to be meat sacrificed to idols." (47).

28 Fee, "II Corinthians VI. 14-VII.1," 151. Cf. also John C. Brunt, "Rejected, Ignored, or Misunderstood? The Fate of Paul's Approach to the Problem of Food Offered to Idols in Early Christianity" in *NTS* 31 (1985) 113-24, esp. 113.

29 Fee, "Eidolothyta Once Again: An Interpretation of 1 Corinthians 8-10" in *Bib* 61 (1980) 172-97, esp. 181.

30 Fee, *The First Epistle*, 362-363.

31 Gooch, *Dangerous Food*, 94-95, 142, 151, 155. He writes (155): "The scholarly consensus on both these issues – that Paul addresses a divided community, and rejects a so-called superstitious fear of idol-food as vigorously as the strong – is ill-founded and mistaken."

32 Gooch, *Dangerous Food*, 136.

33 Gooch, *Dangerous Food*, 71-72. He bases this on 8:13, 10:28-29; 10:23-24 and 5:9-13. On 5:9-13 he writes (72): "If all that Paul did say in the earlier letter was not to mingle with *pornoi* and other problematic persons, then Paul probably did say more than he intended, and the Corinthians had reason to question his meaning, as Paul himself recognises (5:10)." Paul's clarification in 5:9-13 "shows that Paul has himself provoked the Corinthian concern over food offered to other Gods... Presented with this the Corinthians would have asked how one could associate with these

he says that the issue "is root and branch Paul's problem. It has become a problem to the Corinthian Christians at the time of writing of 1 Corinthians only because Paul's earlier demand to avoid any contact with idolaters has raised questions and objections concerning the eating of idol-food."[34] Accordingly, Gooch argues that in 1 Corinthians 8:1 - 11:1 Paul is responding not to a simple inquiry or a "confusion over what is to be done concerning idol-food." Rather, he is facing "a straightforward position on the part of the Corinthian writers that any limitation of their diet is foolish." His readers "had no problem with idol-food."[35] Paul's objection to his converts' view is not caused by his "concern over consciousness of the weak" but stems from "his own consciousness and his own knowledge, which in turn were conditioned by his Judaism."[36] It is caused by his constant avoidance of idol food[37] which holds "deadly contagion."[38] What Paul is doing, therefore, is not to become a mediator but "a persuader trying to win the Corinthians to a different view of idol-food than that which they hold."[39] So, Gooch argues that the Corinthians' misunderstanding of Paul's previous letter was caused by his missionary techniques. When he was in Corinth he did not raise the issue of their relationship with the avoidance of idolatry because he did not want to "frighten them off with demands which they might not understand and to which they would object."[40] He only raised the issue in his previous letter because he saw them as already in new allegiance with him in the Lord.[41]

Gooch's view is developed by Alex T. Cheung even to the extent of saying that while in Corinth Paul had already informed his converts on his opposition to idolatry. He does not think that there is a division within Corinthian church on the issue, simply because Paul is not trying to change the weak, as he does with the strong. Paul's care for the weak does not allow us to think that the weak were in dispute with the strong.[42] Cheung, however, does not agree with Gooch on the hypothetical existence of the

---

proscribed persons, and apparently came up with a disturbing range of ways that such an exhortation could be understood – disturbing enough that in response to the Corinthians' letter Paul is obliged to clarify his own earlier letter (5:10,11)."

34 Gooch, *Dangerous Food*, 72.
35 Gooch, *Dangerous Food*, 63.
36 Gooch, *Dangerous Food*, 97.
37 Gooch, *Dangerous Food*, 140-143.
38 Gooch, *Dangerous Food*, 86.
39 Gooch, *Dangerous Food*, 147.
40 Gooch, *Dangerous Food*, 142.
41 Gooch, *Dangerous Food*, 143.
42 Alex T. Cheung, *Idol Food in Corinth: Jewish Background and Pauline Legacy.* JSNT Supplement Series 176 (Sheffield: SAP, 1999) 8, 38, 39-81, 87-91, 96-7, 109-12, 124-26, 144, 146, 162, see esp. 38, 76-78.

weak.[43] To him, Paul's rejection of their position of 'eating idol food' was not influenced by the Apostolic Decree, but based on his Christian belief practiced in his missionary work. Paul's belief (see Rom. 1:21-23, 2:22, 2 Cor. 6:16, Gal. 4:8, 1 Cor. 12:2, 1 Thes. 1:9) was consistent with widespread negative (vervasive) attitude towards idol-food within Judaism as shown in Jewish apologetic literature which, unlike in early Judaism, also betrays serious efforts and difficulties faced by Jewish authors to propagate it before the Gentiles. The Christian Paul was different from his fellow Jews on circumcision, Sabbath and dietary laws, but not on idol food, even though his opposition to idol food was caused by his rejection of idolatry rather than by general Jewish perception of Gentile as being unclean. As such Paul must have told his Corinthian converts when he was in Corinth 'whether, or in what context, it was all right to eat idol food.'[44] After he left they ate it and even dined in temples probably because of their enlightened view of Christian freedom and social pressure.[45] Paul is not mediating but warning the whole church against eating specified idol food knowingly, which means participating in idolatry and thereby destroying the eaters themselves and the weak.

However, Gooch overlooks the importance of other evidence from 1 Corinthians of the existence of conflicting groups (such as 1:11-12, 11:18-22, 33-34)[46] and for the dispute over other issues (1 Cor. 12 - 14). This is why, like Hurd, he argues that Paul's mentioning of the weak in 1 Corinthians 8:7 is 'hypothetical'. It does not reflect the existence of some members of the church who, in the case of food offered to idols, held a view different from those who wanted to eat it. Gooch goes so far as to say that "there is good reason to suspect its validity."[47] Unlike in 8:1 and 8:4 where we hear the Corinthians, there is nothing in 8:7-13 and in 10:25-27 indicating "that Paul knows of specific weak Christians or of specific objections they might have raised concerning idol-food."[48] Moreover, to support his view Gooch uses the conditional nature of Paul's sentences in 1 Corinthians 8:9, 10, 13, 10:27, 10:29.[49] He writes: "If there are weak Christians seriously threatened by specific practices of strong Christians

---

43 To Cheung, *Idol Food*, 87-89, the weak are 'recent Gentile converts who are somewhat insecure in their belief or convictions' (126).
44 Cheung, *Idol Food*, 38.
45 Cheung, *Idol Food*, 146.
46 Gooch, *Dangerous Food*, 64-66.
47 Gooch, *Dangerous Food*, 66. Gooch's view is re-asserted by Joop F.M Smit, "The Rhetorical Disposition of First Corinthians 8:7-9:27" in *CBQ* 59 (1997) 476-91, esp. 480. He writes (481-82): "He [Paul] gives the impression that this group [the weak] really exists, though he may very well have made it up." Hence, he considers 8:10-11 as hypothetical example to substantiate 8:9.
48 Gooch, *Dangerous Food*, 104.
49 Gooch, *Dangerous Food*, 66, 69.

Paul would very likely refer more to these in less hypothetical terms."[50] He therefore sees the weak as Paul's own creation to suit his argument against the Corinthian Christians.[51] He writes: "the hypothetical example is Paul's appeal to the most obvious and damaging instance of eating he can imagine, and, like the rest of Paul's hypothetical argument, *may not reflect what is occurring in Corinth.*[52]

It must be noted that Gooch is inconsistent in arguing that the weak is Paul's hypothetical creation on the one hand, but in imagining that there are some from those who possess 'knowledge' who saw food as harmful, on the other. He writes: "The Corinthian appeal to knowledge...makes it likely that the Corinthians would expect to educate any of their group who thought such food harmful."[53] Moreover, it is irresponsible to assume Paul's example in 8:10 as hypothetical without considering how his readers would have responded to such a hypothetical statement. It is unlikely that Paul would have done it without safeguarding his credibility. Paul's extreme care in handling the information he has gathered from his sources (note 1:11, 14-16, 5:1, 15:12) indicates the likelihood that Paul would not have referred to anything that would not be seen as factually accurate by his readers. It is not enough to say that Paul is a great persuader.[54] With D.G. Horrell, we argue that Gooch's reading of 1 Corinthians 8:7 is totally unjustified because even if we can dispense with 8:7, Paul's concluding section (10:31 - 11:1) "clearly reiterates the themes of avoiding offence and consideration for others"[55] which cannot refer to Paul's hypothetical existence of such people. It really points to other members of the Corinthian church to whom eating εἰδωλοθύτων is inseparable from idolatry itself. Besides, Paul's retelling of his apostolic example of not using his right to financial support for the sake of the gospel and salvation of more people, which he says is drawn from imitating Christ (11:1), clearly indicates that Paul is very much concerned about the *real* weak people on the issue of food offered to idols.[56] What is more, Gooch is short of exploring the

---

50 Gooch, *Dangerous Food,* 67.
51 Gooch, *Dangerous Food,* 66, cf. Hurd, *The Origin,* 146-149.
52 Gooch, *Dangerous Food,* 101. Italics is my emphasis.
53 Gooch, *Dangerous Food,* 73.
54 Gooch, *Dangerous Food,* 83-84.
55 D.G. Horrell, "Review of P.D. Gooch, *Dangerous Food: 1 Corinthians 8-10 in its Context*" in *JTS* 46 (1995) 279-282.
56 Joop F.M Smit's view, "*About the Idol Offering*": Rhetoric, Social Context, and Theology of Paul's Discourse in First Corinthians 8:1-11:1 (Leuven: Peters, 2000) 47-65 esp. 57, 60-61 and 65, that Paul's concentration in his discourse is on the question of whether or not the food is 'specified' as public sacrificial meals – in which case it is forbidden (8:1 - 10:22) – does not take into account Paul's deep concern over the welfare of the weak. Smit argues that eating private meals provided by Corinthian hosts – which are of the same nature with meat sold in the market – are

likelihood that it is precisely because of their previous association with idolatry and anything associated with it that they would still find it difficult to think that there was no relationship between idols and things offered to them. Therefore, contrary to Gooch's assumption, it is probable that the voice of the weak would have been echoed in the letter of the church to Paul.[57]

Similarly, ignoring the use of περὶ δέ as an indication of the letter of Corinthian Christians to Paul (7:1, 8:1),[58] Pandang Yamsat[59] argues that there is no letter from Corinth on sacrificial food because there is no division in Corinth on the subject. Rather, there is a conflict between the Corinthian Christians and Paul. To support his suggestion, Yamsat argues that in 1 Corinthians 5:9-13 Paul has not addressed the subject of idolatry, except in passing. He reserves it until 1 Corinthians 8:1 - 11:1. Moreover, the combative tone of Paul in our passage is seen by Yamsat as having been caused by the seriousness of the problem to Paul himself, rather than to his readers. Hence he writes: "The clarification of what he had earlier said on idolatry, immorality and other vices and how the Corinthian Christians should relate to people outside the Christian community, shows to some extent that Paul's directives in this area had met with resistance on the basis that obeying such an instruction would have meant that the Corinthians should separate from idolaters who were non-believers."[60] Yamsat does not see the imposition of the Jerusalem decree as the reason for the conflict between Paul and his converts, as J.C. Hurd and G.D. Fee do. Nor does he go so far as to say, as Gooch does, that the weak is Paul's 'hypothetical' creation. Nevertheless, he still speaks of the same notion. He argues that the weak "do not refer to particular group of Christians or to a group who are

---

not prohibited because they are not 'specified' as temple dining or consuming public sacrificial meals in and around pagan temples. Smit's view on Paul's concentration on public sacrificial meals is maintained by John Fotopoulos, *Food Offered to Idols in Roman Corinth* (Tübingen: Mohr, 2003) 38-9, 189-91, 262, even though he follows Mitchell who argues that Paul's discourse is aimed at calling for unity over the issue (261). Fotopoulos believes that Paul rejects in 8:1-10:22 eating idol meat at pagan temples. It is due to 'the religious meaning attached to such meals' presented before idol statues which represent pagan deities. Those who presented them 'believed that the gods participated in the meal with them.' Christian participation there made them guilty of idolatry also because, according to Fotopoulos, sexual encounter 'oftentimes accompanied such meals' (39).

57 Gooch, *Dangerous Food*, 68.
58 He follows Mitchell's view that περὶ δέ does not necessarily indicate the Corinthian letter, but just a way of beginning a new discussion in her "Concerning ΠΕΡΙ ΔΕ in 1 Corinthians" in *NovT* 31 (1989) 229-256.
59 Yamsat, "Partnership," 204-06, 211, 227-229.
60 Yamsat, "Partnership," 211.

incapable of grasping the deeper spiritual things."[61] To him, the mention of the weak in 8:7 is based on a "supposition that there are likely to be weak persons in the Church who still believe that there are gods and idols."[62] To say that the weak do not form a party at Corinth is one thing, but it is quite another to assume that Paul's mention of the weak is based more on a supposition than on fact.

Coming from a slightly different angle, F.F. Bruce[63] argues that Paul's knowledge of the Corinthians' ethical practices and principles caused him to write his previous letter (1 Cor. 5:9-13). It was the news from Chloe's people that precipitated his writing of 1 Corinthians 1 - 4 in which he addressed party spirit, informed them about the sending of Timothy and signaled his intention to visit them. According to Bruce, before this letter was sent he received the Corinthians' reply to his previous letter in which they sought advice on various questions including food that had been offered to idols. Their letter represented *a powerful viewpoint* of those who felt that anything was permissible.

However, Bruce's suggestion does not answer the question of whether or not all members of the church were of one mind in their ethical practices and principles. Only if we can ascertain the answer to this question will we be able to know about the nature of their letter to Paul (7:1, 8:1, 12:1), either apologetic or in the form of a request for advice. The likelihood that on other issues such as those described in chapters 7 and 12 - 14 they are not of one mind, does indicate the impossibility of a unified view coming from them on the matter of food offered to idols. The fact that there were already divisions among them (hence the appeal for unity in 1:10) and the effect of their disunity already causing a negative form in the litigation case conducted by their members (6:1-11) and in their celebration of the Lord's Supper (11:18)[64] might have contributed to their disagreement on the issue of food offered to idols.

2.1.2 Are Foreign Teachings to be Blamed?

a. The Influence of Judaism

Earlier scholars see the dispute in the context of a conflict between Petrine and Pauline Christianity. This line of inquiry was initiated by F.C. Baur in

---

61 Yamsat, "Partnership," 227-228.
62 Yamsast, "Partnership," 229.
63 Bruce, *1 and 2 Corinthians,* 24, 79.
64 Gooch, *Dangerous Food,* 65-6, is wrong in dismissing the Corinthian leadership alignment as a factor that has to be taken into account in determining whether there was a dispute among Corinthian Christians on the issue of food offered to idols.

1831[65] whose interest in the study of the conflict between Jewish and Gentile Christians in the early church governed his study of 1 Corinthians. In fact he used 1 Corinthians as grounds on which to argue that there was a conflict between Pauline and Petrine Christianity in the early church. Consequently, he identified the factions in 1 Corinthians in the light of this conflict. The four parties mentioned in 1 Corinthians 1:12 were reduced by Baur to two parties to match his hypothesis of the Pauline and Petrine conflict, namely between the followers of Paul and Apollos on the one hand and Peter and Christ on the other, the latter being regarded as the Judaizers.[66] 2 Corinthians (such as 10:7) and traces of the Judaizing movement throughout the authentic Pauline letters are searched to support this view.

Moreover, the uncertainty about Peter's visit to or presence in Corinth prior to the writing of 1 Corinthians has been addressed with the suggestion that those using the authority of Peter might have been the Judaizers.[67] The existence of the Jews in the Corinthian church is also considered to be further support for the existence of Cephas' followers (7:18, 10:1f, 11:31). 1 Corinthians 9 is therefore seen as a response to the criticism launched by his rival missionaries who align themselves to the Jerusalem church leaders, and who regard Paul as failing to fulfil the requirement of being apostle because he does not accept financial support. His discussion in 1 Corinthians 8 is conducive to his apostolic defence in 1 Corinthians 9. It gives him an opportunity to show that what is criticized (i.e., his refusal to accept financial support and its motive [9:4-18]), actually gives a high mark to his apostleship, the basis of which he asserts in 9:1-2.[68]

The influence of Baur's work has been felt in many countries since his work was published. Scholars who have had to react to, if not be influenced by, his thesis are quite numerous.[69] In relation to 1 Corinthians 8 - 10, C.K. Barrett[70] is one who takes the hypothesis of this kind of conflict in his

---

65 Baur, "Die Christuspartei." See Munck, "The Church without Factions," 135, Hyldahl, "The Corinthian 'Parties'," 19-32, esp. 19.
66 Baur, "Die Christuspartei," 24-76; See Hyldahl, "The Corinthian 'Parties,'" 19.
67 Barrett, "Cephas and Corinth" in *Essays on Paul,* 28-39, argues that Cephas had visited Corinth and informed the Corinthian Christians of the Jerusalem decree.
68 F.C. Baur, *Paulus, der Apostel Jesu Christi.* Vol. 1 (Osabrück: Otto Zeller, 1968) 299, 301.
69 See chapter one above (12-13).
70 Barrett, *The First Epistle,* which is a repetition of his earlier view in "Things Sacrificed," "Christianity at Corinth" in *BJRL* 46 (1960) 269-97, esp. 284; "Cephas and Corinth," 21-2, 23-34, 53. He argues that there was an attempt made "by or at least under the *aegis* of Peter, to introduce into the Church at Corinth the Jewish Christian ortopraxy of the [Apostolic] Decree" ("Things Sacrificed" [53]). Cf. G. Lüdemann, *Opposition to Paul in Jewish Christianity* (Minneapolis: Fortress Press,

reading of the origin of the problem. He argues that the Judaizers (i.e. Jewish Christian missionaries) introduced the Jerusalem decree in Corinth and urged abstinence from idol-food, and the Gentile Christians ate idol-food on the basis of rational knowledge of the non-existence of idols.[71] The general Jewish practice of avoiding idol-food (Acts. 15) and the existence of the Petrine party (1 Cor. 1:12) are thought to lend support to this view. Similarly, based on his examination of Jewish customs and debates about eating meat, W.T. Sawyer argues that the weak were over-scrupulous Jewish Christians,[72] and hence the controversy in Corinth was understood by Paul "to be related to a larger issue, the growing rift between Jewish and Christian wings in the Church."[73] Paul's position is in between the two.[74]

Nevertheless, as shown by F. Watson[75] and G.D. Fee,[76] it is clear from 1 Corinthians that there is no strong indication of Judaizing activity in Corinth and no explicit mention of 'Petrine' theology.[77] If there was such Judaizing activity that would threaten Paul's teaching, Paul would have naturally written in a clearer manner than he did in 1 Corinthians. Moreover, we can see that the name of Cephas is mentioned twice in early chapters (1:12 and 3:22) without any explanation. In 9:5 and 15:8 Cephas is mentioned with no sense of opposition against Paul. It must also be said that although in 9:20 and 10:32 Paul speaks of the Jews, there is no

---

1989) ET., 263 n. 71; D. Engels, *Roman Corinth: An Alternative Model for the Classical City* (Chicago: UCP, 1990) 111.

71 See also C.K. Barret's latest article, "Paul: Councils and Controversies" in *On Paul: Aspects of His Life, Work and Influence in the Early* Church (Ediburgh: T and T Clark, 2003) 73-107, esp. 76-7. Earlier, F.C. Baur, *Paul, The Apostle of Jesus Christ His Life and Work, His Epistles and His Doctrine. A contribution to a critical history of primitive Christianity.* ET. E. Zeller (London: Williams and Norgate, 1876) 292, argued that it was against Judaizing Christianity. Similarly, W.T. Sawyer, "The Problem of Meat Sacrificed to Idols in the Corinthian Church." DTh. Diss. (Southern Baptist Theological Seminary, 1968) who argues that the weak were mostly over-scrupulous Jewish Christians, and the strong were Gentiles influenced by Gnosticism. Cf. F. Thielman, "The Coherence of Paul's View of the Law: The Evidence of First Corinthians" in *NTS* 38 (1992) 235-53, here 235, who, although favouring the view that Cephas might have visited Corinth, argues that tension between Paul and the Corinthians may have arisen after the latter's contact with Cephas. Yet Thielman rejects the view that the tension involved Jewish law.

72 Sawyer, "Problem," 258.

73 Sawyer, "Problem," 260.

74 Sawyer, "Problem," 178-180.

75 F. Watson, *Paul, Judaism and the Gentiles: A Sociological Approach* . SNTSMS 56 (Cambridge: CUP, 1986) 81-7. Cf. J.T. Sanders, *Schismatics, Sectarians, Dissidents, Deviants. The First One Hundred Years of Jewish-Christian Relations* (Pennsylvania: Trinity Press International, 1993) 207-211.

76 Fee, *The First Epistle,* 57.

77 Thus Horrell, *The Social Ethos,* 113.

indication in 8:7 that those Paul has in mind in this verse are the Jews.[78] N.T. Wright rightly argues that even though Jewish influence could be felt in the Corinthian church, "this strong view of the Jewishness of the Corinthian problem fails completely to explain why it is that Paul never uses in this letter the sort of arguments, or even the tone of voice, that we find in Galatians."[79]

Therefore, it is unlikely that Jewish Christians would have been those in the position described in 8:7. Assuming that the inscription about the 'Synagogue of Hebrews' found in Corinth is from the time of Paul, Graham Harvey suggests that the term 'of Hebrews' is, as in the biblical sources, Josephus, the Mishnah and Christian writings, "associated with loyalty, traditionalism, piety and conservatism."[80] To the users of the synagogue of this kind, the term suggests that its users "were loyal to ancestral traditions and not radical innovators."[81] Harvey identifies this conservatism not with that of 'a Maccabean-style opposition to foreign rule' or that of religious zealots, but that of a 'Josephus-style commitment to Rome,' a liberal one, that which expresses its loyalty not only to their Judaism but also to their citizenship in the city.[82] This would seem to indicate that the Corinthian Jews might not have a strong opposition against food offered to idols.

Given that Judaism was recognized as *religio licita*, however, there is no strong reason to infer that the Jews of Corinth would have been acting in contradiction to the long-cherished prohibition against eating food offered to idols. Rather, they would have their special arrangement with regard to food laws because it was one of the things by which they could safeguard their unique identity, however integrating they might have been at a local level. This is despite the possibility that Jews in *diaspora* were more fluid in their approach to idolatry than those in Palestine,[83] thanks to the recent

---

78 J.T. Sanders, "Paul between Jews and Gentiles in Corinth" in *JSNT* 65 (1997) 67-83, esp. 71, argues that even though the Jewish concept of God was strong in Corinth, the Gentile converts had lived their lives under and with gods.

79 N.T. Wright, "Monotheism, Christology and Ethics: 1 Corinthians 8" in *The Climax of the Covenant in Christ and the Law in Pauline Theology* (Edinburgh: T and T Clark, 1991) 120-36, esp. 123; also A. N. Wilson, *Paul. The Mind of the Apostle* (New York and London: W.W. Norton and Company, 1997) 170, argues that it is unlikely that many of the founding members of the church had "the Judaic life-habits in their blood."

80 Graham Harvey, "Synagogues of the Hebrews: 'Good Jews' in the Diaspora" in S. Jones and S. Pearce (eds.), *Jewish Local Patriotism and Self-Justification in the Greco-Roman World* (Sheffield: Academic Press, 1998) 132-47, here 132.

81 Harvey, "Synagogues," 146.

82 Harvey, "Synagogues," 146-147.

83 Cf. Peder Borgen, "'Yes,' 'No,' 'How Far?'" in Troels Engberg-Pedersen (ed.), *Paul in His Hellenistic Context* (Edinburgh: T and T Clark, 1994) 30-59, esp. 36, who shows that some Jews participated fully in Gentile culture; they said "yes" to pagan

acknowledgement of the existence of "a plurality of Judaisms and Jewish identities in antiquity" in Palestine and the *diaspora*.[84] It would have been odd for Paul to see the Jews as being in the position as described in 8:7 and 10, unless we can prove otherwise.[85] To say that because the Corinthian church consists of Jews and Gentiles the influence of Jewish food laws might have been felt in their dispute over food offered to idols is one thing.[86] But it is quite another to say that it was this influence that triggered their dispute. Not only is it because we cannot ascertain who are those who

---

society, although probably without renouncing Judaism; S. Applebaum, *Jews and Greeks in Ancient Cyrene* (Leiden: E.J. Brill, 1979) 186-90, who points to Jews participating in pagan cult such as dedication of names; A.T. Kraabel, "The Roman Diaspora: Six Questionable Assumptions" in *JJS* 33, Essays in Honour of Y. Yadin, 1-2 (1982) 445-64, esp. 448, where, on the basis of excavation of Jewish synagogues in Sardis, he says that Jewish community in Sardis "participated fully in the community life." However, as shown by Tomson, *Paul,* 45-46, here 46, Jewish diaspora communities were in close contact with Palestine. Envoys and letters regarding calendar matters, halakhic instructions and collections were issued from Palestine. This must be taken into account in our judgment of the diaspora attitude towards Jewish practices. Acts 6:9 and 9:29 indicate the likelihood that their awareness of their existence as a minority made the diaspora Jewish communities to "stick together and keep to their tradition." Hence the warning made by John Clayton Lentz, Jr, *Luke's Portrait of Paul* (Cambridge: CUP, 1993) 35, is right. He writes: "just as one can no longer contend that all Diaspora Jews sought to erect protective walls around their faith, neither should one go to the opposite extreme and say that all Jews, in all places, became fully involved in all aspects of the social and political life of their city. The diversity of Judaism both before and after the destruction of the Temple is far too complicated to allow for an uncritical acceptance of either position."

84 See S. Pearce and S. Jones, "Introduction: Jewish Local Identities and Patriotism in the Graeco Roman Period" in S. Jones and S. Pearce, *Jewish Local Patriotism,* 13-28, here 15. For literature on the plurality of Judaisms, see 15-16 n. 9, 17 n. 18.

85 Although arguing for Jewish acceptance and assimilation of the Greek influence, J. Goldstein, "Jewish Acceptance and Rejection of Hellenism" in Sanders, Baumgarten, and Mendelson, *Jewish and Christian Self-Definition,* Vol. II*: Aspects of Judaism in the Graeco-Roman Period* (London: SCM Press, 1981) 64-87, esp. 66-7, shows that the Jews considered as taboo any participation in the gymnasium and unlimited association with Greeks in terms of religious celebrations. See Lentz, Jr, *Luke's Portrait,* 33.

86 Lawson, *First Corinthians 9:24-10:22,* 39, points out that the Jews "maintained a close community with their own feasts and provision for the ritual slaughter and sale of meat." Also W.L. Knox, *St Paul and the Church of Jerusalem* (Cambridge: University Press, 1925) 236 n. 31 who argues that the Jews of Corinth would have butchers of their own. Jewish Christians might have expected other Christians to buy meat arranged for the Jews of the city because any meat in the general market might be polluted by having been offered to idols. Normally, Jews would have to make sure that the meat they wanted to buy must be free from pagan sacrifice.

argue from the standpoint of the monotheistic God, idols' non existence and neutrality of food in terms of religious background (either Jewish or Gentile), but also because the Jews would never allow eating food associated with idols. As noted by Peter J. Tomson, as in any *diaspora* city the Jews in Corinth had their "separate religious and social organization" which included "the supply of wine, grain or flour, oil and meat."[87]

This difficulty seems to be addressed by James A. Davis[88] who, on the basis of his view that the word εἰδωλόθυτον is a Jewish and Christian term and ἱερόθυτον a more neutral Greco-Roman term, argues that those of 1 Corinthians 8:7 are Gentile Christians who had been associated with the synagogue prior to their conversion and who entered the Christian community from paganism "but without apparently assimilating all of the implications of a monotheistic theology." They would use εἰδωλόθυτον.

However, Davis does not venture to explain the background of those who would like to use the term ἱερόθυτον except saying "those who feel an individual freedom in their ethical conscience." He falls short of explaining the identity of those addressed in 8:1, 4-6 and 8. Moreover, it is not certain whether those associated with the synagogue prior to conversion to Christianity would have lacked the knowledge of a monotheistic God (8:7). It is more likely that they would have known about the superiority of the God whom the Jews worshipped. They would also have known about the limitation of their idols. What they were not willing to commit themselves to was not the Jewish knowledge of monotheistic God, but the Jewish exclusiveness in terms of who could be regarded as their members and, correspondingly, how they should behave in relation to Jewish laws including food laws.[89]

It is therefore more likely that those who are accustomed to idols might have been those who did not possess any knowledge of a Jewish monotheistic God. Moreover, given that Christian conversion had always been seen as a break with idolatry (cf. 1 Cor. 6:9-11; 12:1 cf. 1 Thess. 2:9),

---

87 Tomson, *Paul*, 190.
88 James A. Davies, "The Interaction Between Individual Ethical Conscience and Community Ethical Consciousness in 1 Corinthians" in *HBT* 10 (1988) 1-18, esp. 10; also Yeo, *Interaction*, 97. Cf. Paul Andrew Rainbow, "Monotheism and Christology in I Corinthians 8. 4-6." Unpublished D.Phil. Thesis, Oxford, 1987, 136," 135.
89 Paul R. Trebilco, *Jewish Communities in Asia Minor* (Cambridge: CUP, 1991) 145, 164-65, shows that God-worshippers are different from the proselytes in that although attending the synagogues regularly and accepting Jewish customs such as Sabbath observance and food laws, the former did not reach the stage of being circumcised as the latter did. It is small wonder that some newly arrived members of small Jewish communities were not as receptive as the old members were in seeing God-worshippers as members of Jewish communities even though they attended the synagogues regularly, observed Jewish laws and were regarded as an integral and distinct part of Jewish communities.

it is more likely that converts from paganism would have separated themselves from idolatry, even though they were not Jewish.[90] None the less, this is not to say that we should exclude the possibility of the importance of the presence of Jewish Christians from our reconstruction of the origin of their dispute. Their presence in the new church of Corinth could indeed have exacerbated their discussion.[91] Indeed, it may be argued that the Corinthian Christians' awareness of the practice of Jewish laws by the Jews in their city might have influenced them to define their own stance on the same matter. Nevertheless, it is ill-grounded to argue that it was the Jews who instigated their dispute or it was the Jews who opposed those who wanted to eat on the basis of their monotheism.[92]

Perhaps, what Peter J. Tomson suggests is better. He argues that as people facing a dilemma of "how to live in gentile society and not get involved in idolatry?"[93] Gentile Christians at Corinth were not grappling with Jewish dietary laws,[94] nor with the question of 'known idol food offerings,'[95] but with that of what to do with "food of unspecified nature in a pagan gentile setting."[96] Tomson paraphrases their question in this way: "what should a Christian who subscribes to the prohibition of idol food do with food of which he does not know the status in a pagan environment? If he has heard with certainty that it came from a pagan temple or celebration, he would consider it prohibited. But what if this is not clear and nobody is there to ask?"[97] In assisting them to answer such question, Paul uses sophisticated rhetorical technique and halakhic principles.

This 'unspecified' nature of food is dealt with in 10:25-29. Hence, Tomson sees 1 Corinthians 8 as an introduction of the problem, and 10:1-22

---

90 Cf. Tomson, *Paul*, 185: "The early Christian unanimity on the prohibition of idol food makes the accepted scholarly view that Paul condoned it seem quite unlikely. If he did he would not just have been the first, but in effect the only early Christian authority to defend this position."

91 Tomson, *Paul*, 177, points out that during the time of Paul there existed within the Pharisaic movement various views on approach towards gentile idolatry. The more lenient view (under the influence of Hillelites), and the more strictly traditional viewpoint (under the influence of Shammaites). Given that there was a constant communication between the diaspora Jewish communities with the Palestine, the Corinthian Jews would not have been exempted from the influence of these different views.

92 Horsley, "I Corinthians: A Case Study," 247, argues that the term εἰδωλόθυτον "does not occur in Jewish texts prior to Paul...always refers to food eaten in a temple."

93 Tomson, *Paul*, 190, cf. 209.
94 Tomson, *Paul*, 216.
95 Tomson, *Paul*, 219.
96 Tomson, *Paul*, 208, 219.
97 Tomson, *Paul*, 209.

a reiteration of "the general prohibition of food known to be consecrated to idols."[98] 1 Corinthians 10:25-28 is, to Tomson, the crux of the whole passage. In the light of halakhic principle or method of dealing with pagan food's 'unspecified nature,' he translates συνείδησις not as 'conscience' that is to say in a moral sense as in Romans 2:15, but as 'consciousness,' 'conscious intention' or 'conceptional intention.'[99] Idolatry was seen by Rabbinism as being concerned "not so much with material objects or actions as with the spiritual attitude with which these are approached by the gentiles."[100] According to halakhic practice, "the function or condition of the object can signify the intention of its owner."[101] So, according to Tomson, Paul's solution does not advise his readers to inquire about the nature of the food nor abstain from it (10:25, 27).

There is no certainty, however, whether gentile Christians were as specific as Tomson thinks on the issue of food offered to idols. Tomson's description was certainly the case with Christians who were familiar with Jewish halakhic specification of idolatrous food. It is perhaps too much to expect that gentile Christians, especially those who were not familiar with Rabbinic Jewish principles, would see it that way. What is more likely is that for gentile Christians anything related to idols would have been rejected. Nevertheless, this is not to deny Tomson's emphasis on Paul's halakhic approach to the issue. It remains to be asked, none the less, whether Paul would have used halakhic principles when writing to those who, on the basis of their various legitimate arguments, wanted to eat food offered to idols, irrespective of the consequences. His response seems to be motivated by the concern for the weak than by his dependence on the halakhic principle.

While Barrett thinks that the Judaizers were the ones who told the Corinthians to avoid idol food, Michael Goulder argues that it was the opponents of Paul who ate idol food sacrifices at temple restaurants. Wishing to reawaken Baur' thesis Goulder proposes recently that the opponents of Paul were Petrine missionaries. Goulder is different from Baur, however, in that for him the Petrine missionaries were not commissioned by Peter nor by the Jerusalem apostles. They were not of nomistic party, but of pneumaistic party. They were missionaries who were boasting of their γνῶσις gained through visions. This γνῶσις enabled them to reject the view of Scripture as interpreted by scribes on all issues including on idol food sacrifices. They differ from the knowledge of Paul's limited freedom. This γνῶσις made them say that since idols do not exist, sacrifice to them was meaningless, and indeed eating idol sacrifices cause

---

98 Tomson, *Paul*, 208.
99 Tomson, *Paul*, 210-216.
100 Tomson, *Paul*, 214.
101 Tomson, *Paul*, 217.

no harm to oneself. This, so Goulder argues, runs contrary to Paul's propagation of conscious consumption of idol sacrifices and policy of asking no questions. In 1 Corinthian 8:1 - 11:1 Paul addresses them with a relaxed counsel, but in 2 Corinthians 6:14 - 7:1 with a call to excommunicate them.[102] It remains to be questioned, however, whether such pneumaistic group of Jewish Christians, who were independent of, yet from amongst, Jewish Christians in Jerusalem and therefore claimed themselves to be of Petrine, did exist. It is difficult imagine why, if such group and their view on freedom to food offered to idols based on their knowledge gained through pneumaistic experiences did exist, there seems to be a united view amongst Jewish Christians in Jerusalem against eating food related to idolatry as shown by Acts 15, however valid is Goulder's view that early Jewish Christians in Jerusalem did not have a unified view on many matters.

One who sees the cause of the opposition to Paul as coming from the Judaism related factor, yet not that of Palestine but that of Hellenism, is R.A. Horsley who has persistently suggested that the Hellenistic Jewish tradition as expressed in Philo and the Wisdom of Solomon is the most convincing background of the Corinthian's γνῶσις in 1 Corinthians 8:4.[103] According to Horsley, the Hellenistic Jewish missionary movement in the first century tried to convince Gentiles to believe in the monotheistic God of Judaism whose wisdom (*sophia*) created the world. This wisdom of God was identical with the knowledge or γνῶσις of this true God. Those who possessed this knowledge could negate the existence of idols and eat what they liked or anything related to idolatry. It was this knowledge that was taught by some leaders of the Corinthian church. They also backed their attitude with Hellenistic Jewish eschatology which saw idols as demons in disguise.

Wisdom and Philo made a strong critique on idols. *Gnosis* is "understood as given by God or his consort Sophia to people who thereby attain an exalted spiritual status as wise or righteous (Wis. 7:17; 10:10)."[104] Paul is

---

102 Goulder, *Paul and the Competing Mission in Corinth*, 176.
103 Horsley, "Gnosis in Corinth: 1 Corinthians 8:1-6," 32-51, here 40ff. See also "Chapter IV. Building an Alternative Society: Introduction" in R.A. Horsley (ed.), *Paul and Empire*, 206-14, esp. 212, where he argues that in 1 Corinthians Paul is interacting with a form of Hellenistic theology which was formed by Hellenistic Jewish communities. This theology was a kind of "individual spiritual transcendence of the mundane expressed in terms of wisdom, enlightenment theology, and immortality of soul." This theology had probably been introduced to Corinth by Apollos. Paul responds to this by his emphasis on the solidarity and 'building up' of the community.
104 Horsley, "Consciousness and Freedom," 574-589. Wisdom and Philo concentrate on their extensive critique of false gods and idols around an absolute antithesis between ignorance and knowledge of God. Ignorance of God is synonymous with

therefore facing some "enlightened Corinthians who presume that they have the liberty to banquet in temples (since the gods supposedly honoured there do not exist)."[105] Hence what Paul does in 1 Corinthians 10:14-22 is to prohibit such banqueting. Horsley argues that this prohibition is in line with the view of the non-enlightened majority of ancient Greeks and Romans, and with the "biblical traditions of non-enlightened Isralites/Judaeans." Paul does it in order to fight against "the dominant society and its social networks" in Corinth because it is in such a banqueting that the social networks are established.[106]

Yet, it is still debatable whether or not the Corinthian Christians had already been influenced by Philonic teaching. Moreover, it is impossible to make a clear cut distinction between Hellenistic Judaism and Palestinian Jewish eschatology regarding the existence of idols, the former rejecting the existence of idols and the latter seeing idols as demons in disguise.[107]

Building on Horsley's view, N.T. Wright argues that Paul is facing his opponents whose Hellenistic-Jewish γνῶσις enabled them to eat any food related to idolatry even though they knew that there were some people in their society who gave idols and the lesser beings power to rule over themselves, worshipped them and ate food offered to them. In addressing these opponents, Paul comes from the belief in a monotheistic God in terms of Jewish practice, that is to say, that which opposed dualism and paganism. This is why Paul reaffirms in 8:1-4 "the basic Jewish tradition about paganism"[108] and strengthens it in 8:6[109] with "the Christian version of Jewish-style, *Shema-style*, monotheism."[110] This monotheism is called "christological monotheism."[111] Those who believe in this formula of monotheism are expected to have "a new code of family behaviour."[112] Since the cross is at the centre of this belief, those who believe in it must, in response, love those who belong to the family recreated by it.[113] This, according to Wright, is the point of 8:7-13. What his opponents fail to realize is that: "at the heart of Christian monotheism stands a call to love all

---

    supposing that idols and heavenly bodies are gods. Knowledge of God means knowing that other gods do not exist, that idols are mere foolishness (Wisd. 13:1; 14:22: 15:2-3; Philo, *Dec*.7-8, etc. (576)

105 Horsley, "I Corinthians: A Case Study," 248.
106 Horsley, "I Corinthians: A Case Study," 248-249.
107 Wright, "Monotheism," 124.
108 Wright, "Monotheism," 127.
109 1 Cor 8:6: "yet for us there is one God, the Father, from whom are all things and for whom we exist, and one Lord, Jesus Christ, through whom are all things and through whom we exist."
110 Wright, "Monotheism," 128.
111 Wright, "Monotheism," 129.
112 Wright, "Monotheism," 130.
113 Wright, "Monotheism," 133.

those who share the same faith, and to put their interests ahead of one's own permitted liberties."[114] He therefore concludes that Paul consistently bans the eating of meat in an idol's temple.[115]

It remains to be questioned whether Wright is correct in arguing that Paul's response is motivated by his rejection of idolatry and that therefore, his christological monotheism is used to support it. There is no indication in 8:10 that eating food offered to idols in idols' temple is strictly prohibited. From Paul's description in 8:4-13, it is more likely that his exhortation is motivated more by his care for the weak than by his rejection of idolatry.[116] Wright neglects this aspect undoubtedly because, to him, the weak is Paul's hypothetical invention.[117]

b. The Influence of Gnosticism

It was W. Schmithals[118] who argued that the conflict over idol meat was caused by the outside influence of Gnosticism which had already taken root in the Corinthian community. Based on his identification of the nature of Gnosticism, especially with regard to Christology, anthropology and eschatology, he came to the conclusion that Paul's opponents were Jewish Gnostics. His view is based heavily on the concept of γνῶσις present in 1 Corinthians especially in chapters 5-16 which, according to Schmithals, reflect the existence of problems occasioned by or focused on Gnostic libertinism and disparagement of the flesh. He sees the frequent use of γνῶσις in 1 Corinthians 8:1, 7, 10 and 11 as grounds for suggesting that the Gnostics thought of γνῶσις as power, salvation, deliverance and freedom and their possession of it granted the Corinthians freedom to eat idol meat. Their γνῶσις made them insist that idols had no meaning.[119]

Schmithals' view has received strong opposition because of the

---

114 Wright, "Monotheism," 133.
115 Wright, "Monotheism," 134, see also 134-135.
116 Cf. D.G. Horrell, "Theological Principle or Christological Praxis? Pauline Ethics in 1 Corinthians 8:1 - 11:1" in *JSNT* 67 (1997) 83-114, esp. 100.
117 Wright, "Monotheism," 133 n. 36.
118 Schmithals, *Gnosticism*, 150.
119 Schmithals, *Gnosticism*, 150. This is why Schmithals states that the Gnostics "not only exhibit a certain indifference with regard to the sacrifices of idols, but they deliberately partake of fleshly pleasures...in order thus to demonstrate their victory over the powers of the sarx" (226); Cf. J.W. Drane, *Paul: Libertine or Legalist? A Study in the Theology of the Major Pauline Epistles* (London: SPCK, 1975) 105: "there was a 'Gnostic' element in the Corinthian church, which maintained that by virtue of the pneumatic character of its members it was released from the normal rules of society and ethics, and that this was coupled with a quasi-magical view of the sacraments and a realised eschatology whereby the possessor of *gnosis* was considered to have been raised already and to be living an enlightened, 'spiritual' existence in this present world."

uncertainty of the existence of Gnosticism in first century Corinth. Moreover, if the γνῶσις of 1 Corinthians 8:1 and 4 was that of Gnosticism or proto-Gnosticism,[120] Paul would not have said that he was of the same opinion with Corinthian Christians' knowledge of God's existence and of idols' non-existence. There is no indication in these verses that Paul rejects the legitimacy of their theological knowledge. His qualification of their 'knowledge' with 'love' and with the importance of caring for the weak brother does not amount to a negation of its legitimacy, but of its use to justify their right to eat food offered to idols. In other words, it is not necessary to suggest that just because Paul's converts already possessed a theological knowledge about God's existence they had been influenced by foreign teaching (cf. 1 Cor. 1:5). Reaction against Schmithals' view continued to be very strong[121] until eventually in 1966 at the Messina Colloquium on the origins of Gnosticism it was decided that the term Gnosticism belonged to the second century.[122] The suggestion that proto-Gnosticism[123] or incipient Gnosticism[124] might have influenced the Corinthians has also been proposed by some, but rarely accepted by many. Todd E. Klutz has recently tried to make a comparison between the implied author of one of the tractates of Nag Hammadi, namely the *Gospel of Philip* (especially chapter 77.15-30) and the Strong of the Corinthian Christian Community in an attempt to re-evaluate the dismissal of the influence of Gnosticism on the Corinthian problem.[125] But it remains to be awaited whether his subsequent efforts will be successful in looking into the possible existence of philosophical and historical link between the knowledgeable Corinthian Christians and the community of the implied author of the *Gospel of Philip*.

---

120 Yeo, *Interaction*, 130, argues that the strong held a proto-Gnostic theology of Hellenistic Philonic type.
121 R. Mc.L. Wilson, *Gnosis and the New Testament* (Philadelphia: Fortress Press, 1968) 52, for instance, writes: "To speak of Gnosis in Corinth, and then to interpret the teaching of Paul's opponents by a wholesale introduction of ideas from the second-century systems, is to run the risk of seriously distorting the whole picture." Also his essay, "How Gnostic were the Corinthians?" in *NTS* 19 (197-273) 65-74.
122 However, this does not mean that scholars could easily get away from the influence of Schmithals. H. Koester, for instance, in his *Introduction to the New Testament* II (New York: de Gruyter, 1982) 121-22, identifies the strong as gnostics and proto-gnostics.
123 H. Conzelmann, *A Commentary on the First Epistle to the Corinthians* (Philadelphia: Fortress Press, 1975) 15.
124 Bruce, *1 and 2 Corinthians*, 21.
125 Todd E. Klutz, "Re-Reading 1 Corinthians after Rethinking 'Gnosticism' in *JSNT* 26.2 (2003) 193-216, especially 208-216.

c. The Influence of the 'Over-realized Eschatology'

Some scholars have attempted to see the dispute as a result of the Corinthians' over-realized eschatology. This view has been influenced by interest in the realised eschatology of Paul. Scholars such as E. Käsemann,[126] C.K. Barrett,[127] F.F. Bruce,[128] A.C. Thiselton,[129] and G.D. Fee[130] have suggested that Paul's opponents were enthusiastic Hellenists or upholders of a kind of realized eschatology who practiced freedom to the extent that they did not care about the present bodily behaviour.[131] This view has been influential[132] in that it is now generally seen as a sufficient explanation of the theological outlook of the Corinthian Christians.[133] 1 Corinthians 15 shows that there are some Corinthian Christians who claim that there is no resurrection of the dead (15:12, 35-36, 50). Various proposals have been made to explain the background of their claim[134] or

---

126 Käsemann, *New Testament Questions*, see 72-3, 78-81, 120-131.
127 Barrett, *The First Epistle*, 109.
128 Bruce, *1 and 2 Corinthians*, 49-50.
129 Thiselton, "Realized Eschatology at Corinth," 510-26, esp. 515-16.
130 Fee, *First Corinthians*, 389, prefers the term 'spiritual eschatology': their outlook was that of having arrived (see 4:8) - not in eschatological sense, but in a 'spiritual' sense.
131 According to Jack H. Wilson, "The Corinthians Who Say There Is No Resurrection of the Dead" in *ZNW* 59 (1986) 95-7, the idea of a realised eschatology in 1 Cor. 15 goes back as far as John Chrysostom.
132 See Thiselton, "Realised Eschatology," 510-26, esp. 518, for the discussion and defence of this view.
133 As has been pointed out by J.K. Chow, *Patronage and Power: A Study of Social Networks in Corinth* (Sheffield: Sheffield Academic Press, 1992), 117 and A.J.H. Wedderburn, "The Problem of the Denial of the Resurrection in I Corinthians XV" in *NovT* 23 (1991) 233-234.
134 Such as disbelief in life after death, the conviction that only those alive at Jesus' second coming would be entitled to the life of the new age, their inability to perceive a bodily resurrection, their gnostic view that through baptism they were already transferred into the world of πνεῦμα and their possession of a realised eschatology. For information on the summary of scholarship on various background of the deniers of the resurrection of the dead, see A. C. Wire, *The Corinthian Women Prophets*, 229-36; Martinus de Boer, *The Defeat of Death: Apocalyptic Eschatology in 1 Corinthians 15 and 5* (Sheffield: JSOT Press, 1988) 96-97; Joost Hooleman, *Resurrection and Parousia: A Traditio-Historical Study of Paul's Eschatology in 1 Corinthians 15* (Leiden, New York, Koln: E.J. Brill, 1996) 37-40, revives G. Sellin's view that the deniers were holders of dualistic anthropology that had its origins in Hellenistic wisdom traditions as represented by Philo according to which the physical body is only the temporary vessel of the soul which, upon death, moves into a purely spiritual and immortal existence (*Der Streit um die Auterstehung der Töten. Eine religionsgeschichtliche und exegetische untersuchung*

their social status.[135]

However, there is no explicit evidence which shows that they have thought of themselves as being already raised to resurrection life. Nor is there any evidence that they thought of the resurrection as already over or a fact now, and that they would not die. Indeed, 1 Corinthians 15 does point to the fact that not all of them questioned the bodily resurrection of the dead. In fact, others were so enthusiastic about the resurrection of the dead, that they practiced baptism on behalf of the dead (15:29).[136] This indicates that they expected a future resurrection. Moreover, 1 Corinthians 4:8, which has been read in an eschatological sense, can be seen in reference to the arrogance of some Corinthians (4:6-8)[137] because of their economic achievement or hunger for status. In fact, the Corinthian Christians are still concerned about earthly matters, as clearly indicated in chapters 5 - 7.[138]

d. The Influence of Epicureanism

Coming from another perspective, Graham Tomlin argues that the influence of Epicureans could not be excluded from the whole picture of various influences that caused the emergence of the issue.[139] He writes: "the kind of ideas current in Epicurean thought provide a notable background for, and plausible origin of, some of the practices and beliefs that had grown in the Corinthian church since Paul's departure."[140] Tomlin does not go so far as to argue, as Norman de Witt[141] did, that the influence of Epicurus in Pauline churches was such that even Paul himself was heavily influenced by it.

---

   von 1 Corinther 15, FRLANT 138 [Göttingen: Vandenhoeck and Ruprecht, 1986] 79-189). For an Epicurean background of the deniers of the resurrection, see Tomlin, "Epicureans," 51-72, esp. 56-62.
135 D. B. Martin, *The Corinthian Body*, 105- 12, 122-23, argues that they were the rich who laughed at the poor's belief in life after death.
136 Richard E. DeMaris, "Corinthian Religion and Baptism for the Dead (1 Corinthians 15:29): Insights from Archaeology and Anthropology" in *JBL* 14 (1995) 678-81, may well be right in arguing that this rather specific baptism was invented by the Corinthian Christian community for a short period of time in order to address the concern brought by their members about the fate of their newly deceased relatives who, according to their contemporaries, should be helped to go through the transition process from the world of the living to the world of the dead by means of rituals. It is difficult to accept the view of Joel R. White, "Baptised on Account of the dead: The Meaning of 1 Corinthians 15:29 in its Context" in *JBL* 116 (1997) 487-99, who argues that the dead in 15:29 were the apostles. The Corinthians were disputing about which people baptised by whom were greater (1 Cor. 1:13-17).
137 Tomlin, "Epicureans," 56-57.
138 See Chow, *Patronage and Power,* 123-124
139 Tomlin, "Epicureans," 70-71.
140 Tomlin, "Epicureans," 53.
141 Norman de Witt, *St Paul and Epicurus* (Minneapolis: University of Minneapolis Press, 1954).

To provide the background of the presence of Epicureanism in Corinth, Tomlin argues that this school of philosophy, including the works of Lucretius, was brought to the newly rebuilt Roman Corinth by the first settlers.[142] Following D. Engels,[143] he goes so far as to infer that in the middle first century the élite of the original settlers defended their social and cultural distinctiveness, including their Epicureanism, from Hellenization. He believes that the widespread influence of Epicureanism in Greece and Asia Minor supported his assumption.[144] Hence he writes: "a significant group within the Corinthian congregation had adopted many principles [of the Epicureanism's understanding of the physical structure of the universe], and imported them uncritically into the church." Epicureanism propagated the irrationality, and therefore the banishment of the fear of death, the gods and all disease.[145] The existence of the gods is not denied, but their involvement in earthly human life is negated.[146] People could be encouraged to participate in pagan worship. But they were taught not to see gods as existing in the way the multitude believed. The boasting of the Corinthians in their knowledge, therefore, is thought by Tomlin to "echo the common Epicurean boast in knowledge of the true nature of gods, which frees them from superstition, and sets them apart from other people who remain in bondage because of that lack of knowledge."[147] Those who believed in Epicureanism were the rich, some of whom were converted to Christianity by the ministry of Apollos. After their conversion they did not abandon their Epicurean philosophical view of life. Rather they "carried many of their previous beliefs uncritically into their new faith." In fact, Tomlin argues that they still "kept their close links with Epicurean groups, either through attending their dinner parties (10.27) or worshipping with them at pagan temples."[148]

It is difficult to assume, however, that it was only Apollos' ministry which converted them and that Paul would have failed to address Corinthian Epicurean devotees, had they come to Corinth as early as 44 B.C. Moreover, the arguments used by some Corinthian Christians to eat food offered to idols were not only the belief in the non-existence of idols, but also that of the monotheistic God (1 Cor. 8:4-6) which could not have been possibly shared by Epicureanism.

---

142 Tomlin, "Epicureans," 54. Epicurus lived in 341-270, and his best follower, Lucretius lived in early 90s to 55 BC.
143 Engels, *Roman Corinth*, 73.
144 Tomlin, "Epicureans," 54-55.
145 Tomlin, "Epicureans," 55
146 Tomlin, "Epicureans," 65
147 Tomlin, "Epicureans," 65
148 Tomlin, "Epicureans," 69, see also 56-57 n. 55.

2.1.3 Internal Dispute.

a. Between the Rich and the Poor (?)

As we have seen above, the above said views on the emergence of the issue has largely used the studies on the possible religious, historical, theological, ideological, and even philosophical backgrounds of Corinthian Christians. Since there is no consensus they all have not been able to present an undisputable explanation of the text in its historical context.[149] Moreover, the scholars' preoccupation with the religious, theological or ideological backgrounds of the Corinthian Christians has tended to move the problem away from social reality. This failure has caused many scholars to argue that the best way of interpreting the text must depend on our understanding of the social composition of the Corinthian Christians,[150] for it is thought that people's behaviour is determined by their social status. Consequently, interest in the study of the social backgrounds of the Corinthian Christians has concentrated not so much on their ethnic and religious backgrounds[151]

---

149 Raymond Pickett, *The Cross in Corinth. The Social Significance of the Cross of Christ* (Sheffield: Sheffield Academic Press, 1997) 45, writes: "it is doubtful that one theological misconception would account for the manifold problems Paul confronts in 1 Corinthians. Moreover, if Paul conceived of the different problems in the letter as having their origin in a misunderstanding or misappropriation of the gospel he first preached to them, then why did he not provide them with a more explicitly theological corrective as he does, for example, in Galatians."

150 This interest has been made possible by the statements in 1 Corinthians regarding the different levels of the Corinthians from an economic point of view. For instance, 1 Corinthians 1:26-29 indicates the social and economic background of the Corinthians before they were called (some of them were of high status but the majority were of low status) and 1 Corinthians 7:21-23 indicates that there were some slaves and masters among the household-churches. According to S. Scott Bartchy, *Mallon Chresai: First Century Slavery and the Interpretation of 1 Corinthians 7:21* (Missoula, Mont: SBL, 1973) 58, these slaves were economically secure and confident of their eventual manumission. Cf. Judge, *Social Pattern*, 60 who says that even though they lacked freedom, slaves still enjoyed security, and a moderate prosperity. Acts 18:8 suggests that the conversion of the Corinthians had to do with the conversions of their household owners/masters (1 Cor. 1:11, 16:15 and Acts 18:8). Economically, the members could make collection on an individual and a weekly basis. Those who had weekly incomes could not have come from the lowest strata of the society, the destitute (16:2). When they celebrated the Lord's Supper there were divisions and factions among them, caused by matters related to eating and drinking. Each went ahead with their own meal without waiting for one another, causing those who had nothing to get hungry and, with the church, be humiliated (11:17-24).

151 On reading 1 Corinthians we have the impression that the Corinthian Christians were ethnically pluralistic: Greeks and Jews, uncircumcised and circumcised (see 1 Cor. 1:23-24; 7:17-20, 10:32). There were free people and slaves (7:21-23; 12:13).

as on their social levels.

This shift of interest from theological/religious aspects to social aspects coincides with a long-standing interest among scholars to investigate the social composition of the early Christians. In this quest, theories of modern social sciences have been employed to study the composition of the early Christians. In recent years, with the aid of the expertise of ancient historians, instead of using modern social sciences some New Testament scholars have used social history as the best way of understanding the social condition of the early Christians. This is particularly so because social relations in the first century AD cannot be described by modern social sciences which are used to describe a different type of social relation.[152] The use of both modern social science and social history has resulted in the so-

---

Religiously, the Corinthians came from different backgrounds. Some of them seem to have originally been adherents of religions associated with idols (8:6-7 and 12:2) and sinners of various sorts (6:9-11). Others were new converts still living with the unbelievers in their families (7:13-16). In fact they lived very closely with other faith adherents so that their worship was open to outsiders (14:23). As Christians, they differed from the point of view of spirituality which manifested in the fact that some already had monotheistic knowledge of God's existence and idols' non-existence, but others still believed that idols existed (8:6 and 7). It also manifested in the fact that they received different gifts of the Spirit (Chs. 12-14). Some questioned the reality or feasibility of the bodily resurrection of the dead (15:12, 35) to the point that their morality was influenced by it (15:33-34). In fact, their women were already playing some kind of role in their worship to the point that they dared not to have their head covered while praying and prophesying (11:2-16 and 14:34-36). From a marriage point of view, they ranged from the unmarried to the married and widow. In short their differences in knowledge and in backgrounds posed too many questions to answer that even Paul thought that writing could not substitute a visit to answer all their inquiries (4:17; 11:34b), and this visit was not just a short visit (16:7). In his letter Paul dealt with the urgent issues which concerned the community's unity, integrity and worship (12:2).

152 For instance, Bruce W. Winter, "Civil Litigation in Secular Corinth and the Church: The Forensic Background to 1 Corinthians 6.1-8 (1991)" in B.S. Rosner (ed.), *Understanding Paul's Ethics. Twentieth Century Approaches* (Grand Rapids: Eerdmans, 1995) 85-103, esp. 101-02 charges that the dichotomy of the rich and the poor is "imprecise and misleading." Instead, he argues for the use of 'the haves' and 'the have-nots' (1 Cor. 11:22). The latter are those who do not belong to or nor have any link with any household, and therefore are in an economically less secure position. Cf. M.I. Finley, *The Ancient Economy* (London: Chatto and Windus, 1973) 49-51; P.J. Richter, "Recent Sociological Approaches to the Study of the New Testament" in *R* 14 (1984) 77-90, esp. 85, who writes that: "the historical distance of the New Testament data precludes many of the typical empirical techniques of sociology... Sometimes there is simply not enough extant documentation to support the use of sociological models."

called 'New Consensus'[153] on the composition of the early Christians. Scholars such as E.A. Judge,[154] G. Theissen,[155] R.F. Hock[156] and W.A. Meeks[157] are some of the major proponents of this quest. They all suggest that among the Corinthian Christians there were some well-to-do people who were influential and likely to be the instigators of the conflict in the congregations. This suggestion has been followed up by scholars such as P. Marshall,[158] S.M. Pogoloff,[159] J.K. Chow,[160] A.D. Clarke,[161] D.W.J. Gill,[162] and D.B. Martin,[163] D. Liftin,[164] Ben Witherington III,[165] David G. Horrell,[166] Timothy L. Carter,[167] and R. Pickett,[168] in studying 1 Corinthians.[169]

The New Consensus is actually the result of efforts made by scholars to refute the 'Old Consensus' which in the beginning of the twentieth century was championed by A. Deissmann who argued that, based on Paul's words

---

153 A.J. Malherbe, *The Social Aspects of Early Christianity* (Baton Rouge: LSUP, 1977) 31.
154 Judge, *Social Pattern*, 60; E.A. Judge, "The Early Christians as a Scholastic Community" in *JRH* 1 (1960) 4-15, 125-37; also in "St. Paul and Classical Society" in *JAC* (1972) 19-36.
155 Theissen, *Social Setting*.
156 R.F. Hock, *The Social Context of Paul's Ministry: Tentmaking and Apostleship* (Philadelphia: Fortress Press, 1980).
157 Meeks, *Urban Christians*.
158 Marshall, *Enmity*, esp. 217, 243, 326-40, 359, 397, also his recent article, "The Enigmatic Apostle: Paul and Social Change. Did Paul Seek to Transform Graeco-Roman Society?" in T.W. Hillard et al., (eds.), *Ancient History in a Modern University. Vol 2 Early Christianity, Late Antiquity and Beyond* (Michigan, Cambridge: Wb. Eerdmans, 1998) 153-69, esp. 169.
159 S.M. Pogoloff, *Logos and Sophia: The Rhetorical Situation of 1 Corinthians* (Missoula: MT Scholars Press, 1992) 278-279.
160 Chow, *Patronage and Power*, 112, also "Patronage in Roman Corinth" in R.A. Horsley (ed.), *Paul and Empire. Religion in Roman Imperial Society* (Pennsylvania: TPI, 1997) 104-25.
161 A. D. Clarke, *Secular and Christian Leadership in Corinth: A Socio-Historical and Exegetical Study of 1 Corinthians 1-6* (Leiden: E.J. Brill, 1993).
162 D.W.J. Gill, "In Search of the Social élite in the Corinthian Church" in *TynBul* 44 (1993) 323-37, esp. 337.
163 D.B. Martin, *The Corinthian Body*, 56, 68.
164 D. Liftin, *St Paul's Theology of Proclamation. 1 Cor 1-4 and Greco-Roman Rhetoric* (Cambridge: CUP, 1994) 160-161.
165 Ben Witherington III, *Conflict and Community in Corinth: A Socio-Rhetorical Commentary on 1 and 2 Corinthians* (Grand Rapids: Eerdmans, 1995) 96.
166 Horrell, *Social Ethos*, 91-101, 120-23, 199-235.
167 Timothy L. Carter, 'Big Men,' 48, 54-5, 68-69.
168 Pickett, *The Cross in Corinth*, 102-03, 107.
169 On 2 Corinthians, see F.M. Young and D.F. Ford, *Meaning and Truth in Second Corinthians* (London: SPCK, 1987).

in 1 Corinthians 1:26-29, early Christians came from the middle to lower strata of society.[170] His view was first[171] challenged in full force by E.A. Judge in 1960 who argued that the early Christians did not come from the lower strata alone but from a mixture of high and low classes.[172] A lot of ink has been spilled on this issue, but it is Gerd Theissen who first takes the issue to 1 Corinthians. He accepts both Deissmann's and Judge's theses and

---

170 A. Deissmann, *Light From the Ancient East*. ET. by L.R.M. Strachan (London: Hodder and Stoughton, 1927) 7. For other proponents of the 'Old Consensus,' such as A.D. Nock, A.H.M. Jones, E.R. Dodds, see John G. Gager, "Religion and Social Class in the Early Roman Empire" in S. Benko and J.J. O'Rourke (eds.), *Early Church History. The Roman Empire as the Setting of Primitive Christianity* (London: Oliphants, 1971) 99-120, esp. 112-13.

171 According to J.J. Meggitt, *Paul*, 102 n. 134, it was actually E. von Dobschütz, *Christian Life in the Primitive Church* (New York: PG. Putnam and Sons, 1904) 14, who argued that Paul's use of 'not many' rather than 'not any' in 1 Corinthians 1:26 indicates that among the earliest of Pauline Christians some came from more exalted circles.

172 Judge, *Social Pattern*, 60, said ["far] from being a socially depressed group, then, if the Corinthians are at all typical, the Christians were dominated by a socially pretentious section of the population of the big cities. Beyond that, they seem to have drawn on a broad constituency, probably representing the household dependents of the leading members." They were in the main stream of its culture. See Judge, "Scholastic Community," 4-15, 125-37; also in "Classical Society," 19-36. Before Judge, F.V. Filson in 1939, "Significance," 111, already expressed that ["t]he apostolic church was more nearly a cross section of society than we have sometimes thought." The debate on the social level has continued ever since, as described by Malherbe, *Social Aspects*, 29-59, who in the prolegomena surveys the sociological works on the early Christians. He carried further Judge's judgment on "the social level and literary culture." Based on his analysis of Paul's literary style Malherbe argues that Paul's personal education was higher than that accorded him by Deissmann (59). There have been many scholars debating on what Malherbe considers as the new consensus. B. Holmberg has described the debate in his *Sociology of the New Testament: an appraisal* (Minneapolis, MN: Fortress Presss 1990) 44. He says that "Judge's interpretation of the prosopographical information available in the texts is more down-to-earth and plausible than the generalisations of Deissmann on "the unliterary masses." In particular, Meeks' view is worthy of mention in this regard. Meeks, *Urban Christians*, 55, 73, argues that generalisation is not plausible to describe the social level of early Christians because one's personal status depended on several different variables such as power, wealth, occupation, ethnic background, education and family connections. The rank one achieved from several different aspects would determine one's status. So there is status inconsistency. The Pauline congregation in particular reflected a fair cross-section of urban society and the most active members were people of high status. The leading members suffered from status inconsistency. In response B.J. Malina, "Review of The First Urban Christians by Wayne A. Meeks" in *JBL* 104 (1985) 346-49, regards Meek's view as too modern.

says that the early Corinthian Christians were internally stratified.[173] Evidence in 1 Corinthians is said to abound in support of his view: a) those mentioned by name, judged from their position as the head of the households and their ability to travel, are from relatively high status;[174] b) the missionaries' competition with Paul seemed to revolve around self support provided by the economically well-off; c) the themes of chapters 1-4 especially 1:10-17 for which 1:18-25ff is transitional are conflict within the congregations which involves primarily those of higher status;[175] d) criticism of Paul by others belonging to other parties on his manual labour could have originated from them;[176] Paul's information on the *schismata* comes from those from below who view party strife negatively.[177] Theissen shows that nine of the seventeen names of Corinthian Christians mentioned in Acts 18, Romans 16 and 1 Corinthians were of high status.[178]

Hence, Theissen argues that the Corinthian conflict was caused more by the nature of the congregations as sociologically stratified than by theological or religious differences. This is said to be particularly supported by 1 Corinthians 1:26 and 11:17-34. Hence the body analogy found in 1

---

173 Theissen, *Social Setting*, 69-119, esp. 69. Meeks, *Urban Christians*, 73, elaborates Theissen's view by saying that the typical Pauline congregation reflected a fair cross-section of urban society with "the extreme top and bottom Greco-Roman social scale missing from the picture." He argues that "the most active and prominent members of Paul's circle (including Paul himself) are people of high status inconsistency (low status crystallization). They are upwardly mobile; their achieved status is higher than their attributed status."
174 Theissen, *Social Setting*, 72-96.
175 Theissen, *Social Setting*, 55.
176 Theissen, *Social Setting*, 56.
177 Theissen, *Social Setting*, 57.
178 Namely: Achaicus, Aquila, Erastus, Fortunatus, Gaius, Jason, Crispus, Lucius, Priscilla, Phoebe, Quartus, Sosipater, Sosthenes, Stephanas, Titus Justus, Tertius, Chloe's people (Theissen, "Social Stratification," 95). The social status of Erastus (Rom. 16:23) has been the subject of much debate among scholars. Some of the proponents of the "New Consensus" have argued that the Erastus of Romans 16:23 is the same as that of the inscription found in 1928, 1929 and 1947 which describes Erastus as beholder of the office of *aedilis* in Corinth who had the resources to pay for the paving of part of the city's marketplace. But others are more cautious in identifying Erastus of Roman 16:23 with that of the inscriptions. See J.J. Meggitt, "The Social Status of Erastus (Rom. 16:23)" in *NovT* 38 (1996) 218-23, especially 219-20 ns. 10-11, for the literature on this issue. Meggitt himself rejects the identification and suggests, instead, that the economic situation of Erastus of Romans 16:23 "was most likely indistinguishable from that of his fellow believers." Erastus "cannot be used as evidence of the spread of the new faith amongst the socially powerful of the Principate. He is incapable of bearing the weight of the speculative reconstructions that have been placed upon his shoulders by the 'New Consensus.'" (223).

Corinthians 12:22-24 is seen as Paul's attempt to encourage the well-to-do not to consider the poor Christians as of no use to them in the life of the church. This reading is said to be supported by the movement of the analogy from the "eye to hand, head to feet" (12:20-21), the reversal of ἀσθενέστερα to ἀνακγκαῖα (12:22) and ἀτιμότερα to τιμὴν περισσοτέραν (12:23a), τὰ ἀσχήμονα to εὐσχημοσύνην περισσοτέραν (12:23b), and by Paul's theological legitimation in 1 Corinthians 12:18,24 and 28.[179]

Some criticisms have been expressed against the view that the Corinthian problem is class-influenced. For instance, T. Engberg-Pedersen notes that Theissen's emphasis on the social is expressed at the expense of the theological.[180] Scholars developing Theissen's view have also not been spared from criticism. First, we will see how Andrew Clarke's work, for instance, which builds upon Theissen's thesis, comes under heavy criticism. Then we will present Meggitt's attempt to revive the Old Consensus by attacking Theissen's thesis. We will specifically focus on his criticism of Theissen's view on the issue of food offered to idols.

A.D. Clarke suggests that the immoral man of 1 Corinthians 5 is the highest patron of the church. Assuming that the immoral man himself is of high social standing, A.D. Clarke suggests that the reason for the whole community's failure to take action against the immoral man, and instead,

---

179 See for instance, Theissen, *Social Setting*, 56, 72; Fee, *The First Epistle to the Corinthians*, 612; D B. Martin, "Tongues of Angels and Other Status Indicators" in *JAAR* 59 (1991) 547-89, here 568-69; Cf. Witherington III, *Conflict*, 258-59; Horrell, *Social Ethos*, 181.

180 T. Engberg-Pedersen, "The Gospel and Social Practice According to 1 Corinthians" in *NTS* 33 (1987) 269-70. Cf. S.E. Fiorenza, "Toward a Feminist Model of Historical Reconstruction" in *A Feminist Theological Reconstruction of Christian Origins: In Memory of Her* (New York: Cross Road, 1989) 79, regards Theissen's work as superimposing a model into a text; Rainbow, "Monotheism," 136; Tomlin, "Epicureans," esp. 52 and n. 5. He writes: "a purely sociological or rhetorical approach can tend to ignore what earlier studies saw, namely the existence of real ideological divergence from Paul in Corinth." He argues that the Corinthian Christians were trying to justify their behaviour with theological justification. He also points out that it is difficult to see the view of those referred to in 1 Corinthians 15:12 sociologically. Moreover, it is difficult to square the view that the leadership alignment in 1 Corinthians 1 - 4 is between the rich with the view that the σχίσματα existing in the celebration of the eucharist is between the rich and the poor. Yet, Tomlin accepts Theissen's view that the rich "are disparaging poorer members" (55 n. 17). Pickett, *The Cross in Corinth*, 97, 102-03, 115, is inconsistent in his assessment of Theissen's thesis. On the one hand, he argues that one's view of issues is influenced by his or her social status. Hence those propagating individual freedom who eat idol meat are the élite (103). On the other hand, he argues that the dispute in 1 Corinthians 8-10 is not to be defined in socio-economic distinctions (115).

boasting about him, is not only because they are afraid of retaliation by the immoral man or of losing his patronage, but also because they want to show their due gratitude to him. Moreover, even if they want to take action against him, the law will be in favour of the powerful immoral man. Therefore Clarke argues that "the sexual immorality itself is not being exalted, but the offender is the object of boasting, and this despite the fact that he is involved in sexual immorality. Their arrogance over the issues allows them to overlook the far more serious instance of immorality, instead of them approaching the situation with the more appropriate solemn mourning (1 Cor. 5.2)."[181]

Nevertheless, there is no clear evidence in 1 Corinthians 5 indicating that the Corinthians were boasting or arrogant about the man himself and not about the act he committed. Nor does the text indicate that the immoral man was a powerful man of the church or a poor man. As former immoral people, adulterers and sexual perverts (6:9-11), the Corinthian Christians would not have failed to take note of the worst act committed by their fellow Christian. Even if we accept Clarke's suggestion that the immoral man was a powerful man, it would be too much to suggest that the Corinthian Christians were boasting about him despite their knowledge of his immorality. The most they could have done would not have been 'boasting' or 'arrogant,' but, rather, keeping 'quiet' about the case or about the man's misconduct.[182] The laws against sexual misdemeanours were enacted even if there was no one to initiate litigation. Information from a well-paid informant was sufficient for the law enforcers to act against the guilty party.[183] Indeed, the Roman public could ignore the popular justice in acting against the immoral man.[184] Moreover, as suggested by Stephen De Vos, the fact that there existed leadership alignment among Corinthian Christians makes it very unlikely that the rivals of the immoral man would have let his case remain unnoticed,[185] given the fact that both Jewish and Roman legislations would punish severely any sexual relationship between a step-son and a step-mother.[186] On the contrary, they would use it as a

---

181 A.D. Clarke, *Leadership*, 85-87; also Chow, *Patronage and Power*, 139.
182 Suzanna Dixon, *The Roman Family* (Baltimore and London: The John Hopkins University Press, 1992) 47, points out that during the reign of Hadrian in the second century, a father killed his son for allegedly having an affair with his stepmother.
183 See Richard I. Frank, "Augustus' Legislation on Marriage and Children" in *CSCA* 8 (1976). 41-52 esp. 46: "violations of marriage laws were the main subject of informers' reports."
184 Meggitt, *Paul*, 152-53.
185 Stephen De Vos, "Stepmothers, Concubines and the Case of Πορνεία in 1 Corinthians 5" in *NTS* 44 (1998) 104-14, esp. 109.
186 Stephen De Vos, "Stepmothers," 108. Cf. Karl Galinski, "Augustus' Legislation on Morals and Marriage" in *Phil* 125 (1981) 126-44, esp. 126, who shows that the purpose of the *Lex Iulia de adulteriis* was "to preserve the dignity of marriage by

weapon against him.

Stephen De Vos suggests that the woman is not the stepmother of the immoral man, as such behaviour was against the law, but his father's concubine. The latter was not against the law. In fact, he argues that taking a concubine was considered to be virtuous.[187] That is why neither the society nor the church blamed the immoral man.[188] Indeed, Rawson shows that concubinage was frequent among freed persons because status "precluded many couples from legal marriage."[189] None the less, Stephen De Vos' suggestion does not explain why Paul characterizes the case as an act of immorality which is not found "even among pagans" (5:1). He would not have characterized the case in such a way if the relationship had been considered normal by the Romans. Moreover, there is no ruling which allowed a man to have his father's concubine, let alone when his father was still alive.

Another instance is Clarke's suggestion that the litigation in 1 Corinthians 6:1-11 is between the rich and the poor. Yet, this too does not stand up to close scrutiny. It is true that according to common Roman legal practice it was those of high status who were most likely to benefit from court proceedings either to enhance their prestige, honour and status, achieve financial gain or harm their enemies.[190] However, there is no strong evidence to ascertain that the case of Corinthian Christians was between the

---

transferring the jurisdiction concerning marital delinquency from the private to the public sector."

187 Steven De Vos, "Stepmothers," 111. The man, however, was compelled to report his relationship with the woman to the authorities. See O. Keifer, *Sexual Life in Ancient Rome* (London: Constable, 1994) 39.

188 Steven De Vos, "Stepmothers," 112. Hence he argues that ["i]f she were, indeed, the father's concubine, that meant the father and the woman were not legally married and it would not have been illegal for the son to have engaged in a sexual relationship with her after his father's death. Furthermore, it was normal for young men, not old enough that they were legally expected to marry, to take concubines or mistresses of their own. Although it was unusual, and possibly socially unacceptable, for a son to have taken as his *concubina* his later father's *concubina* at Rome, it may have been more acceptable at Corinth."

189 Beryl Rawson, "Roman Concubinage and Other de facto Marriages" in *TAPA* 104 (1974) 279-305, here 304. Some scholars such as Treggiari and Shaw and Dixon (see Dixon, *The Roman Family*, 93-95), have modified Rawson's explanation for the preference of *concubinage* to marriage. They argue that the reason for the preference among the lower classes is not certain. But among the élite, especially the widowed with children, *concubinage* was seen as an honorable alternative to remarriage. If the woman was of a low birth or of disreputable life (prostitute or actress), it was not considered as a fornication and therefore not punishable because it did not threaten legitimate marriages. See also Sarah B. Pomeroy, *Goddesses, Whores, Wives and Slaves* (London: Pimlico, 1975) 159-160.

190 Theissen, *Social Setting*, 97.

rich and the poor. J.A. Crook rightly claims that "the whole Greco-Roman world was litigiously minded, and there is plentiful evidence for litigation at levels of society below and beyond the élite, not only in Egypt."[191]

The most recent attack on the New Consensus is launched by J.J. Meggitt.[192] Criticisms of his arguments have been expressed by D.B. Martin[193] and by G. Theissen himself.[194] But Meggitt has defended his work.[195] The dialogue between them will continue. Meggitt accuses the proponents of the 'New Consensus' of failing "to stand up to close scrutiny."[196] In fact, by so doing Meggitt wishes to revive the Old

---

191 J.A. Crook, *Legal Advocacy in the Roman World* (London: Duckworth, 1995) 125. Cf. P. Garnsey, *Social Status and Legal Privilege in the Roman Empire* (Oxford: Clarendon Press, 1970) 217, who argues that, though not frequently, men of humble origin and position brought suits against men of rank. Also J.M. Kelly, *Roman Litigation* (Oxford: Clarendon Press, 1966) 62-68, who shows that poor merchants could sue their fellow weak merchants for defraud in business; Meggitt, *Paul*, 122-25 who points out that the élite did not monopolize litigation.

192 Meggitt, *Paul*, 97-154.

193 D.B. Martin, "Review Essay: Justin J. Meggitt, *Paul, Poverty and Survival*" in *JSNT* 84 (2001) 51-64. Martin accuses Meggitt, for instance, of defining the Roman populace notwithstanding Corinthian Christians in a simplistic dichotomy of the elite (1%) and those in 'abject poverty' (99%), of misrepresenting the positions of scholars he criticizes, of selective and tendentious use of ancient sources (56-57) and of not substantiating the concept of mutualism used to face the said economic deprivation (62-63).

194 G. Theissen, "The Social Structure of Pauline Communities: Some Critical Remarks on J.J. Meggitt, *Paul, Poverty and Survival*" in *JSNT* (2001) 65-84. Theissen rejects Meggitt's portrayal of those in abject poverty as structurally homogenous, and argues that although early Christians were below local upper class, some of them were better than the rest (72-75). He also uses the existence of professional and religious clubs to challenge Meggitt's contention (75-79). Also in his "Social Conflicts in the Corinthian Community: Further Remarks on J.J. Meggitt, *Paul, Poverty and Survival*" in *JSNT* 25 (2003) 371-91, Theissen defends his view of Paul as having better social and economic status than those in abject poverty, the economic status of Corinthian Christians as being better than that of the Macedonian and Jerusalem Christians, the role of the pattern of the rich eating more and better food in the Lord's Supper conflict, the *poppinae* function not for ordinary need, but for banquets, and the *macellum* selling expensive meat for the rich. The latter awaits Meggitt's response. In the latter Theissen defends his thesis by questioning Meggitt's arguments.

195 J.J. Meggitt, "Response to Martin and Theissen" in *JSNT* 84 (2001) 85-94.

196 Meggitt, *Paul*, 100-101. He writes: "not only are many of the reconstructions of the 'New Consensus' dependent upon anachronistic and inappropriate interpretations of first-century society but the specific evidence adduced by its followers in support of this interpretation cannot stand up to close scrutiny. Their arguments cannot provide grounds for maintaining that the early communities' experience of life was in any way distinguishable from the common urban experience..." (100). Hence, he

Consensus propagated earlier this century by Deissmann.[197] On the basis of his analysis of the economic condition of the Roman Empire in the first century - that 99% of the population lived in deprivation and subsistence - Meggitt argues that *"Paul and Pauline churches shared in this general experience of deprivation and subsistence. Neither the apostle nor any members of the congregations he addresses in his epistles escaped from the harsh existence that typified life in the Roman Empire for the non-élite."*[198] In this light, Meggitt refutes those who have read 1 Corinthians 1:26 as evidence of the existence of some members of the Corinthian church coming from the élite or the ruling class of the society. He writes: "By itself Paul's words in 1 Cor. 1:26 can tell us nothing concrete about the social constituency of the congregation he addresses except that a small number were more fortunate than the others...the verse can no longer be taken as unambiguous evidence of the presence of the élite, or near élite, within a Pauline church. It is far too equivocal. Indeed, it would be unwise to assign to it any role, however minor, in describing the social make-up of the Pauline congregations."[199]

According to Meggitt, these more fortunate people are "a small group of literate, *ingenui*, artisans - who amongst the urban poor would have appeared relatively more privileged but whose lives would still have been dominated by fears over subsistence."[200] He simply says that the gap between the more fortunate and the less fortunate is not very great. To him, Paul sees the whole congregation as 'foolish, weak, despised, nothings' in 1:27-28. Hence, he states that ["e]ven if such people held leadership position *within* the church it does not follow that they held such position *outside* it. Nor can we legitimately see in the apostle's attack upon those Corinthians who criticised him for refusing to take any material support from them [1 Cor 9:1-27]...evidence of the existence of a wealthy group in the congregation."[201] Even if they were supporting other missionaries, it does not follow that they cannot have been 'materially impoverished' because "supporting a missionary is not a sure sign of affluence. It is possible for all except those facing an immediate subsistence crisis."[202] To be consistent with his thesis, it is not surprising that Meggitt reads 1 Corinthians 4:8, which has been seen by the proponents of the 'New

---

charges that among the proponents of the 'New Consensus,' "possibilities too readily become probabilities and are too quickly treated as though they were certainties." (101)

197 Meggitt, *Paul*, 97
198 Meggitt, *Paul*, 74.
199 Meggitt, *Paul*, 106.
200 Meggitt, *Paul*, 106.
201 Meggitt, *Paul*, 117.
202 Meggitt, *Paul*, 117.

Consensus' as indicating the presence high status people, in a spiritual sense.[203]

Thus, in relation to the issue of food offered to idols Gerd Theissen[204] has argued that the dispute was caused by a conflict between the rich and the poor. He reads the weak in 8:7, 11-12 in the light of 1 Corinthians 1:26-27 as a socio-economically defined group, and invents those who insist on eating food offered to idols as the 'strong' even though such a word does not occur in 1 Corinthians 8 - 10. In terms of eating habits, Theissen argues that meat was a daily menu of the strong. Their convictions and perceptions did not see any negative associations with food offered to idols. In contrast, as members of the lower strata, the weak "seldom ate meat in their everyday lives." Even if they did so, it was "exclusively as an ingredient in pagan religious celebration."[205] Consuming such meat was therefore for them religiously problematic because their perceptions and convictions were influenced by taboo. They would consequently reject eating such meat. Theissen bases his thesis of the norms of first-century consumption on his reading of incidents recorded by Tacitus (*Annales* 14.24) and Caesar (*Bellum Galicum* 7.17) which show that "soldiers ate meat only in exceptional circumstances."[206] Theissen's view has been echoed by P. Tomson,[207] A.J. Blasi,[208] D.W.J.Gill,[209] K.K. Yeo,[210] Stephen J. Joubert[211] and D.G . Horrell.[212]

Meggitt, however, criticizes the contention of Theissen that the conflict in 1 Corinthians 8:1 - 11:1 is between the affluent 'strong,' who could

---

203 Meggitt, *Paul,* 106-07, writes: "But the likelihood that Paul is referring to a socially élite group within the Corinthian church by these words is slim. Rather, the apostle appears to be addressing the entire congregation, and is making reference to the Corinthians' sense of spiritual (rather than social) self-importance..."
204 Theissen, *Social Setting,* 121-143.
205 Theissen, *Social Setting,* 126.
206 Theissen, *Social Setting,* 126.
207 Thomson, *Paul,* 189: "In antiquity meat was expensive and very difficult to keep..."
208 A.J. Blasi, *Early Christianity as a Social Movement.* Toronto Studies in Religion, 5 (New York: Peter Lang, 1988) 64-67, argues that status differences would explain eating problems.
209 D.W.J. Gill, "The Meat Market at Corinth (1 Corinthians 10:25)" in *TynBul* 43 (1993) 389-93.
210 Yeo, *Interaction,* 86-90.
211 Stephen J. Joubert, "Managing Household. Paul as *paterfamilias* of the Christian household group in Corinth" in Philip F. Esler (ed), *Modelling Early Christianity: Social-Scientific Studies of the New Testament in Its Context* (London and New York: Routledge, 1995) 213-23, esp. 218.
212 Horrell, *The Social Ethos,* 143, who argues that it is the socially prominent members who demand the right to eat food offered to idols, and the socially weak who consider such practice idolatrous.

afford to eat meat and would not tolerate any restriction on such an important daily menu, and the indigent 'weak' who rarely ate meat and who, therefore, preferred not to eat food offered to idols.[213] Contrary to Theissen's argument that meat was rarely available to the poor,[214] Meggitt argues that low quality meat was more available to the weak than Theissen allows. According to Meggitt, Theissen's thesis on meat consumption "is based upon a fallacious understanding of the norms of first century meat consumption."[215] Referring to Porphory, *De Abstinentia* 2.4.3 and based on the work of P. Garnsey,[216] Meggitt states that "the diets of soldiers are untypical and can tell us nothing about the eating habits of the rest of the Empire." Moreover, referring to Apian's *Iberica* 85, Frontinus' *Strategemata* 4.1.2, Meggitt states that "we have numerous literary references to the Roman army's prodigious meat consumption."[217] To support his contention, he cites Mireille Corbier,[218] who argues for the ordinariness of meat as a daily diet for a soldier during campaigns and garrison duty to the extent that protest would occur when their diet became "*exclusively* meat."

So Meggitt argues that although most people in the Mediterranean world consumed cereals and the cost of meat was relatively expensive, meat was consumed by the non-élite more regularly than Theissen allows. The non-élite frequently consumed meat "in settings which were decidedly unsacral"[219] and available in the urban settlements of the empire including Corinth.[220] These settings were the 'cookshops' (the *poppinae* and *ganeae*), which were "almost proverbially the meeting places of the common people" in which prepared meats were served to the unmoneyed male and from which the non-élite could consume a modest quantity or just as 'bite' of meat as described in Juvenal's Saturae 11.144.[221] Moreover, Meggitt argues that meat was also available for the non-élite at many of the *tabernae* or *cauponae* (wineshops) that filled any town and also from "ambulant

---

213 Cf. Barrett, "Things Sacrificed," 145-46; Rainbow, "Monotheism," 134.
214 Cf. Yeo, *Interaction*, 98, who argues for the scarcity of meat in the ancient world.
215 J.J. Meggitt, "Meat Consumption and Social Conflict in Corinth" in *JTS* 45 (1994) 137-41 and his book *Paul*, 109; cf. also J.T. Sanders, "Paul between Jews and Gentiles in Corinth," 75-76.
216 P. Garnsey, "Food consumption in Antiquity: Towards a Quantitative Account" in P. Garnsey (ed.), *Food, Health and Culture in Classical Antiquity* (Cambridge: Classical Department Working Papers, 1989) 39.
217 Meggitt, *Paul*, 109 n. 160.
218 M. Corbier, "The Ambiguous Status of Meat in Ancient Rome" in *FF* 3 (1989) 223-64, esp. 229.
219 Meggitt, *Paul*, 109.
220 Meggitt, *Paul*, 110 n. 169.
221 Meggitt, *Paul*, 110, 110 n. 164, 112.

vendors who plied the streets and even the baths,"²²² even though it was historically associated with the poor: sausages, blood puddings, tripe and 'off-cuts.' Meggitt recognizes that, as the atmosphere in these establishments was not hygienic, the quality of the meat was therefore questionable. Even though the quality of this meat was low, Meggitt argues, "it was meat none the less. Nutritionally insignificant perhaps but, contrary to Theissen, a familiar enough part of everyday life of the non-élite that 'numinous' qualities could not have been ascribed to it."²²³

Valid though Meggitt's criticism of the confidence of the proponents of the 'New Consensus' in Theissen's thesis of the socially mixed Corinthian Christians may be, it is none the less hard to accept the logic of his arguments. On the one hand, he argues that the majority of the populace of the Roman Empire including the Corinthian Christians lived near the poverty line or were dominated by 'fears over subsistence.' On the other hand, he believes that the low quality meat was more readily available to or affordable by the masses than Theissen would allow. Had Meggitt considered the question of how people living near starvation could afford to buy and eat meat, be it expensive or cheap, he might have revised his contention. It is hard to imagine that meat would have been readily available to people living near starvation. The meat may have been available. But it is hard to believe that those living near starvation or just beyond it could afford to consume meat easily and as their daily diet. Thus Theissen's recent statement in defence of his thesis and in repudiating Meggitt's challenge, that the meat served at *poppinae* was not part of everyday life, but served for personal feasts and banquets, and that the rich bought their meat from expensive *macellum,* is understandable.²²⁴ Moreover, Meggitt does not take into account the undeniable fact that Roman Corinth could not be compared with other cities in the empire in terms of its economic condition. There are various factors that made Corinth a city different economically from others in the empire. Suffice it to say that in contrast to what happened to Greek cities, some of which even disappeared from sight because of depopulation (Strabo 7.7.3), Corinth succeeded at a rocketing pace.²²⁵

Nevertheless, it is difficult to accept Theissen's assumption that the Corinthian dispute over food offered to idols was between the rich and the poor because meat was available to the rich alone. Apparently, the text does not support Theissen's contention. To say that meat was not available to the poor is something, but it is quite another to argue that the conflict between

---

222 Meggitt, *Paul,* 110
223 Meggitt, *Paul,* 112.
224 G. Theissen, "Social Conflicts in the Corinthian Community: Further Remarks on J.J. Meggitt, *Paul, Poverty and* Survival in *JSNT* 25 (2003) 371-91, esp. 383.
225 Cf. Winter, "Litigation," 102.

Corinthian Christians was between the rich and the poor. Paul does not give any indication in his treatment that supports such a view. 'Those accustomed to idols' (8:7) could also come from the rich. Those whose conscience is affected at seeing others eating food offered to idols in a temple or the house of an unbeliever could also come from the rich. Moreover, what is implausible is the contention made by Theissen that the poor would have rejected the eating of meat on a rare religious occasion. If it is true that the poor could not eat meat at their disposal as a daily menu, it is more likely that they would have been more eager to eat it than to denounce it. M. Lyttelton and W. Forman rightly point out that ["f]or the poor, particularly those in the big cities, a sacrifice with many victims would have provided a rarely enjoyed chance to eat meat."[226] In addition, attempts to see Paul's answers in 1 Corinthians 8:1 - 11:1 in their social aspects have tended to move the issue from food offered to idols to Paul's defence against his enemies. In view of the fact that Paul is addressing a community which was on the brink of a formal split and that Paul is appealing to the Corinthian Christians to have a unified view (1:10), it is less likely that Paul would try to exacerbate their division by favouring the poor as suggested by Theissen and his followers. Theissen's theory of the stratified Corinthian Christians may hold true. However, that does not necessarily mean that their dispute over food offered to idols was caused by economic differences.

While Meggitt repudiates Theissen's hypothesis of the consumption of meat as being confined to the rich, P.D. Gooch refutes his confining of idol-food to 'meat.' Although he recognises that "meals and food are markers of social status,"[227] that idol-food was "associated with occasions of major social significance" (i.e. political, weddings, birthdays, funerals, and diverse occasions celebrating good fortune) and that shared meals "were the major means of the maintenance of social relationship" or of "social advancement,"[228] Gooch rejects Theissen's confining of idol-food to 'meat' alone. He writes: "All kinds of food, whether derived from animals or not, could be and were sanctified (or polluted, depending on one's point of view) by ritual acts of thanksgiving or consecration. This makes it possible that even the simplest meal might become idol-food (for example, grain porridge hallowed by rites sacred to the Two Goddesses)."[229] The difference between the upper classes and the lower classes with regard to food is not in 'structure' but in 'scale.' Again Gooch states: "The humble used the sanctuary of Demeter and Kore extensively, and probably its dining rooms;

---

226 M. Lyttelton and W. Forman, *The Romans, Their Gods and Their Beliefs* (London: Orbis, 1984) 40.
227 Gooch, *Dangerous Food,* 38.
228 Gooch, *Dangerous Food,* 46
229 Gooch, *Dangerous Food,* 149.

the lower class carried away...sacrificed chicken (instead of beef) from the Asklepeion; the poor clients needed to angle for invitations for social advancement more than the wealthy; weddings of the humble involved sacrifice just as those of the rich."[230] Gooch's point must be taken into account, even though the validity of the view that the locations of the issue being the temple of Demeter and Kore or Asklepios is still questioned by the proponents of the view that such temples did not exist at the time of 1 Corinthians (see section 2.2 below).

In fact, Gooch criticizes another emphasis on the social nature of our case, that which is propagated by W.L. Willis who emphasizes the importance of the social character of religious meals. According to Willis, what made the difference was the focus of the participants. The motive of Willis' argument is to explain his conviction that Paul is consistent in his whole treatment of the issue in 1 Corinthians 8-10. Willis refutes the attempt made by some scholars who argue that Paul's understanding of pagan meals in 1 Corinthians 10:1-22 is sacramental, and that in 8:1-13 is more 'enlightened.'[231] The social character of religious meals was always present.[232] Thus he says: "while due regard was given the deity and a portion allotted to him, the focus is on the social relationship among the worshippers. The deity is more an observer than a participant."[233] It was the focus of the participants which determined the religiousness or the socialness of the meal.[234] To prove his contention, Willis collects evidence which indicates that there was criticism of the abuse of religious meals for social interests. Hence, cult regulations, satirical accounts critical of parasites at cultic tables and earnest lamentations on the lack of true devotion are explored by Willis.[235] In this light, Paul's rejection of the Corinthians' involvement in the table of *daimonia* (10:16-22) is seen not in the sense of participation with the demons themselves, but with others in idolatry.[236]

---

230 Gooch, *Dangerous Food*, 149-50. However, Gooch recognizes the contention made by Theissen that avoidance of idol-food would affect the rich in their social intercourse than the poor (150).

231 See references for these scholars in W.L. Willis, *Idol Meat in Corinth. The Pauline Argument in 1 Corinthians 8 and 10* (Chico: Scholars Press, 1985) 18, 33.

232 Cf. Yeo, *Interaction*, 95, who argues that people could visit temples for social reasons such as "a marriage, a birth, or a graduation party." So "to the Corinthians eating idol meat was a social expectation and as much a civil obligation as a religious one."

233 W.L. Willis, *Idol Meat*, 20; cf. Richard B. Hays, "Ecclesiology and Ethics in 1 Corinthians" in *EA*10 (1994) 31-43, esp. 37, who, although recognizing that a personal sacrifice to a god in pagan temple would involve participation of friends and family members, argues for dinner parties than religious ceremonies.

234 W.L. Willis, *Idol Meat*, 48.

235 W.L. Willis, *Idol Meat*, 57-61.

236 W.L. Willis, *Idol Meat*, 191.

Paul does not focus on the contagious nature of the food. Rather he concentrates on partnership with others in idolatry. Only in this way can we see the consistency of Paul's emphasis on the effect of eating food on the weak, rather than on the nature of the food in 1 Corinthians 8:1-3.[237]

Willis' emphasis on the social nature of religious food is criticized by Gooch who argues that Willis has done so at the expense of the religious nature of the food sacrificed in the temple of Kore and Demeter and eaten in its dining facilities, or of food sacrificed as thank-offerings by private worshippers which could be eaten by the priests and the participants in the temple itself or in its surrounding area such as at the fountain in Lerna, and which could be taken home by the participants or given to others met with on the way home.[238] Moreover, Gooch goes so far as to argue that even food served at political and social occasions (such as weddings, birthdays, funerals and response to good fortune) could be ritualized to heighten its social character.[239] Hence, Gooch infers that "some Corinthian Christians did eat in what might be considered an idol's temple without any consciousness (at least until Paul's first letter had arrived) and that they had compromised their faithfulness to Christ."[240] Even if they were unanimous about the rejection of involvement in the temple and about eating food sacrificed there as thank-offerings, it was by no means clear whether such food could be eaten around and outside the temple. Similarly, because shared meals were social occasions and since food presented on social occasions might have undergone religious rites, Christians were not sure whether they should risk social friendship and advancement by refusing to participate on these occasions.[241] With this understanding, Gooch criticizes Willis' social emphasis[242] by arguing that social meetings could also be at the same time "deeply religious occasions."[243]

Since for the ancient people there was an integral link between religious and social happenings, or vice versa,[244] it is not possible for us to emphasize

---

237 W.L. Willis, *Idol Meat*, 184-88, 215-219.
238 Gooch, *Dangerous Food*, 15-26, 81-82. Cf. Tomson, *Paul*, 189, who shows that bloodless offerings are included in the term εἰδωλοθύτων. In fact, for the Jews "wine offered to idols was a strongly forbidden as meat."
239 Gooch, *Dangerous Food*, 27-46; cf. Rainbow, "Monotheism," 134-35, here 125. He writes: "temple precinct was the equivalent of a modern restaurant." He also argues that the survival of ancient clubs and societies depended on religious basis.
240 Gooch, *Dangerous Food*, 102.
241 Gooch, *Dangerous Food*, 46.
242 W.L. Willis, *Idol Meat*, 63.
243 Gooch, *Dangerous Food*, 154.
244 Stanley K. Stowers, "Greeks Who Sacrifice and Those Who Do not: Toward an Anthropology of Greek Religion" in L.M. White and L. Yarbrough (eds.), *The Social World of the Early Christians: Essays in Honor of Wayne Meeks* (Minneapolis: Fortress, 1995) 293-333, emphasizes the integral nature of sacrifice

one at the expense of the other. W. Baird rightly claims that even though we need to welcome the sociological approach with enthusiasm "the notion that all the problems are social represents another methodological oversimplification, parallel to the earlier theological oversimplification."[245] Perhaps, it is the awareness of the inadequacy of this methodology which concentrates on the social composition of the members of the Corinthian Church that causes P.D. Gardner[246] to depend on etymological study which is controlled by a syncronic understanding of a language unit in his exegesis of 1 Corinthians 8 - 10, a method which has its own pitfalls.

It seems that to enter into the debate between the 'Old Consensus' and the 'New Consensus' one should have a good command of the first century social history of the Roman society which has to be seen not only from the views of those from above, that is to say the views of those more fortunate people, but also from those below.[247] Until we come with a better, more balanced knowledge of the composition of the early Christians, we must be wary of depending too much on the controversy between the 'Old Consensus' and the 'New Consensus' in reading our passage. Therefore, we cannot as yet conclude with a high degree of confidence that the issue of food offered to idols emerged in the Corinthian Christian community because of the difference between the rich and the poor.

b. Drawing Boundary Lines: A Proposal

Based on Paul's paraphrase of the previous letter (5:9-13 cf. 6:9-13) and his discourse on the issue of food offered to idols (8:1 - 11:1), we may suggest that this issue was a further natural consequence of the attempts made by the Corinthian Christians to associate with other people in their society in which food offered to idols was an accepted practice (cf. also 6:9-11). Some wanted to have full association with their neighbours, others wished to cut

---

    in community life of Graeco-Roman world in antiquity. Sacrifice was present on every social occasions organised by family, guilds, associations, and by the city officials including imperial festivals. Cf. R.A. Horsley, "l Corinthians: A Case Study of Paul's Assembly as an Alternative Society" in R.A. Horsley (ed.), *Paul and Empire,* 242-52, esp. 247, who argues that religion "was often inseparable from political, economic, and other fundamental social forms."

245 Baird, "One Against Another," 131.
246 P.D. Gardner, *The Gift of God and the Authentication of a Christian: An Exegetical Study of 1 Corinthians 8-11:1* (Lanham: University Press of America, 1994) 10-13.
247 See Meggitt, *Paul,* 14-15; Pace F. Gerald Downing, "A Bas Les Aristos. The Relevance of Higher Literature for the understanding of the Earliest Christian Writings" in *NovT* 30 (1988) 212-30, who is very confident of the higher literature in describing the life of the low masses so much so that he concludes: "There is no sign of a culture-gap between the highly literate aristocracy and the masses." The higher literature is capable of "indicating at least elements in the popular oral urban culture of the day."

any link with other people especially in the area in which the danger of returning to their old belief and practice was greater than scholars have thought.[248] Although both are committed to their Christian faith, they differ in their relationship with other people outside their Christian community.[249] Both have their justifications or reasons and fears for having one view rather than the other. It is more than just a conflict between the Gnostics or a group of 'radical spiritual enthusiasts, who scoffed at scruples' and 'a conservative group' who thought that eating such meat constituted entering into communion with the idols,[250] or with the power of demons.[251]

In ancient time association with idolaters necessarily involved eating which, in itself, was intrinsically related to social, political, economic and religious occasions.[252] Because of the outsiders' close association with food offered to idols, some Corinthian Christians thought that a boundary should

---

248 Pickett, *The Cross in Corinth,* 99-100, argues that, on the one hand, Paul recognises the fluidity of the social boundaries separating believers from non-believers (5:9-10, 7:12-7, 10:25-27), but on the other hand, he propagates the sense of separateness from pagan society. According to Pickett, the latter is because continuing relationship with their society would decisively influence interpersonal relationship between Christians (1 Cor. 5-14). This interpersonal relationship is influenced by one's social position in Roman social ranking system. Both Paul and the Corinthian Christians were facing a crisis of "a discrepancy between social and baptismal identity" (102).
249 We cannot say, as Taylor does, that those who wanted to eat food offered to idols are less committed to their Christianity than those who did not want to eat and therefore wanted to have a total alienation from the world from which they had been called, namely their previous idolatrous practices (Nicholas H. Taylor, "The Social Nature of Conversion in the Early Christian World" in Philip F. Esler [ed.], *Modelling Early Christianity,* 128-36, esp. 134).
250 R. Jewett, *Christian Tolerance. Paul's Message to the Modern Church* (Philadelphia: Westminster Press, 1982) 48.
251 M. Rauer, "Die Schwachen in Korinth und Rom" in *Biblische Studien* XXI (1923) 1-192, esp. 53ff., as noted by R. Jewett, *Paul's Anthropological Terms. A Study of Their Use in Conflict Setting* (Leiden: E.J. Brill, 1971) 34, who identifies the weak as "Gentile Christians who could not rid themselves of the superstitious belief that demonic powers lurked behind idols to whom meat was dedicated and before whom temple meals were celebrated."
252 Cf. Sawyer, "The Problem," 88, warns against any classification of life in the ancient world. He writes: "It is difficult, if not impossible to compartmentalise life into religious, economic, and social areas, for there is an inevitable overlapping of these categories especially in the ancient world." Cf. also S.R.F. Price, *Rituals and Power - the Roman Imperial Cult in Asia Minor* (Cambridge: CUP, 1984) 1, who points out that politics and religion are inseparable in the Greek cities of Asia Minor.

be drawn between themselves and non Christians,²⁵³ whatever the circumstances. As people formerly involved in the worship of idols they knew what offering sacrifices to idols meant and what used to be in their mind when they ate food offered to idols, irrespective of the place (i.e. they saw it as really offered to idols, 1 Cor. 8:7). Their conversion to the gospel meant a break with idolatry and anything associated with it. No relationship should be carried out with idolatrous outsiders. No contact should be made with anything associated with idolatry or anyone who is not a believer (cf. 1 Cor. 7:12-16). Hence, food offered to idols in the temple (εἰδωλόθυτον) or anything sold in the meat market ἐν μακέλλῳ and at a meal prepared by an unbeliever, most probably in his house, could not be eaten.

It is interesting to note that, according to F. Braudel, some of the rich people in Castille fed their dependents and servants directly from their estates rather than from the market.²⁵⁴ If such a case was prevalent in Corinth, it would not be difficult to imagine that the weak might have thought that even such kind of food could not be eaten so long as it had been sacrificed to idols. To them, their contact or interaction with the immoral men of the world would certainly create an opportunity to dine with the idolaters, either in the temple precinct, in the meat market or even at the invitation of an unbeliever (8:10, 10:15 and 28), and eventually lead to their attendance at the sacrificial acts themselves. They feared the thought of interaction with the idolaters of the world for it would gradually, if not automatically, cause them to take part in the sacrificial act of the worship of idols and its post-worship activities including dining.²⁵⁵ This fear caused them to protest against it for they knew what it would involve.²⁵⁶

---

253 Cf. Meeks, *Urban Christians*, 97-98, 100; Tomson, *Paul*, 190, rightly notes that the Gentile Christian in Corinth and elsewhere faced a dilemma of "how to live in gentile society and not get involved in idolatry."

254 See F. Braudel, *The Mediterranean and the Mediterranean World in the Age of Philip II*, ET. by S. Reynolds (London: Collins, 1972) as noted by C.R Whittaker, "The Consumer City revisited: the vicus and the city" in *JRA* 3 (1990) 110-18, esp. 112.

255 Cf. J.E. Staumbaugh, "The Functions of Roman Temples" in *ANRW* 2.16.1 (1978) 554-608, here 591, has shown that many Roman temples were built not just as an obligation to idols, but also to celebrate military victories, and to demonstrate the prestige of builders, generals and benefactors. In particular he says that temples served "not only for the worship of the gods, in this case the patrons of the 'collegium'. They also served as a community centre and private club, where a good meal could be found on specific occasions, and where agreeable company could be found at least once a month."

256 It is D. Newton, "Food Offered to Idols in 1 Corinthians 8-10: A Study of Conflicting Viewpoints in the Setting of Religious Pluralism in Corinth." Unpublished PhD. Diss. (Sheffield University, 1995) 75-76, who argues for the possibility that Paul's previous letter was misunderstood by the Corinthians leading

This fear must have been communicated to Paul by the Corinthians' official letter and oral reports.[257] There is reason to infer that it was probably the awareness of their viewpoint that made Paul write in the way he did in 1 Corinthians 8-9 and more strongly in 10:1-22. In particular we may note that Paul's clear acknowledgement - ambiguous though it seems to be to us[258] - of the existence of the idols in 8:5 and his description in 8:10 of the impact of reclining at the temple on the weak conscienced brother, must have been formulated because of his awareness of this danger. Moreover, in 10:20 he directs the attention from idols to demons.[259]

According to Paul's description in 1 Corinthians 8:7, 10 these people are vulnerable to going back to their old idolatrous practices and therefore to fall back into idolatry, because apart from their conscience they had nothing with which to defend their position. They were likely to be influenced by their fellow Christians to whom eating food offered or sacrificed to idols was theologically as well as sociologically sound. It must be acknowledged that it is difficult for us to know how they expressed their opinion in their relation to those who wanted to eat food offered to idols, whether in an aggressive way or otherwise. Given that even in 'trivial cases' (κριτηρίων ἐλαχίστων) one of the church members dared to take his brother to secular court (6:1-2), there is a possibility to argue for an aggressive attack on those

---

to confusion caused by the failure of the text to provide a clear distinction or definition of the term 'idolater.' And possibly, some Corinthians understood such terms as εἴδωλόν, εἰδωλοθύτον, εἰδωλολάτρες, and εἰδωλολάτρια in ways different from those perceived and communicated by Paul. But I think it was not so much a different understanding between Paul and his readers about those terms as different awareness between the Corinthians about the danger of associating with idolaters that caused the conflict. Those accustomed to idols could instantly pinpoint what would happen if a believer associated with an idolater. But those with knowledge of monotheistic God would not see this anymore.

257 Cf. Ben Witherington III, "Not So Idle Thoughts about EIDOLOTHUTON" in *TynBul* 44 (1993) 237-254, here 241 n. 10 and 243, who argues that Paul never went to the temple and would not know what happened in the temple and its adjacent buildings. But this might be too strong a suggestion because, even though he might not enter the temple while in Corinth, his knowledge of religious life in his world could have been wider than Witherington III allows.

258 J.D.G. Dunn, *The Theology of Paul the Apostle* (Edinburgh: T and T Clark, 1998) 36-37.

259 Again Dunn, *The Theology,* 37, asks: "was Paul simply reflecting the real fears of the "weak" members in the Corinthian Church, naming realities of which he himself was less than certain? Or indeed, was his use of the term 'demons' simply the result of his deliberate echo of Deut. 32.17, with further echo in 10.22 of Deut. 32.21 implying that the idol is "no god" (Deut. 32.21)?" P.D. Gooch, *Dangerous Food,* 77, is therefore wrong in saying that ["w]hile Paul would certainly understand *daimonia* to be demons, the Corinthians might not hear that nuance but understand the term as a general references to deities."

who wanted to eat. However, our text does not allow us to make such an inference simply because Paul does not point in that direction.

Those who want to exercise their right to eat food offered to idols (8:9) use various legitimate reasons.[260] First, their theological knowledge of a monotheistic God, and therefore of the non-existence of idols led them to conclude that food is neutral before God (1 Cor. 8:1,4-6,8).[261] Their view on this indifference to food is not much different from that expressed by Paul in his response to their question. Paul says ["f]ood will not commend us to God. We are no worse off if we do not eat, and no better off if we do" (1 Cor. 8:8) and "the earth is the Lord's, and everything in it" (1 Cor. 10:26). They also thought that since the provision and distribution of food (including meat) was in their society handled by those who were likely to be non-Christians and therefore likely to have been related to their idolatrous religious ceremonies, the thought of abstaining from food offered to idols or of dissociating from those who distributed it was unacceptable not only because it would deprive them of food and of social contact in their society, but it would also, and more importantly, run counter with their theological knowledge. Secondly, such abstinence would contradict their freedom status upon which their right as Roman citizens was based, a status highly prized in the whole empire mainly because of the privileges it offered to its holders (1 Cor. 8:9). In fact, as Roman citizens living in a highly Romanized city, they were entitled to food provision administered by the city magistrates especially when there was a shortage of food.[262] Hence, it would be against their right and, correspondingly, against their freedom status to deprive them of food even though it had been offered to idols. Besides, they knew that offering food to idols was, to their fellow non-Christian citizens, aimed at securing the stability and prosperity of the city. Furthermore, such abstinence would also contradict what was already accepted by some people in their society, namely the aphoristic saying that

---

260 Those who want to eat food offered to idols cannot necessarily be classified as people who were less committed to Christianity, as suggested by Nicholas H. Taylor, "The Social Nature of Conversion," 134, because we cannot regard the weak as more committed to Christianity than those who wanted to eat it and therefore had a fundamental alienation from their previous life and relationship with the world. If they were, Paul would not have seen them as being vulnerable to going back to their previous practice (1 Cor. 8:10-12).

261 Tomson, *Paul*, 193, rightly argues that γνῶσις here does not refer to the 'proto-gnosis' in the city but 'within the church.' It is 'the rational insight that idols are nothing and that dedication to the gods does not make food any different.' Furthermore, Tomson argues that there was at the time a climate of "rational criticism towards idolatry" which was shared by the Pharisaic-Rabbinic and Cynico Stoic traditions and, by Paul even though with qualification.

262 Cf. P. Garnsey, *Famine and Food Supply in the Graeco-Roman World* (Cambridge: CUP, 1988), see esp. 272.

'everything is permitted' (10:23 cf. 6:12) which, they might have thought, was in essence supported by the gospel of freedom proclaimed by Paul.

In other words, some were not open to their society, but others were totally open.[263] Their differences were so intense that Paul's apparently general exhortation in his previous letter (1 Cor. 5:9-13), in which he allows Christians to have contact with the immorals and idolaters of the world but commands them to have no association with Christian immorals and idolaters, could not solve their dispute.

This boundary creation was a concern both to Corinthian Christians themselves[264] and to Paul who, himself, had experienced the importance of defining his Christian identity when he was converted from his old-belief system, Judaism.[265] If a transition from Judaism to Christianity posed a complicated problem for Paul and other contemporary Jewish Christians,

---

263 Marshall, "The Enigmatic Apostle," 155. Although Marshall is right in saying that Pauline letters dealt with his converts' "complex and difficult transition from old to new...yet within the old" and with Christians who were involved in "an independent-dependent form of existence, in which church members were seeking to adjust to a new and collaborative way of thinking and acting distinct from the neighbourhood upon which they relied for their existence," he is wrong in saying that the Corinthian church "appears to be open in its relations with the wider networks in Roman Corinth." The fact that there existed factions among Corinthian Christians (1 Cor. 1:12 - 4:21) and that there were too many issues about which they differed (1 Cor. 7 - 16) does not allow us to infer that they were *all* open to the wider networks of their society.

264 Cf. William A. Breadslee, *First Corinthians. A Commentary for Today* (St. Louis: Chalice Press, 1994) 82.

265 There is no reason to think that this boundary definition was a problem only to Paul himself and not to his converts, even if we accept the view that their environs was not hostile to them, as suggested by J.M.S. Barclay, "Thessalonica and Corinth: Social Contrasts in Pauline Christianity" in *JSNT* 47 (1992) 49-74. The fact that they wrote to Paul (7:1), whatever our reconstruction of Paul's correspondence with them prior to their letter to Paul and his previous letter to them (5:9-13) may be, clearly indicates that their concern about their distinct identity in their society was greater than is normally thought (see for instance the issue of religiously mixed marriage in 7:12-16). If the interplay between the church and the society was a problem to Paul himself, as rightly pointed out by Marshall, "The Enigmatic Apostle," 172, how much more it must have been for his converts, most of whom had come from religions in which idols had long been and continued to be worshipped by their adherents (6:9-11; 12:1). They must have had some difficulty in undertaking the process of transformation from their old identity into their new distinct identity, especially as there had never been any new set of ethos already laid out for them to observe and that their old-belief systems had been observed from generation to generation. We must not undermine the importance of the latter in their lives, especially when we come to the identity of those who are accustomed to idols (1 Cor. 8:7).

how much more it must have been for most of the Corinthian Christians who had to make a transition from paganism to Christianity.[266]

To the ancient people, including the Graeco-Roman Corinthian populace, a solid distinction of religious life from social, economic and political life virtually did not exist as it has been in some societies in our modern world. Social life to them was religious as religious life was social. In this regard, Newton's suggestion that the Corinthian Christians might have varying perceptions of the issue of εἰδωλοθύτων[267] deserves our acknowledgement. His suggestion helps us to appreciate the complexity of the issue among Paul's first century readers. Similarly, Mitchell argues that given the 'variability and awkwardness of terminology' in 1 Cor 8:1 - 11:1 what Paul is asked to give advice on is "at heart a definitional one: who is an idolater?"[268]

None the less, Newton's suggestion is so general that it fails to acknowledge the likelihood that for Corinthian Christians who had been converted from idolatry and Judaism there must have been a clear knowledge of idols and what was involved in the sacrifices to idols. He therefore fails to exploit the reasons for some Corinthian Christians insisting on eating food offered to idols as we have described above. Equally, Mitchell's suggestion that the issue focuses on the question of who is an idolater may be too general. Rather, the issue centers on the question of the reasons whereby any relationship with idolatry and anything or anyone related to it is carried out.

Our description of the existence of two conflicting views among Corinthian Christians on the issue of εἰδωλοθύτων helps us to understand why Paul takes great care in his response in 1 Corinthians 8:1 - 11:1. To face such a dispute, Paul must have found it hard to respond.[269]

---

266 Cf. D.G. Horrell, "The Development of Theological Ideology in Pauline Christianity. A Structuration Theory Perspective" in Philip F. Esler (ed.), *Modelling Early Christianity*, 224-36, here 228, who, in referring to 1 Corinthians 7, rightly argues that Paul is responding to a situation "which may in part be an unintended consequence of Paul's earlier teaching." And so what he is doing is to reformulate, reshape and expand the Christian symbolic order.

267 Cf. B.R. Magee, "A Rhetorical Analysis of First Corinthians 8:1-11:1 and Romans 14:1-15:13." Th.D. Dissertation (New Orleans Baptist Theological Seminary, 1988) 12 argues that there is a barrier between Paul and his readers in their understanding of the issue which could lead to miscommunication.

268 Mitchell, *Rhetoric*, 237.

269 W.A. Meeks, "And Rose Up to Play: Midrash and Paraenesis in 1 Corinthians 10:1-22" in *JSNT* 16 (1982) 64-78, see esp. 73-5. Meeks argues that Paul's answer does not draw a clear cut boundary line in his dealing of the issue in chapters 8-10. The result of his arguments points to an ambiguous boundary line. But this is because his concentration is not on maintenance of boundary line but on "the solidarity of the Christian community."

Commanding those who had no reservation about eating food offered to idols to abstain from it would not do justice to their legitimate arguments. Yet allowing them to act according to their views would also be seen as a legitimation of idolatry and certainly encourage those accustomed to and acknowledging the existence of idols to return to their old belief and idolatrous practices (1 Cor. 8:9-13). He does not agree with the view of those who want to cut relationship with outsiders (10:19), but he loves them as those for whom Christ died (8:11). He does not want them to be injured by their brothers who possess legitimate arguments. Nor does he want the latter to be ignorant of the danger of eating food offered to idols simply on the basis of their legitimate arguments (8:11-13), namely that it would destroy not only their weak brothers but also themselves (10:1-22).

The fact that Paul is at pains in trying to prevent those who wanted to eat food offered to idols from doing so must not be seen as an indication that he is facing some, if not all of the church members, who oppose his stance on the matter, because, as we shall show, the text clearly shows that he also addresses those who refuse to eat but who are likely to eat it because of the influence of their fellow Christians (8:10, 10:19, 25-26). Rather, it must be seen as his attempt to prevent those who want to eat it not only from injuring their fellow Christians but also from destroying themselves. In essence, Paul is trying to hold the community together. Mitchell rightly observes that the larger concern of Paul is "how the Corinthian community can retain its internal unity when faced with pressures from the outside culture which pull the community apart."[270] Hence, we can see why Paul does not want to answer in such a way that they would cease to believe in their legitimate arguments. He does it in a way that would help them to abandon their desire to exercise their right to eat without destroying their legitimate arguments. We will show the benefit of seeing the origin of the dispute in this way later in section 2.3.2 when we attempt to see the overall interpretation of Paul in 1 Corinthians 8:1 - 11:1.

We have seen above that 1 Corinthians 5:9-13 helps us to set up the general context of the Corinthian Christians' dispute over food offered to idols (i.e., dispute around boundary marking). It is appropriate to note in this connection that, as a matter of fact, Paul does not deal with problems related to idolatry (8:1 - 11:1) until he has finished addressing the immoral brother issue which had been addressed in his previous letter and went unheeded (5:1-8 cf. 5:9-13). Their neglect of an immoral man among themselves might have been caused by their preoccupation with the issue of re-association with the idolaters from outside their community. They enjoyed passing judgment on idolaters, but neglected judging their own immoral brother. They judged outsiders, and debated on the problem of

---

[270] M.M. Mitchell, *Rhetoric,* 237; cf. Terry, *Discourse,* 56-7, who points out that the conflict in 1 Corinthians is between Christ against cultures and customs.

associating with immoral men of the world, but neglected their own immorality. A report has reached Paul's ears, saying that one of them has committed an action which is not found even among the pagans (ἐν τοῖς ἔθνεσιν, 5:1). Their arrogance in regarding themselves as better than others, which had exacerbated their leadership alignment, had no ground. They ought to have mourned (5:2). Hence Paul's challenge: "For what have I to do with judging outsiders? Is it not those inside the church whom you are to judge? God judges those outside, 'Drive out the wicked from among you'" (5:12-13).[271]

The question of why this self-definition picked up the issue of food offered to idols will be pursued later after a presentation on scholar's discussion on the possible location of εἰδωλόθυτον itself in Corinth. If the location was in a normal temple as in any other Greek city, the question of why the issue became one major concern in Corinth is crucial. This means that we must seek to find the location in the uniqueness of Corinth of Paul's time.

2.2. The Location of εἰδωλοθύτων: Determining the Historical Context

A glance at 1 Corinthians 8:1 - 11:1 enables us to see the selection of

---

271 In 5:2c-5 and 6-8 he has emphasised the need to expel the immoral man with his own authority from a distance, with an appeal to the assembly to take action, and with the theology of the sacrifice of the paschal lamb. In chapter 6 he develops this by encouraging the Corinthians to have their own internal judiciary system on trivial matters, rather than going out to court before the unrighteous, the least esteemed by the church and believers (1, 4, 6) because, eschatologically speaking, the Corinthians and Paul will judge the world and are about to judge angels (6:2-3). They were asked to continue associating with outsiders, though not being allowed to have an illicit relationship with prostitutes (6:15-16). And in chapter 7 Paul continues to deal with the danger of immorality (7:2,9,36). Deming, *Paul on Marriage and Celibacy*, 139, argues that "the Corinthians objected to living with non-Christian spouses out of fear that physical association with unbelievers polluted them, thereby threatening their relationship with God." Even those married to unbelievers were asked not to divorce them but to continue to live with them (7:12-16), and to care for their sexual life in the face of the danger of immorality in order not to repeat what is committed by the immoral brother. Only after dealing with what he intended most in his previous letter (5:13-19) does Paul tackle the idol-meat issue which is set in the context of associating with idolaters. So, Paul deals first of all with the internal affairs (both leadership alignment and sexual immorality with the proposal of the need to have an internal judgment (chps. 1-7) and then with issues related to outsiders occasioned by idol-meat (8:1 - 11:1), before returning to the internal problem in worship and the Lord's Supper (11:2-34), competition of spiritual gifts (12 - 14) and disputes over the resurrection of the dead (15) and over the collection to the saints in Jerusalem (16:1-4). Lastly, he deals with the issue of local leadership (16:12, 15-18).

various locations of εἰδωλοθύτων. Presumably, it was at these locations that the action of eating εἰδωλοθύτων took place in the city. The Corinthians might have mentioned these locations during the course of their intense debate. Not only did they discuss their presence and participation in temples where εἰδωλοθύτων were likely to have been offered and eaten, and idols worshipped (8:10; 10:21-23),[272] but they also talked about eating "anything sold in the meat market" supposedly to have previously been sacrificed to idols (10:25)[273] and meat presented on social occasions, at a dinner by an unbeliever (10:27-28). Since some of the rich might have fed their dependents and slaves directly from their estates and not through the market, the mention of the house of an unbeliever as the location of the dispute over the food sacrificed to idols is not surprising.[274]

All these locations cover both religious and social life of the Corinthians: from the very religious activity in the sacrificial act (either in temples [8:10] or at other venues such as at the table of δαιμόνια [10:21],[275] houses, theatres or others), to the economic activity away from the temple yet still related to religious sacrificial acts (in the meat-market), and to social activity after religious occasions (at dining tables in and around the temples, and at the invitation of an unbeliever). There might have been many other

---

272 For a recent discussion on the meaning of εἰδωλοθύτων, whether it is simply a general term for food sacrificed to idols that may refer to that eaten in a cultic meal in a temple or strictly sacrificial food eaten at a cultic meal in the temple area and therefore in a pagan worship, see E. Coye Still III, "The meaning and uses of ΕΙΔΩΛΟΘΥΤΟΝ in First Century Non-Pauline Literature and 1 Cor 8:1-11:1: Toward Resolution of the Debate" in *TJ* 23 (2002) 225-234. Coye Still III is for the former.
273 The Corinthians must have had plenty of opportunities to indulge in sacrificial meat. See Ehrhardt, "Social Problems," 279-80; W.L. Willis, *Idol Meat*, 265-266.
274 Braudel, *Mediterranean*, 425, as noted by Whittaker, "The Consumer City," 112 n.15.
275 The phrase ἐν εἰδωλείῳ κατακείμενον (8:10) presents two items of information. First, it refers to an action of being in an idol's temple. Secondly, it points to an act of 'reclining at a table.' If the act of eating was not inside the temple, but in the dining area of the temple - which was still seen as part of the temple -, it would have been the precise reason for some to want to eat food offered to idols, because they were not involved in the act of worship in the temple. Moreover, it would make it easier for others to see than if it was carried out inside the temple. Perhaps, this is why Paul in 10:1-22 stresses the act of 'sitting down, eating and drinking' and in 10:19 which remind them of the fact that the Israelites who ate the sacrifices were also 'partakers' of the altar. In other words, Paul makes a link between the eating and the 'altar' where the sacrifices are offered. It is likely that since their conversion, Christians did not want to enter idols' temples, much less to partake in the act of sacrificing to idols. What they might be tempted to do was not to offer sacrifices to idols, but to eat food which had been offered to idols, not inside the temple itself but in the dining facility adjacent to the temple.

The Interpretive Context 63

locations in the life of the Corinthians in the multi-ethnic city of Corinth, yet Paul's choice of the locations we have in 1 Corinthians 8-10 might have been the ones referred to by his readers in their letter to Paul. Since these locations cover not only the very place where religious rituals were strictly conducted (i.e. temples)[276] but also social meeting places (i.e., market and houses), there is no reason to doubt the likelihood that the issue of εἰδωλοθύτων was very real, delicate, complicated and divisive to the members of the Corinthian church who, having left their former religions and committed themselves to the gospel preached by Paul, had to live in their society from which they were called and to which they were sent to live as Christians.[277]

This way of reading prevents us from the danger of making too much of a distinction between the different terms on the subject matter of εἰδωλοθύτων used by Paul and their locations in chapters 8 and 10, as shown by scholars who emphasize the question of 'where to eat' food offered to idols (see below G.D. Fee and Ben Witherington III), or those who make a case of different meanings of εἰδωλοθύτων (8:1,4,7,10; 10:21) and ἱερόθυτον (10:28) to the point of ignoring the general consensus that to the ancient people there is no distinction between food offered and eaten at the temple with that sacrificed and eaten in the house.

---

276 Cf. A. Watson, *The State, Law and Religion. Pagan Rome* (Athens and London: The University of Georgia Press, 1992) 5, shows that the ceremonies of the state religion of the Roman Empire was conducted by the priests who made sure that "ceremonies were correctly and formalistically carried out in every detail."

277 A cursory reading 1 Corinthians 8-10 shows that Paul does not repeat the same word every time he writes about the location and things associated with it. But we can be certain that since the issue being addressed throughout 8:1 - 11:1 is 'food offered to idols,' εἰδωλοθύτων (8:1) he speaks about the same issue, except in places where he clearly gives other precise contexts of his discourse. For instance, in 8:1,4,7, and 10 (cf. 10:19) Paul uses εἰδωλοθύτων, but in 10:1-22 εἰδωλολάτραι (10:7 cf. εἰδωλολατρίας in 10:14). He also gives a sacrificial context, hence the use of θυσίας in 10:18. This is why in 10:28 he uses ἱερόθυτον which clearly implies that there is an association between what is offered and the temple. We can also note the shift of concentration from εἰδωλόθυτόν/εἴδωλον to δαιμονίοις (10:20-23) which is a subtle way of, on the one hand, not debating with those with knowledge that idols do not exist at all, but on the other hand, of warning the Corinthians not to participate in any pagan sacrificial act related to idolatry, which he says is devoted to demons. In 8:8, Paul's use of βρῶμα does not mean that he thinks of general food, but in the framework of εἰδωλόθυτον, food offered to idols. Eating or not eating it does not have any bearing on one's future relationship with God. Similarly, when Paul uses βρῶμα and κρέα in 8:13 he is speaking about the same food. βρῶμα and κρέα may speak of general meaning of food and meat or point to other notions, but it would be too much to read this general meaning into the immediate context, namely εἰδωλόθυτον, for otherwise we would see Paul as saying that he would not eat any meat or food at all.

It is likely that the issue for the first century Corinthian Christians is not where they ate it, as if eating in the house was different from that in and around the temple, but on what basis they did so.

Granted, before we propose the historical surrounding of the emergence and intensification of the issue among Corinthian Christians, it is appropriate to present briefly the dispute among scholars about the location of the εἰδωλοθύτων. Much of the debate revolves around the questions of the nature of the destruction of the old city of Corinth, of its condition prior to being rebuilt in 44 B.C., and of whether there was any attempt in the Roman Corinth to revive or restore the Greek culture.

Some scholars have argued for the continuation or renovation of the old Corinth. The reasons are that some of its people continued to live after the Roman attack in 146 B.C. because Cicero reported in *De Lege Agraria* 1.2.5 and 2.87 in 79-77 of Corinth being 'most excellent and fruitful land' (W. Willis),[278] its gods and goddesses being worshipped continuously by those people themselves (V.P. Furnish)[279] either because of the nature of Greek religion being slow to change (F.C. Grant)[280] or at the encouragement of the Roman colonists themselves (Oscar Broneer).[281] And so, according to Robert M. Grant, the temples at Corinth are primarily Greek along with a few Roman with equivalents.[282] The following Greek and Egyptian temples are therefore thought to have been the locations that Paul had in mind when writing 1 Corinthians 8-10: the cult of Demeter and Kore at which dining flourished,[283] the cult of Asklepios[284] and its relation to Lerna, the public

---

278 W. Willis, "Corinthusne deletus est.?" in *BZ* 35 (1991) 233-41. See Newton, "Food Offered to idols," 48. Similar view is shared by J.C. Gordon, *Sister or Wife: 1 Corinthians 7 and the Cultural Anthropology*. JSNT Suppl. Series 149 (Sheffield: SAP, 1997) 66.

279 V.P. Furnish, "What Can Archaeology Tell Us?" in *BAR* 15 (1988) 15-27, who argues that the city Romanization did not stop the worship of gods and goddesses.

280 F.C. Grant, *Ancient Roman Religion* (Indianapolis: The Bobbs-Merrill, 1957) 15, see Newton, "Food Offered to Idols," 49. cf. Yeo, *Interaction*, 94: "An ancient city occupied since the Neolithic times, Corinth was, in Paul's day, a cosmopolitan city with rich Greek and Roman cultures." Earlier, Robert Lisle, "The Cults of Corinth." Ph.D. Dissertation (John Hopkins Univ., Baltimore, Maryland, 1955) 2, 32, using Pausanias and accumulated archaeological material, noted that the survival of wooden images of Heracles and Athena Chalinitis well into the second century A.D. could indicate their preservation which was possible if the city was not totally deserted in between 146 BC and 44 AD.

281 O. Broneer, "Corinth - Centre of St. Paul's Missionary Work in Greece" in *BA* 14 (1951) 82.

282 Robert M. Grant, *Paul in the Roman World. The Conflict at Corinth* (Westminster: John Knox Press, 2001) 65.

283 N. Bookidis and J.E. Fisher, "Preliminary Report on Demeter and Kore" in *Hesperia* 41 (1972) 283 ff., but later cast doubt on her earlier suggestion; N.

bath which might function as the venue in which the sacrificial food of private thank-offering was likely to be consumed,[285] the Egyptian cults of Isis[286] and Sarapis,[287] and the cult of the dead and heroes.[288] These temples

---

Bookidis, "Ritual Dining in the Sanctuary of Demeter and Kore at Corinth: Some Questions" in Oswyn Murray (ed.) *Sympotica: A Symposium on the Symposion* (Oxford: Clarendon Press, 1990) 86-94, here 87, identifies 52 dining complexes at the sanctuary from late 6th to 2nd centuries B.C. P.D. Gooch, *Dangerous Food*, 34, here 13, argues that the rites of Demeter worship is in view when Paul speaks of the table of δαιμονίων in 10:21 b. He writes: "To eat from the *kernos* in the sanctuary of Demeter, or to share in pork from a sacrifice offered to her, or to eat a cake representing the fertility brought by Demeter would be to eat food sacred to Demeter, and to share in the rites of her worship."

284 Fotopoulos, *Food Offered to Idols*, 49-70, 92, 128, 154, 176-78, prefers the Temple of Asklepios to other temples (Demeter and Kore, Isis and Sarapis, and at Ishmia) as the possible context. To him, the possibility of the latter depends on the future result of the excavation in Anaploga. Formal meals held at Asklepios temple and in private settings and offered to free citizens provided food, wine, entertainment, sexual opportunities.

285 Witherington III, *Conflict*, 15. The site of this cult is reported by C. Roebuck, *Corinth Vol. 14 The Asclepion and Lerna ASCSA* (Princeton, N.J. 1951) to be in the north of Corinth, adjoining the city wall. J. Murphy O'Connor, "The Corinth That Paul Saw" in *BA* 47 (1984) 147-159. J. McRay, *Archaeology and the New Testament* (Grand Rapids: Baker 1991) 322, criticises J. Murphy-O'Connor for squeezing more out of the dining practice in the temple of Asklepios as a background to Paul's discussion in 1 Corinthians 8 than the situation would allow. P.D. Gooch, *Dangerous Food*, 21-26, esp. 25, is particularly in support of this view. To him the problem faced by Paul's readers might have something to do with the ambiguous relation between the temple of Asklepios and the public fountain, Lerna. Although the use of food was not central in the cult, people brought food to the cult to be sacrificed. There were ritual food which could be eaten by the priest and by the worshippers in the sanctuary or taken out to be consumed elsewhere (in the facilities in and near the Asklepeia or taken home), and ordinary food prescribed to affect the cure. So the problem with Paul's readers was on the question of whether eating in the dining rooms of Lerna was "reclining in an idol's temple" (1 Cor. 8:10) or "sharing the table of *daimonia*" (1 Cor. 10:21).

286 Rainbow, "Monotheism," 289, 291, argues that Corinth's port, Cenchraea, was an important center of the worship of Isis. There was a polytheism in Corinth of the first century.

287 D.E. Smith, "The Egyptian Cults at Corinth" in *HTR* 70 (1977) 201-231, shows that based on archaeological data it is possible to assume that these cults of Egyptian deities were worshipped in Corinth from the time of the Hellenistic period, such as in Cenchraea where a first century temple has been excavated. Apuleius, the second century Latin author [*Metamorphoses* Bk. II) was converted to the worship of Isis.. E.J. Milleker, "Three Heads of Serapis from Corinth" in *Hesperia* 54 (1985) 121-35, has noted that some representations of other Egyptian deity, namely Sarapis, are present.

functioned both socially and religiously.[289]

However, since there is a great uncertainty about the presence and function of the Greek and Egyptian temples from the time of the destruction of the old Greek Corinth in 146 B.C. by the Roman army under the leadership of L. Mummius Achaicus and its resurrection by the Roman Colonizers in 44 B.C. until around the time of the writing of 1 Corinthians, some have understandably expressed their doubt over these temples as the locations of the issue of 1 Corinthians 8-10. The following scholars have expressed this doubt: D.W.J. Gill[290] C.K. Williams,[291] Walbank,[292] Ronald S.

---

288 It is generally understood that these lesser cults may have fallen into decay during the desolation of Corinth, but could have been revived after 44 BC. This is especially argued by O. Broneer, "Hero Cults in the Corinthian Agora" in *Hesperia* 11 (1942) 153. Broneer argues that it is the case because many of the new settlers "were doubtless descendants of the original population" and because "the more important temples were probably not altogether abandoned, and there are reasons to believe that a few settlers began to move in shortly after the destruction" of Corinth. Hence Broneer believes that "it is possible to account for the survival of some of the early cult practices, and the reflection of their continued existence may be traced among the remains from the Roman city" (161). However, Latin writers disagreed over this. Pausanias (*Paus.* 2,3,7) said it disappeared after the destruction of Corinth. But before the close of the second century, Aelian (*Varia Historia* Bk. 5 Ch. 21) in the work of Johannes du Vivie and Isaacum Severinum MDCCI 402-403 argues for its continuation. It is C.A. Kennedy, "The Cult of the Dead in Corinth" in John Marks and Robert M. Good (eds.), *Love and Death in the Ancient Near East Essays in Honor of Marvin H. Pope* (Connecticut: Four Quarters Publishing Company USA, 1987) 229-230, who argues that the temples of 1 Cor 8:10 were not those of the Olympian gods but of tombs. The meals were memorial offerings to the deceased.
289 W.L. Willis, *Idol Meat,* 47-64, emphasises the social aspect of communal meals. His view is refuted by Gooch, *Dangerous Food,* 27-46, who argues that social occasions were heightened by sacrificial acts.
290 D.W.J. Gill, "Corinth a Roman City in Achaea" in *BZ*37 (1993) 259-64, esp. 262-64. Earlier, W. Rees, "Corinth in St. Paul's Time Part 1 Topography" in *Scripture* 2 (1947) 71 and H. Cadbury, "The Macellum of Corinth" in *JBL* 53 (1934) 136, and also M.H. Walbank, "Abstract of Early Roman Corinth" in *AJA* 90 (1986) 220-221.
291 C.K. Williams II, "The Refounding of Corinth. Some Roman Religious Attitudes" in S. Macready and F.H. Thomson (eds.) *Roman Architecture in the Greek World* (The Society of Antiquarians of London, 1987) 31. Williams II records that "For 102 years Corinth remained a ruin, probably with squatters, but without a political life."
292 Mary E. Hopkins Walbank, "Pausanias, Octavia and Temple E at Corinth" in *ABSA* 84 (1989) 398, writes: "in lay out, organisation and religious practice, Corinth was a Roman colony and not simply a restoration of a Greek city."

Stroud,[293] D.G. Romano,[294] D.E. Engels,[295] and recently, Bruce W. Winter.[296]

Winter is the strongest and the latest to have argued for the Romanness of the city. The establishment of imperial cult, the naming of the city and the establishment of divine patronage for Corinth, the policy of dismantling enacted on Corinth in its fall, the use of centuriation and the modernization rather than restoration of Corinth ancient sanctuaries makes Winter to conclude that Corinth was "not a Greek city with a Roman facade." Rather, it was "conceived of, and deliberately laid out as a thoroughly Roman colony".[297] Based on the Argive petition - in which the people of Corinth asked for financial assistance for the extravagant cost of the Imperial cult -, Winter argues that the Corinthians preferred the Roman values to Greek heritage. The petition indicates the loyalty of the people to the Roman values.[298] His view is based on the work of A.J.S. Spawforth[299] who discusses a Greek 'letter' which he claims to be a petition from the city of Argos to the Roman governor of Achaia. Argos begged to be exempted from fulfilling its responsibility to pay the cost needed for the extravagant celebration of the imperial cult at Corinth. Spawforth suggests that member cities of the Achaean League might have been forced to pay the sum on

---

293 Ronald S. Stroud, "The Sanctuary of Demeter on Acrocorinth in the Roman Period" in Timothy E. Gregory (ed.), *The Corinthia in the Roman Period* (Ann Arbor, MI 1993) 65-77, esp. 65

294 D.G. Romano, "Post-146 B.C. Land Use in Corinth, and Planning of the Roman Colony of 44 BC" in Timothy E. Gregory (ed.), *The Corinthia in the Roman Period* 9-30, who argues that when founded as a Roman colony there was a fresh laying out of the site according to the Roman town-planning grid called *centuriation*.

295 Engels, *Roman Corinth,* 62, 69, here 62. Citing L. Shoe, "The Roman Ionic Base at Corinth" in L. Freeman Sandler (ed.), *Essays in Honor of Karl Lehmann* (New York, 1964) 300-304, Engels writes: "The city reflects its Italian origins of many of its citizens in its architecture, from the Roman podium-style temples on the West Terrace down to details of the mouldings of its column bases."

296 Bruce W. Winter, "The Achaean Federal Imperial Cult II: The Corinthian Church" in *TynBul* 46 (1995) 169-178.

297 Winter, *After Paul Left,* 11.

298 Winter, "The Achaean Federal Imperial Cult II," 178, states that: "...it is clear that the Argive petition provides important literary confirmation of Corinth's loyalty, preference for, and adherence to Roman customs and laws." Cf. Theissen, *Social Setting,* 99, who says that ["n]othing in Corinth was more than a century old, whether the constitution, buildings, families, or cults." Similarly, Witherington III, *Conflict,* 8, believes that there was a trend to Romanise the city. The buildings are said to have patterned on the buildings in southern Italian cities such as Pompeii supposedly the homes of the first settlers, veterans and freedmen-women. Furthermore, he points to the significant quantities of Italian wares and goods imported from Italy.

299 A.J.S. Spawforth, "Corinth, Argos and the Imperial Cult: Pseudo-Julian, Letters 198" in *Hesperia* 63 (1994) 211-232.

Nero's accession in A.D. 54 when a cult of the emperors was erected at Corinth. In addition, Winter argues that the Romans applied its policy of dismantling conquered cities to Corinth, and brought its riches to Rome.[300] There is indeed evidence that the building projects conducted in Rome by Lucius Mummius after the sacking of Corinth were funded partly from the sacking of Corinth.[301] Moreover, the amount of booty captured from Carthage and Corinth in 146 B.C. was such that there was a major infusion into the Roman economy. The building of the Marcian Aqueduct in Rome at the cost of 45 million denarii was carried out after the sacking of Corinth and a few years later, after the booty had run out, the building construction ceased.[302] This clearly indicates the extent of the destruction of Corinth. In this light, the locations that are in view in 1 Corinthians 8-10 are said to be Roman domestic cults,[303] the Imperial Cult,[304] and the athletic contests of the Isthmia Games[305] where there was a Poseidon temple.[306]

---

300 K.W. Arafat, *Pausanias' Greece: Ancient Artists and Roman Rulers* (Cambridge: CUP, 1996) 110.

301 T.R.S. Broughton, *The Magistrates of the Roman Republic* (Atlanta, Georgia: Scholars Press, 1986) Vol. 1, 474.

302 E. Badian, *Publicans and Sinners: Private Enterprise in the Service of the Roman Republic* (Oxford: Blackwell, 1972) 53.

303 Which, according to D.G. Orr, "Roman Domestic Religion: the Evidence of the Household Shrines" in *ANRW* 2.16.2 (1978) 1557-1591, here 1564 and 1575, survived over centuries. Their purpose was to seek particular protection of particular powerful deities. Even the Roman emperors had their own *Genius*, the attendant and protecting spirit which could accommodate a great variety of roles. Cf. also M. Lyttelton and W. Forman, *The Romans*, 24-25.

304 The consensus on the Imperial Cult is that it was established and functioning in Corinth long before Paul's visit to Corinth. There are two major arguments which point to its early existence, namely a) the building of temple E (possibly in AD14-37) within a magnificent court in the centre of the city to house the Imperial cult, b) the deification of Livia in AD 23 as divine Julia Augusta with poetry contest even before her death. See C.K. Williams II, "A Re-Evaluation of Temple E and the West End of the Forum in Corinth," 156-62; J. H. Kent, *Korinth* Vol. 8 Pt. 3 No. 153. In addition, the discovery of a number of inscriptions point to the dedications of the Emperor and his house. See. Newton, "Food Offered to Idols," 67. Recently, A.J. Spawforth, "The Achaean Federal Cult Part 1: Pseudo-Julian, Letters 198" in *TynBul* 46 (1995) 151-68, esp. 161-68, claims that the Greek letter, dated in AD 8-120 was written by the official of the city of Argon making a petition to the Roman Govemor of Achaea in which the Argives asked to be exempted from paying towards the cost of celebrations of the Imperial Cult at the Roman colony Corinth. These evidences point to the existence of the Imperial Cult which might have been the background of 1 Corinthians 8-10.

305 The importance of the games was such that a special leadership, the *agoranomos* or the *agonothetes* was elected to take care of the facilitation of the games, including "the sheltering of the crowd and the supervision of the multitude of vendors and

Winter's arguments strengthen earlier arguments for the Roman nature of Corinth, the city of Paul's readers. Earlier it has been shown that Cicero himself mentioned in his *Epist ad. Fam.* 4.5.4 that in a letter written to him in 45 B.C. by Servius Sulpicius Rufus he was informed that the city was lying desolate and demolished.[307] The following strong indications of the Romanness of the city are shown by D.W.J. Gill: the disappearance of the the old traditions of the local sacrifices as noted in Pausanias 7.3-6, signified in boys no longer cutting their hair for Medea's daughter and wearing black clothes, the preference to use Latin names by the people such as Aquila, Priscilla and Crispus indicating the commonality for people to take on "the mantle of Romanness"[308] the naming of the city as *Colonia Laus Julia Corinthiensis*, the issuing of coinage with Latin texts by the magistracy, the use of public inscriptions in Latin until the second century, the architecture of public buildings, the possibility that Temple E overlooking the forum reflected the layout of the Forum of Augustus in Rome, the tombs of the social élite such as that of Lucius Castricius Regulus overlooking the harbour at Cenchreae, the images of the emperor in Roman guise, and lastly the portrait of Augustus looking like an Italian magistrate with his toga worn over his head.[309] Indeed, a process of redesigning the temple of Apollo in Roman style, the change of the image of the Aphrodite Temple in Acrocorinth from the goddess of war to become the goddess of love, the absence of any intention on the part of the Colonists to evoke the glories of Aphrodite Hoplismeni, and the placement of Venus at the city center and thereby as Mother of Roman colony, are cited by C.K Williams II.[310] Moreover, Stroud stresses that Demeter's sanctuary was abandoned soon after Mummius departed. There was speedy rather than gradual transition,[311] and a change of the way Demeter was

---

food merchants." See Daniel J. Geagan, "Notes on the Agonistic Institutions of Roman Corinth" in *GRBS* 9 (1968) 75-76. Giving banquet to the inhabitants was also included in their responsibility, such as done by Lucius Regulus, the first Agonothetes of the first Isthmian Games of the Roman Corinth in 6 or 2 BC.

306 Winter, *After Paul Left*, 6.
307 Cf. Pausanias 2.1.2, 2.3.7 and 5.21.1.
308 Gill, "In Search of the Social élite," 323-37, esp. 327-328.
309 In 1911, A. Robertson and A. Plummer in *A Critical and Exegetical Commentary on the First Epistle of St. Paul to the Corinthians* (Edinburgh: T and T Clark) xii, said that "[l]ittle was done to show there was any wish to revive the glories of Greece." Furthermore, they said that the descendants of the survivors of the Roman attack did not return to the defeated city and Greeks avoided staying there. Yet, Robertson and Plummer argued that in Paul's time the city was already Hellenised.
310 C.K. Williams II, "A re-evaluation of Temple E and the West End of the Forum of Corinth" in S. Walker and A. Cameron (eds.), *The Greek Renaissance in the Roman Empire* (London, 1989) 156-62, esp. 157.
311 Stroud, "The Sanctuary of Demeter," 65.

worshipped from Hellenitic to Roman was took place. This is shown by their different topography, architecture and finds from both phases of the Sanctuary.[312]

The controversy between the proponents of the continuation of Greek culture and of the Romanness of the city have caused some scholars to express caution in emphasizing one or the other. For instance, R.E. Oster, cautions: "...it would be a grave error to suppose that the inhabitants of colonial Corinth lived in a setting which was mono-cultural and homogeneous at the time of nascent Christianity."[313] Similarly, D. Liftin states that "the populace of Corinth was made of an alloy of peoples drawn from across the Mediterranean. Though no doubt dominated by Greeks and Romans, with its various travellers and minority residents Corinth must have represented as much of a cross section of the empire as one was likely to find in any single location. More Greek than Rome, more Roman than Athens .."[314] Hence he warns: "We need argue no more than that Corinth was a significant Greco-Roman city which partook in an ordinary way of the features of Greco-Roman culture. In the end it can only be misleading to claim otherwise without concrete support for doing so."[315]

In any case, given that Corinth was made a Roman colony only 100 years after its destruction and that, according to the Roman policy of colonization, colonists were not settled before the Roman authorities carried out "detailed and meticulous planning" and "careful surveying and purposeful supervision,"[316] it may be argued that unlike other cities which were colonized not long after their defeat by the Roman army, in which case local natives would have been either expelled or allowed to stay alongside the colonists yet with different rights,[317] the colonization of the long-abandoned city of Corinth would not have had to deal with the natives, for they were already brought into slavery immediately after its fall. Therefore, even if we accepted that some people might have lived in the

---

312 Stroud, "The Sanctuary," 68-69.
313 R.E. Oster Jr. "Use, Misuse and Neglect of Archaeological Evidence in some Modern Works in 1 Corinthians (1 Cor 7, 1-5; 8, 10; 11, 2-16; 12, 14-26)" in *ZNW* 83 (1992) 52-73, esp. 55.
314 Liftin, *Proclamation*, 142. Cf. Chow, *Patronage and Power*, 152, who argues that "Corinth was both a Roman colony and a city with a Hellenistic past in a Hellenistic world." He holds this view in order to say that Corinthians held two attitudes towards the imperial cult: the Roman and the Greek traditions. The former saw an emperor deified only after his death and only if he was worthy. To the latter there was a confusing line between the emperor and a god. (153).
315 Liftin, *Proclamation*, 143.
316 E.T. Salmon, *Roman Colonization under the Republic* (London: Thames and Hudson, 1969) 19-25, here 19.
317 Salmon, *Roman Colonization*, 25-26; P.A. Brunt, *Italian Manpower 225 B.C. - A.D. 14* (Oxford: Clarendon Press, 1987) 246-247.

ruined city, they would not have been able to resist the Romanization of the entire life of the city right from the beginning.

Moreover, it may be argued that although at the time of the writing of 1 Corinthians Corinth was undoubtedly a pluralistic and bilingual society the political practice followed the Roman practice of politics. The social structure and dynamics that controlled the social interaction of the population could not have been other than that of Roman, as reflected by its architectural look, its statutes, its inscriptions and its civic laws. The Romanness of the city must have very strongly influenced the individual cultures. At least, people must have found it difficult to escape from the Roman trend.[318] Even if each of the Corinthians might have cherished his immediate ethnic and cultural backgrounds, none the less each had no choice other than to follow the pattern of the larger society. The social structure and dynamics of the city motivated, controlled, and directed the spirit of the whole population. The controlling and dominating values were those related to the Romanness of the city in all aspects of its life. E.T. Salmon rightly claims that any *colonia* of the Roman empire regarded itself as "a community that traditionally originated from Rome" and "an extension of Rome itself."[319] He goes so far as to say that under the reign of Caesar "the greatness and unrivalled prestige of Rome and her Empire made cities, especially provincial ones, very eager to be styled *coloniae* since they could then exuberantly claim to form part of the grandeur and majesty of Rome."[320] In fact, cities which had never been formally colonized would see the bestowal of the title *colonia* as "a mark of imperial favour" upon them, and their proud display of it was therefore not surprising.[321]

Therefore, it is safe to argue that although it is possible that other cults might have been reintroduced by the new settlers and that their influences might have been present in Roman Corinth, the extent of the destruction of the old Greek Corinth and the Romanness of the new Roman Corinth do give cause to infer that the Imperial Cult and its related activities might have been the major concern that intensified the dispute over food offered to idols. In other words, although the issue of food offered to idols had already become a natural issue for Christians coming from idolatrous

---

318 Cf. D.B. Martin, *Slavery as Salvation*, xviii, who argues that Roman influence must have been evident in cities and people of those cities "could scarcely have avoided such influence."

319 Salmon, *Roman Colonization*, 136.

320 Salmon, *Roman* Colonization, 136, see also 153, where Salmon concludes: "the title was a badge, an irrefutable proof of their loyalty." Their status as Roman *coloniae* "carries with it very great prestige...Even towns, that were Roman *municipia* and as such indistinguishable for all practical purposes from *coloniae*, thirsted after the title..." (cf. 157).

321 Salmon, *Roman Colonization*, 136-37.

backgrounds (1 Cor. 6:9-11; 12:1 cf. 1 Thess. 2:9),[322] it could become more serious because of the presence of a local imperial cult in Corinth. Moreover, since this cult was associated with the Isthmian Games and benefited the economy of the city, there is reason to suggest that people of whatever religious backgrounds living in the city could not ignore it. Even if they could, it would have been done with some difficulty and against the mood of their contemporaries. There is no reason to suggest that Paul's converts in this city would have easily overcome such difficulty.

Moreover, Paul's acknowledgement that "there may be so-called gods in heaven or on earth - as indeed there are many 'gods' and many 'lords'" in 1 Corinthians 8:5 could have been conditioned by the reality of these gods and lords in Corinth itself. This is even more likely if it is true that the creation of a provincial or federal imperial cult (called the new Achaean Cult) in Corinth by the cities of the Aegean League, as against a local one, took place in A.D. 54 with the accession of the emperor Nero, as argued by A.J. Spawforth.[323] Prior to this erection, there must have been some preparation involving the Corinthians. According to Spawforth, this enterprise "is likely to have pleased the local population because of the great honour and substantial pecuniary advantages that accrued for the Roman colony."[324] This is especially so if the choice of Corinth as the venue of the new cult owed "more to the Roman authorities than to the wishes of the League's membership"[325] as is indicated by the complaint made by the city of Argos in Letter 198 about their contribution to the financing of the games. The games included those of *venationes* which required beasts such as leopards or cheetahs and lions all of which were very costly. Such a preparation for the erection of the new cult could also have been made possible even while Claudius was still in power. This emperor is known to be one who, like Tiberius, did not want himself to be seen as a god, but at the same time allowed his statues to be carried in procession on the days consecrated to the Emperor, as shown in his letter to the Alexandrians in A.D. 41.[326] This attitude of Claudius, which was inseparable from his desire to preserve the Roman tradition,[327] would create

---

322 Cf. Stowers, "Greeks Who Sacrifice," 294-96, who describes the ubiquitous nature of sacrifice in the Greco-Roman world; Harold S. Songer, "Problems Arising from the Worship of Idols," in *RE* 80 (1983) 363-75, esp. 363, writes: "the worship of the gods was a pervasive and prominent feature of social and civic life."
323 Spawforth, "Corinth, Argos and the Imperial Cult," 211-32.
324 Spawforth, "The Achaean Federal Cult," 151.
325 Spawforth, "Corinth, Argos, and the Imperial Cult," 228.
326 See Jane F. Gardner, *Leadership and the Cult of Personality* (London, Hahhert, Toronto: J.M. Deut and Sons, 1974) 121-22, for Claudius' letter to Alexandria.
327 A. Momigliano, *Claudius. The Emperor and his Achievement.* ET. by W.D. Hogarth with a new bibliography (Cambridge: W. Heffer and Sons, 1934, 1961) 24-29.

a fertile ground for a division among the populace over the imperial cult. Yet, given the importance of getting the favour of the Emperor, there is no reason to doubt that the Corinthians would be more than happy to make themselves appear to be citizens grateful to the emperor by having not only a local imperial cult, but also the federal one.

In addition, Spawforth argues that the notables of the Roman colony might have played their part in convincing the Roman authorities to choose Corinth as the venue of this annual federal cult. Spawforth writes: "Corinthian inscriptions show that the colonial élite took full advantage of the fact that Corinth was the seat of the provincial procurator and closely associated with the proconsuls to cultivate personal ties with Roman officialdom."[328] In other words, the gods and lords that Paul had in mind in 1 Corinthians 8:5 might have included the reigning emperor and living members of the imperial family.[329] For Paul to mention the names of the gods and lords from among the Roman emperors' families would have been very insensitive. However, for him to fail to mention them in his address of the issue would equally mean his ignorance. Hence his general mention of them.

Those who insisted on eating on the basis of theological knowledge of a monotheistic God and non-existence of idols as well as the neutrality of food before God to justify their right to eat might have done so in order not to be alienated from this project of the creation of a federal imperial cult in their city which would improve their city's favour in the eyes of Claudius, his successor and their families. This could certainly be the case particularly because it was during the reign of Claudius (A.D. 41-54) that in the eyes of the provincial cities, particularly those that had never been formally colonized, the bestowal of the title of Roman *colonia* "had acquired the great prestige" because it was seen as a mark of imperial favour.[330] In this *mileu*, Corinthians would not have dared to do anything, such as refusal to practice the Imperial Cult that would jeopardize their city's over one hundred years old cherished status as a Roman colony. Any behaviour displeasing to the emperor would cause imperial disfavour. The question of loyalty would have been raised by the populace of Corinth.[331]

It is true that the worship of the emperors and their families in the east was more of a desire coming from below than as an act imposed from above.[332] However, as shown by Spawforth, the choice of Corinth as the

---

328 Spawforth, "Corinth, Argos, and the Imperial Cult," 228.
329 Gill, "The Roman Empire as a Context for the New Testament," 403.
330 Salmon, *Roman Colonization*, 137.
331 Winter, *Seek the Welfare of the City,* 123-43.
332 Dio LVII, 8, 4 shows that Tiberius and Gaius and Claudius prohibited sacrifices to themselves (see S.R.F. Price, "Man and God: Sacrifice in the Roman Imperial Cult" in *JRS*70 (1980) 28-43, esp. 30, 36. Price argues that, since the status of the

venue of the federal cult was partly a political move of the Roman authorities, but also partly a result of the hard work of the Corinthian élites. The latter is not surprising because although it was the Romans who judiciously encouraged the founding of the imperial cult as an expression of international solidarity, its development was "more likely to be hurried on by local governments anxious to express their loyalty, than by the Romans."[333] This show of loyalty would enhance their political position.[334] Moreover, as pointed out by E.A. Judge, it coincided with the fact that the local leader would always see his power as being by permission only. His privileges could therefore be suspended if he failed to show good behaviour or efficiency.[335] As the games became increasingly popular, like their contemporaries, the Corinthian Christians would not have refused to attend.[336] It is possible that their decision not to attend would have been

---

emperor in relation to man and god was ambiguous, unlike the Greeks the Romans regarded the deified emperor as *divus* and therefore did not have any problem in making sacrifices not only on behalf of, but also in some cases directly to, the emperor.

333 Judge, *Social Pattern*, 25.
334 Gager, "Religion and Social Class in the Early Roman Empire," 104.
335 Judge, *Social Pattern*, 23; cf. F.F. Abbott and A.C. Johnson, *Municipal Administration in the Roman Empire* (Princeton: Princeton University Press, 1926) 146, who points out that, with regard to finances, the central government "adopted the policy of rewarding those who were friendly and of punishing those who were hostile."
336 Lyttelton and Forman, *The Romans*, 74, are right in saying that there was a sense in which the emperor's subjects tried their best to enhance his majestic status in order, also to enhance their own self esteem. They write: "Numerous statues of the emperors and of other members of their families were set up throughout the Empire, games were held in their honour, and temples and altars were erected to them. Indeed in the provinces the institution of the cult and worship of the emperor afforded opportunity for the members of the local élite to safeguard and increase their own status by participating in an official capacity in the rites and observances of the cult. By taking part in the festivals and sacrifices honouring the emperor's birthday or other imperial anniversaries, and by assisting at dedication ceremonies, they emphasized their special relationship with the emperor and their association with his authority, while, at the same time, they communicated their loyalty, and that of their city or province, to the emperor." See also S.R.F. Price, "From Noble funerals to divine cult: the Consecration of Roman Emperors" in D. Cannadine and S. Price, *Rituals of Royalty. Power and Ceremonial in Traditional Societies* (Cambridge: CUP, 1987) 85, who shows how a provincial, a distinguished barbarian, treated emperor Tiberius as reported by a knight, Velleius Paterculus ii. The man said to the emperor who had given a permission to shake his hand: "Our young men are insane, for though they worship you as divine when absent, when you are present they fear your armies instead of trusting to your protection. But I,

seen by themselves and by the city dwellers as running counter to the popular mood of the city. So, although those who were accustomed to idols would have found it difficult to eat food offered to idols, their desire to attend the games - which were related to the imperial cult - and the encouragement by their fellow Christians might naturally encourage them to eat food offered to idols. Paul takes note of this in 1 Corinthians 8:10.

Seen in the context of the patron-client relationship between Corinthian élites or notables and the Roman authorities or emperor, or between the Corinthian public and their local municipal aristocracies, it can be said that the popularity of the games was not to be divorced from the Corinthians' desire to get better favour from the Roman authorities. We know that the patronage-clientele system between the Caesars and the eastern cities' magistrates was strategically introduced by Augustus in order to create dependency of the eastern upper classes on the emperor.[337] As pointed out by R.A. Horsley, despite the fact that the empire did not develop an imperial administration to deal with the complexity of the large empire, it was this patron-client system that kept the whole empire together.[338] Indeed, the social and economic as well as religious relations in the colonies themselves were very much dependent on and controlled by the system of patron-client relations. Just as the support of Rome enjoyed by the municipal aristocracies demanded allegiance of the latter, so the local patrons supported their clients in order to secure their loyalty.[339]

As a Roman colony and as 'the centre of *Romanitas*' in Greece,[340] Corinth must have been influenced by this patronage-clientele system. The name of the city, *Colonia Laus Julia Corinthiensis* must have constantly reminded the populace of the benefaction bestowed on them by Julius Caesar, the emperor who helped refound the long dead city. They knew that the purpose of its refounding was "to revive the merchantile glories of the

---

by your kind permission, Caesar, have today seen the gods of whom I merely used to hear; and in my life have never hoped for or experienced a happier day."
337 Meeks, *Urban Christians*, 12.
338 R.A. Horsley, "Patronage, Priesthoods, and Power: Introduction" in R.A. Horsley (ed.), *Paul and Empire*, 88-95, esp. 88. In fact, it was G.E.M. de Ste. Croix, *Struggle in the Ancient Greek World* (London: Duckworth, 1981) 364, who said that ["p]atronage, indeed, must be seen as an institution the Roman world could not do without." J.K. Chow, "Patronage in Roman Corinth," 105, argues that this institution was that which enabled the limited number of Roman officials to rule the huge empire.
339 See Horsley, *Patronage*, 94-95
340 A. Spawforth and P. Cartledge, *Hellenistic and Roman Sparta: A Tale of Two Cities* (London: Routledge, 1989) 104.

old Corinth."[341] Their gratitude to the emperor did not cease after Julius died. On the contrary, the Corinthians made known their support of the Roman emperor not only on the occasion of the coronation of Caligula[342] or on a successful campaign such as Claudius' victories over Britain,[343] but also on the safety of the emperor from a vicious plot against Tiberius.[344] The erection of the cult of the emperor was the form by which they made known their support of the emperor.

This erection of the cult by the local élites was understandable not only because one of the primary aims of founding a colony was to propagate the imperial cult,[345] but also because it was they themselves who became the priests of the cult. They were the ones who led the practice of sacrifice.[346] They did so on the basis that it was the emperor himself who led the sacrifice in Rome. His role could not be separated from his massive scale benefaction. This role became a model for the élite in Rome and in the provinces. As argued by Richard Gordon, this role was in line with the fact that there was no sharp distinction between "magistry and priesthood" within the traditional Graeco-Roman cult.[347] Using the example of Cleanax, son of Sarapion of Cyme in the Aeolid, Gordon states that: "Religious celebrations provide a privileged context within which a certain notion of community can be evoked: all are united in gratitude to the generosity of Cleanax."[348] In fact, Gordon goes so far as to conclude that this system of

---

341 Salmon, *Roman Colonization,* 135; Brunt, *Italian Manpower,* 256, argues that the sending of the many freedmen to Corinth was inseparable from Caesar's wish to revive Graechus' policy of "emigration for social and economic reasons."
342 By sending envoys of Achaea to congratulate the coronation of Caligula in 37 AD. The envoys proposed to honor him in different parts of the province by offering sacrifices for his safety, holding festivals and erecting his statues in various place, including in Isthmia. See David C. Braund, *Augustus to Nero: A Sourcebook on Roman History 31 BC-AD 68* (London, Sydney: Croom Helm, 1985), no. 564.
343 A.B. West, *Latin Inscriptions, 1896-1926. Corinth: Results,* VIII.2 (Cambridge, Mass.: HUP 1931), nos. 86-90.
344 West, *Latin Inscriptions,* no. 110.
345 Salmon, *Roman Colonization,* 148-49, 152. Other functions of *coloniae* are centers of the propagation of Roman influence, ideas and ways, of law and order, sources of prosperity and city-life, defenders of Roman majesty, affording protection against bandits and foreign foes, absorbing veterans and supplementing the Roman army.
346 Ross Shephard Kraemer, *Her Share of the Blessings: Women's Religions among Pagans, Jews and Christians in the Greco-Roman World* (New York and Oxford: OUP, 1992) 84-85, points out that additional power and social position were garnered by those who performed cultic offices, including that of the Imperial cult.
347 Gordon, "The Veil of Power: Emperors, Sacrifice and Benefactors" in M. Beard and J. North, *Religion and Power in the Ancient World* (Ithaca: Cornel University, 1990) 201-231, here 126-27.
348 Gordon, "The Veil Of Power," 134.

sacrifice "is one of the key links between the imperial system organised at the center and the local control exercised by the local élites at the periphery."[349]

Another form of support of the emperor was the holding of the imperial games or contests at the Isthmian and Caesarean games. It is not insignificant to note that the name of the contests was changed as the emperor changed.[350] In fact, as shown by J.K. Chow, Corinth had the names of their voting tribes and political divisions taken from "members of the imperial families or close friends and associates of Augustus."[351] Given that every emperor since Augustus to Trajan, with the exception of Tiberius and Marcus Aurelius, would not only make every effort to provide spectacles or be present at the games but also show to the people that he was with them and that, like them, he had a passion over the games, the local élites' attempt to honour the emperor with the provision of games in their area could not just have had a localised interest. Indeed, Claudius was one of those that would do his best to become "one with the people."[352] As argued by Roland Auguet, the aim of the presence of the emperor at the games was to control the people. In fact, Auguet goes so far as to say that the provision of the games for the people had more political significance than the distribution of food in times of famine. It prevented the people from being used by usurpers to challenge the emperor. Auguet writes: "There was in fact no reason why the people should not exchange for another a master who scorned what every poor Roman regarded as his right and, in the strict sense of the word, his privilege - to take his seat almost daily at the amphitheatre or the circus."[353]

Other factors that bear witness to the Romanness of the city such as the coins bearing the images of the emperor, images of Augustus, the erection of a Roman temple or Temple E for the cult of the imperial family, must have influenced the attitude of Corinthians to their supreme patron, the emperor.[354] In this patron client system, both obligated themselves to each other. The patron on the one hand possessed the power. But he could not get the honour without their inferiors or clients. The patron provided

---

349 Gordon, "The Veil of Power," 137.
350 Under Tiberius they were called Tiberea Caesarea Sebastea (Kent, *Inscriptions*, nos. 153, 156), to Isthmia et Caesarea et Tiberea Claudiea Sebastea under Claudius (West, *Latin Inscriptions*, no. 82), then to Neronea Caesarea et Isthmia et Caesarea under Nero (West, *Latin Inscriptions*, nos. 86-90). See Chow, "Patronage in Corinth," 108.
351 Chow, "Patronage in Corinth" 106. These names are "Agrippia, Atia, Aurelia, Calpurnia, Claudia, Domitia, Hostilia, Livia, Maneia, Vatina and Vinica."
352 R. Auguet, *Cruelty and Civilization: The Roman Games*. ET. (London: George Allen and Unwin, 1972) 185-88, esp. 186.
353 Auguet, *Cruelty,* 188.
354 Chow, "Patronage in Corinth," 106-07.

financial resources, employment, legal protection, influence and other benefits to his client. In exchange the client supported his patron by providing information and service.[355] The relationship between them was both interdependence and hierarchical. It meant that each depended on the other in the hierarchical structure. It involved the idea of giving and taking on both sides. The generosity of a patron would be publicly advertised, for instance by the clients' following the patron walking through the city doing his business and prominent provincials publicising "their gratitude to the Roman patrons in public inscriptions in every major city of the empire."[356] A patron would receive not only honour but also gifts and wills from their clients.[357] In other words, the tie between patron and client is asymmetrical. In the control of resources they are unequal, and they differ in terms of power and status.

The top patron was the emperor. He was patronless. All senior officials in the administration of the empire were his clients.[358] He was also the supreme patron of the whole Roman populace. This structure went down to the lowest level, to the level of relationship between a master and his former slaves within the household and in business associations. The head of a household was legally a patron to his freedmen. He was also a patron in a subtle and informal way to friends skilful in literature, such as philosophers[359] and religious persons, and to those who sought help.[360] The competition between patrons was so strong that a powerful patron would not receive a gift from a less powerful one, because his receiving the gift would be seen as degrading his power. If the patrons of the Corinthian Christians supported the imperial cult and the games,[361] there is no reason to suggest that they would not have shown their support of their patrons on this issue. If they were their slaves, moreover, their showing loyalty to their masters would have meant a great deal to their desire to gain their freedom

---

355 E. Ferguson, *Backgrounds of Early Christianity* (Grand Rapids: Eerdmans, 1989) 45.
356 Horsley, "Patronage, Priesthoods, and Power: Introduction," 94.
357 See D.B. Martin, *Slavery As Salvation*, 26.
358 Gager, "Religion and Social Class," 100, rightly points out that the network of patron-client relationship between the emperor and his subjects was indispensable for the maintenance of his rule.
359 Hock, *Social Context*, shows that the philosophers' means of support were charging fees, entering a household as resident intellectual, begging and working.
360 Chow, *Patronage and Power,* 70, 72.
361 It is important to note that, as argued by R.P. Saller, "Promotion and Patronage in Equestrian Careers" in *JRS* 70 (1980) 44-59, esp. 57-58, personal ties, that is to say, patronage rather than seniority and specialization played "a major influence on imperial decisions concerning the advancement of equites."

status.[362] We know that the manumission of slaves was carried out not only as a reward for long and good service, but also for gaining the political support or votes of the manumitted.[363] The poorest freemen[364] members of the Corinthian church (cf. those who have nothing to eat in 1 Cor. 11:22) or those who did not belong to any household, the less secure,[365] would have resorted to public benefaction (euergetism), such as that provided by the president of the Isthmian games, for their survival. This would especially be so when charity, kinsmen, neighbours and, in the case of peasants, fellow villagers, could not provide support or find a patron for the poor man.[366]

Moreover, it is in this patron-client conscious society that some former slaves of the imperial family, called *Familia Caesaris* enjoyed a privilege which was envied even by freeborn citizens or free upper classes.[367] The slaves of the imperial family were trained to carry out their tasks in and outside the households of their masters. They could use the imperial power in carrying out their own or their masters' businesses. In the highly

---

362 Thomas E.J. Wiedemann, "The Regularity of Manumission at Rome" in *CQ* 35 (1985) 162-75, esp. 175, concludes that the ideal that slaves would eventually be manumitted was not regular (see also 164-66). In fact, masters of the Roman world were prepared to free their slaves "when it was in their own interest." This is similar to the view of Greek writers who saw the promise of freeing slaves as "an encouragement to co-operation and a disincentive to resistance."
363 Susan Treggiari, "Social Status and Social Legislation" in A.K. Bowmann, et al., (eds.), *The Cambridge Ancient History*. 2nd ed. Vol. X. *The Augustan Empire 43BC-AD. 69* (Cambridge: CUP, 1996) 873-904, esp. 894.
364 P. Garnsey and G. Woolf, "Patronage of the rural poor in the Roman world" in A. Wallace-Hadrill (ed.), *Patronage in Ancient Society* (London and New York: Routledge, 1990) 153-67, here 153, define the poor as "those living at or near subsistence level, whose prime concern is to obtain the minimum food, shelter and clothing necessary for life, whose lives are dominated by the struggle for physical survival."
365 Winter, "Civil Litigation," 101-02.
366 Garnsey and Wolff, "Patronage of the rural poor," 154 argue that patronage is optional or voluntary, and coexist with charity, euergetism and the support of the poor's family.
367 Meeks, *Urban Christians*, 63, who makes use of the study of R.P.C. Weaver, *Familia Caesaris* (Cambridge: CUP, 1972). The resentment of the high status against the low status is reflected in the dream-books in which the violation of the accepted social norms of the status-concerned society is seen as an indication of a less pleasant future (See A.J. Pomeroy, "Status and status-concern in the Greco-Roman Dream-books" in *AS* 21 (1990) 51-74, esp. 51, 74. According to Meggitt, *Paul*, 126-27, not all members and former members of Familia Caesaris enjoyed a prestigious positions. In fact, the majority were "employed in menial domestic or agricultural relations" (126). Meggitt goes so far as to say that the fact that through Bulla's rebellion some members were involved in open revolt against Caesar does indicate that they had "low or virtually non-existent pay" (127).

enterprising city of Corinth, with its location as a commercial centre, these freedmen emerged as powerful entrepreneurs and, quickly amassed wealth.[368] Corinth proved to be a place of fortune for them.

There is a strong piece of evidence from Latin writers who describe four Corinthians of servile descent emerging as important Corinthian benefactors (i.e., C. Babbius Philinus, C. Julius Laco and his son Spartiaticus[369] who were direct descendants of freedman C. Julius Eurycles,[370] and C. Cornelius Pulcher of the second century). In a city which highly depended on the benefaction of its citizens for its development, such an achievement must have been very substantial. It provoked jealousy amongst others especially among the less successful lettered élite, the less fortunate and less skillful or lesser-means freeborn, especially as it was common for the successful freedmen to display their achievements in public buildings, monuments, statues, small temples and inscriptions.[371]

With their wealth and through their contribution to the special need of the city the successful freedmen could also gain power. For instance, T. Claudius Dinipus, a mid first-century freedmen, was elected as *duumvir quinquennalis* and *agonothetes* because of his contribution to famine relief (Kent nos. 158-63; West nos. 80-86). There is a possibility that one of these successful freedmen was a member of the Corinthian congregation, Erastus, who laid the pavement of Corinth in return for his election to aedileship of

---

368 Keith Hopkins, "Elite Mobility in the Roman Empire" in Ed. M.I. Finley, *Studies in Ancient Society. Past and Present Series* (London and Boston: Routledge and Kegan Paul, 1974) points out that in the first century AD some notorious imperial freedmen, such as Pallas and Narcissus of Claudius, held some of the highest administrative positions of the empire and possessed some of the largest personal fortunes ever amassed in Rome. According to P.R.C. Weaver, "Social Mobility in the Early Roman Empire: the Evidence of the Imperial Freedmen and Slaves" in M.I. Finley, *Studies,* 121-40, esp. 123, 133, they did so not only because of their ability/skill and nature of their duties, but also because of their legal and personal relationship with the emperor.

369 Spartiaticus was a grandson of C. Julius Eurycles. Under Claudius he became part of the imperial system which, according to Ronald Syme, *The Roman Revolution* (Oxford: OUP, 1939) 506, was a subtle move on the part of Claudius to form trustworthy clients without arousing unnecessary opposition. See Chow, "Patronage in Corinth," 109 n. 32. Spartiaticus was honoured by the Corinthians in the form of an inscription. See West, *Latin Inscriptions,* no. 68.

370 C. Julius Eurycles helped Octavian to win victory at Actium. In return he was granted Roman citizenship and the control of Sparta in 30 B.C.

371 Witherington III, *Conflict,* 6 n.16, points out that the establishment of the Imperial cult was one of the factors in the rise to prominence of freed slaves. In fact he refers to ILS 607:3 in which it is suggested that "over eighty-five percent of the officials in the cult of Augustus were freedmen."

Corinth. The office of *aedelis* was just one step lower than the highest magistrates of the city which were held by two *duumviri*.[372] Based on his examination of the well-known local notables of Corinth, J.K. Chow summarises the way the larger community of Corinth organised social relationships by concluding that ["t]he populace had to look to the rich to provide them with entertainment like games, to bring a better environment and honour to the city through new buildings, and at times to provide food relief. Honourable offices and honourable titles like 'patron' were usually offered to the benefactors for them to enjoy."[373]

In this connection, the relationship with the Roman authorities and the influential men of the city was a decisive factor in getting a leading role in the competition especially when a noble family background was absent.[374] As shown by P. Zanker, in some cities the local authorities were competing not only with their own rank, but also with the wealthy freedmen who wanted to set up a cult of the emperor in their city because they saw it as an opportunity to gain recognition and honours. Setting up the imperial cult gave freedmen the opportunity to play an active role in the public life of the city. They could sponsor games and public meals and thereby enjoy "if only temporally, certain prerogatives of public officials, such as the *toga praetexta*, an honorary seat, and official attendants."[375] By so doing they could "try to establish themselves as a kind of recognised class, second to *deuriones*, at least in outward appearances."[376]

Thus, given the importance of patron-client relations between the Corinthian élites and their clients on the one hand, and also between themselves and the Roman authorities on the other,[377] it would not have been surprising that the people of the city supported the cult, even if there

---

[372] It is still being debated whether or not the Erastus of Romans 16:23 whose greeting Paul sent to Christians in Rome was that of the pavement. See T.B. Savage, *Power Through Weakness: Paul's Understanding of the Christian Ministry in 2 Corinthians* (Cambridge: CUP, 1996) 40 n. 153, for scholars who regard both Erastus as the same person. Others such as H. Cadbury, "Erastus of Corinth" in *JBL* 50 (1931) 42-58, doubts it as being the case. In fact, Meggitt, *Paul,* 141, concludes that "Erastus' economic situation was most likely indistinguishable from that of his fellow believers." See also his article, "The Social Status of Erastus (Rom 16:23)" in *NovT* 38 (1996) 218-23, esp. 223.

[373] Chow, *Patronage and Power*, 63.

[374] Chow, *Patronage and Power*, 64.

[375] Zanker, "The Power of Images," 79-81, here 80.

[376] Zanker, "The Power of Image," 81.

[377] Chow, "Patronage in Roman Corinth", 106, rightly argues that the populace could not have overlooked the image of the emperor dominating the life of the colony. In fact, Chow concludes that the strong promotion of the imperial cult in Corinth was related to the patron-client system (110).

was no sanction against those who refused to do so.[378]

The above analysis of the historical context of our issue enables us to draw two conclusions regarding the historical context of the Corinthian Christians' dispute over food offered to idols. First, it is important to emphasize that the emergence of the issue of food offered to idols among Corinthian Christians was related to their attempt to draw boundary lines between themselves and the people from outside their Christian community. It was customary that meat sold in the meat market and consumed in the people's houses had been previously offered to idols. Indeed, people might have sacrificed meat and other kinds of offerings (e.g., cake, wine, milk) to their household deities in their household shrines.[379] Hence the term 'ἱερόθυτόν' (10:28), rather than εἰδωλόθυτόν (8:1, 10:19). Associations too had their own deities and patrons. The Jews' prohibition of eating food offered to idols could also have been felt. The fact that Paul apparently reveals three contexts of the issue, namely the temple (8:10), the meat market (10:24) and at the invitation of an unbeliever most probably in his house (10:27) justifies this conclusion.

Secondly, however, it is equally important to acknowledge that the strong presence of the Imperial Cult in their city might have intensified efforts amongst Corinthian Christians to have a clear stance on the issue of food offered to idols in general. Although they may not have been forced to participate in the worship of the Imperial Cult,[380] as is evident from the fact that Gallio did not bow to the demand of the Jews to judge Paul within the

---

378 Indeed, the works of Price, "Rituals and Powers" in ed. R.A. Horsley, *Paul and Empire*, 47-71, and Zanker, "The Power of Images" in ed. R.A. Horsley, *Power and Empire*, 72-86, and Gordon, "The Veil of Power, 126-37, have shown that the patronage system "was articulated parallel to and eventually in fusion with the political-religious system of sacrifices and emperor cult." In fact, the élite were hungry for officiating public sacrifices, including the emperor cult, which they themselves sponsored and controlled. There was an intense competition between the élite to be seen to honour the emperors with "festivals, temples, and monuments." See Horsley, "Patronage, Priesthoods, and Power: Introduction," 95.

379 T.G. Tucker, *Life in the Roman World of Nero and St. Paul* (London: Macmillan 1910) 376-77; Gooch, *Dangerous Food,* 31, 37.

380 Neil Elliott, "The Anti-Imperial Message of the Cross" in R.A. Horsley, *Paul and Empire*, 167-83, esp. 171, shows that imperial cult and ceremonial was a terror on the ideological plane, among many other forms of terror such as crucifixion, to secure peace. If the Corinthian Christians were aware of this, there is no reason to doubt that the issue of food offered to idols was a very important matter to Paul's readers. Moreover, given that Corinth was a colony of Rome and that its municipal aristocracies were or must have tried to appear to be the loyal clients of Roman authorities, it is not totally unlikely that in return for the support given by the Roman authorities to Corinth the local authorities would show that they supported the imperial cult. Their own clients would certainly follow suit.

Roman law but regarded his case as belonging to Jewish law (Acts 18:12-17) and the Christian community as a sub-group of the *religio licita*, Judaism,[381] they themselves must have thought about their role in the city where the cult was being promoted. This would surely have caused them to think about their involvement in the activities associated with the worship of the cult, including dining, and about any food associated in one way or another with the worship of idols. Apparently, they did not have a unified view on the matter. Hence, Paul's primary concern must have been with the question of how he could help the community of his converts to preserve their unity which was being pulled apart by outside cultural pressures prevailing in their society.[382]

Recently, in addition to the importance of the imperial cult and the extravagant erection of the federal cult in Corinth, Bruce W. Winter has proposed three more possible reasons for the issue of food offered to idols to emerge amongst Corinthian Christians after Paul left Corinth, namely [383] (a) the shortage of food in the city caused by a serious famine, (b) the invitation of the President of the extravagant Isthmian Games for the (Roman) citizens of the city to attend festivals held in Isthmia, where the temple of Poseidon possibly was, and (c) the withdrawal of the provision of the Jewish *kosher* food from the market (*macellum*) of Corinth, which is an attempt on the part of the city populace to show their support of the emperor, Claudius, who had earlier expelled the Jews from Rome.[384] The latter is proposed by Winter on the basis of a possible link between the action of the crowd of Corinth to attack the leader of the local Jewish Synagogue soon after Gallio's dismissal of the legal case made by the Jews against Paul and the arrival of Prisca and Aquila to Corinth from Rome after Claudius expelled the Jews from Rome. When Paul was still in Corinth they were not obliged to participate in the imperial cult because they were still seen as part of Judaism of which adherents had the right to stay away from Imperial cult.[385] All those events are seen by Winter to have caused Corinthian Christians to grapple with their own prestige and the prosperity of their city yet at the same time their personal misery caused by social dislocation, and to search for possible answers to vexed questions.

---

381 Winter, *Seek the Welfare of the City*, 142-43.
382 On the nature of the pressure on Christians to participate in political and social activity, which was always related to religion, see Paul J. Achtemeier, "Gods made with hands: The New Testament and the Problem of Idolatry" in *Ex Auditu* 15 (1999) 43-61, esp. 51-53. In fact, Achtemeier shows that actually the warning against idolatry was one of the ways used by Christian leaders to refuse participating in political and social activities related to idols.
383 Winter, *After Paul Left*, xi, 4, 6, 271, 275-76, 279.
384 Winter, *After Paul Left*, 299-301.
385 Winter, *After Paul Left*, 275-76, 279-280.

Put together,[386] the five events would really have forced Corinthian Christians to eat any food that is related to idols, wherever they are.

While I share the first two reasons proposed by Winter, as I have shown above, it remains to be questioned whether the invitation of the Roman citizens in Corinth by the president of the Isthmian Games could be seen as one of the reasons for the emergence of the issue amongst Corinthian Christians. The famine and the withdrawal of the provision of Jewish market for *kosher* could have taken place. But I find it difficult to imagine why εἰδωλόθυτον became an issue to Corinthian Christians when the raw materials for εἰδωλόθυτον were not even available. Indeed, even if it became an issue at all during famine period, I still find it difficult to see why according to Paul's letter the Corinthian Christians were concentrating on their right to eat εἰδωλόθυτον and Paul asking them to forgo that right. During famine the question was survival, not ethical, even if the patrons of the city had to provide food during famine and that food, before being given to the populace, had to be first offered to idols.

In any case, when Paul was still in Corinth questions such as those raised by the Corinthian Christians in their letter to him had not yet been asked because they did not yet begin raising the questions of self-definition, which - normal though they might have been - could only take place after a while. Their raising of the questions was, though natural, became more crucial in Corinth than in other place because of the longstanding importance of the worship of the imperial cult and the preparation to build a federal cult in Corinth. Which came first, the need to define themselves in relation to their fellow citizens and their accepted values, or the imperial cult and the preparation to build a federal cult, is difficult to determine. As far as Corinth was concerned they were integrally and strongly interrelated.

With such historical backgrounds to the urgent need to have self-definition which caused the Corinthian Christians to be in dispute with each other and therefore need Paul's counsel on the matter, we now turn to see Paul's counsel itself in 1 Corinthians 8:1 - 11:1. What kind of counsel does Paul give? We need to see how unified is Paul's answer in terms of getting his counsel across. The answer to this question is important for us in order to see the role of 1 Corinthians 9 in the whole argument.

2.3 Literary Context: Paul's Unified Arguments

2.3.1 The Unity of 1 Corinthians 8:1 - 11:1

Various descriptions have been given to explain the apparently different material of 1 Corinthians 9 in comparison with that of 1 Corinthians 8 and

---

386 Winter, *After Paul Left*, 27-28.

10. Those who support the partition theories will quickly regard chapter 9 as an aside belonging to different letters, time and context.[387] It is often seen as editorially misplaced,[388] loosely related to its context and therefore, a digression[389] or an interruption.[390] Hence, it is regarded as a defence of Paul's apostleship independent of, or unrelated to, the present subject matter under discussion in 8:1-13 and 10:1 - 11:1.[391] It is Paul's defense

---

387 As noted by W. Willis, *Idol Meat*, 271-72; see also M. Goguel, *Introduction au Nouveau Testament*, Vol. 4 (Paris: Editions Ernest Leroux, 1926) 72-6, 408-09, as shown by Russell Barrett Sisson, *The Apostle as Athlete: A Socio-rhetorical Interpretation of 1 Corinthians 9*. Ph.D Diss. Emory University (Ann Arbor: UMI, 1994) 15; A.R. Jewett, "The Redaction of 1 Corinthians and the Trajectory of the Pauline School" in *JAAR* (44 Supplement B, Dec. 1978) 396-404. For detailed information on the scholars who argue for partition theories, see Mitchell, *Rhetoric* 238-39, especially ns. 293 and 295. In fact, in 1876 H. Hagge, "Die beiden überlieferten Sendschreiben des Apostels Paulus an die Gemeinde zu Korinth," in *Jahrbücher für protestantiche Theologie* II (1876) 481-531, as shown by Sisson, *The Apostle as Athlete*, 10-11, regards 9:1-18 as a fragment of the lost letter which included 2 Corinthians 10-13.

388 J. Weiss, *Der Erste Korintherbrief*. KEK 5 (Göttingen: Vanderhoeck and Ruprecht, 1910) 210-13, 231-49; also his *Earliest Christianity* I (New York: Harper and Torchbooks, 1959) 223-32. Weiss argues that there is a lack of continuation between the theme of 8 with that of chapter 9. J. Héring, *The First Epistle of St. Paul to the Corinthians* (London: Epworth, 1961) xiii-ixiv, 75.

389 Barrett, *The First Epistle*, 200, who sees Paul as a person who is quite used to digression; W. Wuellner, "Greek Rhetoric and Pauline Argumentation" in W.R. Schoedel and R.L. Wilken (eds.), *Early Christian Literature and the Classical Tradition. In Honorem Robert M. Grant* (Paris: Beauchesne, 1979) 177-88, and "Where Is Rhetorical Criticism Taking Us?" in *CBQ* 49 (1987) 448-63, esp. 458, who argues that Paul is consciously using a rhetorical device of digression. This device is meant to turn away from the previous topic but at the same time prepares the audience to be cooperative to a forthcoming task, namely to judge on the basis of proofs already set out (10:14-22); Marshall, *Enmity*, 284: "Paul digresses to rebut an invective of inconsistency against him by the hybrists in relation to his refusal of aid." Paul's refusal generated their hostility towards him (245-47, 233-51). The hybrists wanted to keep their freedom. But it was challenged by Paul's teaching and practice. So this invective is related to their expression of freedom which is addressed by Paul in chapters 6, 8 and 10.

390 Conzelmann, *First Epistle*, 151-53.

391 Héring, *The First Epistle*, 14, classifies 1 Cor 9 as belonging to letter b (10:1-22; 11-15 [with 16 and 13 special additions]). Hurd, *The Origin*, 131-157, presents a review of attempts to divide 1 Corinthians into originally different letters. Similarly, Conzelmann, *First Epistle*, 151-53, suggests that Paul enters into a new subject (i.e, his apostleship). 1 Cor 9 is an *apologia* against Paul's opponents who had questioned his apostleship occasioned by his refusal of financial support. Cf. Barrett, *The First Epistle*, 220; Yeo, *Interaction*, 81-2; Sisson, *The Apostle as*

against those who challenge his position.³⁹² This view is thought to be supported by the suddenness of 9:1, the defensive tone of 9:3 and the compositional breaks in 1 Corinthians 9:19 and 24.³⁹³

However, this reading does not take into account the fact that, as pointed out by David G. Horrell, there is no "compelling textual or literary grounds" for rejecting the integral nature of this chapter. It also overlooks "the fact that chapter 9 falls into the ABA' pattern with an apparent digression at its heart."³⁹⁴ M.M. Mitchell lists six strong reasons to refute the partition theories and defend the coherence of the unit.³⁹⁵

Those who argue for the integrity of 1 Corinthians propose exegetical, theological and rhetorical points of view to support the present position of 1 Corinthians 9 in the context of 1 Corinthians 8 and 10.³⁹⁶ Some see 1 Corinthians 9 as Paul's apostolic example, but others regard it as an

---

Athlete, 43; Goguel, *Introduction*, 72-86, argues that chapter 9 is a fragment of a later letter (letter C) and of later controversy.

392 Barrett, *The First Epistle*, 220, writes: "Paul would hardly have spent so long on the question of apostolic rights if his own apostolic rights had not been questioned in Corinth." Lawson, *First Corinthians 9.24-10.22*, 47 argues that 1 Cor 9 is Paul's defence against challenges to Paul's position.

393 Schmithals, *Gnosticism*, 92-93.

394 Horrell, "Theological Principle," 84. Cf. Hurd, *The Origin*, 131-41, and Tomson, *Paul*, 77, who argues that 1 Corinthians 9:1 - 10:22 "are rhetorical digression giving moral examples from life and from biblical history. This reflects a Hellenistic rhetorical device."

395 Mitchell, *Rhetoric*, 239-40. These are: a) the apparent link between the content of 8:9-13 and its end (8:13) with chapter 9; b) the lexical as well as topical unity of the whole section. Lexically, we have the repetition of key terms and word groups [ἐξουσία/ἐλεύτερος/ἐλευθερια; πρόσκομμα/ἐγκοπὴ/ἀπρόσκοπος; συνείδησις, ἀσθενής, μετέχειν and οἰκουδομεῖν]. Topical unity is the discussion of εἰδωλοθυτα/εἰδωλολατρία; c) the overall argument and the structure of our section has parallel with Romans 14-15; d) exegetically, our section can be understood without any impression that Paul contradicts himself; e) exegetical emphasis on the unity of the church and f) the link between every subsection of 1 Corinthians 8:1 - 11:1 with Corinthian factionalism.

396 Such as J. Jeremias, "Chiasmus in den Paulusbriefen" in *ZNW* 49 (1958) 156, who compares the position of 1 Cor 9 with that of 1 Cor 13 in between chapters 12-14. Also, Dungan, *The Sayings of Jesus*, 3-40, who regards 1 Cor 9 as an explanatory digression which offers Paul's example to the strong. The apologetic note is subordinate to pedagogical intention. Wuellner, "Greek Rhetoric and Pauline Argumentation," 177-88, here 186-87, points out that 1 Cor 9 is a conscious attempt by Paul to use a rhetorical device of digression to add weight to his argument. Similarly, C.A. Kennedy, "The Structure of 1 Corinthians 8-10," in *SBL American Academyof Religion Abstracts 1980*, Abstract n. 426: "Chapter 9 does not have to be re-assigned to another hypothetical letter, it becomes an integral if somewhat protracted comment to the argument's development."

example and defence,[397] commonly known as "killing two birds with one stone."

W.L. Willis is the strongest proponent of the former. For him, 1 Corinthians 9:1-2 is too slim to be regarded as a defence. The themes discussed in these verses are not taken up in subsequent verses (9:4ff.).[398] Moreover, it is apparent that it is not the right to support that is being discussed by Paul, but his renunciation of it.[399] Yet to support this view, Willis and others have translated ἀνακρίνουσιν of 9:3 in future sense, and consequently see verse 3 as anticipatory,[400] fictitious,[401] conative,[402] or

---

397 See Dungan, *The Saying of Jesus*, 3-40. He recognizes the apologetic function but gives priority to its pedagogical function. Paul's behaviour in refusing financial support is used as an example for the strong in their encounter with the weak on the issue of idol meat.
398 W.L. Willis, "An Apostolic Apologia," 34-35.
399 W.L. Willis, "An Apostolic Apologia," 42 n. 14.
400 W.L. Willis, "An Apostolic Apologia," 33-38. The reasons given for rejecting the view of defence are: a) vv. 1-2 are too brief for a real defence, b) Paul's rhetorical questions assume positive answer, c) his apostleship could not have been contested by the Corinthians who are themselves the seal of his apostleship, d) 9:3 fits well with 9:1-2 and 8:13, and e) the topic of apostleship is not elaborated in the subsequent discussion but previously in 4:9-15. Chapter 9 is a personal example to be imitated by the Corinthians. It presupposes an objection from those who find his restriction in 8:9-12 difficult to bear. Hence, he gives his personal example. W.L. Willis, *Idol Meat*, here 273, 274, concludes that the chapter "is neither an aside on the apostolic office nor a personal defence. It advances Paul's argument about the obligation Christians have to consider the good of others first. In its context 1 Corinthians 9 is another part of Paul's attempt to instruct the Corinthians in the matter of participation in pagan cultic meals." Similarly, P.D. Gardner, *The Gifts of God*, 76, writes: "Paul's ἀπολογία was, therefore, his argument defending his own behaviour (not his apostleship), that is, defending his approach to his ἐξουσία. He was not so much confronted by an opposition as deliberately driving the Corinthians into admitting that, on their basis of making judgments, he must himself fail. He did not flaunt his ἐξουσία in the way that they expected. He was to be seen as 'weak.'"
401 D.B. Martin, *Slavery As Salvation*, 77-79, here 78, conjectures that Paul may be debating with "merely hypothetical adversaries, perhaps for the purpose of delineating a point of view to which his own example will serve as a corrective and counterpoint." Against the view of defence he writes: "if some Corinthians were already criticising Paul for refusing their support, he would be foolish to use the very bone of contention as the prime focus for the behaviour he is advocating...it would not make sense of him to use that action as an analogy for behaviour he is urging his very critics."
402 Malherbe, "Determinism and Free Will," 240 n. 13. Paul's apologia anticipates a retort to the advice he is giving. Paul is anticipating reactions from his readers to his warning in 8:9 where Paul asked them to submit willingly to the limitation of their freedom. Those who would reject his exhortation were the Corinthian Christians

rhetorical in style,⁴⁰³ quite contradictory to the present notion of ἀνακρίνουσιν, a dative plural present participle active.⁴⁰⁴

Others maintain the connection between 1 Corinthians 9 with the issue of idol meat, but see it not just as an example but also as a defence.⁴⁰⁵ Even among those who want to see 1 Corinthians 9 as an original and integral part of 1 Corinthians 8:1 - 11:1, the difficulty of explaining Paul's seemingly inconsistent answer throughout his discourse has remained. It will be argued in the next section below that Paul's discourse must be seen in the context of the existence of conflicting views among Corinthian Christians and from the standpoint of Paul's attempt to prevent one party in the dispute from harming the other and themselves, and more importantly, of his desire to safeguard the unity of his converts. It is in this way that we may see the connection between Paul's desire to bring to an end their dispute over food offered to idols and his defence of his apostolic practice against some people. Therefore, we submit that chapter 9 is primarily an example, the ground of which has to be defended.

2.3.2 The Overall Interpretation of 1 Corinthians 8:1 - 11:1

Related to the dispute among scholars on the role and position of 1 Corinthians 9 is the overall interpretation of 1 Corinthians 8:1 - 11:1. Scholars have failed to appreciate the importance of Paul's acknowledgement of the legitimacy of both positions in the dispute and his careful response. They have failed to see the clear indication in Paul's

---

who were using Stoics deliberations known to them to justify their behaviour in eating idol meat. Their claims were made in popular philosophical slogans. Their reaction has nothing to do with his apostleship nor his forgoing of his rights and enslavement.

403 Mitchell, *Rhetoric*, 244-245 n. 330, 246, here 244 n. 229. She refutes the view that chapter 9 is a defence (from whichever point of views: refusal to accept money, inconsistency, or forensic rhetoric). She also refutes the view that sees chapter 9 as having a dual function, known as "killing two birds with one stone," because "The two birds are not only separate but *contradictory*...Is it not naive...to think that the Corinthians' "charge" played so completely into Paul's hand?" See also her article, "Rhetorical Shorthand in Pauline Argumentation: The Function of the 'Gospel' in the Corinthians Correspondence" in L. Ann Jervis and Peter Richardson, *Gospel*, 62-68.

404 Newton, "Food Offered to Idols," 232, points out that since ἀνακρίνουσιν is in dative plural masculine present participle active, there is no reason to see verse 3 as hypothetical or the like.

405 Such as G. Agrell, *Work, Toil and Sustenance: An Examination of the View of Work in the New Testament* (Lund: Verbum-Haken Ohissons, 1976) 106ff. and Hock, *The Social Context*, 59-62. Hock argues that 1 Corinthians 9 was motivated by a specific occasion.

discourse that he does not oppose the arguments of those who want to eat food offered to idols. Instead, Paul's sentences such as ["w]e all possess knowledge" (8:1), "we know that 'an idol has no real existence' and that 'there is no God but one' (8:4)," "yet for us there is one God, the Father, from whom all things and for whom we exist, and one Lord, Jesus Christ, through whom are all things and through whom we exist" (8:6), and 'this right of yours' (ἡ ἐξουσία ὑμῶν αὕτη) have all been seen as Paul's opposition to his readers' unified view of the matter.

This failure has caused scholars to contradict Paul's answer in 8:1-13 and 10:23 - 11:1.[406] They have argued that Paul's stance in 1 Corinthians 8:1-13, where he seems to adopt a tolerant view, is inconsistent with that in 10:14-22, where there is a clear-cut condemnation of participation in a sacrificial act.[407] Some have explained this seeming inconsistency by dividing the passage historically.[408] Schmithals argues that they are from different letters of different time.[409]

Those who do not want to see a contradiction in Paul's view explain this seeming inconsistency from the point of view of the place of the eating. It is thought that Paul is so condemning in 10:1-22 because he is dealing with the Corinthians' participation in the sacrificial act itself, rather than simply eating food offered to idols. G.D. Fee is the strongest proponent of this

---

406 Barrett, "Things Sacrificed," 40, states that this seeming inconsistency is the centre of the problem 1 Corinthians 8-10. Gooch, *Dangerous Food,* 51, argues that the tensions between the two must be maintained. It "must not be ignored or obscured in an exegesis of these chapters."

407 This issue of Paul's consistency or inconsistency has occupied New Testament scholars. H. Räisänen's conclusion in his *Paul and the Law* (Philadelphia: Fortress Press, 1983) 266-67, which emphasizes Paul's inconsistency, has generated continuous debate among scholars. Indeed, M.M. Mitchell, "A Variable and Many-sorted Man:" John Chrysostom's Treatment of Pauline Inconsistency" in *JECS* 6 (1998) 93-111, has, as the title of her article indicates, drawn an example of how important figures of the early church, such as John Chrysostom, had already struggled with the same question. See 94-97 for a summary of how modern scholars deal with the issue.

408 Weiss, *Der Erste Korintherbrief,* 264, argues that 10:1-22 belongs to the previous letter (5:9-13) and chapters 8 and 10:23 - 11:1 is Paul's later view on the whole subject; cf. Yeo, *Interaction,* 81-82, who suggests that there are 6 letters: A (11:2-34); B (2 Cor. 6:14 - 7:1, 1 Cor. 6:12-20, 9:24 - 10:22, 15:1-15 and 16:13-24), C (1 Cor. 1:1 - 6:11, 7:1-8:13, 9:19-23, 10:23 - 11:1 and 12:1-31a, 14:1c-40, 12:31b - 13:13, 16:1-12), D (2 Cor. 2:14 - 6:13, 7:2-4) E (1 Cor. 9:1-18, 2 Cor. 10:1 - 13:13), F (2 Cor. 1:1 - 2:13; 2 Cor. 7:5 - 9:15).

409 Schmithals, *Gnosticism,* 92-93, assigns chapters 8-9 and 10:23-11:1 to one letter, 9:24-27 and 10:1-22 to another.

view.[410] According to him, there are two different matters being addressed by Paul, and the determining factor is *the place* of the eating. There is a difference between taking part in sacrificial food at the cultic meals or banquets *within pagan temples* (8:7-13 [especially v. 10] and 10:14-22), on the one hand and eating meat in *the meat-market* and that served *in an unbeliever's house* which might have previously been offered to idols (10:23 - 11:1, especially 10:27-28), on the other. The former is strongly condemned, but the latter is conditional upon the weak conscienced brother. Only in 10:23 - 11:1 does Paul encourage the eating of food without concern for its previous relation to idol sacrifice, except when the pagan host of the dinner publicizes its background of having been offered as a sacrifice (10:25-28).[411] In this case, those who want to eat on the basis of knowledge should not do so in order to avoid offending the pagan host and shatter his understanding of Christian morality.[412] He regards 1 Corinthians 8:1-13 as a correction of the Corinthians' mistaken ethics and 10:1-22 as the imperative which comes after the former and after his vigorous defence of his apostleship. In a similar vein, Ben Witherington III argues that Paul does not allow his readers to eat εἰδωλοθύτων at temples or in their precincts where the power and presence of the idols is thought to abide, but allows them to eat ἱερόθυτόν, food that has come from and not to be eaten at the temple.[413] The problem is about the venue of eating such meat.[414]

However, as pointed out by Fisk, Fee's approach does not solve the question of why what is acceptable in chapter 8 is declared idolatrous in chapter 10:1-22. Fisk shows that Fee fails "to explain Paul's toleration in

---

410 Fee, *The First Epistle*, 357-63, 484-85; cf. also Calvin J. Roetzel, *Judgment in the Community. A Study of the Relationship Between Eschatology and Ecclesiology in Paul* (Leiden: E.J. Brill, 1972) 171.
411 See Tomson, *Paul*, 206 n. 95 for other scholars who support this distinction between cultic and non-cultic contexts.
412 Cf. Lawson, *First Corinthians 9:24-10:22*, 40-41; Hays, *1 Corinthians*, 135, 144; Osamu Nakahashi, "Idol Meat and Monotheism: A Study of the Church in Corinth (1 Cor. 8-10)," MTh Diss. (Faculty of Divinity, Univ. of Glasgow, 1992), who argues that those with knowledge held a polynymous monotheism in which several gods merged into one chief. They believed in one God whose power is superior to that of other gods they worshipped. The suggestion that the informant is a pagan is contested by Barrett, *The First Epistle*, 242 who says that "it is not easy to see how a non-Christian's conscience could enter into the matter." See also Meggitt, *Paul*, 113.
413 Witherington III, "Not So Idle Thoughts," 246-48.
414 Ben Witherington III, "Why Not Idol Meat? Is it What You Eat or Where You Eat it?" in *BR* 10 (1994), 38-43, 54-55, esp. 42. Cf. also J. Delobel, "Coherence and Relevance of 1 Corinthians 8-10" in R. Bieringer, *The Corinthian Correspondence* (Leuven: University Press, 1996) 177-90, esp. 183.

chap. 8 of an activity declared idolatrous in chap. 10."[415] He claims that "evidence within chap. 8 suggests strongly that Paul did NOT view those dining in the temple as morally culpable (unless they scandalised someone else), whereas chap. 10 contains a strong warning against idolatry that occurs elsewhere around the idol's temple."[416]

To address the problem Fisk himself proposes that what is at stake is not the meat as such nor the location of the eating but the character of the meat, that is to say, whether or not the meat has "distinctively religious focus" and whether or not the participants "were consciously acknowledging pagan gods." Such an argument is based on Fisk's view that the attendance at temple feasts should not be seen in the religious aspect alone, but also as a social convention.[417] Fisk's appeal to the social aspect of the issue has previously been expressed by W.L. Willis who argues that the social meaning of cultic meals forms the background of the problem. Cultic meals were generally regarded as social occasions.

Although Fisk's critique of Fee's thesis is valid, his and Willis's appeal to the social aspect does not solve our problem, because it is difficult for us to determine whether or not those who do not possess the knowledge of the non-existence of idols would have seen the case as Fisk and Willis do. W.T. Sawyer rightly warns against any classification of life in the ancient world. He writes: "It is difficult if not impossible to compartmentalise life into religious, economic, and social areas, for there is an inevitable overlapping of these categories especially in the ancient world."[418] Moreover, in 1 Corinthians 8:10 Paul does not seem to indicate that there is a distinction between the social and religious aspects of the case. This is clearly pointed out by Derek Newton who shows that there might have been different conceptions held by the Corinthian Christians of the food offered to idols. These conceptions were a mixture of sociological, religious and political factors which might not have been clearly identified by the Corinthian Christians themselves.[419] Social and religious factors might probably not be the main issue here. It seems that the primary issue at stake might be that the weak conscienced brother saw a man of knowledge "at table in an idol's temple" (8:10). This does not allow us to make any distinction between social or religious, sacrificial or social motives. It is more likely that Paul's

---

415 Bruce N. Fisk, "Eating Meat Offered to Idols: Corinthian Behaviour and Pauline Response in 1 Corinthians 8-10 (A Response to Gordon Fee)" in *TJ* 10 (1989) 49-70, here 59. Cf. Lawson, *First Corinthians 9:24-10:22*, 99-100.
416 Fisk, "Eating," 62.
417 Fisk, "Eating," 63-4; cf. Lawson, *First Corinthians 9:24-10:22*, 101-05, who argues that 8:1-13 is social in nature and therefore the concern for the weak determines the eating, but 10:1-22 is religious (i.e. idolatry).
418 Sawyer, "The Problem," 88.
419 See Newton, "Food Offered to Idols," 10-11 for his criticism of Willis' work.

readers would have seen any activity around the temple in a religious sense, even though the activity might be socially or politically motivated. Even eating food offered to idols in areas other than the temple could have been associated with a sacrificial act. The Corinthian Christians would not have made a distinction between food which had been associated with idols in temples and in other areas. The determining factor was that the food had association with idols.

Fisk's critique of Fee's proposition has been followed up by D.G. Horrell who rightly points out that the sacred and the secular cannot be neatly divided. He argues that this is perhaps part of the reason why Paul does not give a clear answer about which precise settings are acceptable or unacceptable.[420] Moreover, he points out that in 8:10 there is no indication that being present or eating at the temple itself is seen to be idolatrous or acceptable. It is not commendable 'only if it causes problems for the weak.'[421] Hence he states: "Paul does not condemn or prohibit εἰδωλοθύτων but εἰδωλολατρία – worship of idols."[422] Horrell argues that what is Paul doing in chapter 8 is to give concern for the weak, which is built up in chapter 9 and reiterated in 10:23 - 11:1. But chapter 10 is to warn "the strong against complacency, against regarding themselves as immune from judgment and punishment and against idolatry -- their gnosis is no protection (10:1-14)...against the delusion that they can unproblematically share in opposing spheres of κοινωνία (10:15-22)."[423] Hence he writes: "Paul does indeed want to warn the strong Corinthians against participation in pagan sacrificial cultic celebrations, but this does not amount to a ban on εἰδωλόθυτα, nor *necessarily on activities at the temple*."[424]

Although I share Horrell's reading of the unified discourse of Paul in 1 Corinthians 8:1 - 11:1, I part company with him in following Theissen's definition of the nature of the conflict as between the 'strong' and the 'weak.' Moreover, it is rather unfortunate that, in emphasizing the unitary approach of Paul in the whole section, Horrell minimizes the importance of 10:1-22. He writes: "in view of chs. 8-9, 10.1-22 does not contain the dominant focus of Paul's ethical instruction here."[425] We maintain that chapter 10 too has an equal value with the preceding (8:1-9:27). Paul introduces his arguments in chapter 10 to add more weight to his exhortation in chapter 8 and 9.

Those who want to maintain the inconsistency in Paul's discourse do so

---

420 Horrell, "Theological Principle," 101.
421 Horrell, "Theological Principle," 99.
422 Horrell, "Theological Principle," 100.
423 Horrell, "Theological Principle," 100.
424 Horrell, "Theological Principle," 100.
425 Horrell, "Theological Principle," 101.

by supposing that Paul is in conflict with the Corinthian Christians as a whole, and what he says in 1 Corinthians 8:7-13 is conditional. This is particularly the case with P.D. Gooch who dismisses the reality of the weak and who charges Paul as being responsible for the emergence of the issue. He differentiates the two by seeing 8:10 as Paul's incomplete 'estimate' of eating in an idol's temple, but 10:14-22 as a "true estimation of the reality of other Gods and Lords."[426] He considers it as Paul's strategy of persuasion.[427] Similarly, Ralph Bruce Terry argues that in 8:1-13 Paul is employing a conditional approach by seemingly accepting his readers' arguments (8:1-6) as valid for the moment and proceeding with a discourse on two points, namely the negative effect of eating food offered to an idol and the importance of forgoing his right for the sake of the gospel (8:9-9:27).[428] This is then supported by 10:1-22. In other words, by using conditional sentences Paul does not validate the Corinthians' arguments. According to Terry, this is an Oriental (Jewish and Greek)[429] way of reading, a subtle one, which is different from the Western approach which looks "for explicit markers to lay out an argument in unambiguous terms." What Terry means by an Oriental approach is: "the listener or reader is given the argument, but is supposed to figure out what the speaker or writer is saying and what the relationship is between the parts of discourse."

However, against Terry, we may argue that there is no indication that Paul does not accept the validity of the arguments of those who want to eat food offered to idols.[430] *It is more likely that the crux of the issue does not*

---

426 Gooch, *Dangerous Food*, 83.
427 Gooch, *Dangerous Food*, 84, 103, here 84, writes: "Where passion and persistence count Paul is effective; where our standards of consistency and logical development are applied Paul's arguments are less effective."
428 Terry, *Discourse*, 47, 51, here 47, paraphrases Paul's conditional notion of his approach: "Let's assume for a minute that you are right, that if you are not personally worshipping the idol, you have a right to eat food offered to idol, even in its temple."
429 Terry, *Discourse*, 47, 51, argues that the Old Testament gives evidence to this approach. In it "the setting is missing from passages and transitions are made from one item to another without explicit conceptual markers showing the relationship." For the Greek style Terry quotes Demetrius's reference to Theophrastus (*On Style 4* [Loeb 222]): "that not all possible points should be punctiliously and tediously elaborated, but some should be left to the comprehension and inference of the hearer."
430 Cf. Brunt, "Rejected," 113-15, 120-21, who argues that Paul is personally in agreement with the position of those who wanted to eat food offered to idols. However, it is not this agreement that determines his treatment of the problem. Rather, it is the concern for the weak. Hence the importance of love and of the setting aside of one's right. This treatment was unique, ignored and then misunderstood in early Christianity.

lie in the place of eating food offered to idols nor the act of eating itself, but in the ground on which one based his or her decision whether to eat or not, and on the fear of acting against such a ground. Some defend their right to eat on the basis of the non-existence of idols, but others refuse to do so because of their awareness of idols' existence and its link with food offered to them (8:1,4-6,7,8). The crux of the problem lies here. Those who wanted to eat on the basis of their right justified it with their knowledge that idols did not exist and with other related arguments. But others, who might still possess right,[431] thought that idols did exist. They thought that food offered to idols were inseparable from idols themselves. If they ate it they would do so with the understanding that they ate a substance which was associated with idols.

Paul's whole discourse is better seen in the context of the existence of this intense dispute among his readers as we described above (2.1.2b). Their encounter with the social and religious conditions known to them before their entry into the church and which they had to view from their new identity as Christians necessitated them having to reflect on what it meant to be Christians in their society in which people acted upon some social and religious practices which might not be compatible with their new identity as Christians.[432] On food offered to idols, they were not sure as to what should be eaten, on what ground and with whom.[433] As they did not yet have a well defined or well-written set of ethos with which they could live in their environment, writing to Paul for advice must have been necessary (8:1, cf. 7:1,25, 11:34b; 12:1; 16:1).[434] As we can see from 1 Corinthians, this process of reflections did not go smoothly. On the contrary, it caused disputes among themselves to the extent that there were σχίσματα among them (1:10, 11:18 and 12:25). In fact, their differences were such that they had quarrels or contentions (ἔριδες, 1:11).

This reading gives us the advantage of not having to contradict Paul's approach in 8:1-13 and 10:23-30 with that in 10:1-22, as has been done by many who emphasize the different place of the act of eating the food under consideration, at the temple or in the market or at a private dinner, and who differentiate between the act of eating communal meals (8:10) and personal

---

431 Note that unlike in 8:1, 4 and 7 Paul does not state in 8:9-10 that the weak do not have any right.
432 Cf. Engels, *Roman Corinth*, 110, who points out that the Corinthian Christians retained their traditional values even after they were converted.
433 See Judith Lieu, "'Impregnable Ramparts and Walls of Iron': Boundary and Identity in Early 'Judaism' and 'Christianity' in *NTS* 48 (2003) 297-327, especially 305-07 who shows the existence of dynamism and permeatability in the reconstruction of boundaries in the Second Temple text including in 1 Corinthians 8.
434 D. Wenham, "Whatever went wrong in Corinth" in *ExpTim* 108 (1997) 137-141.

involvement in an act of sacrificial offering (10:1-20).[435] It does not allow us to simply see Paul as being reconciliatory at the expense of the validity of the arguments of those who want to eat food offered to idols,[436] because, as we shall show, there is a strong indication that in a tactful way Paul tries to prevent those who want to exercise their right to eat food offered to idols from destroying *the weak brother* (8:1-9:27) and *themselves* (10:1-22) without refuting the validity of the arguments of the former nor accepting the position of the latter. Therefore, there is essentially a position being taken by Paul, namely 'flee from idolatry.'[437] He does it in a tactful manner in 8:1 - 9:27 and 10:23 - 11:1, but with a strong one in 10:1-22. This would have been understood by his readers.

Furthermore, our reading prevents us from thinking that Paul allows them to eat so long as it does not affect the internal harmony,[438] for Paul's answer was addressed to a community which was already in dispute on the issue and rocked by the existence of leadership alignment. It is doubtful that he would give an ambiguous answer, for it would certainly make his readers remain in their position and divide the community further. The intended message to be received by the recipients of the letter must have been that εἰδωλόθυτον should not be eaten. This means that one position must be given up. Hence the importance of 8:9-9:27. However, Paul does it in a way that does not repudiate the validity of the arguments of this one position. This is the craft of an apostle who loves his converts!

Lastly, our reading has the advantage of avoiding any attempt on our part to emphasize Paul's agreement with the view of those who wanted to eat food offered to idols in such a way as to claim that Paul is not concerned about their presence and eating of εἰδωλόθυτον in the temple. The locations and the food itself are not unrelated to each other.

Both views are irreconcilable and therefore extremely divisive. Little surprise then that the Corinthian Christians had a serious debate over it and that they sought advice from Paul (8:1, cf. 7:1). Given his previous stay in

---

435 For a short review of various views regarding the controversy over the relation between 1 Cor 8 and 10:1-22, see Newton, "Food Offered to Idols," 286-88.

436 Mitchell, *Rhetoric*, 238, resorts to Paul's reconciliatory strategy to explain the existence of different points of view on the part of Paul. She writes: "Paul tried (perhaps unsuccessfully) to hold two balls in the air by allowing the eating of idols (unless in particular situation it hurts the fellow Christians) but condemning idolatry. This is because Paul's overriding concern here is not merely idol meats in themselves, but the impact of conflicts over idol meats on the concord of the church community."

437 Similar view is held by Coye Still III, "Paul's Aims Regarding εἰδωλόθυτα: A New Proposal for Interpreting 1 Corinthians 8:1-11:1" in *NovT* 44 (2002) 333-43.

438 Meeks, *Urban Christians*, 160, says that Paul "is confirming the right and freedom of Christians to participate in the macro-society so long as that participation does not upset the internal harmony and development of the Christian community."

Corinth and based on the information he received from his converts, Paul must have been familiar with the position of both sides. Paul's answer in 1 Corinthians 8:1 - 11:1 indicates that the solution to the conflict demands a series of arguments which will convince those who have valid arguments to abandon their insistence to exercise their ἐξουσία (right) to eat food offered to idols. Hence, the importance of his emphasis on the negative effect of ἐξουσία on the weak in the same community,[439] and on his apostolic example of renouncing his ἐξουσία for the sake of the gospel and others.

Firstly, he counters 'knowledge' with 'love' (8:1). Then he elaborates the practicality of this love by speaking about the negative effect of exercising the right to eat εἰδωλοθύτων on other members of the community, in this case those who cannot separate idols with food offered to them (8:10).[440] To support this, he brilliantly uses terms which are already shared by his readers, namely the συνείδησις of the brother being weak, the sense of family of brotherhood within the community, and what Christ has done to the brother (note the use of 'your brother' in 8:11).

In other words, Paul strengthens his point by saying that because of their inconsiderate exercise of their ἐξουσία the weak brother, for whom Christ died, is essentially *destroyed*.[441] Moreover, Paul adds that by sinning (ἁμαρτάνοντες) against their brethren and wounding (τύπτοντες) their συνείδησις they essentially sin against Christ (8:11-12). Paul is so concerned with the negative effect of their exercising their 'right' on their weak conscienced brother that he issues a very strong statement to prevent it from happening. He states: "Therefore, if food causes to fall (σκανδαλίζει) my brother, I will never eat meat for ever, lest I cause my brother to fall" (8:13).[442]

Had Paul concluded his treatment with 8:13, it would have been understandable. But he did not end there. Indeed, had he terminated there, we would not have grasped the strength of the position of those who insist on eating and the existence of conflicting views among his readers. Paul is not satisfied with his statement in 8:13 which, understandably, could have

---

439 Thus W.A. Meeks, *The Moral World of the First Christians Library of Early Christianity* (Philadelphia: Westminster Press, 1986) 134-36, and "'And Rose Up to Play,'" 73-75, who argues that in order to maintain the unity of the church Paul uses arguments which take into account fully the arguments used by both to protect their interests and concerns.

440 Note the use of the negative notion of a word which has been used throughout 1 Corinthians positively. This word is οἰκοδομηθήσεται ('be built up or encouraged') to eat food offered to idols which to the weak brother is related to idols).

441 Note the importance of the place of ἀπολλυται in the beginning of the sentence in 8:11 (cf. 1 Cor. 1:18 where those who see the cross as folly are called 'those who are perishing,' ἀπολλυμένοις)

442 Horrell, "Theological Principle," 90-91

been seen by his readers as 'lip-service.' Given the strength of the opinion of those he wants to discourage from eating food offered to idols, Paul has to substantiate his exhortation in 8:9-13 with his own historical personal example, even though and precisely because such example has been seen by some as grounds for questioning his apostolic status (9:3).[443] In addition, Paul did not stop in 8:13 because he still had to address two more arguments being used by those who insist on eating food offered to idols, namely their freedom status and their aphoristic saying that 'everything is permitted' (10:23). Hence the important role of 1 Corinthians 9 in addressing their right (vv. 4-18) and their freedom status (vv. 19-23), and in encouraging them to exercise self-discipline in everything (vv. 24-27). The latter is a direct opposition to the aphoristic saying that 'everything is permitted.'

However convincing and compelling the attempts made in 8:9-13 and 9:1-27 may have been, as I believe it was, it would be wrong for us to expect Paul to have stopped there. He is aware of some who, for various reasons which are related to their different conditions, would not have been convinced by his argument in 8:9-9:27 and would still find great difficulty in carrying it. This is despite the fact that, by way of athletic imagery and his own example in 9:24-27, he has encouraged them to exercise self-control and made them aware of the negative consequence of their failure to give heed to his exhortation by speaking about the imperishable wreath, a theological idea which was common to every believer in Paul's churches. In fact, as in 8:13 Paul does it by saying that he himself does not want to become disqualified (9:27).

Paul then substantiates his warning against missing eschatological reward with another down-to-earth warning against the real danger in present life which may occur if they ignore the danger of idolatry in the event of eating εἰδωλοθύτων. He warns them against the danger of the sins of idolatry, of immorality and of invoking God's punishment in 10:1-

---

443 Again Horrell, "Theological Principle," 94-95, rightly argues that "Paul cites and accepts the theological principles which the strong use to justify their ἐξουσία to eat εἰδωλοθύτα. Paul never questions this ἐξουσία or the principles upon which it is based, but what he does do is to maintain that Christian conduct involves a Christ-like self-giving for others, a self-enslavement, a setting aside of one's own rights for the sake of the gospel. This, Paul demonstrates, is precisely his own practice. He has an unquestionable right to financial support from the congregations, but he sets it aside in order to place no barrier in the way of the gospel and in order to become weak alongside the weak whom he seeks to gain...it is about acting on the basis not on knowledge, but of love; a love whose paradigm is Christ."

22.[444] For this purpose, he draws on various sources.

First, from the history of the Israelites recorded in the books of Exodus and Numbers (1 Cor. 10:1-10) which were very central in Jewish history and known to Jewish Christian members of the church and to those who used to have association with the Jewish synagogue (such as the proselytes). From these books Paul draws paraenetic lessons to make sure that his readers get the point of this message (see especially vv. 6-12 and 14). He *then* brings the language of participation in the Christian eucharist and Israel's sacrificial practice in 10:15-19 to "illustrate how eating and drinking in a cultic context established κοινωνία which embraces those who partake and that which they share"[445] and uses it as a better ground for his strong prohibition in 10:21-22. It is striking to note that even in 10:1-22 Paul does not abandon the method he has used before in 8:1-6,8 and 8:10 where he does not negate the knowledge of his readers but encourages them to consider the effect of their action. Here in 10:20-22 he moves from the issue of the knowledge of idols' non-existence, which is the battleground of his readers' dispute, to the demonic world or to the world of intermediary beings, thus the use of δαιμονίοις an idea which was shared by everyone, irrespective of their educational level and social class.[446] As pointed out by J.D.G. Dunn, Paul never mentions 'demons' again in his so-called undisputed letters (note 1 Tim 4.1). It shows the ambiguous status of idols and demons.[447] What is important for us is to note that with the introduction of 'demons' Paul directs their dispute from a very divisive aspect to something about which both parties in the dispute have common knowledge. He moves from acknowledging the existence of the so called gods and lords as he has done in 8:4-5, to downgrading their existence (see 10:19-20). Strong though his arguments are, Paul does not force them to obey his exhortations blindly. Rather, he leaves it to their logic. He says:

---

444 Cf. J.S. Sibinga, "The Composition of 1 Cor. 9 and its context" in *NovT* XL (1998) 132-63, esp. 138 who regards 9 as an interruption, accordingly argues that 1 Corinthians 9:24-27 is not part of but connected to 1 Corinthians 10:1-22.

445 Horrell, "Theological Principle," 97.

446 See T.P. Paige, "Spirit at Corinth: The Corinthian Concept of Spirit and Paul's Response as Seen in 1 Corinthians." Unpublished PhD Thesis (Sheffield University, 1993) 222-24, 267-68, 271-72, who shows the importance of δαιμονία in the life of the first century AD Greek speaking Romans, irrespective of their educational level or social class. For many, δαίμονες were part of a daily life. Their understanding of δαίμονες ranged from a guardian spirit of the home to individual δαίμον like Roman *zenus*, to the fearful and mysterious δαίμον which were believed to be mere phanthoms hounding the night. In fact, Paige goes so far as to argue that δαίμονες were seen as intermediary beings between the humans and gods that Corinthian Christians could have some problems distinguishing the Judaistic idea of πνεῦμα τοῦ θεοῦ from δαίμονες.

447 Dunn, *Theology*, 37.

"judge for yourselves what I say" (10:15).

The strong exhortations (8:9-9:27 and 10:1-22) are aimed at the extreme position we have described, that which says that εἰδωλοθύτων can be eaten anywhere whatever the circumstances. Up to this point, Paul has not addressed the other extreme directly. He has indirectly done so in 10:20-22 where he downgrades the reality of idols. He does the same in 10:23 - 11:1.

The elaboration of his answer to those who want to eat on the basis of their aphoristic saying that 'everything is permitted' (10:23-27, 29b-30) has a direct effect on the other extreme.[448] Before reaching the point in which he cares for the weak (10:28-29a) and defends them against their counterparts (10:28-29a), Paul speaks of a point in 10:25-27 which basically favours those who want to exercise their slogan that 'everything is permitted' and yet, by implication, shocks the weak.[449] He admonishes those wanting to have a full contact with the people of the world to eat not only anything sold in the meat market (10:25),[450] but also any food served by an unbeliever in his house (10:27), even though the possibility for it to have association with or previously been sacrificed to idols is high.

The reasons given for this admonition are very strong indeed. In verse 26 he says: "For 'the earth is the Lord's, and everything in it.'" This is a confession drawn from Psalm 24, 50:12 and 89:12. If it is true that some food came to the houses of the rich directly from their estates, this quotation must have been deliberate. It was meant to give a theological legitimation of eating anything sold in the market and in the house of an unbeliever, whatever its background. Here, at no point is there any indication of Paul bowing to the position of those who want a strict boundary in their relationship with the world and anything in it. Rather, it is a very clear cut opposition to their demand, and rightly so. It would have been foolish of Paul to prohibit people eating any food sold in the meat market, whatever the conditions of the meat market might have been in terms of its association with idolatry. Total disengagement with the world, either by

---

448 Pace Rainbow, "Monotheism," 138, who argues that Paul addresses only those who want to eat. Also Cheung, *Idol Food*, 89.

449 Both groups are addressed in 10:23 - 11:1: one directly, the other indirectly. It is true that the holders of the slogan that 'everything is permitted' are directly addressed, but the position of the weak is also challenged. Cf. Ramsaran, *Liberating Words*, 61; F.W. Grosheide, *Commentary on the First Epistle to the Corinthians* (Grand Rapids: Eerdmans, 1953), 241; B. Hall, "All Things to All People: A Study of 1 Corinthians 9:19-23" in Robert T. Fortna and Beverly R. Gaventa (eds.), *The Conversation Continues* 137-57, esp. 155 n. 19, tries to determine which group is addressed in which verse (s).

450 Given that idolatry might have been present around the *macellum* of Corinth and was considered as a matter of course by many people, and given that meat was only one of many food sold there (see Tomson, *Paul*, 190), Paul's allowing them to eat Πᾶν τὸ ἐν μακέλλῳ (10:25) must have been very shocking to the weak.

means of the *kosher* laws of the Jews or anything else, has no place in Paul's answer. This is substantiated in 10:29b-30: "For why should my liberty be determined by another man's scruples? If I partake with thankfulness, why am I denounced because of that for which I give thanks?"[451] This admonition must have really shocked those who wanted to abstain from eating food associated with idols anywhere. Moreover, given that in 8:7, 10-12 Paul is very concerned about the conscience of the weak, his strong rejection of any qualm of conscience on the part of the weak here in 10:25-27 must have shocked the weak.

Shocking though Paul's permission for anything sold in the market and meat served in a house of an unbeliever to be eaten must have been for those who did not want to eat it, Paul's answer was none the less contextually understandable. How would his converts consume meat if he admonished them to refuse to eat it? Even if it is true that food served in the house had already been sacrificed by the host to his household deities in his household shrine, Paul's permission for them to eat it was still logical. Had Paul exhorted them to ask the host beforehand about the condition of the food being served, they would have faced unnecessary fatal consequences. The invited believers would lose contact with the outside world (cf. 1 Cor. 5:10). Even if the invited believer knew from general knowledge that the food being served may have been sacrificed to idols by religious officials before it was sold in the meat market or by the host in his house, it would be very presumptuous of the believer to ask his host about the background of the food.

However, Paul does not stop there. Rather, knowing that in their dispute the weak conscienced brother argued that even meat served in the house of an unbeliever was related to idolatry and could therefore not be consumed, and being aware of the fact that their view was rejected by those who wanted to eat food offered to idols, Paul admonishes that if the weak made their voice known the meat should not be consumed, whatever the consequences (10:29).[452] This admonishment must have shocked those who wanted to eat food offered to idols. None the less, they would have known that they were asked to refrain from eating not because their freedom could be curbed by the scruple of the weak. Rather, it was because of their concern for the conscience of the weak. They were expected to show a voluntary restraint.

---

451 Clarence E. Glad, *Paul and Philodemus* (Leiden: E.J. Brill, 1995), 292-93, 293 n. 168, rightly points out that 9:29b-30 is an impersonation to support the wise. Pace D.F. Watson, "1 Corinthians 10:23-11:1 in the Light of Graeco-Roman Rhetoric" in *JBL* 108 (1989) 313 n. 54, who rejects impersonation in these verses.

452 Since the emphasis on conscience here is related to the conscience being discussed in 8:7 and 10, it is likely that the informant Paul has in mind is a Christian brother. It is this person and those holding the same view as his that Paul wants to help.

Paul's answer in 10:28-29a is therefore meant to care for the weak, without negating the validity of the argument of those who want to eat food associated with idols in the house of an unbeliever. Just as in 8:10 - 10:22 Paul makes a great effort in preventing them from eating food offered to idols in idols' temple and injuring the weak conscienced brother, valid though their right to do so is, so does he here try to prevent them from doing any harm to the man of conscience, even if the meat is consumed in a house, away from the temple, and even if their aphoristic saying that 'everything is permitted' gives them a justification to do so. The care for the weak and his conscience is the principle that has to be taken into consideration even in the house of an unbeliever.

None the less, it must be remembered that, as we have shown above, this consideration of the weak does not cause Paul to bow to their extreme scruple. Hence, a total permission to eat whatever is sold in the meat market, even though Paul knows that, in one way or another, it is also related to idolatry (10:25). The summary of his advice in 10:31 - 11:1 is therefore appropriate: giving glory to God, which is the motivation of all actions. It is translated by Paul as the act of not causing offence to the Jews, Greeks and the church of God, and also of seeking not one's own advantage but that of many, with the purpose that they may be saved. It is only after such a long discourse that Paul issues his call for them to imitate him (11:1).

We have seen that 1 Corinthians 9 is an attempt on the part of Paul to use his apostolic practice to substantiate his exhortation already expressed in 8:9-13, but in doing so and being aware of the criticism of his apostolic status by some Corinthian Christians the chapter functions also as his defence against his critics. Though both are interrelated, the primary function is his intention to use it as an example.[453] Yet it must also be acknowledged that this example carries less weight if it does not stand up to criticism and if the basis upon which it is carried out (i.e. his apostolic status) is being questioned.

In short, it can be argued that our reading gives more justice than otherwise to the present text. It acknowledges that Paul himself consciously wrote chapter 9 not simply because 1 Corinthians 8:13 would appropriately be followed by chapter 9, but more importantly because Paul wanted to encourage his readers to draw a lesson from something which, material wise, is not directly related to the issue of food offered to idols itself, but

---

453 Horrell, "Theological Principle," 92, expresses this succinctly. He writes: "Certainly there are elements of defensiveness here in relation to Paul's apostleship (vv. 1-3) and perhaps also in relation to his refusal of financial support from the Corinthians. Yet in the argument of the passage as a whole it clearly serves as an example, spelling out for the strong the pattern of conduct that Paul calls them to imitate, and that he perceives as an imitation of Christ (11:1)."

which - in giving more weight to his purpose of encouraging his readers to move away from exercising their right to eat εἰδωλοθύτων - is highly significant.

Paul wants to give an example to those who wish to exercise their right about how to cope with a condition in which they have every legitimate reason to exercise their right on the basis of their theological knowledge of idols' non-existence and its relation to food offered to idols, their freedom status, and their slogan that 'everything is permitted,' yet for the sake of others should refrain from doing so. It is in this light that we have to see Paul's arguments in 1 Corinthians 9 where he clearly shows how difficult it has been for him to do something which runs counter to his right *for* the sake of the gospel and others. This is reflected in 1 Cor 9:12b,15,16-18 and 19-23, where he shows some paradoxes that he has undertaken for the sake of a greater purpose.

In fact, his argument in chapter 9 brings him into two interrelated issues which have been examined by some of his readers (9:3), namely his apostolic example of forgoing his right to financial support and, consequently, his apostolic status. He has to do this significantly because he knows that this example will add more weight to his exhortation already given in 8:9-13. Paul would not have opted for such a risky discourse had he not understood and recognized the legality of the position of those who wanted to eat food offered to idols. Nor would he have done so were it not for his great desire to prevent them not only from exercising their right and thereby destroying their weak brother for whom Christ died and sinning against Christ (8:9-13 cf. 10:32), but also from destroying themselves (10:1-22). Furthermore, given the existence of their leadership alignment, Paul would have expected that the success of his whole discourse here would at least prevent the church from disintegrating further.

Therefore, I submit that since Paul's answer was addressed to a community which was already in dispute on the issue and which was sacked by the existence of leadership alignment, it is doubtful that he would give an ambiguous or one sided answer, for such an answer would certainly cause his readers to remain in their position and divide the community further. The intended message to be received by the recipients of the letter must have been that εἰδωλοθύτον should not be eaten. Hence the importance of 8:9 - 9:27 to encourage them to have the capability to do so. However, Paul does it in a way that does not repudiate the legality of the arguments of this one position nor accepts the position of the other. This is the reason why, while allowing the former to eat food that has been sacrificed to idols and served by an unbeliever in his house (10:25-27), he nevertheless goes on pleading that when the position of the latter is made known the food must not be consumed (10:28-29a). This is the craft of an apostle whose suggested solution to the issue is driven by his desire not only to prevent the community from disintegrating further but also, and perhaps more substantially, to discourage them from destroying others (i.e.,. the weak), and themselves.[454]

2.4. Some Concluding Remarks

1 Corinthians 9 is part of a comprehensive and unified discourse of Paul in 1 Corinthians 8:1 - 11:1 on the issue of food offered to idols which was debated by Corinthian Christians. Some wanted to eat it, but others refused to do so. The former advanced valid arguments to justify their insistence on eating food offered to idols on the basis of their right. These arguments are: their theological knowledge of the existence of monotheistic God and non-existence of idols (8:1, 4-6), and the neutrality of food before God (8:8), their freedom status and their enthusiasm in the aphoristic saying of 'everything is permitted' (10:23). However, the latter refused to eat simply because they were accustomed to idols and their perception was determined by their conscience. Given that the arguments of the former were valid it was likely that their insistence would influence the latter.

Read against the background of the imperial cult and the Isthmian Games, it is now possible to infer that, while acknowledging the ordinariness of the issue, the intention of the former to insist on exercising their right to eat food offered to idols, which was based on various valid arguments, might also have been associated with their desire to participate in both occasions.

Knowing that the former possess valid arguments, that they were likely to influence the latter and thereby would cause them to fall into the sin of idolatry, and not wanting the former to destroy their weak brother and thereby sin against Christ, and in his attempt to prevent the former from falling into the sin of idolatry themselves, Paul arranges his discourse in a way that would help the former to abandon their insistence on eating food offered to idols, yet in a way that will not lead them to think that their arguments are illegitimate and those of their counterparts were valid.

We have seen that in facing the intense dispute, Paul uses a very tactful and passionate method. He accepts the validity of the arguments of the former *in insisting on their right* to eat food offered to idols which is justified by their theological knowledge of the existence of monotheistic God, the non-existence of idols, the neutrality of food before God, their freedom status and their slogan that 'everything is permitted' (8:1-6, 10:23). But he asks them *not to exercise their right* to eat food offered to idols for *the sake of the weak*. He does so by emphasizing the destructive effect of

---

454 Cf. Morna D. Hooker, *Paul. A Short Introduction* (Oxford: Oneworld, 2003) 127, who notes the importance of 1 Corinthians 10:1-14 to ensure that those who want to eat meat offered to idols are aware of the danger not only for the weak as described in chapter 8 and 9 but also for themselves.

eating food offered to idols in idols' temple on the brother weak in conscience (8:9-13) and urging them to learn from and imitate his apostolic examples of forgoing his right to financial support in order not to cause a stumbling block to the gospel (9:12b, 15-18; cf. 10:24, 29b-30), enslaving himself in order to win the more (9:19-23) and exercising self-control in order not to be disqualified (9:27). Moreover, he challenges them to think about the immortal wreath which would be the destiny of those who can exercise self-control, but which would be denied to those who eat food offered to idols and thereby sin against the weak conscienced brother and Christ (9:25, 8:10-13).

While in 8:9-9:27 Paul warns some of his readers of the negative effect of the use of their right to eat food offered to idols on the brother weak in conscience, in 10:1-22 he intensifies his discourse by asking them to be aware of the danger of their involvement in idolatry and immorality. Hence his call for them to shun the worship of idols in 10:14. In fact in 10:23 - 11:1 he tells them that the concern for the weak conscienced brother is still applicable even if the location of the eating is not in the temple and the nature of the food in terms of its relation to idols is not so obvious, namely in the house of an unbeliever (10:27-29a).

In his discourse, it is clear that Paul does not reject the validity of the arguments of those who want to eat food offered to idols, nor supports the position of those who want to have a complete separation from the world (i.e., those who emphasize that being involved in activities related to idols, whether in the market or in the house of an believer and, how much more, in temple, is forbidden). Hence his rejection of the identity of idols in 10:19 and his unconditional allowance and strong support of eating any food sold in the meat market (10:25-26, 29b-30).

By 11:1, the readers of both positions will have understood that Paul does not want them to eat food offered to idols, neither because the arguments for eating are invalid nor the arguments for abstinence are valid, but because of its effect on the weak conscienced brothers. It is by reading Paul's discourse in this way that we are able to explain the seemingly inconsistent treatment of Paul of the issue of food offered to idols in 8:1-13, 10:1-22, and 10:23 - 11:1. In this regard, the role of 1 Corinthians 9 is crucial.

CHAPTER 3

Understanding Paul's Apostolic Paradigm (1 Corinthians 9)

3.1 Defending the Ground for the Paradigm: 1 Corinthians 9:1-3

3.1.1 Introductory Remarks

We have established in chapter 2 above that in writing 1 Corinthians 9 Paul has in view two interrelated arguments used by some Corinthian Christians to justify their position in matters related to food offered to idols. First, they argue that they have the ἐξουσία to eat food offered to idols (8:9). This ἐξουσία is justified by theological knowledge of a monotheistic God, of idols' non-existence and of the neutrality of food before God. 1 Corinthians 9:4-18 is meant to address their insistence on using their ἐξουσία. Secondly, forgoing their ἐξουσία can be conceived to be contradicting their freedom status. Hence, it is sensible that Paul's calling for the Corinthian Christians to take care of their ἐξουσία (8:9-13, 9:14-18), must be backed up by a further argument which will help them to grapple with this fear of acting in contradiction to their freedom status (9:1,19-23). This is the reason why Paul feels that he ought to address this fear and why he immediately speaks of his own freedom in 9:1a, pending a full address in 9:19-23 which comes after writing about the renunciation of his rights (9:4-18). This is particularly important because Paul has already encouraged his readers to seize the opportunity to be freed and forbidden them to be slaves of men (1 Cor. 7:21-23). In fact, he does not speak of the latter until he defends his apostolic status which is being examined by some people (9:1-3). Moreover, in the context of 1 Corinthians 8:1 - 11:1, there seems to be a close link between ἐξουσία as right (8:9, 9:4-6, 12, 15, 18) and πάντα ἔξεστιν (10:23, cf. 6:12: πάντα μοι ἔξεστιν). Those who insist on their right and are reluctant to act contrary to their freedom status are likely to support their position with the aphoristic saying that 'everything is permitted.' Since the slogan has already caused some to have sexual relationship with prostitutes (6:12-20),[1] it is likely that the same slogan could have been used by some members to back up their insistence on exercising the right to eat food offered to idols (10:23).

Therefore, what we expect to find in 1 Corinthians 9:1-27 is an attempt on the part of Paul to push some of his readers further into forgoing their right to eat food offered to idols for the sake of the weak. He does this by providing personal examples of how to forgo his right as an apostle (9:4-18), how he makes himself a slave to all (9:19-23), and how he carries out self-control (9:24-27). In each of these examples he always emphasizes the goal of his practice, namely in order not to become an ἐγκοπή to the gospel (9:12b), to win and save the more (9:19, 22b) and, not insignificantly, to safeguard his share in the gospel (9:23) and prevent himself from being

---

[1] Scholars have recently raised the question of which kind of prostitution that Paul has in mind in 6:15b-16. The old view that it is a temple prostitution in the temple of Aphrodite of the old Corinth where 1000 prostitutes worked (see Fee, "II Corinthians VI.14-VII.1," 149), one that is based on the remark of Strabo (8.6.20) is still held by some scholars (see for instance F. Thielman, *Paul and the Law* (Illinois: IVP, 1994) 94; Roman Garrison, *The Graeco-Roman Context of Early Christian Literature* [Sheffield: Sheffield Academic Press, 1997] 35-39; J.A. Glancy, "Obstacles to Slaves' Participation in the Corinthian Church" in *JBL* 117 [1998] 481-501, esp. 493, argues that most of the prostitutes were slaves). This view has been doubted not only on the basis of the rarity of such case in Hellenistic religions and the silence of ancient authors on the issue (see Murphy-O'Connor, *St. Paul's Corinth*, 56; B.S. Rosner, "Temple Prostitution in 1 Corinthians 6:12-20" in *NovT* XL [1998] 336-51, esp. 347-48, argues that sexual engagement took place only on festive occasions at the temple [348, 351]), but also because of the fact that in the Roman era the Aphrodite had become a dignified deity. See Bruce W. Winter, "Gluttony and Immorality at Elitist Banquets: The background to 1 Corinthians 6:12-20" in *JD* 7 (1997) 77-90, esp. 79, who argues that the background to 1 Corinthians 6:12-20 is not brothel prostitution, but the after-dinner sexual activities of the élitist banquets. The participants Paul has in mind are the élite, especially the youth who, when reaching the age of 18 and thereby having the right to wear a *toga virilis,* have access to *symposium* and licence to recline at the banquets (*convivium*). Like the men of their time, the youth used the first century Platonic anthropology and philosophical hedonism to choose the path of gluttony, drunkenness and whoring. Winter argues that it was the acceptable practice of the élite to bring into their banquets the prostitutes to satisfy the physical hunger of their quests. In fact, travelling prostitutes could be brought into grand civic dinners such as the Isthmian Games to entertain the honourable guests. Cf. Ramsaran, *Liberating Words,* 58, who, following Stanley K. Stowers, "A Debate over Freedom: 1 Corinthians 6:12-20" in Everett Ferguson (ed.), *Christian Teaching. Studies in Honor of LeMoine G. Lewis* (Abilene, Tex.: Abilene Christian University, 1981) 59-71, suggests that this maxim (10:23, 6:12, note the use of 'for me') "represents an individualistic unrestrained freedom characteristic of Cynics and more strict Stoics" which was different from the 'responsible freedom' propagated by the Stoics.

disqualified (9:27). This emphasis on the goal is crucial in convincing his readers to forgo their right. However, knowing that the apostolic example of renouncing his right to financial support has been seen by some people as an indication of the invalidity of his apostleship (9:1b-2), Paul has to defend his apostolic status in 9:3. Without doing this, whatever he says about his apostolic example after verse 3 will have no value. It will fail to convince his readers of the importance and benefit of forgoing their right to eat food offered to idols.[2]

The questions of who his examiners are and why they examine him have occupied many scholars. In fact, they have influenced scholars' explanations of why Paul regards receiving financial support as an ἐγκοπή to the gospel (9:12b). In their interpretation, scholars have read the examination of Paul's apostleship against the background of the means of support of itinerant missionaries and popular philosophers believed to have been known or probably cherished by Paul's readers. We will propose, however, that according to the text Paul's apostolic practice has been consciously carried out not because of his attempt to be independent of the congregations or his desire not to be labelled as an itinerant missionary or popular philosopher, but by his own characterizing of the gospel he preaches (9:18). We shall show in chapter 4 (see 4.3) that this proposal may shed light on the question of why Paul strongly claims that he has never made use of his right to live off the gospel (9:12b), but at the same time receives support from churches (Phil. 4:15-16, 18; 2 Cor. 11:7-11; 1 Cor. 16:5-6, 15-18).

3.1.2 The Enigma of 1 Corinthians 9:3: What Is Examined?

The dispute over the nature of 1 Corinthians 9, whether it is a defence[3] or an example,[4] is partly to blame for the absence of any consensus on the question to which verses 9:3 refers (either verses 1-2 or verses 4-27). If it refers to verses 1-2, Paul is seen to be defending himself against the 'others' to whom he is not an apostle (9:2). Accordingly, 9:3 is translated as follows: "*My* reply to those who examine *me* is this."[5] It is argued that this

---

2 Horrell, "Theological Principle," 92, rightly states that the reason for Paul to defend his apostolic status is "that it is a necessary prerequisite for the validity of the argument that follows. Paul will go into some detail about his refusal to use his rights as an apostle, but if he were not a true apostle then the whole argument becomes completely worthless."
3 Hurd, *The Origin*, 126-31; G. D. Fee, *The First Epistle*, 390 n. 71, 392-394.
4 W. Willis, "Apologia," 35, and Mitchell, *Rhetoric*, 243-50, are the strongest proponents of this view. See also P.D. Gardner, *The Gifts of God*, 67-69.
5 Robertson and Plummer, *The First Epistle of Paul to the Corinthians*, 179, write: "That I have seen the risen Lord, and that you are such a Church as you are, -- there you have my defence when people ask me for the evidence of my apostleship."

reply or defence does not refer to the following because verses 4-11 "are not so much a defence as a statement of *claims*...People blamed him for maintaining his independence, but they could not deny his right to do it."[6] Their criticism of his apostolic status revolves around the question of whether or not Paul has seen the Lord (9:1c) and whether he has any seal of his apostleship (9:1d and 9:2b). Both are related.[7] Although his defence in 9:1c-2 is short, it is defence none the less. Our view of the reality of this defence does not depend on our understanding of Paul's rhetorical questions in 9:1a-d (i.e., whether or not the questions reflect the confrontation between Paul and his readers) as has often been done by scholars,[8] or on 9:1b ("Am I not an apostle?") as emphasized by G.D. Fee.[9] Rather, it depends on Paul's acknowledgement in 9:2a that there are 'others' to whom he is not an apostle.[10] This is despite the fact that, in Paul's eyes, he is an apostle to his readers, as confirmed by the expected positive answer to his rhetorical question: "Am I not an apostle?" The question of who the 'others' are will be discussed below.

Others, however, argue that 1 Corinthians 9:3 refers to the verses that follow. This is said to be supported by the use of αὔτη at the end of the sentence.[11] As a corollary, it is argued that Paul is not defending his apostolic status but his apostolic behaviour, especially with regard to his approach to ἐξουσία.[12] Paul is seen to be defending his own practice of

---

6   Robertson and Plummer, *The First Epistle*, 179.
7   Robertson and Plummer, *The First Epistle*, 178, capture this link: "Preachers who were not apostles might convert many, but the remarkable spiritual gifts which the Corinthians possessed were a guarantee that one who was more than a mere preacher had been sent to them."
8   While W. Willis, "Apologia," 34, argues that the expected positive answer rules out the possibility that Paul's apostolic status is debated by the audience, Fee, *The First Epistle*, 394-96, argues that the questions presuppose the confrontation on each question raised between Paul and the audience.
9   Fee, *The First Epistle*, 395.
10 Although admitting the problem dealt within 1 Cor 9 as internal, Fee, *The First Epistle*, 396-97, acknowledges the presence of outsiders within the Corinthian church and regarding them as the start of the confrontation in 2 Corinthians 10 - 12. Gardner, *The Gifts of God*, 71, is indecisive on the presence of the others. On the one hand, he accepts the possibility that the others are those who claim that by virtue of his rejection of support Paul is not an apostle. On the other hand, he regards it as a hypothetical possibility, used by Paul "to confirm Paul's apostleship as the premise for the forthcoming argument." Similarly, Malherbe, "Determinism and Free Will," 239, contends that the first part of verse 2, "If I am not an apostle to others" is hypothetical, and the stress is on the second part "at least I am to you; for you are the seal of my apostleship." However, each part of the verse must be given due weight.
11 Weiss, *Korintherbrief,* 233; Barrett, *The First Epistle,* 202.
12 Dungan, *The Sayings,* 5-6; Hock, *Social Context,* 60-61; Gardner, *The Gifts of God,* 72-76, esp. 72, 76.

forgoing his apostolic right to financial support (9:4-18) and his changing behaviour (9:19-23).[13] Some have even argued that Paul's defence covers his qualification to exert his authority over them,[14] and his failure to show consistency in matters of eating or not eating food offered to idols (referring to 8:9-13)[15]

None the less, it is quite obvious that those who have rejected the presence of defence in chapter 9 have done so at the expense of the literal translation of 9:3. As we pointed above,[16] they have inevitably translated ἀνακρίνουσίν in a future sense, rather than as dative plural present participle active,[17] and consequently seen verse 3 as anticipatory, fictitious, conative, or rhetorical in style. M.M. Mitchell's rejection of defence is such that she goes so far as to say that there is no charge against Paul in the chapter, even with regard to receiving money. She writes: "the only possible charge which one can unearth is an historically implausible one, that Paul did not take the Corinthians' money."[18] What will be defended is his "use of himself as the example for imitation...because he is well aware of the risks he takes in using himself as the example for imitation."[19] She explains that: "Using oneself as the example to be imitated is a strategy which is fraught with danger, the most obvious being that it might be read as self-praise, which is rhetorically unacceptable."[20]

We argue that there is no need to make a sharp distinction between the two notions. Both are present and, therefore, have to be taken seriously.[21] In those times when the role of apostles was of paramount importance in the growth of the newly founded churches, apostolic status could not be separated from apostolic practice and vice versa. In other words, not only is Paul's apostolic status under attack,[22] but his past and present missionary

---

13 H. Chadwick, "All Things to All Men (1 Cor. IX. 22" in *NTS* 1 (1954-5) 261-75, reprinted in *Heresy and Orthodoxy in the Early Church* (Aldershot: Variorum, 1991), argues that Paul's statement in 9:22b is seen by his critics as an inconsistency.
14 Sisson, *The Apostle as Athlete*, 57,65,77, 167-68.
15 Fee, *The First Epistle*, 293.
16 See page 84.
17 Newton, "Food Offered to Idols," 232 points out that since ἀνακρίνουσίν is in dative plural masculine present participle active, there is no reason to see verse 3 as hypothetical or the like.
18 Mitchell, *Rhetoric*, 246.
19 Mitchell, *Rhetoric*, 246-247. Mitchell uses comparable examples from ancient literature where a defence speech is simultaneously an appeal to one's example. She refers to Isocrates (*Or*.15.8) to show that the use of *fictional* defence for rhetorical purpose is paralleled in ancient rhetorical texts.
20 Mitchell, *Rhetoric*, 57 n. 166.
21 Thus Horrell, *Social Ethos*, 205.
22 Hays, *First Corinthians*, 146-47.

practice is being criticized.²³ The examination of his apostolic status may possibly have been occasioned by his practice which is not in harmony with that of others who received financial support from Corinthian Christians. The latter received financial support on the basis of the Lord's command (1 Cor. 9:14). E. Best rightly claims that Paul refers to himself as an apostle only when his apostleship is being questioned. In our context, the questioning came about because of his refusal to be maintained financially by the church.²⁴ Similarly, Gerd Lüdemann,²⁵ who claims to concentrate on texts which he sees as unambiguously presupposing an anti-paulinism, argues that the indication of attack against Paul can be found in passages where Paul quotes his opponents and of apologetic nature.²⁶ So, according to Lüdemann, Paul's argument to be supported by the congregation is his answer against attack on his apostolic status.²⁷ What is important to note, however, is that Paul would not have presented his apostolic practices, which were already used by some to question his apostleship, were it not because of his belief that it was these practices that could convince some of his readers to abandon their desire to eat food offered to idols on the basis of their right. This belief could not succeed if his apostolic status itself, upon which his apostolic practices are based, is being questioned. Burton L Mack²⁸ rightly states that "Paul turns a criticism to positive advantage. His behaviour could now be seen as absolutely commendable."

3.1.3 The Use of the Defended Apostolic Practice as a Paradigm

The use of his apostolic practice as a source of exhortation is standard in Paul's apostolic task as a leader of newly founded congregations. He uses his behaviour to support his commendation.²⁹ His practices of not using his

---

23 Cf. Wright, "Monotheism," 135.
24 E. Best, "Paul's Apostolic Authority" in *JSNT* 27 (1986) 3-25, esp. 10-11; also his *Paul and His Converts.* The Spurnt Lectures 1985 (Edinburgh: T and T Clark, 1988). 113; cf. Barrett, *The First Epistle*, 200, rightly states that "Paul would hardly have spent so long on the question of apostolic rights if his own apostolic status had not been questioned in Corinth."
25 Lüdemann, *Opposition to Paul in Jewish Christianity.*
26 Lüdemann, *Opposition*, 31-32, 64.
27 Lüdemann, *Opposition*, 66-67.
28 Burton L. Mack, *Rhetoric and the New Testament* (Minneapolis: Fortress Press, 1990) 60-64.
29 According to Stephen Barton, *Invitation to the Bible* (London: SPCK, 1997) 145, such a usage is in common with the practice of Graeco-Roman moralists of his day; Carl R. Holladay, "1 Corinthians 13. Paul as Apostolic paradigm" in D.L. Bach, et al., (eds.), *Greeks, Romans and Christians* (Philadelphia: Fortress Press, 1990) 80-98, esp. 84, argues that such a usage was based on their conviction "that example was far

right to financial support, of enslaving himself and of self-control are three examples of such a usage.

In his missionary endeavour in Corinth and elsewhere, Paul has constantly conducted a practice of not using his apostolic right in order not to put any obstacle in the way of the gospel (1 Thess. 2:9; 4:11; 2 Thess. 3:6-13; 1 Cor. 4:12; Acts 20:33-35). He uses that example in encouraging the Thessalonian Christians not to be idle but to work for a living (1 Thes. 2:9; 2 Thess. 3:6-13). Now, writing from Ephesus to Corinthian Christians who are in dispute over food offered to idols, he uses his refusal to accept financial support for a different purpose, namely as an example to those who want to eat food offered to idols on the basis of their right (1 Cor. 11:1).[30] Later on, as shown by Luke (Acts 20:33-34), in his farewell speech to the elders of the Ephesian congregation, Paul uses his working with his hands to meet his and his colleagues' needs for a slightly different purpose, namely as an example for the Ephesian elders to help the weak among them.

When using this example to both Thessalonian Christians and Ephesian elders Paul does not have in mind any criticism of his practice of working with his hands. But this is not the case when he writes to Corinthian Christians. Due to the existence of some who examine his apostleship, the use of the same example needs defending. The existence of leadership alignment amongst his Corinthian readers and, more importantly, the presence of other missionaries in Corinth who have received financial support from Corinthian Christians (1 Cor 9:2,11) are the reasons for such defence. If we look back to 1 Corinthians 1 - 4, we see the justification of Paul's defence here in 1 Corinthians 9:3. Paul has been made aware of the fact that, because of their leadership alignment, there existed among his readers some arrogant people who had refused to align with him because of his failure to perform eloquent wisdom while he was in Corinth (1 Cor. 1:10-12,17,18-25; 3:4; 4:3-4,6; cf. 1:10-18) and who in fact, as a result, made a big fuss about his failure to return to Corinth (4:18-19, cf. 1 Cor.

---

superior to precept and logical analysis as a means of illustrating and reinforcing appeals to pursue a particular mode of life."

30 Andrew D. Clarke, "'Be Imitators of Me': Paul's Model of Leadership" in *TynBul* 49 (1998) 327-60, esp. 340-47 here 47, rightly refutes Castelli's contention in her *Imitating Paul: A Discourse of Power* (Westminster: Louisville, 1991) 112-13. Castelli argues that in his discourse on imitation of himself and of Christ (1 Cor. 11:1) Paul is setting a hierarchy in order to reassert his own authority. Clarke, instead, argues that Castelli's idea is not present in 1 Corinthians 8-10. Hence, Clarke rightly states that "the intention underlying his exhortations to imitation of himself is to point to the real example of Christ which is the ultimate goal, in a self-effacing recognition of his own indebtedness to Christ."

16:3f.; 2 Cor. 1:15-2:2).³¹

It is striking to note, and this will be made clear in our interpretation, that in his defence Paul does not negate the ground upon which his critics base their criticism of his apostolic practice, namely the command of the Lord (9:14). In fact, he speaks positively of this command. The reason for Paul to introduce his criticized and defended apostolic practice is precisely that he wants to use it as an example for those whom he encourages not to use their right to eat food offered to idols. By way of analogy, he wants to let them know that just as his apostolic practice of renouncing his right to financial support has aroused criticism because it runs counter to the Lord's command upon which the other missionaries based their acceptance of financial support, so will the Corinthian Christians be seen as acting contrary to their legitimate right to eat food offered to idols. They will have to do this in order not to become a πρόσκομμα to and thereby destroy their weak conscienced brothers (9:9-12), just as Paul has done in order not to create an ἐγκοπή to the way of the gospel (9:12b).

3.1.4 Identifying Paul's Examiners: An Intractable Task

We have established above that there are some people who examine Paul, and they are likely to be those to whom Paul is not an apostle (9:2). Who are Paul's examiners? Are they some Corinthian Christians or other missionaries or both (9:2, 12a)?

Since the discourse is conducted between Paul and Corinthian Christians, the non-Christian Jews or pagans in Corinth may be excluded from our investigation. They did not have any interest in Paul's apostolic status. It was an issue only to his Christian communities. Due to leadership alignment among his readers (1 Cor. 1:10-4:21), it may be argued that Paul might have in mind some Corinthian Christians who aligned with other leading figures. Their alignment with leaders other than Paul must have been caused at the very least by their lack of interest in Paul and, consequently, their doubt as to his apostleship.

However, other missionaries cannot be excluded from our reconstruction. In fact, it will be argued that they are our primary suspects. It is these missionaries who are likely to have raised the importance of being the witness of the resurrection of Jesus and having the evidence of apostleship. Their criticism of Paul's apostolic credibility might have lent support to the critique of Paul's apostleship launched by some Corinthian

---

31 Dunn, *1 Corinthians*, 32-33, points out that Paul's sharp response in passages like 1:17, 3:1-3, 4:18-21, 8:1-3, 11:16 and more particularly his defence in 4:3 and 9:3 would seem to be odd if Paul was not "confronted by some sharp criticism if not outright opposition from within the church" and if he was not aware "that he had come under criticism from within the Corinthian assembly."

Christians, both on the issue of eloquent wisdom (1:18-25) and on the renunciation of his right. The issue of 'having seen the Lord' was more a concern to those compelled to preach the gospel (i.e., the missionaries) than to its recipients (i.e., the Corinthian Christians themselves). The latter could not be interested in the issue of 'having seen the Lord' if the former did not introduce it to them. The other missionaries, to whom Paul is not an apostle, may have raised the issue of 'having seen the Lord' because they were told by the Corinthian Christians that Paul did not receive money from them while he was in Corinth.

We argue, therefore, that both are involved in criticizing Paul's apostolic status. The other missionaries are involved because they accepted financial support from Corinthian Christians (9:12a, 9:14). Since Paul did not receive financial support when he was in Corinth and these other missionaries accepted material support from Corinthian Christians, it is not difficult to imagine that when asked by Corinthian Christians why, unlike Paul, they accepted support from Paul's converts in Corinth they would refer to the command of the Lord (9:14) to justify their practice. Moreover, they would have in turn questioned Paul's apostolic status for refusing to accept financial support. They would also raise the issue of apostolic proof, namely 'seeing the Lord' and 'the seal of apostleship' (9:1c-d). The Corinthian Christians would then point to the weaknesses of the proof of Paul's apostolic status in their leadership alignment in which Paul's lack of eloquent wisdom had been used by some not to align with him.

But our question remains: who are the other missionaries? One way of answering this question, the safest one, is to focus on the proof of apostleship that Paul introduces by means of rhetorical questions which expect positive answers. One of these is the importance of 'seeing the Lord.' Based on 1 Corinthians 15:8 it is clear that the Corinthian Christians knew to whom Jesus appeared. They knew from Paul's own proclamation (15:3) in Corinth that he himself was not excluded from the first witnesses (cf. 15:1 with 15:11). The case here is not who saw Jesus while on earth and in his appearance (1 Cor. 9:5 and 15:8), but who had seen or claimed to have seen Jesus at the time of the writing of 1 Corinthians. Those Paul had in mind could not have been those who saw Jesus on earth and on his post-resurrection appearances, that is to say the twelve disciples and many other witnesses of the resurrection of Jesus (15:8).[32] The other missionaries

---

32 In 15:3-7 Paul's reference to the witnesses of Jesus' resurrection is not to defend his apostleship or against the other witnesses including the apostles, but in a positive manner, namely to give ground to the validity of his proclamation on Jesus' resurrection which is needed to address those who doubt the bodily resurrection of the dead (15:12). His description of himself as the least apostle is not because he is under attack from the witnesses of the resurrection including the twelve, but simply because he persecuted the church (15:9).

(9:1c+12a) are not likely to be those of 1 Corinthians 9:5 nor of 15:8, because it is difficult to prove that all names cited in the latter verses had visited Corinth. Rather, they were the others who claimed to have seen the Lord themselves and used it in defending their status and questioning Paul. Who are they?

Theissen suggests that Paul's examiners might have been the charismatic itinerant missionaries who practiced pious poverty as commanded by Jesus in the synoptic tradition (Lk. 10:7-8; Mt. 10:9-10).[33] As a community organizer in the Greek urban cities, Paul did not conform to this charismatic poverty practice, as it was no longer relevant in the new environment. Instead, he worked to support his livelihood for his evangelistic activity. The Corinthians received his gospel, but their knowledge of the itinerant missionary practice caused them to criticize Paul's policy of forgoing his rights. Hence in 1 Corinthians 9 Paul is defending himself against the Corinthians who became influenced by the itinerant charismatic missionaries and, in 2 Corinthians, Paul was defending himself against the itinerant missionaries themselves.[34] In relation to the issue of 1 Corinthians 8-10,[35] Theissen argues that it was the rich who were interested in observing the different practices of Paul and the itinerant missionaries. They accepted the latter to stay in their houses and paid them while in Corinth and on their way to other cities.

However, to relate these missionaries to Theissen's thesis of the issue of food offered to idols as a conflict between the rich and the poor is wrong, not only because such a thesis is not supported by the text, but more importantly because it is against logic to imagine that these itinerant missionaries who have come from Judea would not have criticized the rich for holding the fluid view towards food associated with idols or with idolatry. More fundamental is that we have no evidence to ascertain that the supposedly élite Corinthian Christians had already so cherished the spirit of charismatic poverty at the time of the writing of 1 Corinthians that they would support the itinerant missionaries who practiced it.[36]

Others argue that they are followers of Peter. This is in line with the view of F.C. Baur who regards 1 Corinthians 1:12 as an indication of the presence of conflict in the Corinthian Church between Pauline Christianity

---

33 Theissen, *Social Setting*, 27-67.

34 Theissen, *Social Setting*, 41-46.

35 Theissen, *Social Setting*, 121-143; Meeks, *Urban Christians*, 69-70, regards Theissen's thesis as convincing. Neil Elliot, *Liberating Paul: The Justice of God and the Politics of the Apostle* (Maryknoll: Orbis Books, 1994) 205-206, takes up Theissen's interpretation without question.

36 Thus Chow, *Patronage and Power*, 108.

and Jewish Christianity.³⁷ Along this line, Robertson and Plummer argue that they are Judaizers who for various reasons questioned Paul's genuine apostleship.³⁸ In relation to 1 Corinthians 9, C.K. Barrett suggests that the 'others' of 1 Corinthians 9: 2 and 9:11 were Cephas' followers.³⁹

Based on his calculation of the length of time involved in Paul's visit to his congregation in Macedonia, J. Murphy-O'Connor argues that the missionaries were not emissaries coming from Palestine to mislead Corinthian Christians about Paul's apostleship,⁴⁰ but Antiochian Judaizers who had come to Corinth while Paul was on his visit to Macedonian churches and who wanted to uproot Paul of his missionary basis which he found while under the commission of the Antiochian community. In Corinth, so Murphy-O'Connor goes on to argue, these Antiochian Christian Judaizers changed their tactics by not concentrating on the law. Instead they focused on Paul's missionary practice which was in contradiction to the practice of missionaries from the Mother church.⁴¹ However, it seems that Murphy-O'Connor's view is based on a speculation of the length of time taken to travel by land and sea in those times. Moreover, it is doubtful whether they would have conducted that strategy at the expense of ignoring the intention of some Corinthian Christians to insist on eating food offered to idols, something which they themselves would have refused to do.

Wishing to refute the view that outside trouble-makers had come to Corinth, but ignoring the plural ἄλλοι (9:2, 12a), Ben Witherington III unjustifiably suggests that the others is 'Apollos.'⁴² G.D. Fee argues that they are the itinerant philosophers and missionaries, who "peddled" their wisdom or religious instructions (cf. 2 Cor. 2:17; 1 Thess. 2:5-10). Fee is not certain, however, whether they are the same as those of 2 Corinthians 11:20.⁴³ Jeffrey A. Crafton argues that Paul's opponents in 2 Corinthians were Christian missionaries of Hellenistic origin who arrived in Corinth

---

37 Baur, "Die Christuspartei," 1-146 See Munck, "The Church Without Factions," 135, Hyldahl, "The Corinthian Parties," 19.
38 Robertson and Plummer, *Critical Commentary*, 179-81. These reasons are his refusal of maintenance, his view of himself as being better than the Twelve, his pride as to refuse hospitality, his using the new religion to make money for himself.
39 Barrett, *The First Epistle,* 204. In his paper presented to the New Testament seminar at the Faculty of Divinity of Cambridge University on the 3rd February 1998, entitled "The Jerusalem Council," he reiterated that, if there was a leader of the Judaizing campaign in Corinth, there would be no more suitable candidate than Cephas.
40 C.F. Kling, *The Epistle of Paul to the Corinthians* (New York: Charles Scribner and Co, 1869) 181.
41 Murphy-O'Connor, *Paul*, 283-90, 293-295.
42 Witherington III, *Conflict*, 208.
43 Fee, *The First Epistle,* 411.

shortly after the reception of 1 Corinthians.[44] We would argue, however, that these missionaries had worked in Corinth and examined Paul's apostolic status even before he wrote 1 Corinthians (1 Cor. 9:3). They are Christian missionaries of Hellenistic origin[45] who are attacked by Paul in 2 Corinthians 12:16. They are those who claimed to have seen visions and revelations. Other than identifying the others of 9:2-3, 12a with those of 2 Corinthians,[46] therefore, we can only follow Hans Conzelmann's restraint when he said that the Corinthian readers would understand.[47] Those who do not agree with the view that other missionaries had visited Corinth at the time of 1 Corinthians would totally reject this view.[48] Yet, by rejecting their presence we would have to dispense with 9:1-2, 3 and 12a where they are said to have reaped material benefits from the Corinthian Christians.

---

44 Jeffrey A. Crafton, *The Agency of the Apostle: A Dramatic Analysis of Paul's Responses to Conflict in 2 Corinthians* (Sheffield: Academic Press, 1991) 54.

45 Pace Fee, *The First Epistle,* 409-410, who thinks that the "others" are Apollos and Peter.

46 Cf. Jerry L. Sumney, *Identifying Paul's Opponents: The Question of Method in 2 Corinthians* (Sheffield: Academic press, 1990) 189-190, who, after analysing all the previous methods of identifying opponents of Paul in 2 Corinthians, has concluded that the opponents were not Judaizers, Gnostics or divine men, but Pneumatics, especially those of 2 Corinthians 10-13. According to Paul, they like telling visions. The opponents of 2 Corinthians 1-9 and 10-13 raised the issues of pay for apostles, the practice of presenting evidence for apostolic status, and the proper criteria for evaluating apostles. If this is the case, it is small wonder that Paul in 1 Corinthians 9:1b puts as evidence of his apostleship his having seen the Lord Jesus. Cf. Marshall, *Enmity,* 346-47, 399, who regards Paul's enemies as those unnamed in 1 Corinthians (4:18-19), and in 2 Corinthians (2:17; 5:12, 10:12, 18 and 3:1, 12:11, 11:4, 11:12 and 13). They were Hellenistics Jews who had been educated in rhetoric and belonged to the mainstream of the Graeco-Roman cultural tradition. They influenced Paul's enemies in Corinth by virtue of their written self-commendation. Their opposition against Paul was not on the aspect of the legitimacy but authority of Paul on social rather than theological standing Paul's inconstancy in terms of the Greek standards of morality, his many humiliating experiences including his social debilitating disease or his ineffectual speech were all regarded as shameful. Moreover, his standard of apostleship provided none of the things highly regarded by the Corinthians. The criteria he developed were the antithesis of their standards

47 Conzelmann, *First Epistle to the Corinthians,* 152. Cf. Barrett, *The First Epistle,* 202, who could only guess that ["e]vidently, there were some in Corinth (local and visitors) who wished to put him to the test - with some presumption that examination would expose his lack of authority."

48 Witherington III, *Conflict,* 203. n. 3; Gardner, *The Gifts of God,* 71.

3.2. The First Paradigm: Forgoing ἐξουσία (1 Corinthians 9:4-18)

3.2.1 Introductory Remarks

Paul's discourse on his refusal to exercise his ἐξουσία to financial support from Corinthian Christians is meant to give a counter-example to their insistence on using their ἐξουσία to eat food offered to idols (1 Cor. 8:9). Our recognition of this plain analogy needs to be substantiated with an appreciation of the Corinthian Christians' ἐξουσία in order to grasp the strength of Paul's argument in 9:4-18. This appreciation cannot be achieved without a proper understanding of what it means to some Corinthian Christians. The suddenness of the imperative βλέπετε δὲ μή πως ἡ ἐξουσία ὑμῶν αὕτη in 8:9 after a discussion of γνῶσις in 8:1-7 and a statement on the neutrality of food in 8:8 is very significant in this regard. In the following, therefore, we will first of all show the importance of their ἐξουσία in Paul's eyes, its significance in relation to both their ἐξουσία and their desire to eat food offered to idols, and then try to ascertain what Paul means by ἐξουσία in 8:9. We will also read this ἐξουσία against the historical context, and argue that the insistence of some Corinthian Christians on exercising their ἐξουσία to eat food offered to idols was not only motivated by their γνῶσς, but also strengthened by the mood of their contemporaries to enjoy their rights as Roman citizens.

3.2.2 The Importance of Corinthians' ἐξουσία in Paul's Eyes

It is evident that from 8:9 up to 9:12 Paul compares the Corinthians' ἐξουσία to eat food offered to idols and the concern of the weak conscienced brother with his ἐξουσία to financial support, the concern for the gospel (8:9-13 and 9:4-12) and the beneficiaries of the gospel proclamation. In the former (8:9-13) he encourages the Corinthians not to exercise their ἐξουσία in order not to become πρόσκομμα to the weak conscienced brother. Their exercise of their ἐξουσία to eat εἰδωλόθυτον in the temple - the act of eating is described in 8:10 as ἐν εἰδωλείῳ κατακείμενον - would cause the weak conscienced brother who sees it to be encouraged (οἰκοδομηθήσεται)[49] to eat εἰδωλόθυτα. This cause and effect action is spoken of by Paul in a personal way in 8:13 where he appropriately uses the verb σκανδαλίζω.

In his own case, Paul shows extensively and strongly that he has not made use of his ἐξουσία to financial support in order not to become ἐγκοπήν to the way of the gospel of Jesus Christ (vv. 12b,15,18, cf. v. 23).

---

[49] It is important to note that here Paul uses a negative sense of οἰκοδομέω (cf 8:1; 10:23; 14:26).

In 1 Corinthians 9:12b and 15-18 he makes it very clear that he does not want the Corinthians to misunderstand his point. He is writing about his legitimate ἐξουσία not because he wants to obtain it from them, although he has every reason to do so, but to tell them that he has forgone it and continues to do so. By so doing he expects them to imitate it in their exercise of their own ἐξουσία to eat food offered to idols (10:24, 25-27, 28-29a, 10:31 - 11:1).

Paul appropriately uses different words in describing the cause and effect of a certain action. In 8:9-10 he uses πρόσκομμα and οἰκοδομηθήσεται as the effects of the exercise of ἐξουσία by εἰδωλείῳ κατακείμενον. In 8:13 he uses σκανδαλίζει[50] as the effect of φάγω βρῶμα or κρέα; in 9:12b, 15a he uses ἐγκοπὴν δῶμεν τῷ εὐαγγελίῳ τοῦ Χριστοῦ as the effect of making full use of ἐξουσία to financial support. Finally, in 10:32 he commands his readers not to become ἀπρόσκοποι to the Jews, the Greeks and the church of God. Even though we do not make an extensive etymological study of the different words used and the possibility of them having different meanings, as is being done by P.D. Gardner,[51] the point being made by Paul is clear, namely the idea of the negative effect of an action on somebody or something.

The close analogy between 8:9-13 with 9:4-18 indicates that Paul respects the ἐξουσία of the Corinthian Christians and at the same time is aware of the effect of its exercise on others. It is this close analogy that enables us to see that the way Paul presents his legitimate ἐξουσία in a detailed argument and his reason for forgoing it indicates the difficulty that the Corinthians would have faced should they wish not to exercise their ἐξουσία to eat εἰδωλοθύτων.[52] Paul is addressing people who had strong grounds and a great deal to offer if they were to give up their ἐξουσία.

Having established the importance of their ἐξουσία in Paul's eyes, we now need to determine its function in relation to γνῶσις and food offered to idols. P.D. Gardner suggests that here Paul is trying to make an analogy

---

50 In 1 Corinthians 1:22 Paul reveals that the preaching of the gospel of Christ crucified by him and his companions is seen as a stumbling block, a σκάνδαλον to the Jews, and a μωρίαν to the Gentiles. The Jews see the proclamation of Christ crucified as something unacceptable. It causes great trouble to them. In this sense, there is similarity of meaning in 8:13 with 1:22.

51 Gardner on πρόσκομμα, *The Gifts of God,* 57-61, here 61-62. Gardner concludes that πρόσκομμα was "an *entirely appropriate word* for the Corinthian situation in which Paul regarded the action of the 'strong' as sinning against Christ and leading people to worship other gods...Πρόσκομμα should therefore be allowed its full weight in signifying that which stopped people either being identified with or actually being the people of God."

52 Cf. Fisk, "Eating Meat Offered to Idols," 51-52 n. 7, who shows that Paul's rights defended in chapter 9 "presuppose the existence of parallel rights in chap. 8 to which the Corinthians were entitled, but upon which they should not insist."

of how an ἐξουσία should function in *authenticating group membership*, be it that of those who posses knowledge or that of the apostles of whom Paul is a member. Hence, he argues that γνῶσις is an authenticator to the Corinthian Christians' secure status in the covenant community. They eat food offered to idols in order to demonstrate their γνῶσις. So, Paul is using his apostolic position as an analogy. However, this analogy is not meant to address the different attitudes to idol meat. Paul is not asking the 'strong' to behave like him in their use of ἐξουσία. Rather, Gardner suggests that his apostleship is "an analogy of group membership that carries a particular ἐξουσία."[53] Those who possess knowledge belong to one group, and their membership of that group in the covenant community is authenticated by their demonstration of their ἐξουσία. And so, eating food offered to idols is a demonstration of their status as members of the group. Therefore, Gardner thinks that what Paul is doing in speaking about his ἐξουσία that comes from his apostleship is not to encourage the Corinthians "to behave like him in their use of their ἐξουσία, but to tell them that ἐξουσία does not authenticate apostleship." Hence Gardner states that *"just as an apostle's ἐξουσία does not authenticate apostleship, so a Christian ἐξουσία does not authenticate those who are God's."*[54] However, Gardner's reading diverts the use of ἐξουσία from the desire on the part of some Corinthians to eat food offered to idols to something else, namely to authenticate group membership. It is difficult to square his notion of 'authentication' with Paul's overall purpose of exhorting some Corinthian Christians to imitate him as he imitates Christ in making it the concern of others the determining factor in their ethical action (11:1).

Given the sudden and emphatic exhortation (βλέπετε δὲ μή πως ἡ ἐξουσία ὑμῶν αὕτη) in 8:9, there is strong reason to argue that the desire on the part of some Corinthian Christians to insist on exercising their ἐξουσία might have been the central element of their contention. They wanted to exercise their ἐξουσία to recline at a temple. In order to justify this ἐξουσία, they put forward their theological knowledge of God's existence, of idols' non-existence (8:4-5) and of the neutrality of food (8:8).[55] It is for this reason that, although Paul does not repudiate the legitimacy of their theological knowledge - in fact he agrees with them -, he none the less puts the blame on its use in the event of the destruction of their weak brother because of the exercise of their ἐξουσία.[56] He writes in

---

53 Gardner, *The Gifts of God*, 77.
54 Gardner, *The Gifts of God*, 77.
55 Cf. Fee, "Eidolothyta Once Again," 180.
56 Cf. Bruce W. Winter, "In Public and in Private: Early Christian Interactions with Religious Pluralism" in Andrew D. Clarke and Bruce W. Winter (eds.), *One God, One Lord in a World of Religious Pluralism* (Cambridge: Tyndale House, 1991) 112-34, here 132, who writes: "He [Paul] condemned those who placed pressure on other

8:11: ἀπόλλυται γὰρ ὁ ἀσθενῶν ἐν τῇ σῇ γνώσει ("for the weak man is destroyed *by your knowledge*"). Indeed, it is striking to note that because of the exercise of their ἐξουσία, the weak brother becomes similar to those for whom the word of the cross is 'folly': "those who are perishing" (ἀπολλυμένοις, 1 Cor. 1:18,23, cf. 2 Cor. 4:3). Their destruction is no different from that of those who reject the cross. If this is the case, then, the exercise of ἐξουσία is actually very central in the Corinthian Christians' dispute. Their desire to exercise it has a strong theological justification.[57] It is therefore not surprising that Paul has to address this heart of the matter as he continues his discourse.

It is evident that Paul does not negate the rightness or the legitimacy of the ἐξουσία itself (8:9). What he does do is to make his readers aware of the negative effect of its exercise on others (8:10). To strengthen this, Paul speaks of the victim as one's own brother for whom Christ died (8:11-12) and of his own example of having to forgo his own ἐξουσία for the sake of a greater purpose, the proclamation of the gospel and the salvation of many (9:4-12a, 12b, 15-18). Whereas his readers use theology to justify the exercise of their ἐξουσία Paul uses theology to discourage its use for the sake of others. *To him, the concern for others is the starting point of his theology. And this theology is derived from Christ himself and the gospel of Christ crucified.* This is also what he describes in his apostolic life (9:4-18): he wants others to be saved more and more (9:19). Hence, his appeal in 11:1: "Become imitators of me, as I am of Christ."[58]

Thus we may surmise that Paul's treatment of his own apostolic ἐξουσία in 9:4-18 is an attempt to draw an example or a paradigm of *what*, *why* and *how* one has to do when facing the problem of possessing a legitimate ἐξουσία to do something, in this case to eat food offered to idols, and yet being encouraged not to use it because of the effect it will have on others with whom one disagrees, in this regard the weak conscienced brother.[59] In other words, Paul is saying that they must not insist on exercising their

---

Christians to attend pagan feasts. This would lead the weaker brother back into the world of religious pluralism and destroy him 'for whose sake Christ died."

57 Rainbow, "Monotheism," 137, acknowledges this theologization of their right, but leaves unanswered the question of the precise nuance of their argument and other grounds for the legitimacy of their practice.

58 Winter, "In Public and in Private," 134, is right in emphasizing that "Paul operated like that, the Messiah also functioned like that, and so too must the Christian church as it interacted with the world of religious pluralism in public and in private (10:32 - 11:1)."

59 G. Didier "Le salaire du désintéressement (1 Co. 9.14-27)," in *RecSciRel* 43 (1955) 228f., rightly says that Paul is simply proving that "to live at the expense of the congregations is, technically speaking, his right - just as incontestable as the right of the Corinthian Christians to eat of the meat sacrificed to pagan idols," as noted by Dungan, *The Sayings of Jesus*, 5.

ἐξουσία, valid though it may be, when they have a dispute with each other, particularly over issues such as food offered to idols which, in nature and character, are intrinsically related to the pluralistic social and religious contexts from which Christians have been called, in which they are living and into which they are called to witness.[60]

3.2.3 The Meaning of ἐξουσία in 1 Corinthians 8:9 - 9:18

How have scholars understood ἐξουσία in 1 Cor 8:9? Depending on the perspective from which one comes to the text, the word has been translated differently. In most of the translations, ἐξουσία of 8:9 is differentiated from that of 9:4-18. As a result, although in 9:4-18 ἐξουσία is translated as 'right,' in 8:9 it is translated differently.[61] Because of the fact that there are various meanings of ἐξουσία in the New Testament,[62] it is not surprising that scholars have translated ἐξουσία of 8:9 differently:[63] authority,[64] power,[65] freedom,[66] freedom of action or of choice,[67] the right to judge on the basis of having the potential to evaluate or free choice,[68] liberty,[69] duty

---

60 Cf. Winter, "In Public and in Private," 132.
61 See for instance Horsley, "I Corinthians," 249.
62 J.P. Louw and E.A. Nida, *Greek-English Lexicon of the New Testament Based on Semantic Domains*. Vol. II (New York: UBS, 1988, 1989) 147-8, 473, 476, 477, 681 list the following: authority to rule, the domain or sphere over which one has the authority to control, symbol of authority, ruler, control, power and supernatural power.
63 See for the summary of the translations of this word, Ronald Trail, *An Exegetical Summary of 1 Corinthians 1-9* (Dallas: Summer Institute of Linguistics, 1995) 355.
64 Fee, *The First Epistle*, 384-85, 402; Stephen Barton, "All Things to all people: Paul and the law in the light of 1 Corinthians 9:19-23" in James D.G. Dunn (ed.), *Paul and the Mosaic Law* (Tübingen: Mohr, 1996) 271-85, esp. 272, for that of Paul (9:4-18), but 'liberty' for 8:9; also his *Invitation to the Bible* (London: SPCK, 1997) 146.
65 A. Denaux, "Theology and Christology in 1 Cor 8, 4-6: A Contextual-Redactional Reading" in Bieringer (ed), *Corinthian Correspondence* (Leuven: Leuven University Press, 1996), 593-606, esp. 597.
66 Mitchell, *Rhetoric*, 242 and 242 n. 219.
67 Conzelmann, *First Epistle*, 148, and Bruce, *1 and 2 Corinthians* 8, who give 'right' as an alternative; R.A. Horsley, "I Corinthians," 246, 269. This translation is not surprising because as shown by J.H. Moulton and G. Milligan, *The Vocabulary of the Greek New Testament from the Papyry and other non-literary sources* (London: Hodder and Stoughton, 1930) 225, the basic meaning of ἐξουσιανδ α is 'power of choice' or 'liberty of action.'
68 Louw and Nida, *Greek-English Lexicon*, 865.
69 Héring, *The First Epistle*, 72; Trail, *An Exegetical Summary*, 355. This liberty is said to refer to that of eating sacrificial meat; KJV, NASB, NRSV, REB.

or responsibility,[70] and recently, right.[71] Those who define it as 'freedom' have assumed that it is either Paul's teaching on the freedom from the law[72] or Gnostic influence[73] or Stoic philosophical moral teaching (i.e. that it is the person who is free that has ἐξουσία)[74] that led some Corinthian Christians to eat food offered to idols.

However, if we are to see the Corinthians' ἐξουσία in the light of Paul's usage in 1 Corinthians 9:4-6,12,15, and 18 where the word is used in connection with the ἐξουσία (right) to eat, be accompanied by wives, and live from one's job, there does not seem to be any indication that Paul is speaking of 'freedom' in 8:9. Perhaps, it is the failure to see how Paul uses the word in 1 Corinthians 9 that causes Foerster to render it as 'freedom,'[75] even though he knows that in ordinary Greek usage ἐξουσία is that which is granted by a higher norm or court and therefore means "the right to do something or the right over something"[76] and in Jewish usage such as *Ant.*

---

70 Thus Witherington III, *Conflict*, 229; Winter, *Seek the Welfare of the City*, 166, with a specific meaning in 'civic privilege' which entitled the Corinthian citizens to dine in 'civic' occasions in the temple. Malherbe, "Determinism and Free Will," 235, 237 who sees it to be tied very closely with γνῶσις, and as such to be equated with the Stoics' view that the person who is free has ἐξουσία . The freedom is 'the knowledge of what is allowable and what is forbidden, and slavery as ignorance of what is permissible (ἔξεστιν) and what is not' (Dio Chrysostom, *Or.* 14.18). Paul's response to the question of idol food is informed by the Stoics view which was held by the Corinthians.
71 Winter, *Seek the Welfare of the City*, 167. Winter questions the normal translation of ἐξουσία of 8:9 as 'liberty' on the basis of the fact that Paul uses the same term repeatedly in the following chapter and that for freedom Paul uses ἐλευθέρια (9:1). Cf. also V.P. Furnish, "Belonging to Christ: A Paradigm for Ethics in First Corinthians" in *Interpretation* 44 (1990) 145-57, here 154, who sees the 'right' as that of 'before God.'
72 W. Foerster, "ἔξεστιν, ἐξουσία, ἐξουσιαθαζω" in G. Kittel (ed.), *Theological Dictionary of the New Testament.* Vol. II (Grand Rapids: Eerdmans, 1964) 560-75, esp. 570.
73 H. Lietzmann, *Messe und Herrenmahl. Eine Studie zur Geschichte Liturgie* (Bonn, 1926) 39, as noted by Gardner, *The Gifts of God*, 55; Reitzenstein, *Hellenistic Mystery*, 461-62.
74 Malherbe, "Determinism and Free Will," 235-41, here 238, writes: "the idea of freedom was integrally related to that of *exousia* and is implicit in 8:9-13. It becomes explicit in chapter 9, and Paul's mentioning of his freedom in 9.1 and repetition of it in 9.19 should cause neither surprise nor caution as it has done. According to the Stoics, one's freedom is inextricable from one's *exousia*, and Paul also argues from freedom (9.1) to *exousia* (9.3 following)." Marshall, *Enmity*, 292; cf. also Conzelmann, *First Corinthians*, 109 n. 5.
75 Foerster, "ἔξεστιν," 570.
76 Foerster, "ἔξεστιν," 562. This meaning of ἐξουσία is also present in John 1:12, as pointed out by W.J. Dumbrell in his *The Search for Order: Biblical Eschatology in*

4.247 the word denotes the right given or protected by the law.⁷⁷

Since there is no indication in 9:4-6,12,15, and 18 that Paul thinks of 'freedom of choice' or 'authority' when using ἐξουσία, it is unlikely that he speaks of this notion in 8:9. Rather, he speaks of the right that is guaranteed by common law and practice. It is like the right of a soldier to be supported by the government when he goes to war or that of a worker to live from what he is and does. It is a right to have something. It is not about the right to do whatever one wants to do. Since Paul wants them to imitate him in forgoing the kind of right that is similar to the right of a soldier who goes to war and is supported by the state, it is likely that the right they are expected to forgo is of the same nature. If that which he wants his readers to forgo is the right of a different nature (i.e., that of freedom of choice), Paul will likely use ἐλευθέρια (liberty, cf. 10:29b) in 8:9 and, consequently, in 9:4-6,12,15, and 18, rather than ἐξουσία to financial support.

The context of 1 Corinthians 8:9 - 9:18 does not allow us to render ἐξουσία as freedom or authority even though other contexts, such as that of 1 Corinthians 7:4, do.⁷⁸ It is true that there is a connection between ἐξουσία in 8:9, 9:4-6,12, and 18, and παντα ἔξεστιν in 10:23 (cf. 6:12). As shown by Thiselton,⁷⁹ the latter is derived from the verbal form of the Greek ἔξεστι (= it is permitted) and its cognate noun ἐξουσία (right). Accordingly, he translates παντα μοι ἔξεστιν as "I have the right to anything" or, "I have the right to do what I like." However, this does not necessarily mean that Paul thinks of this slogan in 8:9, 9:4 - 6,12, and 18 where he speaks of an ἐξουσία that is guaranteed by common law.⁸⁰ Paul does not deal with the slogan until 10:23. This is perhaps the reason why he mentions ἐλευθερία (liberty) in 10:29b. In other words, Paul deals with

---

Focus (Michigan: Baker, 1994) 237. Jesus as Logos gave those who believe in him the ἐξουσία to become the children of God. This ἐξουσία is "the right to do something, or to dispose of something; and the ability to do it." See also his "Law and Grace: The Nature of the Contrast in John 1:17" in EQ LVIII (1986) 25-37, esp. 26.

77 Foerster, "ἔξεστιν," 564.

78 Delobel, "Coherence," 184, is right in arguing that the ἐξουσία in 1 Cor. 8:9, 9:4,5,6, 12, 18 is "specific to 1 Cor, and differs from its meaning elsewhere in Paul." However, he is still influenced by the scholars' usual association of it with liberty. Hence, he defines it as "personal right and liberty."

79 A.C. Thiselton, "Human Being, Relationality and Time in Hebrews, 1 Corinthians and Western Traditions" in EA 13 (1997) 76-95, esp. 88-89; cf. S. Zodhiates, The Complete Word Study Dictionary New Testament (Iowa: World Bible Publishers, 1992) 606, points out that ἔξεστι "denies the presence of a hindrance" and that it is used "either of the capability or the right to do a certain action."

80 Marshall, Enmity, 285 and 289, sees ἐξουσία as etymologically related to freedom (eleutheros and eleutheria) in 1 Corinthians 6-10 (6:2, 10:23; 8:9, 9:1,4,5,6,12a,b, 18,19, 10:29, and therefore translates it as freedom.

right as guaranteed by common law in 8:9-9:18 and its basis (i.e, freedom status/ἐλεύθερος) in 9:19-23, and then with a different kind of ἐξουσία (i.e., that of 'doing what one likes' or 'freedom to do anything') in 10:23 following. Hence Paul's mention of ἐλευθερία in 10:29b.

Therefore, with Bruce Winter, we contend that the best way of translating ἐξουσία of 8:9 is to see it in the light of the user of the word in our textual context, Paul himself, and therefore translate it as 'right,'[81] such as that of being supported financially because of his status as an apostle and his profession as a preacher of the gospel. The Corinthian Christians' knowledge of God's existence, idols' non-existence and of the neutrality of food before God gives them a right to eat food offered to idols.

3.2.4 The Historical Context of Corinthians' ἐξουσία

We have established above that, because of their knowledge, ἐξουσία was very central in the eyes of those who wanted to eat food offered to idols. Since the meaning of ἐξουσία is 'right,' we will propose in the following that their insistence on exercising it may also have been related to the high regard of citizenship status and the rights therein among the populace of Corinth, the highly Romanized city. In other words, theological justification of their right was even strengthened by their legal rights as Roman citizens.

What was ἐξουσία within the context of Corinth as a Roman colony under the reign of Claudius? With the exception of Bruce W. Winter (see below), because of the rendering of ἐξουσία as 'authority' or 'freedom,' this aspect of 1 Corinthians 8:9 has been overlooked. There has been virtually no attempt to see the insistence by some on eating food offered to idols on the basis of their ἐξουσία in the light of the fact that under the reign of Claudius there was a strong encouragement for the whole people in the empire to gain their Roman citizenship and thereby enjoy its legal privileges.[82]

Bruce W. Winter[83] suggests that the ἐξουσία of the Corinthians is related to the right of a Roman Corinthian citizen to a specific privilege which entitled him to dine on 'civic' occasions. Winter specifically argues that not

---

81 Winter, *Seek the Welfare of the City*, 167; Morris, *The First Epistle*, 125 and 131. The use of 'we' in vv. 4-5, 10, 12a, 12b 'Barnabas and I' in v. 6, 'others' in v. 12a, 'I' in 15, and 'my' in v. 18: all indicate that he is speaking of his and others' ἐξουσία. Cf. Gardner, *The Gifts of God*, 56, 76-77, who translates it as 'the exercise of your legal right' which becomes theirs because of their knowledge.

82 M. Goodman, *The Roman World. 44 BC-AD 180* (London and New York: Routledge, 1997) 136, argues that "Claudius deliberately encouraged the spread of citizenship; none is known to have opposed it."

83 Winter, *Seek the Welfare of the City*, 171-72, and *After Paul Left Corinth*. Chapter 5, "Elitist Ethics and Christian Permissiveness (1 Corinthians 6:12-20; 10:23; 15:29-34)," esp. 93-96.

all Corinthian dwellers were entitled to be invited to such occasions.[84] Those who stayed in Corinth but did not possess Roman citizenship (i.e., the *incolae*) did not have this right.[85] The occasion that Winter suggests is the Isthmian Games. The president of the Isthmian Games invited the Corinthian citizens to attend the Games and other festivities involved in and around the Games, including dining and related sexual activities, and the worship of imperial cult with its idols. He argues that on the occasion of the transfer of Games from Corinth to Isthmia in AD 23, Lucius Castricus Regulus celebrated it with a banquet for all the citizens as an act of benefaction. This particular event was subsequently seen by the citizens as their right, and extended by the subsequent presidents of the game (Plutarch, *Moralia,* 723). In line with the fact that this honorary office of the president of the game was conditional upon the promise of the candidate to offer something for the people, Winter goes so far as to argue that the subsequent presidents would not offer less than what had been offered by their predecessors. Since the temple of Poseidon was integrally related to the site of the games, it is likely that the banquets took place in this temple. Not using their right to accept the invitation would deprive them of the benefits of the invitation, and make them act in contradiction to the enthusiastic mood of the population about the games.[86] It would be understandable that every one would have been happy to be present at such famous games. Winter's suggestion is supported by the possibility of the relationship between Paul's mentioning of 'the so called gods in heaven or on earth' and many 'gods' and 'lords' in 1 Corinthians 8:5 which can allude to the imperial *divi* that were likely to have been worshipped in the celebration of the imperial cult which was often carried out along with the imperial games. The desire to be present at the games and recline at idols' temples is therefore thought to have been very strong.

However, we must be wary of confining the exercise of ἐξουσία to the specific right to be invited to and privilege to be present at the Isthmian games. Since Paul reads the Corinthians' ἐξουσία in the same context as the common right to live from one's employment, Winter's suggestion might be too specific. Paul might have included what is suggested by Winter, especially with the use of the example from the temple service

---

[84] For an information on the legal difference between the citizens and aliens, see Garnsey, "Legal Privilege," 141-65, here 165, who claims that: "The Romans rejected juridical equality, the equality of all citizens before the law, as easily as they rejected political equality."

[85] Pace John R. Lanci, *A New Temple at Corinth: Rhetorical and Archaeological Approaches to Pauline Imagery* (New York: Peter Lang, 1997) 105-06, who argues that all, irrespective of their social strata and gender, had access to all public occasions.

[86] Newton, "Food Offered to Idols," 215 n. 30, regards Winter's proposal as an argument from silence and appears to rest totally on the Roman background.

(9:13). Imperial cults had official priests.[87] None the less, Paul might have intended a broader sense than that proposed by Winter. It is a right to eat food offered to idols which is not only guaranteed by theological knowledge of God's existence, non-existence of idols and of the neutrality of food before God, but is also supported by the importance of general civic rights of Roman citizens.

There was a generousity of granting Latin rights as a preparation for full citizenship. In fact, this encouragement continued to develop until eventually under Caracalla, probably in A.D. 212,[88] when it became almost universal. Caracalla's edict alleviated "the fundamental distinction between Roman and non-Roman citizens within the empire."[89] Claudius, however, made sure that there was a strict check on the abuse of citizenship status. As pointed out by Garzetti: "He punished severely any overstepping of the bounds by non-citizens who illegally acquired citizenship, by citizens who did not speak Latin and by people who falsely pretended to be knights."[90] He made sure that the bond between former masters and their freedmen was kept.[91] As argued by Sherwin-White, it was Claudius who began the practice of granting citizenship of honour.[92] He writes, "the readiness of Claudius to assimilate citizen-soldiers and peregrine troops is manifest."[93] In fact, he argues that the importance of the possession of citizenship status during the reign of Claudius was such that there was a traffic in Roman citizenship[94] and a competition between people who already possessed it.

---

87 Price, "From noble funerals to divine cult," 56-105, 88.
88 Finley, *Ancient Economy*, 51.
89 Dixon, *The Roman Family*, 91.
90 A. Garzetti, *From Tiberius to the Antonines. A History of the Roman Empire. AD 14-192*, ET. by J.R. Foster (London: Muthuen and Co Ltd, 1974) 132.
91 Garzetti, *From Tiberius*, 132.
92 A.N. Sherwin-White, *The Roman Citizenship* (Oxford: Clarendon Press, 1973, 1996) 248-249.
93 Sherwin-White, *The Roman Citizenship*, 249. It was Claudius who granted the privileges of citizenship to the builders of ships which were destined for the transportation of grain. This was due to Claudius' concern for corn supply. See Garzetti, *From Tiberius*, 138. Goodman, *The Roman World 44 BC-AD 180*, 118, argues that the practice of auxiliary soldiers being issued a diploma of 25 years service on their retirement as evidence of citizenship was not known before Claudius. Pace Brunt, *Italian Manpower*, 142-44, who argues that the system of granting citizenship to auxiliaries troops did not originate with Claudius, but was a result of a gradual evolution, starting with Augustus himself who, later in his reign, exercised a degree of caution in granting citizenship and preferred a gradual extension of citizenship.
94 Judge, "St. Paul and Classical Society," 25; Lentz, Jr, *Luke's Portrait*, 40, refers to Dio Cassius, *Roman History*, ET. E. Cary, lx, 17, 5f, who describes the devaluation of Roman citizenship. According to Dio Cassius, while in the first year of Claudius'

As a result it was Claudius who made sure that "a balance is maintained between the citizenship as a reward for services and as the ground of duty; the material content and the dignity of the *civitas* do not suffer, although the tendency, due to the enthusiasm of the provincials themselves, that created degrees of honour within the citizenship, a sort of *civitas*-within-*civitas*, is just beginning to appear."[95] Under Claudius women were freed from the power of the guardianship of agnates. Under this guardianship, women could not issue any legal transactions without the assistance of their guardians.[96]

The status of Corinth as a Roman colony and the centre of the Achaian province, and the fact that its first settlers were mostly freedmen from Rome help us to see the likelihood that most, if not all of its citizens, viewed their Roman citizenship very highly.[97] In the Roman empire, some people were even willing to sell themselves into slavery to a Roman citizen in order to gain Roman citizenship upon manumission by their masters and to enjoy the privilege of being under the members of a high status Roman family. Various methods were used to grant citizenship to slaves[98] on whose skill and energies the economy of the whole empire greatly depended. At a time when slaves and freedmen of the imperial *familia* could enjoy great privilege, such a case was possible. Indeed, it has been noted that the members of Claudius family, especially his freedmen (such as Narcissus and Pallas), were very influential in the imperial family. Claudius' *familia* was very influential in the imperial court in which many policies of government were decided.[99] Moreover, placed in the context of the local and federal imperial cult and its relation to the patron-client system in the city and in the empire (see chapter 2 above), the desire for the Corinthian Christians to make use of their right as Roman citizens was consonant with the mood of all segments of the Corinthian society. Indeed, it is not impossible to suggest that all Roman citizens living in Corinth might have been aware of the need to safeguard their right, given the practice of the Roman authorities to grant better citizenship to those seen to be loyal to the empire and the withdrawal of the citizenship status of cities perceived by the Roman authorities to have failed to live up to that status.[100] The only

---

reign the price of a citizenship was very high, it was later very cheap that "even a broken piece of glassware" was sufficient to pay for a citizenship.
95 Sherwin-White, *Roman Citizenship,* 249-50.
96 Pomeroy, *Goddesses,* 152.
97 Lentz, Jr, *Luke's Portrait,* 43, rightly points out that in Greek cities "citizenship was a distinction of no small degree and was jealously guarded."
98 See the detail in A. Watson, *Roman Slave Law* (Baltimore and London: The John Hopkins University Press, 1987) esp. 23-34.
99 See Garzetti, *From Tiberius,* 141-43.
100 Garnsey, "Legal Privilege in the Roman Empire" in M.I. Finley (ed), *Studies in Ancient Society. Past and Present Series* (London and Boston: Routledge and

way they could safeguard their citizenship right was to show their loyalty to either their local patrons or to the emperor as their supreme patron or to those close to the emperor.

If this is the case, it is small wonder that Paul, for the sake of the weak in conscience brother, warns his readers very emphatically: "βλέπετε δὲ μή πως ἡ ἐξουσία ὑμῶν αὕτη" in 8:9 against their insistence on making use of their ἐξουσία. It is because of Paul's recognition of the legitimacy of their right based on knowledge, civil perspective and from common sense that he has to choose his own intrinsic apostolic right in order to persuade the Corinthians not to exercise their right to eat εἰδωλόθυτον. It is true that Paul does not use his right as a citizen of the Roman empire to counter their desire to use their right to eat food offered to idols. He uses his right as an apostle. Nevertheless, he speaks from his position as the one who legally has the right to be supported by them financially.

The legitimacy of the ἐξουσία of Corinthian Christians is of equal value to that of Paul. It is his acknowledgement of their ἐξουσία that motivates him to emphasize his ἐξουσία in 9:4-12a, 13-14 only to deny it in 9:12b, 15a, 18. And this denial is meant to be a paradigm for his readers who want to exercise their legitimate ἐξουσία to eat food offered to idols. As we shall see, Paul's discourse is full of notions which can clearly be understood if read within the context of his attempt to discourage some of his readers from exercising their right to eat food offered to idols.

3.2.5 Paul's Renunciation of his ἐξουσία (1 Cointhians 9:4-18): The Paradigm

Paul's elaboration of his rights in 1 Corinthians 9:4-12a, 13-14 is very comprehensive and progresses into a climax in 9:14 only to be juxtaposed first in 9:12b and then more strongly in 9:15a. Scholars have tended to generalize on the value of Paul's arguments for his rights by saying that Paul starts from common sense in 9:4-8, and develops it with argument from the law of Moses (9:8-10), temple practice and, finally, alludes to the Lord's command (9:13-14).[101] Other scholars emphasize one over the other. For instance, without regarding the three authorities used by Paul in his argument (daily life, Old Testament and Jesus tradition - for they mutually

---

Kegan Paul, 1974), 164, shows that the Emperor "was interested in the welfare of citizens in the provinces." He notes that Cyzicus and Rhodes are two cities which lost their freedom. The latter because of violence committed against Romans or for putting them to death. He refers to Dio, liv. 7.6; lvii.24.6; Taac., Ann, iv. 36. 2-3; cf. Suet., Tiber., xxxviii. 3). See 164 n. 83.

101 D. Prior, *The Message of 1 Corinthians* (Downers Grove: IVP, 1985) 153, shows that Paul argues from "common practice, scriptural precept, intrinsic justice, Jewish custom and Christ's command."

support each other), W. Schrage gives different values to them. The everyday-life proof of Paul's right is least significant, the Old Testament evidence more significant and the Jesus tradition is the climax.[102] Frank Thielman makes a distinction between the human evidence in 9:4-8 and the divine evidence in 9:9-14.[103]

However, the emphasis on the flow of Paul's argument, from common sense to Christ's command, has caused scholars to overlook another more important aspect of the text in terms of Paul's attempt to make his discourse on the importance of setting aside one's right for the sake of others to be understood by the readers. There has been no appreciation given to, nor investigation carried out on the question of why Paul uses specifically the examples given in 1 Corinthians 9: 4-10 and 13-14. The issue of eating and drinking is very basic and understandable to any one of any age. But the issue of being accompanied by a woman on a missionary journey is more conceivable to those who are involved in travelling than to those who never travel. Then the issue of working as a soldier, a farmer and a shepherd, temple service workers as well as proclaimers of the gospel are fully accessible to people working in these workplaces. It is therefore necessary that we should not simply pass any of these examples of rights because of the presence of the apparent movement from ordinary to climax in Paul's discourse.

It is important to note that right from verse 4 through to verse 12b Paul speaks not only of his rights but also of his associate's, that of Barnabas. This is clear in his consistent use of the first person plural: μὴ οὐκ ἔχομεν ἐξουσίαν (vv.4-5), ἡμᾶς (v. 10), ἡμᾶς...ἐσπείραμεν...θερίσομεν v. 11), ἐχρησάμεθα... στέγομεν (v. 12b). In other words, what Paul says here is representative of the group of missionaries to which he belongs. The apostolic practice he commends here has already been carried out by his fellow missionaries, such as Barnabas, and his fellow workers.[104]

It is also significant to note in verse 4 that Paul speaks not only of the right to eat but also to drink, probably in order to prevent his readers from misunderstanding his point. He does not want them to think that the right he is talking about is that of eating food offered to idols, for this he has ruled out in 8:9-13, but to something more general. None the less, there is reason to argue that in speaking about his right Paul does so first of all in terms directly related to the Corinthians' right to eat food offered to idols. Paul seems to be saying: "If you have the right to eat εἰδωλοθύτων, so do we the right to eat and drink as apostles."

Moreover, by speaking about the right to eat and drink, Paul argues from

---

102 W. Schrage, *The Ethics of the New Testament* (Philadelphia: Fortress, 1982) 205-206.
103 Thielmann, "The Coherence," 240-241.
104 Dungan, *The Sayings of Jesus*, 8.

the most basic. In the light of what he will say in 9:11 it is possible to argue that what he is saying here is that as their apostle he has the right to eat and drink at their expense.[105] He is talking about the right to receive physical nourishment and sustenance.[106] As his arguments point out, this right is his due based on very strong grounds, namely the secular principle of work and pay, the support of the scripture, and the decree of the Lord.[107]

Paul then writes about another right which is directly related to the right to eat and drink: the right to be accompanied by a sister as wife, as the other apostles and the brothers of the Lord and Cephas (v. 5). While in verse 4 he directs the attention of his readers to his physical needs, here in verse 5 he talks of the need to be accompanied, not by a fellow worker, but by a wife who is termed as a sister (cf. 8:12). Since he is a missionary who is involved in travelling, it may be argued that by such a talk of being accompanied Paul is claiming about his right to marry - an idea which is supported by the fact known to his readers that he is not married (7:8; cf. 7:40) - and the right to be accompanied by her on his missionary journey.[108] If this is the case, the corollary is that the figures mentioned in this verse (the other apostles, the brothers of the Lord[109] and Cephas) are married and accompanied by their wives in their mission. This is particularly so because of the positive response expected by Paul from his readers to his rhetorical question.

The importance of these figures must have been known to the Corinthian Christians. Paul himself could have introduced their names when he preached on the account of the resurrection of Jesus (1 Cor. 15:1-8). Hence, Dungan goes too far in arguing that all these figures might have visited Corinth and that their practice of accepting financial support was to blame for the creation of Corinthian factions.[110] The special mention of Cephas is probably not caused by the existence of a party aligning to his name,[111] but because of the role that Cephas played in the early church (cf. Gal. 2:6).

---

105 F. Godet, *Commentary on St. Paul's First Epistle to the Corinthians* (Edinburgh: T and T Clark, 1898) 6; cf. Robertson and Plummer, *Critical Commentary*, 179, and Barrett, *The First Epistle*, 202.
106 C. Blomberg, *1 Corinthians* (Grand Rapids: Zondervan, 1994) 174.
107 Cf. Hooker, *Paul*, 127.
108 C.F. Kling, *The First Epistle*, 182. Cf. also Robertson and Plummer, *Critical Commentary*, 180, "Paul is claiming that they have a right to maintenance at the cost of the Church, and that, if they are married, the wife who travels with them shares this privilege."
109 See Mark 3:31-35 and Acts 1:14.
110 Dungan, *The Sayings of Jesus*, 7, 19, 21, cf. 37-38, 37 n. 2. In fact, Dungan goes so far as to argue that these apostles might have different view with Paul on the issue of food offered to idols, indicating the existence of many deep divergences in practice and belief in the leadership of the early Church (19, 21).
111 Pace Blomberg, *1 Corinthians*, 174; Hays, *1 Corinthians*, 150.

The Corinthian Christians' knowledge of his name may not have been gained from Cephas' visit to Corinth, but from Paul's mentioning of his name when he preached on the account of the appearance of Jesus to Cephas, the twelve and others (1 Cor. 15:1-8). This mention indicates Paul's acknowledgement of the role of Cephas in the early church.[112] Hence some Corinthian Christians did not hesitate to align with Peter, even though they might never have met him face to face in Corinth.[113] What is more important for us is that Paul's point in referring to the practice of these figures might have been aimed at reminding his readers of the general practice of the apostles, in order to lay a strong ground for him to claim that, as their apostle and like other apostles, he too had the right to be accompanied by a sister as wife.

Although still speaking in missionary context, in verse 6 Paul shows the intensification of his argument: "Or is it only Barnabas and I who do not have the right not to work for our living"? Here, the figure of Barnabas is being introduced to strengthen his own argument. The Corinthians might have at least heard from Paul or others about Barnabas and his work with him. Paul's mention of him does not necessarily mean that Barnabas had visited Corinth. Although Barnabas was not amongst those mentioned in verse 5, his important role in the early church is emphasized by Luke (Acts 4:36, 9:22ff; 13:14).[114] If we were to use Luke's account, we would know that Paul's mission to the Gentile world began with Barnabas (Acts 11:25, 13:2, but see Gal. 1:17,21, and 2:1). Given the probability that the conflict between them must have taken place (Gal. 2:13; Acts 15:37-40), Paul's mentioning of him as an important figure who, together with him, has the right not to work for a living cannot be without reason. This reason is obvious: his practice of refusing to accept financial support has been used

---

112 Thus N. Taylor, *Paul, Antioch and Jerusalem. A Study in Relationships and Authority in Earliest Christianity* (Sheffield: SAP, 1992) 176-81, here 179.

113 Barrett, *The First Epistle,* 204, unnecessarily uses the singling out of Cephas in verse 5 as an argument for him to say that Cephas "has himself visited Corinth, presumably bringing his wife with him...Perhaps it was those who 'belonged to Cephas' who had questioned Paul's apostleship." But Paul's singling out of Cephas cannot necessarily be taken to mean that Cephas had visited Corinth. If he had, Paul would have indicated it, as he did with Apollos by the use of the phrase "I planted, Apollos watered" (3:5). If we insist that Cephas had visited Corinth because some aligned to him and Paul singles out his name, we also have to be prepared to assume that "the other apostles and the brothers of the Lord" had also visited Corinth, something which is unlikely.

114 J. Read-Heimerdinger, "Barnabas in Acts: A Study of His Role in the Text of Codex Bezae" in *JSNT* 72 (1998) 23-66, esp. 21, 34, 40, 53, 56, 57-62, suggests that it was the apostles' lack of understanding that caused Barnabas' failure to be elected to replace Judas and his disappearance from the picture after Acts 15 despite his importance in the early church.

by some to examine his apostolic status. He wants to say that his refusal to accept financial support does not mean that his apostolic credibility should be questioned. Hence, by mentioning Barnabas, Paul emphasizes that together with this important figure he has the right to financial support, and that this right has been his possession since his early mission with him, that is to say since the time when he did not yet think of himself as an apostle equal to Peter and the twelve. There is no reason to exclude them from the right not to work for a living.

In verse 7 Paul moves from the missionary context to the people's workplace or profession in society: military, agriculture and husbandry. He says: "Who serves as a soldier at his own expense? Who plants a vineyard without eating any of its fruit? Who tends a flock without getting some of the milk?" The Corinthians, who must have had a good knowledge of these three occupations, must have answered: 'no one.'

These three professions are not directly related to specialized religious duties such as temple sacrifice and gospel preaching (9:13-14). It is part of Paul's creativity in making his readers not miss his point. He speaks right from their daily life. It indicates, as it were, the mind of a theologian at work. Why does Paul single out these three jobs in describing the legality of his rights?[115] Of course, it may be said that Paul sees them as representation of people's professions. Indeed, it may also be argued that the choice of the last two may be deliberate and arranged to suit the agricultural context of the scripture which he is about to cite (9:8-11). Similarly, the function of a soldier in war was very much known even in ancient times.

However, seen from the point of view of Paul's attempt to enable his readers to follow his point, we can gain some insights from his choice of these professions. We will argue that Paul's choice of 'soldier' going to war as an example was motivated by his knowledge of the importance of veterans and soldiers in the Roman empire not only during the expansion campaigns carried out by the Roman army, but more importantly in keeping peace within the whole empire in a period of stability. Some scholars have argued that some veterans might have been included in the composition of the first settlers of Corinth in 44 BC.[116] The soldiers of the Roman empire, especially those who could become senators, were Roman citizens to whom the issue of right was highly prized. In Paul's time, in the era of stability,

---

115 For occupations of lower classes, see M. Maxey, *Occupations of the Lower Classes* (Chicago: University of Chicago, 1938).

116 Brunt, *Italian Manpower,* 256; pace Lanci, *New Temple,* 27, who fails to mention the veterans as the first settlers; Williams II, "Roman Corinth as a Commercial Center" in Gregory, *The Corinthia in the Roman Period,* 31-46, esp. 32, argues that Roman Corinth was not refounded to settle ex-soldiers, but the freedmen-agents were sent to Corinth to serve the interest of the wealthy families of Rome who foresaw the colony as potentially strong centre.

the role of soldiers was indispensable. In the victorious Roman expansion and in the era of stability no one could dispense with the important role of soldiers, and no one would be ignorant of the cost of preserving a good army.[117] The military profession was entitled to support by the Roman empire. Meat, grain, fruit had to be provided for soldiers who went to war. In the Roman world, those who had military experience would get a better job in society.[118] In fact, land was distributed to veterans in return for their service. Under Claudius the number of Roman citizens entering imperial service and holding important posts increased, and they did it through the service of auxiliary forces. This was in line with the policy of granting a gift of citizenship to individuals in return for service. The mark of the period was the promotion of status as a reward in service and loyalty.[119] So far as Paul's purpose in highlighting the importance of the logical and legal right to support is concerned, his choice of soldier as a profession fully supported by the empire must therefore have been deliberate. Every Roman citizen of the Roman colony of Corinth would have known the cost of maintaining the Roman army and its auxiliary soldiers on the border.

Paul does not choose traders, however important their role must have been in the famous trade city of Corinth, because their enterprise and economic success depended on their own initiative. The city of Corinth or the empire was not responsible for their welfare. Rather, it was these traders, who depended on the safety of the sea from the pirates and the road from bandits[120] that were grateful to the military and had to pay taxes for it.

Nor does he choose the city magistrates, the most highly respected office in the city, for it was the people of this profession that had to pay in order to be elected to their offices. In fact, prior to election they had to promise to give some enormous amount to the populace if elected. Entering public office was a costly business, causing some people of noble background who were landowners and, as such, lacked cash, to borrow large amounts of cash

---

117 See W. Ramsay and R. Lanciani, *A Manual of Roman Antiquities* (London: Charles Griffin, 1894) 428-30.
118 Thomas Wiedemann, *Adults and Children in the Roman Empire* (London: Routledge, 1989) 159, argues that even though the individual interests in military career decreased by the first century AD, "military service normally continued to be a condition for entry to a political career under the empire as it had been in the time of the republic. The career structure for officers appears to have become more standardised under the early empire." Saller, "Promotion and Patronage," 59, concludes that in the Principate period "men with military experience were preferred for procuratorships with military duties..."
119 See Sherwin-White, *Roman Citizenship*, 244-45.
120 J.P. Campbell, *The Roman Emperor and the Roman Army 31BC-AD 235* (Oxford: Clarendon Press, 1984) 5, points out that in addition to security and defence, protecting local trade routes and shipping is the soldiers' task.

from moneylenders.[121] Moreover, they had to provide their town with "splendid buildings, endowments, gladiatorial shows, beast-baitings and other forms of entertainment."[122] In the event of food shortage, they were even expected to supply the needs of the populace in the city.[123] In this connection, it must be borne in mind that much of the public works of Roman cities depended on the personal expenditure of the wealthy who in return expected to receive honorific titles from the city and, for some, be appointed to the Roman *ordo equester* or rank of senator.[124] The competition of honor was indeed encouraged in order to keep the system going.[125]

Rather than choosing traders and city-magistrates, Paul opts for the most important example which will help describe his point, a soldier which does not exist without the full support of the empire. Thus Paul's question is very striking: Who serves as a soldier at his own expense?[126] Paul's choice of the soldier is no accident. In describing the contributions of the army to the economic well-being of the empire, James L. Jones acknowledges that "the maintenance of the army was a drain upon the economy of the Empire."[127] Soldiers had the right to have the support of the empire. To keep the army away from rebellion and to hold on to power, every emperor had to make sure that the needs of the army were met.[128]

In addition, writing to his readers in whose society the agricultural work

---

121 See M. Gelzer, *The Roman Nobility* (Oxford: Basil Blackwell, 1969) 110-112, 114-15; Finley, *Ancient Economy,* 53-56.
122 Salmon, *Roman Colonization,* 155.
123 Finley, *Ancient Economy,* 40, states that until the third century AD even resident citizens were entitled to be the beneficiaries of food supply provided by the authorities, including the emperors. It was a political necessity they would not dispense with.
124 See Gager, "Religion and Social Class in the Early Roman Empire," 104-05.
125 Judge, *Social Pattern,* 19.
126 According to Gelzer, *Roman Nobility,* 7, an ordinary Roman soldier received one third denarius a day, a centurion two third and an *eques* 1 denarius. The Roman infantryman received two third of an Attic bushel of wheat a month, in contrast to 2 bushels of wheat and 7 of barley for an *eques*.
127 James L. Jones, "The Roman Army" in S. Benko and J.J. R'Ourke, *Early Church History,* 187-217, esp. 211; Campbell, *The Roman Emperor and the Roman Army,* 164, conjectures that in first century AD the cost of maintaining the army was 40% of the available revenue of the state.
128 Campbell, *The Roman Emperor and the Roman Army,* 6-8, 128, 158-57, 163, shows that the emperor uses various means of maintaining the loyalty of the soldiers. These are: an oath of loyalty sanctified by religious rites, providing benefits such as prompt payment of regular wages, booty or donations, discharge bonus taken from the Bonus Fund which was founded by Augustus with 170 million sesterces' donation from his own fund. Failure to satisfy the needs of the army could cost political catasthrope.

force consisted most of slaves and their masters were obliged to provide their necessities of life (food, clothing and shelter),[129] Paul's choice of a farmer who plants a vineyard and eats from its fruit, and of one who tends a flock and gets some of the milk (9:7b-c) is not an unthoughtful choice either. Readers who are unaware of the urban nature of Corinth would read Paul's statement in an ancient agriculture context.[130] Such a reading is justified since in 1 Corinthians 3:6-9 Paul has described his evangelistic work in agricultural terms and continues to do so in 9:8-11. Indeed, the law of Moses cited speaks of a practice the setting of which was agricultural. Nevertheless, a more comprehensive notion will be perceived by those who read Paul's choice against the background of the economy of Roman cities. Paul's choice of the agricultural professions when speaking about the legal right of workers may have been conditioned by his knowledge of the importance of agriculture in the eyes of his Romanized readers. For its economic success, Corinth could not have overlooked the importance of its limited cultivated soil and agricultural products.[131]

D. Engels has recently argued that Corinth was not a 'consuming city,' which survived on the rental of the apartments of the élite and the rents of their estates, but it was a 'serving city' which survived on the basis of its extensive marketing activity in the city. Engels estimates that the population of the city was between 72,500 and 116,000. Therefore, the product of its limited fertile agricultural land would not have been sufficient to feed the mouths of its populace. It depended on the surplus of goods which were brought into the city by travellers, traders and tourists.[132] Engels' emphasis on the serving nature of the city of Corinth awaits

---

129 Keith Bradley, *Slavery and Society at Rome* (Cambridge: CUP, 1994) 81, 92, 100-01. Bradley notes, however, that even though these provisions put slaves in a better position than that of free poor, it was at the expense of their independence, particularly felt when the masters looked to their own interests, in which case there was no guarantee of the availability of rations, especially when there was a shortage of food.

130 Thus H.A.E. Meyer, *Critical and Exegetical Handbook to the Epistle to the Corinthians* (Edinburgh: T and T Clark, 1892) 257.

131 Meggitt, *Paul*, 42-43, notes that agriculture was central to the life of the Roman Empire, even though he makes a distinction between our modern practice of agriculture, namely that organized along 'rational' lines, with the non-commercial criteria of the Roman empire. Meggitt points out that nearly "90% of its population lived on, or directly from, the land." Various factors such as aesthetic, general meaning of profit/gain, pleasure, prestige, income stability were important.

132 Engels, *Roman Corinth*, 1-2. But see Meggitt, *Paul*, 41 n. 1, who argues that "the inter-regional trade within the empire was limited and largely concerned with the import and export of luxury items" which accompanied Roman political and military expansion and was often shortlived."

validation, however.[133] In his review of Engels' work, A.J. Spawforth has shown various weaknesses of his thesis.[134] This is followed up by J.J. Meggitt who still defends the old view promoted by M.I. Finley[135] who argued that the cities in the Roman Empire of our period "were essentially centers of consumption and not production. They did not generate significant wealth but were dependent upon the incomes accrued from the land holdings of the élite and from taxation."[136]

---

133 D.P. Thompkins, "Review of D. Engels' Roman Corinth: An Alternative Model for the Classical City' in *PMCR* 1 (1990) 20-33, in reviewing Engels' book suggests that Roman Corinth might more appropriately be considered a 'merchant city.' C.K. Williams II, "Roman Corinth as a Commercial Center," 31-46; Winter, "Civil Litigation," 102-03.

134 A.J. Spawforth, "Roman Corinth and the Ancient Urban Economy. Review of Donald Engels: *Roman Corinth: an Alternative Model for the Classical City* (Chicago and London: University of Chicago Press, 1990)" in *CR* 42 (1992) 119-22.

135 Finley, *The Ancient Economy*, 56, points out that the basic wealth of the upper strata was land. Finley's thesis is inspired by Weber's *The Agrarian Sociology of Ancient Civilizations*. E.T. by R.I. Frank (London and New York, 1988) 48. A. Wallace-Hadrill, "Élites and trade in the Roman town" in John Rich and A. Wallace-Hadrill (eds.), *City and Country in the Ancient World* (London and New York: Routledge, 1991) 141-72, esp. 244-50, 257, 261, 265-67, who argues that the property owners had their income not just from their agricultural estates and apartments, but also from trade without engaging in 'sordid occupations' (257). He writes: "although freedmen were clearly prominent in the trade of the area [Pompeii and Herculaneum], and may indeed have emerged as important property owners, both through their own efforts, and as beneficiaries of their masters' wills, it is likely that the ruling élites represented by the members of the local councils were also major owners and exploiters of urban property." (267). He develops this further in his study, *Houses and Society in Pompeii and Herculaneum* (Princeton: NJ, 1994) which directly challenges the scholars' belief in Cicero's account that the élite rejected of the urban center in his *De officiis*, 1. 150-1. The model of the houses in Pompeii and Herculenaum indicates the close link between the élite and the very people directly involved in trade itself (i.e., slaves, freedmen, and clients). See also Bradley, *Slavery and Society at Rome*, 79, who argues that the élite were involved in trade, banking, money lending and other business activities "obliquely rather than openly" through their intermediaries and agents. Helen Parkins, "The 'Consumer city' domesticated? The Roman City in élite economic strategies" in Helen M. Parkins (ed), *Roman Urbanization Beyond the Consumer City* (London, New York: Routledge, 1997) 83-111, here 108, refines Weber's thesis further by arguing that "the city helped to supply more immediate cash needs as well as to meet the unpredictable demands" which were necessary for anyone "playing the status and politics game." In fact, Parkins (87) goes so far ar to argue that the élite "drew electoral support" from traders with whom they were bound.

136 Meggitt, *Paul*, 45 n. 19. Cf. Also R.P. Saller, "Review of Donald Engels, *Roman Corinth: An Alternative Model for the Classical City*" in *CP* 86 (1991) 351-357.

At any rate, it may be said that, although Corinth had the advantage of having a high inflow of traders, the role of the countryside farmers in providing the daily needs of the city dwellers cannot be dismissed altogether. It was on the farmers, almost all of whom were slaves that much of the physical needs of the city depended. They provided what was needed by the mouths of the whole populace of the city. Their masters could not live without them. Besides, given that sea-travel would have taken a considerable length of time before reaching one port or the other, it is more likely that the traders did not provide the daily needs of the city. They provided the more luxurious ones.

Seen in this light, Paul's choice of the two professions could have been deliberately intended to address the readers who knew of and recognized the right of farmers and flock tenderers without whose products their very livelihood and trading activity in the city would not have succeeded as well as they wished. We do not know for certain whether or not some members of the Corinthian Christian household congregations included slaves working in agriculture. 1 Corinthians 1:26 may give us a positive answer. However, we cannot go beyond this in describing their professions. In any case, by speaking of their right to eat the first fruits of their agricultural product and drink the milk of the flock they tend,[137] Paul builds up his argument for his legal right as their apostle to live from his work as a gospel preacher in a language that was well understood by his readers.

Having written about his right to eat and drink and to be accompanied by a sister as wife, and to work for a living and about the right of those involved in three professions known to his readers, Paul then directs his readers to an even stronger argument which was derived from a shared authoritative source and could therefore carry a more authoritative legitimation of his rights, the law of Moses: "Do I say this on human authority? Does not the law say the same?" (9:8).[138] He then elaborates the Mosaic law by referring to the law of Moses in Deuteronomy 25:4, the command not to muzzle an ox when it is treading out the grain (9:9a), and in 9:9b-10 he gives his interpretation of it without the slightest indication of its being interpreted differently or possibly distorted by his readers.

The fact that Paul refers to the law of Moses in a convincing way does

---

137 It is often noted that the wages of the shepherd is a portion of the milk. See Kling, *The Epistle to the Corinthians*, 183.
138 Given that the cotext speaks of the law of Moses, there is no reason to suggest, as Hollander does (see Harm W. Hollander, "The Meaning of the term "Law" (NOMOΣ) in 1 Corinthians" in *NovT* XL [1998] 117-35, esp. 121-22), that the law in 9:8 refers to general laws known in the Roman world of the time, but that of 9:9 is Mosaic law which is a segment or a specimen of the general laws. This is in line with his view that the law of Moses is not the primary or the only reference to the νόμος in 1 Corinthians.

indicate the likelihood that Paul's readers must have been familiar not only with the Law of Moses, but also with Paul's use of scriptural texts in his teaching. Still in rhetorical manner he asks: "Is it for oxen that God is concerned? Does he not speak entirely for our sake? It was written for our sake, because the ploughman should plough in hope and the thresher thresh in hope of a share in the crop" (9:10). Clearly, Paul employs an authoritative scriptural argument to legitimate his and his colleague's rights.

However problematic Paul's interpretation of Deut 25:4 might appear to us,[139] there was no difficulty for the Corinthians in perceiving Paul's point. This is shown by Walter C. Kaiser[140] and D. Instone Brewer. The latter sees Paul as using a rabbinic interpretation, and argues that Paul is here "mustering all his legal expertise to derive a new ruling, using arguments that a contemporary rabbi would have been proud of." With his quotation "as it is written in the Law of Moses," Paul "was using legal terminology, quoting legal rulings, and employing legal exegetical techniques" to demonstrate that under the Law of Moses he has a legitimate right to live from his apostolic work.[141] Paul's interpretation of Deut 25:4, which

---

139 See Walter C. Kaiser, "The Current Crisis in Exegesis and the Apostolic Use of Deuteronomy 25:4 in 1 Corinthians 9:8-10" in *JETS* 21/1 (1978) 3-18, who discusses this puzzling manner of Paul's interpretation of Deut 25:4. Kaiser highlights the various viewpoints that have been proposed so far. Some accuse Paul of erroneously using the Old Testament, of interpreting allegorically or mystically. Others see Paul as using a rabbinic principle of argument or a Hellenistic Jewish Exegesis.

140 Kaiser, "The Current Crisis," 17-18, concludes: "If the principle that all workers have a right to be paid for their services (be they animal or human) is what is written, and that is what Moses meant, then that is what God meant. The issue was settled..." He follows Godet's Commentary on *The First Epistle of St. Paul to the Corinthians*, 2, 11-16, who, using literal theological exegesis, shows that Moses' concern "was not for the oxen alone but to develop gentleness and gratitude in their owners." Cf. Fee *The first Epistle*, 407-408, is right when he says that the text was chosen "because in its original setting it meant precisely what Paul is arguing for here, that the 'worker' should reap material benefit from his labor."

141 D. Istone Brewer, "1 Cor 9.9-11: 'Do not muzzle the ox'" in *NTS* 38 (1992) 554-65, here 564. Istone Brewer has shown that there is no need for us to be concerned about why Paul appears to have played down the ox as if he was not speaking the original intention of Deut 25:4, because 'ox' was equivalent with all labourers, be it animal or human. Brewer concludes: "the understanding that 'ox' in Scripture implied all labouring species was already well established by the time of Paul." (See also 263-364). Witherington III's criticism of Brewer's view on the basis of the possibility that other Corinthians might have understood it allegorically (see *Conflict*, 208 n. 16) is not justified because we cannot judge from that point. What we can assume is the likelihood that the Corinthians might have been familiar with Paul's biblical use in his teaching while he was in their midst, and in this sense Paul's method must have been influenced by his upbringing.

emphasizes God's concern for 'us' rather than for 'the ox' - though it seems odd to us – "would have been regarded as a literal interpretation of the plain meaning of the text."[142] What Paul is doing is to derive from the Law the right of a missionary to wages, and this is based on "a literal interpretation of Deut 25:4 and on the contemporary understanding of the term 'ox' in the Law as a reference to all types of labourer, human and animal."[143] Perhaps, Paul may have this message to send: "just as an ox that is treading the ground has the right not to be muzzled by humans, for it logically would harm the ox, so are the ploughman and thresher not to be deprived of their hope in the share of the crop, for it would oppose God's command."[144]

Paul brings the long and detailed argument in verses 4-10 into sharp focus in verses 11-12 by speaking directly about his and his colleagues' work among the Corinthians in an agricultural language: "If we have sown spiritual things among you, is it too much if we will reap[145] material things from you? If others share this right from you,[146] do not we the more?" Paul

---

142 Brewer, "1 Cor 9.9-11," 545.
143 Brewer, "1 Cor 9.9-11," 559-560.
144 Cf. Kaiser, "The Current Crisis," 15: "Paul wants to give the reason why he said that law was written for our sakes. The meaning of the command is a principle for all men: The workman, be he man or animal, is to be rewarded for his labor. And to whom is the command directed? Only to men [Sic]."
145 Paul's use future θερίσομεν has been overlooked in most translations, neglecting the flow of argument of Paul in the whole 1 Corinthians 9. If we translate it with present 'reap' or 'harvest' we do not fully grasp Paul's intention. Paul and his colleagues have up to the time of the writing of 1 Corinthians never shared any support from the Corinthians. His phrase 'is it too much if we will reap' indicates that Paul is referring to the future. Later in verse 15a he states that he is writing not to secure any such provision. This future tense is spotted by Harry P. Nasuti, "The Woes of the Prophets and the Rights of the Apostle: The Internal Dynamics of 1 Corinthians 9" in *CBQ* 50 (1988) 246-264, here 248. But he does not seem to emphasize its significance in the argument of Paul. This dynamic is crucial if we see 9:4-18 as Paul's attempt to convince the readers not to use their ἐξουσία in eating idol-meat. This helps us to see why Paul uses an example in 8:10 in present tense and with the conditional 'if', both of which clearly reflect Paul's elegant approach to the issue concerned. It may be suggested that Paul's use of 'if' in 8:10 may indicate that the Corinthian Christians had not yet been involved in the act of eating in the temple. Nevertheless, given his strong exhortation in 10:1-22, especially in 10:14 where he asks them to flee from idolatry, it is more likely that they were involved in the eating of idol meat in the temple and that they were trying to encourage their fellow Christians to do the same with their theological knowledge of idols' non-existence. Hence Paul's ironic use of οἰκοδομηθήσεται in 8:10.
146 This translation of Εἰ ἄλλοι τῆς ὑμῶν ἐξουσίας μετέξουσιν is better in expressing the sense that Paul is speaking of in chapter 9. He has been and will speak about 'right' So far as Paul's theme in 1 Corinthians 9 is concerned there is

is here speaking in a down to earth manner about his work and his right to get material things, just like he does in 3:6. In fact he is comparing his right with that enjoyed by others. The closeness of verse 11 with verse 12a undoubtedly indicates that, apart from Paul and his team (2 Cor. 12:17-18), there were others who had sown spiritual things to the Corinthians and, in exchange for their work, received material benefits. The question of what kind of spiritual work they did and, if it was preaching the gospel - what sort of gospel they preached - are beyond our ability to investigate. Nor is Paul concerned about that detail here. Moreover, it is crucial to note that he mentions the 'others' in 9:12a not so as to refute them or their practice, rather, he refers to their practice of reaping material benefit to support his own right to material support.

These missionaries would have no objection to what Paul says in verse 12a. None the less, on close reading, there is in this verse an indication that Paul thinks of himself and his associates as having greater value than the 'others.' This is clearly indicated by the phrase οὐ μᾶλλον ἡμεῖς ('Do we not the more'?). Upon reading this statement, the 'others' would have raised their eyebrows. Paul's attitude is justified, however, by the fact that he is their apostle (9:1, cf. 1:1), the first who planted the seed (3:6), who laid the foundation (3:10), and their father (4:15). He can speak to them like a father to his children (4:21). In fact, he can pass judgment from a distance on the immoral man amongst them (5:3-5)[147] and, because he has the Spirit of God in him, his advice on whether a widow should remain as she is or remarry should be trusted (7:39-40). Indeed, his position as a father to them makes him confident enough to call on them to imitate him in not going beyond what is written (4:6,16) and in how to deal with their right to eat food offered to idols (11:1).

The point Paul makes is that he and his team have the right to material things from their beneficiaries. Yet he also makes clear that he has not received it from them. Hence the future tense θερίσομεν (9:11) and verse 12b: "Nevertheless, *we have not made use of this right*, but we endure

---

no strong ground in translating ἐξουσία as authority. Neither is it necessary to see Paul as being ironical in this verse that we render Εἰ ἄλλοι τῆς ὑμῶν ἐξουσίας with "if others share in ἐξουσία over you," as suggested by Malherbe, "Determinism and Free Will," 241 n.17, when he says "Paul would ironically be saying that while the Corinthians insisted on their own ἐξουσία, they placed themselves in a position where others (including Paul!) had ἐξουσία over them!"

147 For a discussion on the reason for and background to Paul's stern language in 1 Corinthians 5:5, see V. George Shilington, "Atonement Texture in 1 Corinthians 5.5" in *JSNT* 71 (1998) 29-50. He suggests that the atonement ritual text of Leviticus 16 is used by Paul because of the immoral condition of the supposedly holy Christian community.

anything rather than put an obstacle in the way of the gospel of Christ."[148] Indeed, in view of 4:12a it is clear that Paul is still working with his own hands in Ephesus not only for his necessities but also for his companions (cf. Acts 20:34). Paul and his colleagues have not made use of their rights to reap material things and will not do so because reaping material things will put an obstacle in the way of the gospel of Christ. Consequently, Paul and his team endure anything.

In verse 12b Paul introduces two ideas related to the foregoing of their rights. First, the idea of endurance: "we endure everything παντα στέγομεν and, secondly, the importance of not creating an ἐγκοπήν to the gospel of Christ, ἵνα μή τινα ἐγκοπὴν δῶμεν τῳ εὐαγγελίῳ τοῦ Χριστοῦ. Both ideas are related. The former is the consequence of the latter. Waiving rights cannot be achieved without enduring everything. The former idea is not difficult to understand. It is the consequence of not making full use of the right to financial support. It is, as it were, the cost that has to be paid. The scope of the endurance is not small, however. It covers παντα, anything or everything, not just physical labour and hunger.[149] 1 Corinthians 4:10-13 and 15:10 (cf. 2 Cor. 11:23-29) confirm this. It was not his own sufficient financial resources that caused Paul to refuse to exercise his right to financial support from his congregations. He did not pretend. He endured the cost of his own policy. He did it for a reason described fully in 1 Corinthians 9:18. Little surprise then that later in 1 Corinthians 15:10 he says that he labors harder than the rest of the witnesses of the resurrection of Jesus.

In the first place Paul had already given up his comfortable life-style[150] which he enjoyed before being called by Jesus Christ to work as an apostle to the Gentiles. Now in doing his work as a missionary to Gentiles he refuses to exercise his right to have financial support. From 1 Corinthians 9:12b it is self-evident that Paul does not have any money of his own apart from what he earns with his hands (1 Cor. 9:12b cf. 4:12). We do not know whether he received any support from his parents. Nor do we have any evidence whereby we learn anything about Paul's relationship with his parents after his conversion. We do know from Luke's account that Paul has a sister in Jerusalem whose son heard of the Jews' plot to kill Paul and entered the soldiers' barracks to inform the centurion about it (Acts 23:16-7). But we do not know about the identity of this sister, much less about her

---

148 Nasuti, "The Woes," 251, regards verse 12b as much a dividing point as an anticipation.
149 As suggested by Gardner, *The Gifts of God*, 79.
150 Hooker, *Paul: A Short Introduction*, 19, is right in arguing that Paul's insistence on working hard with his hands to support himself means that he could have avoided it, he was not from 'working class.' Hooker is also right in referring to Philippians 4: 11-12 as ground to say that Paul's was not alien to living with plenty.

financial support of Paul's work. The amount of money he earned did not enable him to dispense with his need for endurance.

Moreover, the fact that he determines to refuse to accept financial support from his Corinthian converts (9:12a-b) may indicate that his Corinthian readers might have been trying hard to give him financial support as they would later to other missionaries (9:12a) after he left Corinth. This could explain the economic ability of his readers. It would be unlikely that a poor community would have insisted on helping Paul financially. If they were poor, they would be grateful that Paul did not seek their assistance. However, we must not push this too far, because the Macedonian Christians begged to be allowed to take part in the relief of the saints in Jerusalem, even though they were not economically well-off. They gave beyond their means (2 Cor. 8:1-5). The saints in Jerusalem expected financial assistance from Christians in other places, and not the other way around, undoubtedly because they did not have sufficient funds to survive. If anything, the economic condition of Corinthian Christians could not be lower than that of the saints in Jerusalem. The fact that the Corinthian Christians failed to collect the contribution does not necessarily indicate that they were poor economically. It could be caused partly by their suspicion of Paul's handling of the money, as has been suggested by most scholars,[151] but partly also by the lack of harmonious perception among themselves about Jewish Christians in Jerusalem and about the practicalities of the distribution of the collection (16:1-4). They might not have been of one mind regarding this project of Paul which purported to bring about the unity between the Jewish and Gentile segments of the early church.[152]

We now come to the task of explaining a more difficult phrase of Paul, ἵνα μή τινα ἐγκοπὴν δῶμεν τῷ εὐαγγελίῳ τοῦ Χριστοῦ, for it has a bearing on our understanding of the reason why he refuses to exercise his right to financial support. In this regard, scholars have been preoccupied

---

151 See Verlyn D. Verbrugge, *Paul's Style of Church Leadership Illustrated by His Instructions to the Corinthians on the Collection* (San Francisco: Mellen Research University Press, 1992) 61-66, who argues that because of the nature of the commanding letter of 1 Corinthians 16:1-2 Paul is not responding to the Corinthian question but to his knowledge of the sign of the Corinthians' reluctance to participate in the relief project they had promised earlier (2 Cor. 8-9). Cf. Jewett's paper presented at the Conference of Midwest Region of SBL, Feb. 2, 1988 as noted by Verbrugge, *Paul's Style,* 61 n. 85, in which Jewett argues that the infighting in the house-churches might have caused the Corinthians to lose interest in continuing the collection of the contribution, the reluctance to keep on with the collection. Wire, *The Corinthian Women Prophets,* 177, argues that perhaps the women known for single devotion to the community and leadership in it may have been the ones who handled food donations, including food or money for the hungry, and the collectors of the money.

152 Verbrugge, *Paul's Style,* 3, 368

with the question of the perception of the Corinthian Christians about the means of sustenance of their contemporary philosophers and Christian missionaries other than Paul and his colleagues and what impact it might have on their perception of Paul. With the exception of P.D. Gardner,[153] less attention has been given to what Paul himself says in our passage as the reason for his own statement that accepting financial support would constitute an ἐγκοπή to the way of the gospel.

Judging from Paul's discourse in 1 Corinthians 9:15-18, I propose that both Corinthian Christians and other missionaries are not to blame for Paul's practice of renouncing his rights. Rather, it is Paul's own attitude towards his own gospel proclamation that causes him to see it in his own way. Paul deliberately emphasizes this precisely because it is directly relevant to his intention to draw the attention of those who insisted on using their right to eat food offered to idols to a purpose greater than indulging in their right, namely the concern for the weak brother. In the light of 1 Corinthians, what Paul means by the gospel of Christ is that of Christ crucified (1 Cor. 1:23). This must certainly influence the policy of Paul's gospel proclamation.[154] As we have shown above (3.1.2) Paul must have adopted this policy of refusing to exercise his right long before he came to Corinth. Hence his practice in Thessalonica. In fact he was still exercising it in his new base, Ephesus (1 Cor. 4:12).

Paul's typical attitude towards his gospel proclamation and its relation to his means of support was different from that held by other missionaries who reaped material benefit from the Corinthian Christians (9:12a). The latter would not have thought that accepting material support would constitute an ἐγκοπή to the proclamation of the gospel. On the contrary, they must surely have thought of the idea of refusing to accept the material support for their missionary enterprise as constituting an ἐγκοπή to the gospel proclamation itself. It makes sense in practice: how else could they support themselves without the support of those who benefited from their activity? In fact, Paul himself does not see their accepting the support as constituting an ἐγκοπή to their gospel proclamation. There is no indication in his discourse that he has a negative feeling about their gospel proclamation. If he did, he would not have spoken positively of the right to support described in 9:4-14. Yet, Paul states that his proclamation of the gospel is different in character from theirs. It is not that which accepts payment, but it is that which is free of charge (9:18). Nevertheless, it would be surprising if his statements in 1 Corinthians 9:12b, 15-18 would not have generated opposition from those whose gospel proclamation is that in which the right to financial support is fully exercised. Even if there was no quarrel or competition between Paul

---

153 Gardner, *The Gifts of God*, 79-85.
154 See Pickett, *The Cross in Corinth*, for the importance of the cross in Paul's treatment of the issues discussed in 1 Corinthians.

and the other missionaries when he wrote 1 Corinthians 9:12b, Paul's statement that his refusal to exercise his right to financial support would certainly be seen by the other missionaries as saying that by benefiting materially from the gospel they were creating an ἐγκοπή to the gospel, even though Paul did not intend it that way. He did it to encourage some Corinthian Christians to be willing to renounce their right to eat food offered to idols in order that they might not become πρόσκομμα to the weak (8:9).

Why would exercising his right to financial support constitute an ἐγκοπή to the way of the gospel? Before we answer this question, it is important for us to look at Paul's further evidence for his right to financial support. We find this in 9:13-14 after which he repeats what he has said in 9:12b and states that he is not writing to secure his rights (9:15a). Only after this repetition and statement does Paul proceed with his reasons for renouncing his right in 9:15b-18 and in 9:19-23 (note the frequent use of γαρ in verses 15b-17 and 19).

In 9:13-14 Paul makes two important points regarding the foundation of his rights. First, he refers to the temple practice and, secondly, to Jesus' command on the proclamation of the gospel. In verse 9:13 he uses the formula of οὐκ οἴδατε ὅτι, 'Do not you know that' (cf. 5:6, 6:3,9,15,16,18) to strike a point. Paul tries here to associate his discourse with the centre of the issue around which the question of right is discussed by his readers, the issue of eating food offered to idols in a temple and the sacrificial activity at the altar (cf. 8:10; 10:18). It is striking to note that even as he discusses his own way of dealing with his right, Paul tries to make his point as wide and intelligible as possible without ever drawing his readers away from the issue which generates his response in the first place. Here he uses οἱ τὰ ἱερὰ ἐργαζόμενοι [τὰ] ἐκ τοῦ ἱεροῦ ἐσθίουσιν (those who work at the temple eat from the temple). Then he develops it more specifically by writing about those responsible for the important part of the temple activity itself, namely those who serve at the altar. He says: 'those who serve at the altar' (οἱ τῷ θυσιαστηρίῳ παρεδρεύοντες) 'share in the sacrificial offerings' (τῷ θυσιαστηρίῳ συμμερίζονται).

Given that the Corinthian household-churches consisted of both Jews and Gentiles to whom temples played an important, if not central, role in their respective previous religious communities,[155] and given that the priests of Roman religions received a certain amount of salary for their temple service, Paul's reference to those responsible for carrying out the very central activity in the temple, namely the sacrificial act to the deity on behalf of the worshippers, could not have been accidental. Both Jewish and

---

155 Cf. Lanci, *New Temple,* 89, suggests that Paul's description of the church as a temple in 1 Corinthian has to do with the role of some temples in Greco-Roman society to define the community.

Gentile Christians could not have failed to see the reality of Paul's reference. The Jews did not have any temple in Corinth. But they did have their own synagogue where they could worship[156] (Cf. Acts 18:4 and the excavation discovery of the synagogue in Corinth).[157] To the Jewish Christians and former God-fearers, the temple in Jerusalem - that which is the 'central national symbol and institution' of Judaism[158] - reminds them of the importance of the role of the priests performing sacrificial acts. Moreover, it also reminds them of their responsibility to bring burnt offerings to the temple in Jerusalem. Part of these offerings could be eaten by the priests (cf. Num. 18. 8-31). They also had to pay the half-shekel temple tax levied upon all males over the age of twenty, and to carry out pilgrimage.

Similarly, the Gentile Christians who formerly worshipped dumb idols (cf. 1 Cor. 12:2) could well remember the importance of their former temple priests in their previous sacrificial offerings. Their former priests would also have a portion of the meat they sacrificed.[159] Even if they no longer associated themselves with the temples which were very real in the old Graeco-Corinth but now lying in ruins underneath their present city, and even if Paul might not have in mind the priests of the pagan temples,[160] the Gentile Corinthian Christians would have encountered no difficulty in perceiving Paul's mention of priests eating from the sacrificial acts. Indeed, they must have known that Roman traditional religions employed priests in their religious activities. Even the imperial cults paid some priests to conduct their activities, even though they came from the senatorial class.

It is therefore not necessary for us to ponder upon the question of which temple Paul or his readers might have in mind.[161] It is sufficient to say that

---

156 Tomson, *Paul,* 46, shows that the Jewish communities in diaspora "were organized around the 'synagogue,' a building which not only served for prayers and festivities but also for study, administration, law courts, meetings, welfare work and other communal affairs."
157 See Harvey, "Good Jews," 132-147.
158 M. Stone, *Scriptures, Sects and Visions* (Philadelphia: Fortress Press, 1980) 77.
159 Blomberg, *1 Corinthians,* 175. In fact, as is shown by Stowers, "Greeks who Sacrifice," 298, 326-27, the eating of the noble viscera (liver, lungs, hear, kidneys) by the élite inner circle of men near the altar was the central and focus of the sacrifice.
160 R.C.H. Lenski, *The Interpretation of St Paul's First and Second Epistles to the Corinthians* (Minneapolis: Augsburg Publishing House, 1963) 367, rejects that pagan temples are in the mind of Paul.
161 Peter Richardson, "Temples, Altars and Living From the Gospel" in L. Ann Jervis and Peter Richardson (eds.), *Gospel in Paul,* 89-110, esp. 98-104, argues that Paul has in mind the Jerusalem temple, that is to say the support enjoyed by the priests. This support included tax, burnt offerings and other offerings.

temple activity was known to the ancients.[162] What is necessary for us to acknowledge is the likelihood that Paul's use of the practice of people who serve in the temple and share in the sacrificial offerings might have been his attempt to speak about his right in a language that was understandable to his readers who in fact asked him in their letter about their involvement in the act of eating food offered to idols in idols' temples (8:1). The people who worked in the temple where food was offered as sacrifice had the right to eat from the sacrifice. Therefore, Harry P. Nasuti's attempt to see a spiritual meaning in verse 13 in contrast to the secular meaning in verses 7-10,[163] though possible, may be reading too much into what Paul intends, namely describing his right in the most tangible way. Moreover, the σαρκικά of 9:11 indicates that he is speaking in an economic sense, rather than in a spiritual sense. 1 Corinthians 9:11 governs our reading of 9:13-14.

Christian evangelistic activity was a new phenomenon in Corinth, and therefore it may be said that it was in the process of creating its own authoritative tradition and legacy among Corinthian Christians. Accordingly, it is not surprising that a tradition of the word of the Lord had been preserved to authorize this new profession. In this light, we can see the importance of the use of οὕτως in 9:14. Hence, verse 13 is not just a repetition, nor a mere example, or superfluous as suggested by Käsemann,[164] but an intensification of Paul's previous arguments and a preparation for the point he is about to make in verse 15a.

In verse 14, using the Jesus tradition,[165] Paul comes to the strongest foundation of his right in Christian community. He writes: "In the same way, the Lord commanded that those who proclaim the gospel should get their living by the gospel." This verse has been studied very extensively in relation to the quest for Paul's knowledge and use of the Jesus' tradition, and in particular, to the question of which sayings recorded by the synoptic gospels might have been alluded to here. Dungan and Tomson favour the version of Mathews 10:10,[166] but B. Fjärstedt that of Luke 10:7 especially because of Paul's elaboration of μισθός.[167] A middle view is argued by D.C. Allison who emphasizes the ambiguity of evidence which "shows

---

[162] See Lanci, *New Temple*, 90, who describes various functions of temples of the Greco-Roman world.
[163] Nasuti, "The Woes," 251 .
[164] Käsemann, "A Pauline Version of the 'Amor Fati'" in his *New Testament Questions for Today* (Philadelphia: Fortress, 1969) 218.
[165] According to F. Neirynck, "Paul and the Sayings of Jesus" in A. Vanhoye, *L'Apotre*, 320, 1 Cor 9:14 and 7:10-11 are two instances of an explicit reference to a command of the Lord. But in both there is no quotation of the saying.
[166] Dungan, *The Sayings of Jesus*, 79-80; Tomson, *Paul*, 126-27.
[167] B. Fjärstedt, *Synoptic Traditions in 1 Corinthians. Themes and Clusters of Theme Words in 1 Corinthians 1-4 and 9* (Uppsala: Theologiska Institutionen, 1974) 65-77.

points of contact with more than one account."[168]

At any rate, it is important to acknowledge that the saying is known to Paul and his readers. Whether or not the command of the Lord has been misused in the early church even before Paul preached in Thessalonica and that therefore Paul and his associates had decided early in their ministry not to be associated with such an abuse, is impossible to ascertain.[169] What is clear is that in our text Paul does not show any doubt about the authority of the saying. In fact, he puts a great deal of trust in it. Indeed, he is making a very important point here in order to enable some of his readers to relate to his exhortation in 8:9-13. In stating his departure from the common practice of other apostles, Paul is making a very significant point. J. Moffatt was right in emphasizing the lack of any hesitancy on the part of Paul to show that he acts against a highly authoritative saying in the early church, that of Jesus.[170] Paul is not saying in verse 14 that he has been specifically destined by God to transgress the usual norms of early Christian missionary behavior, as suggested by Theissen,[171] nor that he is making a spiritual point about his right as an apostle, as argued by Harry P. Nasuti.[172] Rather, Paul

---

168 D.C. Allison, "The Pauline Epistles and the Synoptic Gospels: The Pattern of the Parallels" in *NTS* 28 (1982) 13.

169 Following W.D. Davies and D.C. Allison, *The Gospel According to Saint Matthew*, vol. II (ICC, Edinburgh: T and T Clarke, 1991) 170, Horrell, "'The Lord Commanded...But I have not Used...': Exegetical and Hermeneutical Reflections on 1 Cor 9.14-15" in *NTS* 43 (1997) 587-603, here 597, refers to Matt 10:8b, Luke 22:35-37 against Luke 9 and 10, Acts 20:33-35 as evidence of the attempt by early Christians to part from the command of the Lord as stated by 9:14. In fact, on Acts 20.33-35, Horrell writes: "In view of the criticism of Paul which emerged in the Corinthian context we may conclude that here Luke is quoting Jesus against Jesus in support of Paul. Luke...clearly considered that Paul needed some (dominical) justification for his policy of self-support, which was in fact a policy which went against the Lord's instruction...It does indeed seem likely that Luke has created a saying of Jesus, already known as a proverbial aphorism, in order to support Paul's stance on the question of support, which Luke also regards as a model for his own time." (598). Similarly Theissen, "Gospels and Church Politics in Early Christianity," The Reid Lectures, Westminster College, Cambridge, June 1994 as noted by Horrell "The Lord Commanded," 598 n. 65; A.E. Harvey, "The workman is worthy of his hire: Fortunes of a proverb in the early church" in *NovT* 3 (1982) 209-21, esp. 216-17. However, it must be said that in our context there is no slight indication that Paul shows any disregard of Jesus' instruction. If Paul has a slight doubt on its authority his example carries less weight.

170 J. Moffatt, *The First Epistle of Paul to the Corinthians* (New York, London, 1930). 118.

171 Theissen, *Social Setting*, 48.

172 Nasuti, "The Woes," 253. It will be very unwise of Paul to subtly direct his readers' preoccupation of mind from the talk of material support, which he has built up since verse 4 and is needed in building up his argument for the right to financial support,

wants to show the necessity or cost of avoiding an ἐγκοπή at least in his gospel preaching enterprise and of prioritizing the interest of the salvation of others, namely acting against the command of the Lord.

In relation to the dispute among scholars over which version of the synoptic tradition is known and used by Paul, the equally crucial matter concerns the audience of the command of Jesus. In alluding to Jesus' saying, what is Paul doing? Is Paul implying that his present readers are the object of the saying, and therefore they should provide his right to financial support? Or, rather, is he trying to establish that just like the apostles, who were the original audience of the saying, he has the right to be supported? Those who deny the implication that Paul, rather than the Corinthian Christians, is acting against the command of the Lord would favour the former question. What Paul is saying is not about his rights but his readers' responsibility to support him. Hence NRSV's translation: "The Lord commanded that those who proclaim the gospel should get their living by the gospel." This is supported by G.D. Fee,[173] F.F. Bruce,[174] and Seyoon Kim.[175]

Yet, the context does not seem to support this, because Paul is clearly building up his argument that although he has every reason to get the support, he has not done so. And therefore, it would be strange that within the immediate context Paul would expect them to perceive that he was asking them to provide the support or that it was their responsibility to support the apostles. Rather, given that he has already stated in 9:12b that he has not made use of his right,[176] he is trying to convey a notion that *he is consciously acting against the command of the Lord*. He is consciously making a blatant point that he continues to act as he has done (i.e., waiving his rights) even though the command of the Lord gives the right to him to live off the gospel. On the basis of the grammar of 1 Corinthians 9:14 and the historical setting of the saying itself, D.G. Horrell is correct in arguing that: "Paul knows and agrees with the synoptic tradition which regards the

---

to the talk of spiritual point which he has not indicated before. Since verse 11 Paul has clearly indicated that he is speaking about his right to τὰ σαρκικά rather than to τὰ πνευματικά.

173 Fee, *First Epistle,* 413 n. 96 writes: "the command is not given to the missionaries but for their benefit."
174 F.F. Bruce, *Paul and Jesus* (Grand Rapids, MI: Baker Book House, 1974) 73.
175 Seyoon Kim, "Jesus, Sayings of" in Gerald F. Hawthorne, *Dictionary of Paul and His Letters* (Downers Grove: IVP, 1993) 475-80, esp. 475, who argues that Paul's failure to make use of his right does not constitute his disobedience to the command of the Lord.
176 Gardner, *The Gifts of God,* 78, rightly argues that Paul "was not seeking 'to establish that he has such rights' but was restating the fact of that ἐξουσία as strongly as possible." The purpose was "to create the strongest possible impression when he stated, in v 12b, that he had given it up."

instruction to live from the gospel as a command of Jesus addressed to the apostles. Paul, however, is prepared to set this command aside, treating it as a right which he chooses not to use."[177] Furthermore he says: "While obligations are thus indirectly placed upon the sympathisers of the Jesus movement who remain resident in the towns and villages, it cannot be claimed that the instruction is in any way directly addressed to them, though there are other passages 'which stress the reward which is gained by supplying the needs of his (sc. Jesus') followers' (e.g. Matt 10.40-2; Mark 9.41)."[178]

We can see the point Paul makes in referring to the command of the Lord in terms of his whole intention to convince some of his readers not to insist on exercising their right to eat food offered to idols. By alluding to the tradition known to the Corinthian as an authoritative saying of Jesus,[179] Paul claims that his right is as secure and legitimate as theirs. But he is also trying to avoid the impression that he expects his readers to give him his due,[180] purely because he wants them to draw an analogy of his refusal to exercise his right with theirs. Again, Horrell is correct in stating that: "If ever there were a right...which could be unquestionably legitimated, this is it. It is undergirded by the logic of human affairs, by the scriptures, by the way the temple operates, and even by a command of the Lord."[181] Paul says: "But I have made no use of this right" (9:15a) and clarifies it in 9:15b-18. Clearly, Paul does not reject the practice of apostles living off the gospel and the congregations providing the support. Rather, as is rightly argued by Dungan, he "made a practice of setting this regulation aside whenever they encountered circumstances where to have kept it would have made them a hindrance to the gospel."[182] Analogically, Paul does not say that the right of some Corinthian Christians to eat food offered to idols must be rejected. Instead, he shows them by his practice that they need to set aside their right especially when they know that exercising such a right would cause their weak brother to perish.[183]

---

177 Horrell, "The Lord Commanded ...," 596 n. 50.
178 Horrell, "The Lord Commanded...," 596.
179 D. Wenham, *Paul: Follower of Jesus or Founder of Christianity* (Michigan and Cambridge: Eerdmans, 1995) 193. Cf. Dungan, *The Sayings of Jesus*, 27, assumes that the saying was well known. Pace Fee, *The First Epistle*, 413, who argues that it cannot be known whether the Corinthians knew the saying well.
180 See Sisson, *The Apostle as Athlete*, 111-12.
181 Horrell, "Theological Principle," 94.
182 Dungan, *The Sayings of Jesus*, 41.
183 Achtemeier, "Gods," 515, is right in concluding the intent of Paul to be conveyed to the Corinthians in the following way: "If being Christian can cost some of the more socially prominent people in Corinth the place in the respectable circles of Corinthian society then for the sake of fellow Christians, that is apparently the price that must be paid."

To Paul, what he has done and will continue to do with his right is no small matter. He risks himself being accused of violating the Lord's command. He runs the risk of acting against one of the sayings of Jesus. In other words, he is willing to distance himself and his companion from the cherished authoritative practice of living off the gospel to avoid the hindrance to the gospel, even though he knows that it will cause others to question his apostolic status and himself to endure hardship.[184] Dungan is right in saying that ["no] sooner has Paul referred to this command of the Lord than he asserts he does not and will not obey it."[185] *Paul has to show that even this command of the Lord can be acted against for the sake of the gospel. This is very strong indeed in encouraging some of his readers not to use their right, legitimate though their right is and their theological knowledge used to justify it.* Therefore, there is no reason to suggest, as Christian Wolff does, that Paul is only apparently disobeying the saying of the Lord.[186]

Paul would not have alluded to the command of the Lord as the basis of his ἐξουσία if it was not because of the strength of the Corinthian Christians' ἐξουσία. What he has described in 9:4-13 would have been more than sufficient. He would not have done this if he had thought that for them to forgo their ἐξουσία was just a matter of throwing rubbish into a bucket. No! To Paul and to the Corinthians, their ἐξουσία was very precious. To abandon it would involve a great risk. It would contradict their contemporaries' high regard of rights granted to Roman citizens. It would mean the rejection of their knowledge of God's identity, of idol's non-existence, of neutrality of food before God, and of their slogan that 'everything is permitted.' Paul would emphasize later in 9:19-23, however, that their willingness to act contrary to these legitimate reasons does not mean that such reasons are illegitimate in themselves. They remain legitimate. To convince them of this, he speaks of his own experience of acting or behaving in ways that would make him look like something but in actuality he is not something. Hence the role of his language of self-enslavement which is described in the form of 'becoming as' (ἐγενόμην ὡς).

Coming back to our question, why would exercising his right to financial support constitute an ἐγκοπή to the way of the gospel? The answer to this question is of crucial importance in our attempt to know the relevance of

---

184 Cf. Dungan, *The Sayings of Jesus*, 36-39, 41. From mission perspective it was effective in winning others, but in terms of his relationship with some Corinthian Christians it caused bitter conflict with them (2 Cor. 11:7-15; 12:16).
185 Dungan, *The Sayings of Jesus*, 3-4.
186 Christian Wolff, "Humility and Self-Denial in Jesus' Life and Message and in the Apostolic Existence of Paul" in A.J.M. Wedderburn (ed.), *Paul and Jesus Collected Essays* (Sheffield: SAP, 1989) 145-60, esp. 149.

this discourse to Paul's purpose of helping his readers to solve their dispute over food offered to idols. This is especially so because of the fact that in the light of what Paul says in 9:15a and in the first part of 9:15b, Paul seems to be very determined to explain that the use of this right to τὰ σαρκικά and other rights which have been mentioned since 9:4 (note τούτων in 9:15a and ταῦτα in 9:15b) will constitute an ἐγκοπή to the gospel. The extent of Paul's determination is such that he goes so far as to say that he is not writing to secure such rights and that he 'will rather die than...' (9:15b).

A considerable amount of work has been carried out to answer this question.[187] Some have referred to Paul's rabbinic background.[188] Barrett simply assumes that it would affect the acceptance of the gospel which they saw could lead to financial commitments, and the insistence of right could affect the presentation of the gospel.[189] Horsley thinks that Paul's refusal is caused by his desire not to be like the apostles who, coming from villages, were familiar with "sharing in the poverty of village life."[190] As a former Pharisee (Phil. 3:5), Paul did not want to repeat what he used to do before his conversion, namely to benefit from the redistribution of revenues which were taken by the priestly rulers of the Jerusalem temple state from the Judaean villagers under the system of tribute. Paul did not want to follow the practice of the early Jesus movement which adapted "the horizontal economic reciprocity of village communities" that in itself followed "the traditional covenantal ideal of maintaining the subsistence level of all community members"[191] not because it was no longer relevant in the cities, as suggested by Theissen,[192] but because of his sensitivity "about continuing to live off of poverty-stricken people once he identified with them in joining the movement."[193]

The fact that Paul receives support from other congregations (see Phil. 4:15f, 2 Cor. 11:8-9; Phil. 2:25-30), that he and the whole congregations received some kind of hospitality from Gaius (Rom. 16:23), that he has been refreshed by the visit of Stephanas, Fortunatus and Achaicus (1 Cor. 16:17-18) - which has been read in both spiritual and material sense[194] - and

---

187 The difficulty in explaining the puzzle is such that B. Holmberg, *Paul and Power: The Structure of Authority in the Primitive Church as reflected in the Pauline Churches* (Lund: Coniectanea Biblica, 1978) 95, argues that the effect of Paul's statement went beyond what he had intended.
188 Harvey, "The workman is worthy of his hire," 213- 14. Cf. Hengel, *The Pre-Christian Paul*, 15-17.
189 Barrett, *First Epistle*, 207.
190 Horsley, "I Corinthians," 250.
191 Horsley, "I Corinthians," 249.
192 Theissen, *Social Setting*, 27-67.
193 Horsley, "I Corinthians," 250.
194 Horrell, *Social Ethos*, 123.

that he expects Corinthian Christians to speed him on his journey from Corinth to somewhere else (1 Cor. 16:6, cf. Rom. 16:24), have caused some controversy among scholars. Some argue that Paul did not accept support from people who had not been converted, and if he accepted support from churches it was not for his work among them but for his work in other mission fields or when he was in prison.[195] This argument has been regarded as a mere theory, one that is difficult to prove.[196] Others explain it from the condition or standpoint of the motivation of the providers of the support. M. Ebner, for instance, argues that Paul does not accept their support in order not to be drawn into any of their factions.[197] Yet if this was so, it would only be applicable to the time of 1 Corinthians. It would not apply to the initial work of Paul in Corinth. D.L. Dungan thinks that Paul's refusal depends on the financial strength of the congregations.[198] However, such an argument can only stand if it can be proven that Corinthian Christians were economically poor, something which cannot be done in view of the fact that, as indicated in 2 Corinthians 8:13-14, Corinthian Christians are not poor.

T.B. Savage, argues that Paul's practice is in harmony with the mould of the Hellenistic missionary because, unlike the highly educated gentlemen who downgraded trading, tradesmen viewed their work highly. Hence, he infers that the Corinthian Christians' rejection of Paul's working with his hand is not because they do not want him to enter into a demeaning profession,[199] but because they want to give to Paul in order to boast selfishly.[200] They disagree with Paul because his refusal "keeps them from boasting in their own generosity and forces them to identify with his poverty."[201] They give not as the Macedonians do, namely in order to conform to the Lord (2 Cor. 8:5).[202] The measure that Paul uses in deciding to receive or reject the support from the congregation is the spiritual maturity of the givers.[203] Hence, apart from teaching them to know that "the rights of an individual are not so dear as the welfare of the brethren," Paul

---

195 Theissen, *Social Setting,* 40; H. Windisch, *Der Zweite Korintherbrief, Kritisch-Exegetischer Kommentar über das Neue Testament begründet von H.A.W. Meyer,* part 6, 9th edn. (Göttingen: Vandenhoeck and Ruprecht, 1924) 336, see Horrell, *Social Ethos,* 213; Bachmann see Gardner, *The Gifts of God,* 82.
196 Savage, *Power Through Weakness,* 98.
197 M. Ebner, *Leidenslisten und Apostelbrief: Unturschungen zu Form, Motivik und Funktion der Peristasenkataloge bei Paulus. Furschung zur Bibel,* Band 66 (Wuryburg, 1991) 75-77, see Horrell, *Social Ethos,* 214 n. 88.
198 Dungan, *The Sayings of Jesus,* 15.
199 Savage, *Power Through Weakness,* 85-86.
200 Savage, *Power Through Weakness,* 95-97, 98.
201 Savage, *Power Through Weakness,* 93.
202 Savage, *Power Through Weakness,* 98.
203 Savage, *Power Through Weakness,* 98.

is also trying to let them know "the folly of boasting about their own generosity."[204] However, as rightly pointed out by Gardner, it is not clear whether the traders saw working philosophers in the same way as they did their own profession. Moreover, if the church members wanted to see Paul as a high ranking member by supporting him and thereby be proud of their leader and boast in their generosity, the Corinthian Christians "would have regarded manual labour as demeaning for a leader and as reflecting badly on them."[205] We may add that Savage overlooks the fact that in 1 Corinthians 9:2,3,11 there is no indication that Paul refuses to accept financial support because of the Corinthian Christians' motivation to boast.

While Savage sees the motivation of the gift as the cause of Paul's refusal, P. Sampley argues that it is the nature or closeness of the relationship between Paul and his congregations that motivates his acceptance or refusal. While with Philippian Christians Paul has a healthy relationship based on good faith and trust, a condition which enabled them to be in partnership with Paul by supporting his mission, and encouraged Paul to receive their support from the beginning, he does not have such faith and trust in his relationship with Corinthian Christians.[206] However, it is difficult to see why Paul uses his refusal to accept support in Thessalonica, Ephesus and Corinth as a paradigm for various purposes if it applies only to some churches and not to others, valid though such distinctions on the basis of the closeness of relationship[207] and on the motivation of the givers may be. The difficulty in explaining the puzzle has caused recent scholars to view Paul's refusal against the sociological and philosophical backgrounds of Corinthian Christians. R.F. Hock, for instance, argues that the Corinthian Christians were familiar with wandering philosophers, in particular the popular Cynic philosophers of the time.[208] Of the four means of the philosophers' livelihood (i.e., charging, staying in the households of patrons to be the household philosophers, begging and working), Paul chose the last even though to himself, as

---

204 Savage, *Power Through Weakness*, 96-97.
205 Savage, *Power Through Weakness*, 96-97.
206 J. Sampley, *Pauline Partnership in Christ* (Philadelphia: Fortress Press, 1980) 86-89, 109.
207 F.C. Baur, *Paul the Apostle of Jesus Chris,* 258, acknowledges the close relation between Paul and his Corinthian converts.
208 Hock, *The Social Context,* 50-65; Stanley K. Stowers, "Social Status, Public Speaking and Private Teaching: The Circumstances of Paul's Preaching Activity" in *NovT* 26 (1984) 59-82, esp. 81; Hock in his "Paul's Tentmaking and the Problem of his Social Class" in *JBL* 92 (1978) 555-64, here 559, sees 1 Corinthians 9:3 as a defence. However, he does see 1 Corinthians 9 as having a paradigm function as that of Thessalonica in his *The Working Apostle: An Examination of Paul's Means of Livelihood.* PhD Yale, 1974 (Ann Arbor: UMI, 1978) 124-32. Blomberg, *1 Corinthians,* 173, follows Hock's view.

someone coming from a high status (1 Cor. 4:11-12),[209] it was demeaning. This choice, which was the least preferred by the philosophers, caused criticism from the rich Corinthians who wanted Paul to be their household philosopher. Furthermore, Hock argues that to Paul, what he did not only maintained his independence of the rich but also gave him an opportunity to preach the gospel to his fellow workers, customers of his tent-making business and others who entered his shop.[210] But to the élite Corinthians, those who wanted to pay him and thereby attempted to make Paul their leader appear as someone of high status, what Paul did was seen as an insult to them. They therefore accuse Paul of behaving in a manner which, in their eyes, was very demeaning and caused embarrassment to them. Therefore, in 1 Corinthians 9 Paul was seriously defending himself against their accusations based upon his decision to work with his hands and his refusal to be paid by the Corinthians.

Peter Marshall has developed Hock's reconstruction. He argues that Paul's enemies in Corinth were high ranking members who are unnamed in 1 Corinthians.[211] They became Paul's enemies in such a short period of time simply because Paul refused their offer of monetary gifts which, to them, was a sign of friendship. This refusal was understood by the Corinthians as a declaration of enmity, an action harmful to their honour, status and power.[212] While in Corinth Paul did not continue to stay in the patron-client relationship with the rich Corinthians.[213] Therefore, Marshall argues, "Paul's refusal of support from certain wealthy Christians initiated the hostilities which underlie chapter 9 and which continue throughout 2

---

209 Hock, "Paul's Tentmaking," 560-62: Paul was not from the class of artisans or practicing the Jewish convention of a rabbi preferring to love labour for independence in order that they can take pupils without charging them. Pace Hengel, *The Pre-Christian Paul,* 15-16, who argues that the practice goes back to the early period in the first century BC and it might influence Paul in forgoing his right to support.

210 Hock, *Social Context,* 41, 67. Cf. Murphy-O'Connor, *Paul's Corinth,* 176-77, who shows the existence of numerous small shops uncovered as part of the city centre of Paul's time. Their position close to the market would give Paul plenty of opportunities to communicate with others. Cf. Wolff, "Humility and Self-Denial," here 146 who argues that what motivated Paul in carrying out his practice was his desire to "guard himself against any mistaken identification of himself with the wondering preachers of his time."

211 Marshall, *Enmity,* viii, xi, xiii, 94, 341-348.

212 Marshail, *Enmity,* 396-398.

213 Pogoloff, *Logos and Sophia,* 151, 271-283, though aware of the differences between 1 and 2 Corinthians, has followed Marshall's work. He sees Apollos' presence and work as being the trigger of the Corinthians' accusation of Paul's refusal to receive their support. Apollos is thought to have received the Corinthians support; Similarly, Chow, *Patronage and Power,* 107-110.

Corinthians."²¹⁴ As a result, the élite Corinthians rejected Paul in favour of the other apostles who were willing to play the Corinthians' game of the convention of friendship by following the sophists who were happy to allow their hosts to pay them with monetary gifts.²¹⁵

Marshall's reconstruction has been criticized for reading back 2 Corinthians too much into 1 Corinthians.²¹⁶ But not a few have followed up his thesis. J.K. Chow, for instance, argues that Paul's refusal of financial support was seen by some rich patrons, who sought to extend their patronage to Paul, as a violation of their norm of supporting a teacher or a missionary worker.²¹⁷ Similar to Marshall's approach, but from a slightly different social perspective,²¹⁸ Carter has recently argued that Paul's refusal to accept financial support from the Corinthians was hated by the 'big men' of the Corinthian Christian community because to them it was a cultural necessity for someone who worked to have received pay in exchange for their service. They were people of upper grip who did not like Paul's lower grip. They were criticizing Paul not only for the sake of criticism but they did so to gain the support of the church members in order to increase their social prestige by using their common cultural values which, in Paul's eyes, were in essence in opposition to his idea of keeping the Christian community unified and separated from their world.

R.A. Horsley has qualified Hock's and Marshall's proposal. He agrees that Paul was personally concerned about being made a household philosopher. However, Horsley argues that in the context of Paul's attempt to prevent his converts from being influenced by "the dominant society and its social networks"²¹⁹ which used the sacrificial banquets as its maintenance, what he wants to achieve most in refusing to accept financial support is to prevent his converts "from replicating the controlling and exploitative power relations of the dominant society."

Following Hock, D.G. Horrell argues that Paul's refusal of support is not a blatant rejection of *any* support. It is a rejection of a *specific* support. Paul

---

214 Marshall, *Enmity*, 284.
215 Marshall, *Enmity*, 243, 276, 326-40, 359, 397; cf. Horrell, *Social Ethos*, 210-16, esp. 216, follows Marshall's view.
216 This reading implies that he sees the existence of a group of anti-Pauline agitators already causing problems at the time of the writing of 1 Corinthians. Pogoloff, *Logos and Sophia*, 151f. This is also noted by Witherington III, *Conflict* 74 n.8, and Stanley K. Stowers, "Paul on the Use of Reason" in D. Bach, et al., (eds.), *Greeks, Romans, and Christians* (Minneapolis: Fortress, 1990) 253-86, esp. 258ff.
217 Chow, *Patronage and Power*, 107-10, esp. 110.
218 Carter, "'Big Men,'" 48, 54-55, 61-64. He uses M. Douglass' theory of Paul's being high-group/low grid as opposed to the Corinthians' low grip/high grid (see M. Douglass, *Natural Symbols: Explorations in Cosmology* (New York: Pantheon, 3rd. ed. 1982. repr. London: Routledge, 1996).
219 Horsley, "I Corinthians," 248.

rejects to be seen as a client to some élite patrons. What is criticized by the élite members is his insistence on working with his hands to supply his needs. It is in this sense that Paul is said to have angered the élite members and created an ἐγκοπή in his relationship with them, because to them his insistence to work with his hands is against the values of their contemporaries.[220] Similarly, Peter Richardson suggests that the support refused by Paul is *defiled food* offered by the patrons, which is therefore offensive, tainted and unacceptable. This form of support is accepted by the others who, according to Richardson, are those with allegiances to Jerusalem, including Peter. Richardson goes so far as to suggest the possibility that the others ate this defiled food *in the kitchen of their patrons*. To justify their acceptance, they used the logion of Jesus (Luk 10:5, 7-8, Mat 10:10b,11; Mk 6:10).[221] However, against both Horrell and Richardson, it must be noted that the context, especially that of 9:14, does not seem to indicate that Paul is talking about such a specific support. In the light of 1 Corinthians 9:16-18 it is clear that he talks about 'pay' or 'living off the gospel.' He talks about support from the audience of the gospel proclamation as a whole, irrespective of their economic and social backgrounds. He does not talk about mere hospitality, basic necessities or maintenance offered by those who host missionaries.[222]

Rejecting R.F. Hock's view,[223] Bruce W. Winter argues that what Paul does in 1 Corinthians 9 is adopting an anti-sophist stance. According to Winter, the sophists were already influential in the Corinthian society at the time of 1 Corinthians. They were known to have charged their students highly.[224] Therefore, knowing their practice and in order to avoid being associated with the sophists and creating an ἐγκοπή to his gospel proclamation, Paul had initially avoided behaving like the sophists.[225] This, Winter believes, is clearly described in 1 Corinthians 2:1-5 where Paul consciously states his anti-sophist stance, and in 1 Corinthians 9.[226] What is not clear in Winter's view is the link between Paul's statement of his stance against the position of the sophists and the Corinthians' view of his

---

220 Horrell, *Social Ethos*, 210-16, esp. 214-16.
221 Peter Richardson, "Temples," 104-10, esp. 107.
222 Dungan, *The Sayings*, 28. Pace John P. Dickson, *Mission Commitment in Ancient Judaism and in the Pauline Communities: The Shape, Extent and Background of Early Christian Mission* (Tübingen: Mohr Siebeck, 2003) 188-94, who argues that Paul is talking about hospitality, basic necessities or maintenance rather than pay.
223 Winter, *Paul and Philo Among the Sophist*, 169.
224 Winter, *Paul and Philo Among the Sophist*, 164-65, argues that two widely-held perceptions circulated by the first century AD, namely: "Firstly, only the wealthy could afford instruction in the sophists' schools; Secondly, the sophists were impostors and flatterers motivated by love of glory and money."
225 Winter, *Paul and Philo Among the Sophist*, 168.
226 Winter, *Paul and Philo Among the Sophists*, 163, 166.

practice. If the populace of Corinth increasingly disliked the sophists' practice of charging high fees to their pupils, why on earth would some Corinthian Christians criticize Paul for taking a stance against the sophists? The same question is applicable to the views of Hock and his followers.

Perhaps, it is his awareness of the various explanations described above that causes Ben Witherington III[227] to argue that all explanations are possible. The purpose of Paul's refusal of support are: a) in order not to be an obstacle to the gospel; b) so as not to be a burden to his new converts c) to avoid being seen as a huckster, a travelling philosopher, peddler of God's word, stealing people's money, abusing the privileges of hospitality; d) not to be caught up in the social web of patronage,[228] and e) in order to be free to work amongst the Corinthian populace. But is it legitimate to include all notions in understanding Paul's reason for rejecting support? We will argue below that, from Paul's point of view, what lies at the heart of his refusal is *his own view of the gospel itself.* We need first of all to set some parameters drawn from the text before justifying our view.

First, it is evident that what he means by the gospel of Jesus Christ here must be no other than that of Christ crucified (cf.1 Cor. 4:23; 2:2). It is this gospel of Christ crucified which influences Paul's attitude towards his own proclamation of the gospel. And it is this attitude that he wants to be used as a model in Christian ethics, in this regard, in addressing the dispute over food offered to idols.

Secondly, the occasion of the preaching of the gospel he has in mind is that of Corinth and of other places (see 4:12; note also ἐχρησάμεθα in 9:12b and 9:22b; cf. 1 Thess. 2). Paul and his associates have constantly refused to exercise (note ἐχρησάμεθα) the right to financial support. The ἐχρησάμεθα covers the time that he and his associates arrived in Corinth and the time of the writing of 1 Corinthians from Ephesus. Not once did they make use of this right. In this light Pogoloff's suggestion that Paul at first accepted patronage and then changed his mind is based on argument from silence, and therefore does not stand up to scrutiny. Paul is not talking about 'hospitality' here, but 'legal right to financial support' which was understood in the workplace at the time. To the Corinthian Christians Paul says that he *has never made use of* his right to financial support which is his due. This must be borne in mind, even though we can find in 2 Corinthians 11:9 that he acknowledges having received some support from the Macedonian churches while he was in Corinth, and that in Philippians 4:7 he says he received support from Philippian Christians while he was imprisoned.[229] It is tempting to suggest that, perhaps, the circumstances of

---

227 Witherington III, *The Acts of the Apostles: A Socio-Rhetorical Commentary* (Michigan, Cambridge: Wb. Eerdmans, 1998) 547-48, also his *Conflict* 208ff.
228 Cf. Glad, *Paul and Philodemus* 269-70.
229 Gardner, *The Gifts of God,* 81.

Corinthian Christians may have influenced Paul's refusal of their support when he was amongst them. However, this suggestion cannot be squared with the fact that Corinth was not the first city where Paul carried out this policy. He had done it before in Thessalonica (1 Thess. 2:9; 4:11; 2 Thess. 3: 6-13) not because of the circumstances of Thessalonians.

Thirdly, there is no indication in 9:4-18 that Paul regards the right to live off the gospel as illegal and therefore those who exercise it should be criticized and their apostleship be questioned. On the contrary, he supports it (9:14). None the less, it is significant to note that the practice of Paul and his colleagues regarding the right to financial support was different from that of the other missionaries. Moreover, the fact that other missionaries had worked in Corinth after Paul's departure (9:2, 12) gives us reason to suggest that the questioning of Paul's and his colleagues' practice by both the other missionaries and, later on, by some Corinthian Christians was nothing extraordinary. It was natural. Different practice would have raised questions. Even if we can reconstruct the attitudes of their contemporaries towards manual work and the means of support of itinerant missionaries or popular philosophers, the answer to our question of why Paul sees making full use of his right to financial support as constituting an ἐγκοπή to his proclamation of the gospel cannot be determined by that construction. The other missionaries accepted financial support not because they wanted to act as the popular philosophers did. Nor did they do so in order to differentiate themselves from Paul and his group. In so far as 1 Corinthians 9:14 is concerned, they did so in total submission to the command of the Lord. It is therefore unjustified to say that Paul refused to exercise his right because of his desire to avoid being labelled as those missionaries. Rather, it is because he does not want to create a stumbling block to the way of the gospel (9:12b, 15). It is his own reason. Thus, what the text says must be of paramount importance in our investigation.

None of the explanations we have outlined above seeks to find the reason in Paul's own view of the character of the gospel itself. E. Best in 1985[230] is correct in claiming that there is no indication whatsoever in 1 Corinthians 9 that Paul holds his pre-Christian background or the perceptions and the economic background of the Corinthian Christians themselves or even the other missionaries' acceptance of τα σαρκικά to be responsible for his own apostolic practice of refusing financial support. *The sole reason is found in his own characterizing or viewing of his proclamation of the gospel itself.* As argued by Best, it is caused by Paul's view of himself as a slave to God and men and of his gospel. Paul decided not to accept financial support long before he ever thought of himself as an apostle on par with Peter and others of the twelve. This is clear in 1 Corinthians 9:18 where we find the paradox of ὁ μισθός. Paul says that he receives μισθός in the form of preaching the

---

[230] Best, *Paul and His Converts*, 103-104.

gospel free of charge. J.H. Schütz rightly points out that it is in 9:18 that Paul states the reason for his refusal of his rights.[231]

From the standpoint of the audience, this characterizing of his preaching of the gospel free of charge has a strong effect on them. They will have no chance to think that Paul's preaching of the gospel is something which needs paying for. Hence, from the standpoint of pay, the chance of creating a barrier to those who want to respond to his preaching is avoided.[232] Yet, from Paul's point of view the reason goes deeper than that. The gospel itself is free of charge. This is the character of the gospel of Christ crucified. According to Schütz, the gospel meant by Paul is not its content or his own *delivery* of it, but the gospel "as a force or agency able to accomplish something, having a purpose toward which it proceeds. Paul will do nothing to thwart that thrust of the gospel towards its own goal. The renunciation of his apostolic 'right' seems to him a small enough price to assure this."[233] *The gospel itself is more important than the exercise of the right to live off the gospel, solid though the grounds for this right is. So his understanding of the nature of the gospel is all that causes Paul to see that exercising his right makes up the ἐγκοπή to its way.*

It is in this light that the role of 1 Corinthians 9:15-18 is very crucial. Here Paul is not just repeating what he has described in 9:12b. The legacy of the command of the Lord is such that it would not be surprising that the readers would think that Paul was asking them to provide for his needs. Anticipating this response, Paul immediately and explicitly rejects such a response by writing two clauses in 9:15a.[234] First, he writes: "But I have not made use of any of these rights." Secondly, to negate such kind of response he adds: "nor am I writing to secure any such provision." In fact, in the first part of 9:15b he writes a very strong and unfinished clause which, none the less, was probably expected by Paul to be completed by the readers themselves with the notion he has so far been trying to describe: καλὸν γάρ μοι μᾶλλον ἀποθανεῖν ἤ (for it is far better for me to die than). After this part there is a break, as if something was missing. The existence of variant readings betray the curiosity of many who read Paul's sentence. Most Bible translators have tried to eliminate the difficulty by erasing the disjointed structure, as has been pointed out by Roger L. Omanson.[235]

---

231 Schütz, *Paul and the Anatomy*, 51-52.
232 Cf. Gardner, *The Gifts of God*, 84.
233 Schütz, *Paul and the Anatomy*, 51.
234 Thus Dungan, *The Sayings of Jesus*, 5,11,13; Horrell, *Social Ethos*, 210; pace D. Daube, *The New Testament and Rabbinic Judaism* (London: The Athlone Press, 1956) 395-396.
235 Roger L. Omanson, "Some Comments About Style and Meaning: 1 Corinthians 9:15 and 7:10" in *BT* 34 (1983) 135-139; Morris, *The First Epistle*, 134, who argues that Paul's emotion shows the importance he ascribed to his practice.

Omanson himself rightly maintains the text as it is to allow it, as he claims, to reflect Paul's emotions.[236]

However, acknowledging Paul's emotion is not sufficient. As I hinted above, it is more likely to imagine that Paul would have expected his readers to continue his sentence. He expects them to fill in the gap in his sentence. It is likely that the logical continuation of his sentence would be related to the exercise of his right, which has been rejected in the second clause of 9:15a: "It is far better for me to die than *to write about my right to financial support so that you might provide it for me.*"

In a way, such an expectation is not only logical, but also shows Paul's attempt to restrain himself from becoming and being seen as a person who speaks out of proportion. In 1 Corinthians 15:10-11 he shows the same restraint. After saying that he works harder than the rest of the witnesses to the resurrection of Jesus,[237] he makes a self-correction, reflecting a man who guards himself from speaking out of proportion. He says: "I laboured more abundantly than they all; *yet not I, but the grace of God* which was with me. *Whether it were I or they...so we preach.*" The same restraint is also shown earlier in 1 Corinthians 1:16.[238] In view of the fact that he is expecting them to imitate him (11:1), his restraint here is understandable. He is not willing to be seen as asking his readers to die rather than use their right. That should be the decision of each individual. When he speaks of himself, he is prepared to say the utmost. He has done this in 8:13 where he says that he "will not eat meat *for ever* that I may not cause my brother to stumble." If this is the case, then, it is clear that for Paul himself the choice of not making use of his right is a matter of life and death. This is how he sees the importance of preventing an ἐγκοπή to the way of the gospel. This strong statement is necessary to match his previous statement in 9:15a: he is not writing that the Corinthian Christians should play their part in supporting him.

Moreover, the strength of καλὸν γαρ μοι μᾶλλον ἀποθανεῖν ἤ is emphasized further by Paul with the high value given to his refusal to exercise his right. He says that in fact he boasts about it. He writes in the remaining part of 1 Corinthians 9:15b the following: τὸ καύχημά μου οὐδεὶς κενωσει (the boast of mine no one will empty). This boast stands firm. This is the reason for his use of οὐδεὶς κενωσει. This is similar to his strong statement in 1:17 that his refusal to preach the gospel with eloquent wisdom (ἐν σοφίᾳ λόγου) is to prevent the cross of Christ from being emptied (κενωθῇ) of its power.

---

236 Omanson, "Some Comments," 136; Gardner, *The Gifts of God,* 85, follows Omanson's view.
237 Cf. 2 Corinthians 11:23b.
238 He says: "I did baptize also the household of Stephanas. Beyond that, I do not know whether I baptized any one else."

At first sight, it seems difficult to understand why Paul, after speaking about his refusal to exercise his right in such a way that he would rather die than exercise it, immediately speaks of his boasting. Why does he suddenly speak of boasting and why does he defend it here very strongly by the use of οὐδεὶς κενώσει? On the one hand he says that he would rather die than have the Corinthians provide the provision he needs. On the other hand he emphasizes that he boasts about not allowing the Corinthians to support him. Why does Paul do this? Why does he regard the forgoing of his apostolic right to live by the gospel, an action which has caused him to exercise endurance in everything, as something about which he boasts and which no one will empty?

Our question seems to be correct, for preaching the gospel itself is, to Paul, not a source of boasting, hence 9:16a, b, c: "For if I preach the gospel, that is not boasting for me. For necessity (ἀνάγκη) is laid upon me. For it is a woe to me if I do not preach the gospel." Logically, since it is a necessity, preaching the gospel itself cannot be a source of and the reason for boasting. This emphasis on the necessity of preaching the gospel is given more weight by Paul in 9:17 (note the use of γαρ) where he undermines the ground for him to have the μισθον, which is here to be seen as a payment for his missionary work rather than an eschatological μισθον.[239] He writes:

εἰ γὰρ ἑκὼν τοῦτο πράσσω, μισθὸν ἔχω
εἰ δὲ ἄκων, οἰκονομίαν πεπίστευμαι.

He preaches not of his own will[240] (i.e. not intentionally, ἑκών),[241] and therefore he has no μισθον. In fact, he preaches as a steward (οἰκονομίαν).

With these arguments (9:16-17), Paul frees himself from any chance of receiving pay. In the context of our passage, this conclusion is deliberate on Paul's part. He wants to emphasize the reason why he boasts about his forgoing of his right to financial support, something which has caused him endurance (9:12b, 15b), and why he would rather die than have this boast stripped of him (9:15c-d). *It is not the preaching itself that is the source of his boasting, but the refusal to accept support.*

Although the ἀνάγκη (necessity) is externally imposed, various suggestions that regard it as internally imposed (such as ethical or psychological ones) have been suggested. E. Käsemann is right in rejecting

---

239 Pace Gardner, *The Gifts of God,* 94, who emphasizes the eschatological notion of μισθός in verse 18.
240 Contrast, Malherbe, "Freedom and Free Will," 251, who says that Paul preaches willingly.
241 Gardner, *The Gifts of God,* 92 n. 152, is right in emphasizing the notion of intention rather than one's will in the word ἑκών.

these suggestions.²⁴² He himself approaches it from the philosophical concept used by Paul to 'delineate the character of the divine power as sovereign, inexorable and ineluctable,' but not as the impersonal force or chance of the Greek ἀναγκη or Roman fatum but as a manifestation of the divine power of the gospel which in itself has challenged Paul and made him its servant. Therefore, the use of ἀναγκη is meant to underline the importance of God as the controlling power and Paul's destiny to preach the gospel.

A.J. Malherbe²⁴³ looks at the term in the context of the debate between the Stoics and the Cynics over the role of choice and compulsion. Paul is different from them because neither of them countenanced the idea of acting under compulsion: "The Stoic only willed himself to conform and the Cynic put even greater emphasis on personal decision, while Paul acknowledged constraint." R.F. Hock, who looks at 1 Corinthians 9 in the light of the traditional debate over the philosopher's means of support in Greek literature,²⁴⁴ argues that Paul's terms have parallels with the Socratic reasoning. To Socrates, the real gain, κέρδος, of teaching is not money but friendship, and by not charging he could converse with many, rich and poor alike. In the same way, Paul does not receive pay in order to win more converts. To both Paul and Socrates the words ἐλεύθερος, ἀναγκη and δοῦλος are important, but they used the words in a different way.

Hock's view has been refined by P. Marshall.²⁴⁵ He argues that unlike Socrates, neither does Paul reject the validity of having the right to financial support, nor is he arguing that by receiving payment he will be a slave and dependent on others. Assuming that Paul is facing his enemies who have accused him of being inconsistent (i.e., being a free man who acts unlike a free man), Marshall sees the use of ἀναγκη, ἄκων and οἰκονομίαν in 9:16-18 in the context of slavery and therefore in antithesis with παντα μοι ἔξεστιν, ἐλεύθερος, ἐλευθερία, ἐξουσία and ἑκων which are championed by his enemies who want to live as free men. In response, while in 9:1-14 Paul speaks of his free status, one who is free to act or choose, in 9:15-18 he speaks of his servile status. As a slave he does what he is told to. However, Paul qualifies that his externally imposed slavery is not that of an ordinary one. It is that with οἰκονομίαν (9:17), a trusted slave with a managerial responsibility.²⁴⁶ Therefore, no μισθός is expected (9:17).

---

242 E. Käsemann, "A Pauline Version of the 'Amor Fati,'" 229. He outlines various meanings (theological, psychological, mystical and ethical); see 228-30. Morris, *The First Epistle,* 136-37, still takes up these psychological and ethical notions.

243 Malherbe, "Determinism and Free Will," 249.

244 R.F. Hock, *The Working Apostle,* 129-31.

245 Marshall, *Enmity,* 295-304.

246 Marshall, *Enmity,* 301-03. Marshall's and D.B. Martin's identification (*Slavery as Salvation*) of οἰκονομος here as a Roman slave with a managerial responsibility

Fulfilling his duties of stewardship, namely preaching the gospel without cost, is what is expected.[247] In this sense, Marshall emphasizes that Paul's response is radical, blatant, deliberate and provocative because, to the Greeks, those who are free in status are not in servile status.[248] It is radical and unconventional because a ridiculed free man would normally assert his free status in defence. If he is defenceless, he would retreat in shame and dishonour.[249]

At any rate, what Paul describes in 9:16-18a (the idea of preaching as a necessity and therefore without μισθός) is introduced in order to emphasize his boasting in enduring hardship because of his refusal of financial support. *His boasting is not the preaching itself, nor the preaching without pay, but his endurance therein.* Receiving provision would certainly deprive him of his boasting. This is emphasized in 9:18 where he says that his activity of preaching is that which is free of charge. Hence accepting a payment or μισθός would automatically bring his preaching to an end. By asking "[w]hat then is my reward," Paul is not speaking facetiously as suggested by D.L. Dungan,[250] or being provocative against his enemies who charged him with inconstancy in not acting as a free man and of behaving in a wilful, servile manner, as suggested by Marshall.[251] But he is preparing his reader for the point he is making: "his preaching of the gospel is that which is free of charge, that which excludes the making full use of the right to live by the gospel." This is the character of his preaching. This is what makes him see that accepting pay will end his preaching activity.

If this is the case, then, we may argue that *the reason for Paul's reluctance to exercise his right does not lie in the other missionaries or in the Corinthians themselves but in the nature of Paul's preaching activity.* Paul does not speak against payment itself or against those who receive payment. On the contrary, he speaks of it as something legal and with the strongest possible arguments. *The Corinthians and the other missionaries are not to blame for Paul's refusal. On the contrary, it is the kind of*

---

has recently been challenged by John Byron, *Slavery Metaphors in Early Judaism and Pauline Christianity* (Tübingen: Mohr Siebeck, 2003) 235-255, here 249, and 245, who argues that the meaning of οἰκονομία in 1 Corinthians (based on 4:1) is not that of an upwardly mobile slave, nor a slave status, but 'Christ voluntary servant.' To him, the status of the οἰκονομία, as an administrator, is ambiguous (slave or free) and can only be determined by the circumstances. Overall, Byron's methodology, which does not take Roman background as serious as Marshall and Martin do, but that of Jewish notion of the slave of God and of Paul's own usage in his letters, is the main reason for his rejection (see 1-19, esp. 7, 18-19).

247 Marshall, *Enmity*, 304.
248 Marshall, *Enmity*, 305.
249 Marshall, *Enmity*, 306.
250 Dungan, *The Sayings of Jesus*, 23.
251 Marshall, *Enmity*, 304-305.

attitude that Paul brings to his gospel preaching that causes his refusal to exercise his rights to live off the gospel. It is therefore strictly a matter of perspective towards the gospel itself that makes Paul conduct his gospel proclamation in the way he has done. This emphasis on the gospel as the reason for his refusal of his right to financial support is deliberate. He wants to use it as a paradigm for his readers whom he expects to forgo their right for the sake of the weak.[252]

We now return to the question that we have raised above and not yet solved completely: Why does he see his endurance of hardship, which is the consequence of his preaching of the gospel free of charge wherein the right to financial support is not used, as his boasting? Why does he boast about it in a way that no one can empty him of, just as preaching without eloquent wisdom is a necessity in order for the power of Christ crucified not to be emptied?

If Paul opposes the Corinthian Christians' boast of their leaders, eloquent wisdom and achievement (1:29,[253] 4:7b) and asks them to boast in God (1:31),[254] why does he boast about his achievement, that of not using his right to financial support which has caused him to exercise endurance in everything? Our curiosity increases when we read it against the background of Paul's rejection of the Jews' boasting in circumcision (Gal. 6:12-15), of the law (Rom. 3:27) and in the flesh (Phil. 3:3). None have expressed this puzzle better than Käsemann.[255] He writes: "It is all the more astonishing that the apostle speaks here without any embarrassment of his boast and the reward which is bound up with it. In so doing, surely he is contradicting the rest of his theology and what lies at its heart - the teaching about justification? Is he preaching to others what he is unable to keep up himself?" Moreover, he writes: "The apostle, who elsewhere rejects all boasting of himself as presumption over against God, here he defends both his own right, and even the obligation laid upon him, to boast of himself and, while elsewhere he reserves for God as eschatological Judge the power of reward, he here describes as his own reward his particular mode of rendering his service without pay."[256] In this regard, Gardner's solution to

---

252 Hooker, *Paul*, 149, is right in her following emphatic statement: "In the Corinthian world, the apostle who accepted honour and privilege did not need to defend himself, because his position and authority were obvious to others. It is the apostle who willingly accepted suffering and dishonour who was forced to defend himself by reminding his readers that this was what the gospel of Christ crucified was about." Again she writes, "...it is only by appealing to the Corinthians to imitate his example (11:1) that he can get them to understand what living out the gospel means."
253 1 Corinthians 1:31 cites Jeremiah 9:22-23.
254 Gardner, *The Gifts of God*, 85-89.
255 Käsemann, "A Pauline Version of the 'Amor Fati'," 219-20.
256 Käsemann, "A Pauline Version of the 'Amor Fati'," 226.

our question by arguing that in the Corinthian context the use of boasting is both pejorative, particularly in rejecting his readers' arrogant behaviour, and positive in terms of differentiating self-centered boasting from that which is God-centered,[257] that is to say that Paul can boast so long as it is centered on God, does not solve the puzzle, because clearly *Paul boasts about his achievement of enduring hardship as a consequence of his policy of forgoing his right to financial support for the sake of the gospel.*

Is it a counter argument against those who see such a refusal as an evidence of weakness, something to be ashamed of because it has caused him to endure 'everything' (9:12b)?[258] According to R.V.G. Tasker, suffering was something "about which the naturally boastful person would say nothing."[259] Some Stoic philosophers regarded working as the last number in their list of means of support.[260] In fact, as argued by Bruce W. Winter, the sophists charged their pupils highly. Indeed, as we have shown in our exegesis of 1 Corinthians 9:13 above, some missionaries and Corinthian Christians examine Paul's apostolic status simply because he rejects financial support.

Or rather, is it because, as argued by John T. Fitzgerald, "boasting in regard to one's hardships was extremely common in the ancient world"?[261] It is generally acknowledged that one of the functions of the *peristasis* catalogue is 'to legitimate a person.' In his *peristasis* catalogue Paul is 'legitimating his claim to be an apostle of Christ.'[262] Of various kinds of catalogue of hardships,[263] Fitzgerald's study on the *peristasis* of the wise man, the ideal philosopher, comes up with the conclusion that the catalogue of hardship is used to furnish the genuine worth of a philosopher.

In terms of Paul's purpose, Tasker's suggestion is likely. Paul's

---

257 Gardner, *The Gifts of God,* 91.
258 C.K. Barrett, "Boasting (καυχᾶσθαι) in the Pauline Epistles" in A. Vanhoye (ed), L´Apôtre Paul: personalité, style et conception du ministère (Bibliotheca Ephemeridum theologicarum Lovaniensium, 73; Leuven: University Press, 1986) 363-68, esp. 365, captures this notion when he writes: "He will not be the rich man who boasts of his riches, but the poor man who boasts of his poverty, and he would rather die than lose this καυχημα."
259 R.V.G. Tasker, *The Second Epistle to the Corinthians* (Grand Rapids: Eerdmans, 1963) 167.
260 R.F. Hock, *Social Context,* 35-36.
261 John T. Fitzgerald, *Cracks in an Earthen Vessel. An Examination of the Catalogues of Hardships in the Corinthian Correspondence* (Atlanta, Georgia: Scholars Press, 1988. PhD dissertation, Yale University, 1984) 4.
262 Fitzgerald, *Cracks,* 2.
263 Fitzgerald, *Cracks,* 203, highlights 7 catalogues of hardships: human hardships, hardships of national groups, occupational hardships, of punishments, of passions, the vicissitudes of particular individuals and of various types such as those of the wise man.

discourse is aimed at convincing some of his readers who are involved in boasting of men (1:12-4:21) not to exercise their right to eat food offered to idols. Perhaps, it is precisely their shock that Paul wants to achieve.[264] If the Corinthians boast about their eloquent wisdom, which in their time was very popular, Paul boasts about that which is considered low or demeaning by the society. By implication, then, Paul expects his readers not to consider their renunciation of their right to eat food offered to idols as something lowly. They should boast about it. Refusing to exercise his right prevents Paul from creating a stumbling block to the gospel. This is why he boasts. Likewise, by not exercising their right, Corinthian Christians will not cause their weak brother to perish. For this reason, they should boast about it.

However, in so far as Paul is concerned, and if the practice of boasting about one's endurance was common knowledge among his readers as suggested by Fitzgerald, he has a reason to boast about his endurance. In the light of 1 Corinthians 9:2 and 3, some have questioned his apostolic status because he has endured hardship, instead of making full use of his right to financial support. If Paul had this in mind, his boasting of his hardship in our passage was not surprising.[265]

We may conclude that both reasons may be present in Paul's mind. On the one hand, Paul was offering his readers an alternative paradigm whereby it is right and proper to boast about the forgoing of one's rights and not the boasting of one's exercise of rights. On the other hand, in keeping with the custom, Paul had reason to boast about his suffering particularly if he had in mind those who had questioned his apostleship because of his refusal to exercise his right. It is imaginable that upon reading Paul's statement the other missionaries would have immediately reacted against Paul, because not only has Paul stated that he would rather die than exercise his right, but he also boasts about not making full use of his right and about his endurance. 2 Corinthians 10 - 13 indicates the possibility that the other missionaries might have been offended by Paul's statement of his boast in not exercising his right and consequently influenced the Corinthian Christians. What Paul meant to be a paradigm was seen as an attack by the other missionaries on themselves and on their practice of receiving financial support in their missionary activity amongst

---

264 Cf. Räisänen, *Paul and the Law,* 266-68, here 267, on Paul's capability to make a statement "which logically contradicts the previous one when trying to make a different point, or, rather, struggling with a different problem."

265 In fact, Paul reasserts in 2 Corinthians 11:12-13 that he and his team will continue to boast about not accepting pay from Corinthian Christians in order to differentiate themselves from false apostles who boast about things. It is, as it were, an added value to him and his colleagues.

Corinthian Christians.[266]

3.3. The Second Paradigm: Self-enslavement (1 Corinthians 9:19-23)

3.3.1 Review of Scholarship

Much of the discussion on this passage has been generated by the view that Paul is facing his opponents who have criticized him for his chameleon behaviour which he showed whilst he was doing his missionary work in Corinth and continued to do during his correspondence with Corinthian Christians and in his entire missionary work. Our assessment of how scholars have approached this question is important in answering our own question of what Paul is actually doing in 9:19-23 in relation to his entire discourse on the issue of food offered to idols. Our ultimate question is this: is Paul defending himself for his inconsistent or chameleon behaviour in his missionary work? Whereas an affirmative answer implies that his praxis is applicable only to himself and not to his converts, a negative answer means that in this passage Paul is setting an exemplary action to be imitated by his converts in relation to their freedom status which, as we argued above, is the basis of their right. Their fear of loosing their freedom status makes them reluctant to forgo their right. We will show that the latter is the case.

The view that in this passage Paul is facing his opponents or enemies who accuse him of being inconsistent is quite common.[267] In this light, various explanations have been given to account for the background of Paul's changing behaviour. Some have argued that this is due to his previous Jewish missionary practice.[268] Others consider Hellenistic practices as the background,[269] and still others argue that the passage reveals Paul's radical self-understanding as an apostle.[270]

The first to have addressed this inquiry and set it in the context of Paul's entire mission activity is H. Chadwick in his famous article, "All Things to

---

266 Cf. Godet, *First Epistle to the Corinthians*, 1.
267 There are various terms used to describe this inconsistency: flexible (G. Bornkamm, "The Missionary Stance of Paul in 1 Corinthians and Acts" in L.E. Keck and J.L Martyn (eds). *Studies in Luke-Acts* [Nashville: Abingdon Press,1966], 194-207 esp. 197), chameleon (H.L. Ellison, 'Paul and the Law – "All Things to All Men'" in W.W. Gasgue and R.P. Martin, eds., *Apostolic History and the Gospel* [Exeter, 1970] 195), inconsistent or contradictory (Stephen Barton, "All Things to All Men' (1 Corinthians 9:22): The Principle of Accommodation in the Mission of Paul." Unpublished BA. Hons. thesis, Macquire University, 1975) 27.
268 D. Daube, *The New Testament and Rabbinic Judaism*, 336; Bornkamm, *Paul*, 10-12.
269 Dungan, *The Sayings of Jesus*, 34.
270 Barton, "'All things to All Men,'" 204-16.

All Men (1 Cor ix. 22)."[271] By choosing 1 Corinthians 6:12-20,7,8,12-14 and even Colossians as specimens and by seeing Paul's treatment in these passages in the context of his apology to his critics for his behaviour of being a 'trimmer,' Chadwick notes the importance of Paul's acceptance of the position of his critics and his qualification of it in such a way that in the end his critics cannot fight back. Chadwick concludes that "Paul's genius as an apologist is his astonishing ability to reduce to an apparent vanishing point the gulf between himself and his converts and yet to 'gain' them for the Christian gospel." Chadwick goes so far as to say that "Paul had an astonishing elasticity of mind, and a flexibility in dealing with situations requiring delicate and ingenious treatment which appears much greater than is usually supposed."[272]

Similarly, P. Richardson notes that the frequent use of ὡς may be regarded as implying a 'pretence' and that thereby Paul lays himself open to the charge of inconsistency and hypocrisy.[273] Hence he argues that[274] since Paul is defending his apostleship and since what he describes in 1 Corinthians 9:19-23 is not accepted by his opponents, Paul does not expect his converts to imitate what he experiences. He writes "the basic text on the question of accommodation does in fact provide evidence that Paul did not generally advise his constituency to adopt the same principle as he advocated for himself."[275]

While accepting the presence of defence in 1 Corinthians 9:19-23, D. Carson rejects Richardson's reading and argues that the principle set out by Paul in 9:19-23 is not the accommodation, but 'self-denial' and 'servanthood' which is reflected in his own practice of accommodation. Carson emphasizes that "Paul's principle of accommodation is an expression of his commitment in his apostolic ministry not to use all his *Exousia*."[276] There is a danger, however, in seeing that Paul is just demonstrating his apostolic ministry and not seeing it as a principle which is worthy of imitation. This is what Philippa Carter does. Following Carson, she writes "there are limitations on how far this principle should be extended, but *all* Christians are bound to practice self-denial and surrender their rights, a responsibility which is partly, but not completely, demonstrated by Paul's practice of accommodation." Furthermore, she says "the accommodation illustrated by 1 Cor 9:19-23 is not, in and of itself, a

---

271 H. Chadwick, "All Things to All Men."
272 H. Chadwick, "All Things," 275.
273 Richardson, "Pauline Accommodation," 97
274 According to P. Richardson, "Pauline Inconsistency: I Corinthians 9:19-23 and Galatians 2:11-14" in *NTS* 26 (1980) 347-62.
275 Richardson, "Pauline Inconsistency," 355.
276 D. Carson, "Paul's Inconsistency: Reflections on I Corinthians 9.19-23 and Galatians 2.11-14" in *Churchman* 100 (1986) 7-45, here 15.

principle, but merely the demonstration of the principle of self-denial in Paul's own life."[277]

Assuming that in 1 Corinthians 9 Paul "digresses to rebut an invective of inconstancy against him by the hybrist in relation to his refusal of aid,"[278] P. Marshall argues that this invective of the hybrists is related to their defence of their 'freedom' which, in itself reflects their social status and their desire to keep their status quo, but is now threatened not only by their association with people of lower social and economic status in the church but also, and more importantly, by "the teaching and practice of Paul."[279] This 'freedom' (ἐξουσία, 8:9) which is found in chapters 6, 8, and 10 "represents an ideal which had long been at the very heart of their way of life and which remained largely untouched by the gospel."[280] Paul's course of conduct runs counter to the standards of morality of these educated Greeks. His expositions in 8:10-13 and 10:27 are of no surprise to them because they know him as possessing an unprincipled character "with his inconsistency in matters of friendship and giving; with his multiple changes of character to suit those with whom he associated. Such willing and deliberate inconstancy was not the mark of a free man but of a servile origin."[281] Paul is therefore seen to be accused of having a hidden motive, and as indicated by 2 Corinthians, of deceiving people and of seeking their property, and therefore not to be trusted.[282] In response, Paul acknowledges that he is a slave of a self-imposed kind, but not for a negative reason (own gain), but to win more converts. Instead of rejecting the accusation, Paul uses it to explain his apostleship, and in fact requests them to imitate his self-imposed slavery to win many by using the language of invective and the notion of shame. This request is considered to be an affront.[283] Paul "would have offended them greatly."[284]

Clarence E. Glad assumes that Paul's endeavour to nurture his proto-Christian communities had affinity to the communal practice among Epicureans.[285] Within this framework of mind and by seeing the conflict in 1 Corinthians 8 -10 not as between groups, parties or theological positions but between "psychological dispositions or character types revealing different aptitudes of students and their maturity"[286] with the wise or more

---

277 Philippa Carter, *The Servant-Ethic in the New Testament* (New York: Peter Lang, 1997) 58.
278 Marshall, *Enmity*, 284.
279 Marshall, *Enmity*, 285.
280 Marshall, *Enmity*, 285.
281 Marshall, *Enmity*, 291.
282 Marshall, *Enmity*, 306-317.
283 Marshall, *Enmity*, 315-316.
284 Marshall, *Enmity*, 317.
285 Glad, *Paul and Philodemus*, 335-336.
286 Glad, *Paul and Philodemus*, 333.

mature harshly trying to educate the weak or less mature by way of example through eating food offered to idols in temples (1 Cor. 8:10),[287] Glad argues that Paul's language in 9:22b is not to be seen negatively as Marshall thinks but positively.[288] She writes: "Paul's statements do emphasize adaptation and flexible behavior which does indeed resemble the practice of flatterers and obsequious persons; however, I suggest that we view it as a positive enunciation of versatile approach needed in recruitment in psychagogy."[289] In facing the wise who attempt to reform the weak by means of giving an example of eating in a temple and thereby destroy them,[290] Paul is responding in 1 Corinthians 9:19-23 with two perspectives. Firstly, in 9:20-21 he uses "the unreserved association with all in light of human diversity." Secondly, 1 Corinthians 9:22a is "psychagogic adaptation requiring attentiveness to students of different dispositions." It is "a solicitous concern for the tender ones."[291] Therefore, Glad argues that "Paul adapts to the disposition of different types of students, using gentle speech toward the insecure while being appropriately harsh toward the stubborn ones."[292] However, Glad does not relate 1 Corinthians 9:19-23 to Paul's attempt to convince those who are reluctant to act against their freedom status.

D.B. Martin regards the *topos* of a populist leader as the background. Regarding the passage as an example rather than a defence, Martin suggests that Paul's language of enslavement in 1 Corinthians 9:19-23 should be seen in the context of the conflict of social status. Building upon the thesis of Theissen[293] that sees the conflict on idol meat as that which is between the rich and the poor,[294] and on R.F. Hock's and A.J. Malherbe's[295] theses, Martin notes Paul's emphasis on the weak in 9:22.[296] He argues that Paul intentionally singles out the weak lastly and fails to mention the strong in order to emphasize his enslavement for the weak. He sees Paul's enslavement in his conflict with the Corinthians,[297] and reads it in the light of the *topos* of the enslaved leader in Graeco-Roman antiquity. Paul is willing to give up his right in order to characterize his act of self-enslavement to all. His enslavement is an intentional self-lowering. Both his refusal of support and behaviour as a manual labourer depict this downward

---

287 Glad, *Paul and Philodemus*, 214-216.
288 Glad, *Paul and Philodemus*, 16.
289 Glad, *Paul and Philodemus*, 16-17.
290 Glad, *Paul and Philodemus*, 278-287.
291 Glad, *Paul and Philodemus*, 335-36.
292 Glad, *Paul and Philodemus*, 334.
293 Theissen, *Social Setting*, 121-143. 289, 290, 291, 292
294 D.B. Martin, *Slavery As Salvation*, 119.
295 Hock, *Social Context*, 67, and Malherbe, *Paul and the Thessalonians*, 55.
296 Cf. Witherington III, *Conflict*, 213.
297 D.B. Martin, *Slavery as Salvation*, 138.

social movement. Moreover, Paul's action was seen by the high status as "the indiscreet and unprincipled demagogue, who shamelessly deserts his true position to cater to the worst elements of society." He thus descends voluntarily in order to appeal to those of low status. This strategy was appealing to the weak, but offensive to those of high status who were embarrassed by Paul's joining those below his station at the workbench. On the one hand, to the manual labourers themselves, Paul's language is appealing. Martin writes: "Had Paul maintained his higher-status position as a non laboring free man, he might have lost the opportunity to gain the weak. By rejecting that form of life and becoming a manual laborer, Paul appeals to the weak -- the lower class."[298] On the other hand, to those accustomed to the *topos* of enslaved leader (the high status), his enslavement would be heard as "the appropriation of a particular model of leadership opposed to the benevolent patriarchal model."[299]

Stephen C. Barton,[300] has some reservation about Martin's view. He argues that Paul might have a motive different from that argued by Martin. The motive might not have been oligarchic or demagogic. Rather the influence of the models of authority and servanthood, especially that of Christ crucified and risen, might have transformed Paul's political stance which enables him to transform every available model. But what is more important is that, whereas Marshall's reading of the passage fails to recognize that Paul is trying to unite the divided Corinthian Christians (1:10), Martin's argument that the passage is received differently by the two types of audience, cannot square with Paul's attempt to unite the divided Corinthian church.

What has been overlooked by the above readings of Paul's self enslavement is its function in relation to his attempt to help those who want to eat food offered to idols in grappling with the fear of acting against their freedom status and their aphoristic saying that 'everything is permitted' (10:23; 6:12) if they refrain from exercising their right. If we see Paul's language in this light, we can perceive what Paul is doing and wants to achieve. He is here speaking of his own experience, most likely known to the Corinthians, of how - in his preaching activity in Corinth in particular - he has acted in interacting with people of different backgrounds in terms of ethnicity (to the Jews 9:20a), law (9:20b-21) and weakness (9:22a). Paul wants to show them that, although to him freedom is basic and is one of the marks of his apostleship (9:1)[301] and slavery is a negative thing, he has set his own freedom aside for a greater purpose. He does it to give an example to those who fear that forgoing their right will contradict their freedom.

---

298 D.B. Martin, *Slavery as Salvation*, 124.
299 D.B. Martin, *Slavery as Salvation*, 140.
300 Barton, "All things to all People," 282.
301 Schütz, *Paul and the Anatomy*, 52.

Moreover, he does it in order to prevent them from clinging to their belief in the saying that 'everything is permitted.' It is toward this purpose that the importance of his elaborations of self-enslavement and the use of 'ὡς μή' in 9:19-23 are meant to achieve.

In order to understand Paul's discourse in 9:19-23, we first of all have to establish the background of his readers in relation to freedom status, after which we will see the purpose of his discourse, interpret the passage and reconstruct the historical context of his self-enslavement.

3.3.2 The Historical Context of Paul's Readers in Relation to 1 Corinthians 9:19

To freedom status-concerned readers living in the centre of *Romanitas* in the East, Paul's statement in 9:19 (["f]or though I am free from all I have enslaved myself to all, that I might win the more") which comes after emphasizing the importance of freedom in 1 Corinthians 7:17-21, must have been very shocking. Even to the eyes of a Greek reader, such a speech on self-enslavement must also have been received with strong reaction. Of the four kinds of freedom under Greek law, none can easily be given up.[302]

As indicated by Paul's discourse in 1 Corinthians 7:17-21 it can be argued that with regard to attitude towards slavery, his readers are of two different kinds. Some sought their freedom, but others wanted to remain in slavery and, perhaps, sold themselves into slavery (7:21, 23). The former knew how difficult it was for them to attain or get back their freedom status[303] and what impact their freedom would have on their social status as Roman citizens in the society of the Roman Empire.[304] Some of them might be freedmen of Roman citizen status or, probably, of Junian Latins

---

[302] Freedom was highly respected by the ancient Greeks, because through freedom one could be his or her own representative legally, not be subject to seizure, may do what he or she desires to do and lastly, he or she may go wherever he or she desires to go. All these are intrinsic rights of a freedman. Thus, says W.L. Westermann, "Slavery and the Elements of Freedom in Ancient Greece" in *Quarterly Bulletin of the Polish Institute of Arts and Science in America* 1 (1943) 341, as noted by Marshall, *Enmity*, 293. Bartchy, *Mallon Chresai*, 94-95, shows that private and public acts of manumission continued to occur frequently in Corinth during the first century A.D.

[303] Lentz, *Luke's Portrait of Paul*, 43, rightly writes: "Citizenship in Greek cities...was not held by everyone. Possession of citizenship was a distinction of no small degree and was jealously guarded."

[304] Clarence L. Lee, "Social Unrest and Primitive Christianity" in S. Benko and J.J. O'Rourke, *Early Church History*, 121-38, esp. 130-131.

struggling to attain citizen status[305] (the Junian Latins were informally manumitted and therefore did not yet have Roman *ciuitas*) or slaves still struggling to gain freedom in their society and, if possible, in the church circle (cf. 1 Cor. 7:21-22).

It must be borne in mind that in Roman society even the *peculium* (savings) of the slaves belonged to their masters, despite increasing support given by the Roman jurists in the first and second century A.D. to protect it.[306] Moreover, slavery was such that even after manumission the freedmen were still associated with and, to some extent, expected to deliver their obligation to their former masters, including that of supporting their patrons in need.[307] In fact, Claudius ordered that failure to fulfil this obligation (such as respecting and working for a number of days for a former master) be penalised with the loss of freedman status and the return to slavery.[308] They could not sue their patrons or the children of their patrons without having special permission from the praetor who would normally stop the case at the outset. Their right to accuse their patrons in criminal cases was also limited. Indeed, even after manumission, slaves would still have to face the attitude of society that they and their descendants had an indelible slavish past.[309] This is markedly shown in their bearing of the *praenomen*

---

305 The procedures of converting Junian Latins to Roman citizen status were very hard to undertake, for not only did they require the participation of the praetor, governor or emperor and were they influenced by family and personal relationship in the household, but they also required a repetition of formal manumission for those 30 or over years of age and proof of a one year old child for those under 30. The Junian Latins did have rights to own property, conduct business, make contract and access to Roman courts, but upon death they were treated as though they had been slaves all along. Their property belonged to their former masters who manumitted them informally. Their children did not have any right to their property. According to Paul Weaver, the law that arranges these procedures, *lex Iunia*, was made to secure the return of capital of the élite and for financial considerations (see Paul Weaver, "Children of Junian Latins" in (eds.) B. Rawson and P. Weaver, *The Roman Family in Italy*, 55-72, esp. 56-60; also Jane F. Gardner, "Proof of Status in the Roman World" in *BICS* 33 [1986] 1-14, esp. 9-10).

306 Young-Gil Cha, "The Function of Peculium in Roman Slavery during the First Two Centuries A.D." in T. Youge and M. Doi (eds.), *Forms of Control and Subordination in Antiquity. Tokyo: The Society for Studies on Resistance Movements in Antiquity* (Leiden: E.J. Brill, 1988) 433-436.

307 Judge, *The Social Pattern*, 31.

308 Bruce W. Winter, "St Paul as a Critic of Roman Slavery in 1 Corinthians 7:21-23" in Παυλεία 4 (1998) 14; A.M. Duff, *Freedmen in the Early Empire* (Cambridge: CUP, 1958) 41.

309 Clarence A. Forbes, "The Education and Training of Slaves in Antiquity" in *TAPA* 86 (1955) 321-60, esp. 321; Cf. P.R.C. Weaver, "Children of Freedmen (and Freedwomen)" in B. Rawson, *Marriage, Divorce, and Children in Ancient Rome* (Oxford: Clarendon Press, 1996) 167-90, esp. 177, 188, who warns that we cannot

and *nomen* of their patron and their own servile *cognomen*. No livelihood could be made without one's revealing his *cognomen*. Though allowed to wear the *toga,* they had to wear a close-fitting cap called *pilleus.* Those who were in slavery would have known very clearly the miserable psychological condition of life as a slave. Roman law distinguishes the free and slaves, freeborn and freedmen, the freedmen of Roman citizens and of Latins or of *dedicticii*.[310] Seen from this legal perspective, the fear of losing one's freedom on the part of Corinthian Christians was understandable.

Given that the worship of the imperial cult was probably the occurrence that exacerbated the dispute among Corinthian Christians over εἰδωλοθυτων (see chapter 2 above) and that, as the dominant force in the *seviri* or *magistri Augustales* in the Roman provinces and cities,[311] freedmen had a major role in promoting the imperial cult by sponsoring public games,[312] the fear of acting against their cherished freedom status on the part of freedmen Corinthian Christians was conceivable. In fact, during the early Empire, particularly under Augustus some laws were passed to restrict the manumission of slaves. Tax on manumitted slaves was enforced. Manumission by will was curtailed, and owners under twenty years of age were forbidden to manumit.[313]

However, there are also some who wanted to remain in slavery even though the opportunity to be freed by their masters occurred. Against their intention Paul has already told them to seize that opportunity to be freed (7:21b). In fact, it can be shown that the reason Paul commands them not to become slaves of men (7:23) has something to do with the fact that some people, especially of freeborn status, make themselves slaves of rich patrons in order to have social and economic benefits.[314] Still, the society

---

use what happened to the slaves of the family of Caesars to picture the condition of slaves in general. The stigma of being a slave or of having been the descendants of slaves remained until the next generation. They did not have the luck or talent of Horace to rise above their inherited inferiority. Perhaps, this could be seen as part of the reasons why they did not use in their tombstones the status-indicators available to them to clarify to which status they belonged.

310 Treggiari, "Social Status and Social Legislation," 872.
311 J.J. O'Rourke, "Roman Law and the Early Church" in S. Benko and J.J. O'Rourke, *Early Church History,* 165-86, esp. 168, points out that under Claudius, it was freedmen from his own household that constituted the *de facto* governors of the Empire.
312 Gager, "Religion and Social Class in the Early Roman Empire," 108-109.
313 Gager, "Religion and Social Class in the Early Roman Empire," 99,108; O'Rourke, "Roman Law and the early Church," 178.
314 As shown in the record of Satyricon Petronius 58 in which Hermeros, a freedman of the wealthy Trimalchio who, in his quarrel with Asoylton, describes the reason and benefit of his slavery in terms of gaining higher social status. Satyricon Petronius wrote about aspects of Nero's rule. In his oration 14 and 15 (written in AD 70-110),

did not consider it a popular course of action, because the stigma of slavery remained, however good the living conditions in the house of a rich patron into which one sold oneself might have been.

To both freedom status seekers or defenders and those who wanted to remain in or sell themselves into slavery, Paul's self-enslavement in 9:19-23 is shocking, for he has exhorted both to avail the opportunity to be freed (7:21)[315] and to reject self-slavery (7:23)[316] because freedom from bondage of slavery is important[317] and slavery is not socially and morally good.[318]

Dio Chrysostom speaks of freeborn who sold themselves into slavery. Epictetus, *Diss. 4.37* speaks of a man who prefers being a slave to being freed, because in the former he is cared for by his master in return for his limited service, and in the latter he has to care for himself. (See Winter, "St Paul as a Critic," 4-12, 15). I am indebted to the author's generosity for allowing me to read his article before the appearance of the journal. It is regrettable that I cannot get hold of the journal itself. Hence, the pages cited here may not be the same as in the journal. Winter rejects J.A. Harrill's dismissal of Petronius and Dio Chrysostom as evidence for self-slavery (J.A. Harrill, *The Manumission of Slaves in Early Christianity* [Tübingen: J.C.B. Mohr, 1995] 31) and supports Rose's analysis of Petronius' historical reliability (F.S. Rose, *The Date and Author of the Satyricon* (Leiden: E.J. Brill, 1971) 75. Moreover, Winter uses Lucian's "On the Salaried Posts in Great Houses" and "Apology for the 'Salaried Posts in Great Houses'" to support his use of Petronius and Dio as evidence. The enthusiasms among the provincials to perceive a different degree of honour among Roman citizens is seen by Winter as a probable reason why, like their contemporaries, Corinthian Christians were tempted to opt for self-slavery. Hence, Paul's emphasis on their free status as the 'class' or 'calling.'

315 The controversy among scholars over the interpretation of the enigmatic verse of 1 Cor 7:21b revolves around the question of whether or not in the society of Roman Corinth it was possible for slaves to refuse to be freed by their masters. If it was not (thus Bartchy, *Mallon Chresai*, 119), then what Paul says in 1 Corinthians 7:21 is not advising them whether or not to accept manumission. But if it was (thus Harrill, *The Manumission of Slaves*, 6), then what Paul is saying is to command those who have the opportunity to be freed, whether by their effort or by their master's decision, to make use of the opportunity. This is confirmed by 1 Corinthians 7:23.

316 Winter, "St Paul as a Critic," 12-16.

317 This is despite the fact that, in ancient times, negative attitudes towards slavery was absent. See Bartchy, *Mallon Chresai*, 116-17; Bradley, *Slavery and Society at Rome*, 72-73, 101-02, regards the multiplicity of slave occupations and statuses, differences of origin and geographical location and competition between slaves for the favour and support of the master, lack of material incentive, the prospect of manumission and the stability of the household as some of the reasons why slaves were prevented from having a common cause to protest.

318 Pace K.R. Bradley, *Slaves and Masters in the Roman Empire: A Study in Social Control* (Oxford: OUP, 1987) 38, who uses 1 Corinthians 7:17-21 as evidence of how ingrained slavery had become that even Christianity could not dispense with it.

Moreover, it is shocking because Paul does it not for his own gain, but to win others the more. However, it is precisely their shock that Paul wants to arouse, and this is the purpose of his whole discourse on the importance of caring for the weak. To those who think that forgoing their right to eat food offered to idols contradicts their freedom status, Paul's example of self-enslavement conveys a very strong message. He is saying that he himself, who has exhorted them to see slavery as a negative factor, has to do what is contrary to his freedom for a greater purpose.

3.3.3 The Purpose of Paul's Discourse

It is against the historical background we established above that Paul's emphasis on the purpose of his self-enslavement, which is characterised by the phrase 'in order that I might win the more' (ἵνα τοὺς πλείονας κερδήσω, 9:19), plays its significant role. He does not simply say ἵνα κερδήσω ('in order than I might win'). Rather, he says 'in order that I might win *the more*' (τοὺς πλείονας). It means that he can still win some by not enslaving himself. But he wants to win *'the more,'* and this can only be done by making himself a slave to all. By implication he is telling his readers that in his life as an apostle his self-enslavement has *an added value* and achieves more than otherwise. This emphasis on the added value must have been well-thought out by Paul, if only to achieve his goal of encouraging his audience not to use their freedom status as a reason to refuse forgoing their right to eat food offered to idols.

While in 8:9-13 Paul warns them against destroying their weak conscienced brother if they eat food offered to idols on the basis of their right which is justified by their knowledge, here he is trying to let them know the positive result of refusal to exercise their ἐξουσία and of acting against their freedom status and their aphoristic saying that 'everything is permitted.' In other words, he wants to show them *how important 'winning others' in great number is in his life and how crucial 'self-enslavement' has been for this purpose. What is cherished by him, namely freedom, is sacrificed for 'others.' What is dreaded by him, namely slavery, has to be undertaken to win the more.* There would be no more convincing way of opening the minds of his audience living in a slave-master society than his language in 9:19.[319] Given that slavery was to Paul a negative thing,[320] his

---

He sees 7:17-21 as a Christian "unqualified acceptance of the existing social structure" in which Christians found themselves.
319 Barton, *Invitation to the Bible*, 146.
320 Harrill, *The Manumission of Slaves*, 3-10, 93-102, cited here 3, argues that since the slaves could refuse manumission, and given that in the ancient slavery was "a fundamental given in daily life, and virtually nobody thought to question its morality" what Paul is doing in 1 Corinthians 7:21b is to advise slaves to avail the

discourse on constant self-enslavement (ἐδούλωσα), must speak very compellingly to the Corinthians. Even near the conclusion of his discourse on his self enslavement Paul still repeats this emphasis: τοῖς πᾶσιν γέγονα πάντα, ἵνα πάντως τινὰς σώσω (I have become all things to all, that I might by all means save some [9:22b]).

Furthermore, 1 Corinthians 9:19-23 is also related to vv. 14-18 since it is closed with that which he used in closing the latter: "I do it all for the sake of the gospel" (v. 23 cf. vv. 12b,15 and 18). In other words, just as his forgoing of his rights is necessitated by the offering of the gospel freely, so his enslavement to and identification with "all" is caused by his concern for the gospel. In fact, in verse 23 Paul seems to be speaking highly of his enslavement to and identification with all, so much so that he is prepared to say that his own interest is also safeguarded. He says that he does it all not just for the sake of the gospel (i.e., for the gospel to be preached) and in order to win and save many, but also that he "may become a sharer in the gospel" (ἵνα συγκοινωνὸς αὐτοῦ γένωμαι).[321] In other words, *in enslaving himself, he also benefits from the gospel*. In view of its purpose to convince his readers to forgo their right and not to be afraid of contradicting their freedom status, this hint on his having a share in the gospel is crucial. Clearly, the gospel is the power that forces Paul to do what he has done. Just as in forgoing his right Paul has a purpose (i.e., not causing an ἐγκοπή in the way of the gospel, see 9:12b), so in making himself a slave to all Paul has a clear aim, namely *to gain* (κερδαίνειν, vv. 19, 20b,21, and 22b) or *to save* (σώζειν, v. 22) others, and *himself to become* a sharer in the gospel (v. 23). These three purposes must be seen in relation to each other. To win is to save others by means of the proclamation of the gospel. Little wonder that he closes his discourse in 1 Corinthians 9 by saying: "*I pommel my body and subdue it, lest after preaching to others, I myself should be disqualified*" (9:27).

What 'a sharer in the gospel' means is certainly determined by Paul's high view of the gospel of Jesus Christ and its proclamation. In 9:16c he

---

opportunity to be freed. In other words, Paul criticizes slavery even though for some staying in slavery, especially that of high status family, would mean gaining better economic and social benefits than being free and yet not related to households. Harrill's view is followed and developed by Glancy, "Slaves," 499-501, who suggests that Paul has in mind also the "slaves who are sexually vulnerable to their masters" (499) and without freedom could not integrate into the Christian body. Winter, "St. Paul as a Critic," 13-14, strengthens Harrill's view by emphasizing the importance of the positive command of the aorist form of χράομαι. This is in line with his heading of 1 Corinthians 7:23 where, he argues, Paul denounces those who are tempted to undertake self-slavery even though, in their society, self-slavery helped to boost their social status.

321 Hall, "All Things to All People," 138, is correct in noting the radical nature of verse 23: "Radical identification with all people is what the gospel requires of him."

considers ceasing to preach the gospel as a curse on himself. He is therefore likely to be speaking about his part in the preaching of the gospel. Clearly, Paul here is operating not on the basis of his apostolic right or privilege, but on a more authoritative one, namely the demand of the gospel. His refusal of his right is in order to submit to the demand of the gospel.[322]

3.3.4. Paul's Elaboration of His Self-enslavement: A Historical Narration

The questions of how and why Paul has enslaved himself to all (9:19) are described in historical happenings in 9:20-22.[323] This is indicated by the use of ἐγενομην, a past experience known to Paul and most probably also to the Corinthians. This must be borne in mind when we try to read Paul's statements in 9:20-22a. Before we explore the detail of Paul's elaborations and then reconstruct their historical contexts, we need to address the question of what kind of accommodation Paul is expressing in 9:19-23.

It revolves around the question of whether or not Paul is accommodating theologically (i.e., Paul gives up some items of his belief in certain things), or epistemologically/methodologically (i.e., Paul changes his method so as to be in the same tone with that of others to whom he preaches the gospel), or ethically (i.e., Paul behaves in certain ways without having to sacrifice his belief). None has opted for the first meaning. Chadwick[324] and Longenecker[325] opt for the second. But this is rejected by Richardson and Gooch who argue for the third.[326] At any rate, Paul's emphasis on becoming

---

322 Schütz, *Paul and the Anatomy*, 235.
323 Cf. H.C. Kee, "From Jesus Movement toward Institutional Church" in Robert W. Hefner (ed.), *Conversion to Christianity. Historical and Anthropological Perspectives on a Great Transformation* (Berkeley, Los Angeles, Oxford: Univ. of California Press, 1993) 47-63, here 57, who argues that in 1 Corinthians 9:19-23 we can see Paul's adoption of strategies and norms "that seem to be appropriate to local situation." Pace Gooch, *Dangerous Food*, 107, who thinks that Paul's description in 9:19-23 is historically 'vague,' "it cannot be taken as a description of his missionary practice in concrete social terms."
324 Chadwick: "All Things to All Men," 264, 270, 275, argues that in his missionary activity Paul employed accommodation to "minimize the gap between himself and his potential converts" (275). In fact, even now he does not directly challenge his readers' position. Rather "he begins by accepting unhesitatingly their fundamental position...he begins from where they are" (264).
325 R. Longenecker, *Paul, Apostle of Liberty* (New York: Harper and Row, 1964) 234, 236, Paul "begins on their own ground, at the point where he finds agreement with them, and leads them on from there" (234). "Paul's approach to the question is that he begins in agreement with those he seeks to correct" (236).
326 P. Richardson and P.W. Gooch, "Accommodation Ethics" in *TynBul* 29 (1978) 89-117, esp. 99-103, 102-05, here 105, argue that what Paul is doing is not in terms of method but his personal behaviour. They write: "Paul here discusses not his

"all things to all" (9:22b) does not allow us to limit his accommodation to one sense or the other. It indicates all forms of accommodation. What he describes in 9:20-22a are some examples of his accommodation, probably the most urgent, real, relevant, tangible and readily understandable of his self-enslavement in the form of 'becoming as' someone not of his own identity or belief.

Our task is to try to reconstruct as far as possible the historical experience of Paul's becoming what he mentions in 9:20-22a, for only by so doing can we appreciate his effort in encouraging his readers to imitate his example. It is illegitimate to dispense with the need for this reconstruction and the groups mentioned, as has been done by J. Weiss, W. Willis, Stephen C. Barton and E.P. Sanders.

Weiss argues that in 9:20 Paul does not speak of a series of actual cases.[327] Despite his attempt to see 1 Corinthians 9 as an apostolic example of renunciation of rights, Willis thinks that when writing 9:20-22a, except on the weak, Paul does not have a particular occasion in mind.[328] Stephen C. Barton, who follows W.L. Welborn's and M.M. Mitchell's reading of political factionalism in the Corinthian church,[329] argues that 9:19-23 must be seen rhetorically. It is Paul's rhetoric to encourage the strong to "imitate his example of self-denial in order to stave off harmful division and faction and unite in Christ's body as many people as possible."[330] Similarly, E.P. Sanders regards it as hyperbolic. He equates Paul's statements in 1 Corinthians 9:20-22a with his broad exhortation in 10:32 because both passages refer to Paul's conduct and are concerned with how to live for the benefit of many.[331]

However, Paul's attempt to draw the attention of his readers to his self-example cannot bear much fruit if he speaks of that which is based on concept rather than on real experience. Paul speaks of a concept drawn from or manifested in historical experience. The danger involved in the issue dealt with in the whole discourse is too great to require just an hyperbolic example or rhetorical force.

Paul begins his discourse on his past experience in verses 20-21 with one ἐγενόμην and does not use it again until 9:22a when he comes to a different

---

dialectical or apologetic method, but his behaviour, his personal conduct. He does not say that he adopted the language of those within law or outside it; he does not present himself as agreeing with the basic premises of Jew or the weak. Instead he claims that he has become as one of those he is trying to win; he has adopted, not terminology, but ways of behaving."

327 Weiss, *Korintherbrief*, 233.
328 W. Willis, "Apologia?," 37-38, 46 n. 43.
329 Welborn, "On the Discord," 88, 98-100,107-08; Mitchell, *Rhetoric*, 300.
330 Barton, "All things to All People," 277, 280.
331 E.P. Sanders, Paul, *The Law and the Jewish People* (Philadelphia: Fortress Press, 1983) 186.

object of becoming, the weak. Moreover, the resumption of the use of ἐγενομην in 9:22a is specified by the absence of the use of ὡς and μὴ ὤν.³³² There are several important points in Paul's elaboration of historical self-enslavement in 9:20-22a.

First, Paul informs the Corinthians that at one point in his life he became 'as³³³ a Jew to the Jews' (9:20a). What does Paul, a Jewish Christian, mean by saying that he became a Jew to the Jews? This is quite puzzling. Some resort to a chiastic structure to explain it.³³⁴ Others appeal to 9:20b which is thought to clarify 9:20a. It is argued that what Paul has in mind in 9:20a is what is described in 9:20b. In verse 20a he addresses only the Jews, but 'those under the law' includes not only the Jews but also "proselytes, God-fearers, and all who accepted (at least in part) the requirements of the Mosaic law."³³⁵ 1 Corinthians 9:20b explains that, as a Christian, Paul is submitting voluntarily to the Jewish Torah, which is distinguished from the non-Christian Jewish obligatory obedience to it.³³⁶ However, if we quickly resort to 9:20b, we do not do justice to 9:20a.³³⁷ Paul may have deliberately used 9:20a to speak of his becoming as a Jew to the Jews in a sense different from that in 9:20b.³³⁸ Moreover, if 9:20b includes the Jews, there is no reason for Paul to mention specifically his becoming as a Jew. It is therefore more justified to treat 9:20a separately from 9:20b. Paul really

---

332 It is surprising that in his translation of the passage Daube, *The New Testament and Rabbinic Judaism*, 336, still includes ὡς in 9:22a.

333 Some manuscripts omit the ὡς in 9:20a, undoubtedly because of the strange nature of Paul's statement of his becoming as a Jew to the Jews. However, omitting it will certainly abandon Paul's point of 'becoming as' which is needed in his discourse. It is rather unfortunate that Tomson, *Paul*, 277, regards it as a later insertion based on his assumption that at the time the anti-Judaism trend was strong.

334 See N.W. Lund, *Chiasmus in the New Testament: A Study in Formgeschichte* (Chapel Hill: University of North Caroline Press, 1942) 147-48: A= 19; B=20a; C=20b; C1 = 21; B1=22a; A1= 22b.

335 K.V. Neller, "1 Corinthians 9:19-23. A Model for Those Who Seek to Win Souls" in *RQ* 29 (1987) 129-42, here 134; Gardner, *The Gifts of God*, 100.

336 See C.H. Dodd, "Εννομος Χριστου" in *More New Testament Studies* (Manchester, 1968) 134-35. By removing the ambiguity he writes: "in one sense, it is true, Paul is a Jew, but not in the sense of one who submits to the authority of the law of Moses; in that sense he is not a Jew, but behaves as *if* he were a Jew, that is, as if he were subject to the Mosaic law...When Paul is endeavouring to convert Jews, he means, he voluntarily submits to the precepts and prohibitions of the Torah, although as a Christian he holds himself to be free from them."

337 Cf. Ellison, "Paul and the Law – 'All Things To All Men,'" 196 who writes: "it must not be too readily assumed that these two groups are completely synonymous."

338 Robertson and Plummer, *Critical Commentary*, 191: "The one refers to nationality, the other to religion; and there were some who were under the Mosaic Law who were not Jews by race."

became as a Jew to win the Jews. This is to be differentiated from his becoming as under the law.

This separation is supported by the fact that in his statement of his becoming as a Jew Paul does not qualify it with μὴ ὡς Ἰουδαῖος as he will with his becoming as ὑπο νομον and ἄνομος. This is understandably because he is a Jew. It also indicates that he is not simply speaking about his ethnic identity, for ethnic identity is not omissible. He must be speaking about something with which Jewish people would like to be seen or appear. This could be cultural or social, not just in matters related to food as suggested by G.D. Fee.[339] Paul became Jewish-like, as it were, to win the Jews. Paul no longer sees himself as a Jew. He does not see himself as being controlled by his Jewishness. He is a man who goes beyond his own cultural and religious *mileu*. It is true that in his other letters he shows his loyalty to his people (Rom. 9:3; Phil. 3:5; 2 Cor. 11:22). But he also plays down his previous Jewish achievement. Hence his cross-boundary or egalitarian gospel (Gal. 3:28). Although the immediate context of chapter 9 discusses the matter of eating food offered to idols, we can see Paul's statement of becoming as a Jew as covering the whole characteristic of Jewish people in his time: social and cultural.

In other words, he wants to show his readers that even though he did not have any obligation anymore to live culturally or socially in the Jewish way, he did live as a Jew. Realistically, his status as a Christian missionary who was commissioned to different nations did require him not to live any longer in a manner that was Jewish-like or Jewish-bound.[340] Even deeper than this is the probability that, after his conversion, Paul was no longer bound by his previous cultural and social boundaries. Therefore, when he brought the gospel to the Jews in Corinth he became, once again, as a Jew. In other words, he returned to live in a Jewish manner. This idea is crucial in encouraging those whom he expects to understand the position of the weak conscienced brother. The strength of his encouragement would have been stronger than otherwise if his readers had been aware of the historicity of his "becoming as a Jew to the Jews." He wants them to be like the weak with their scruples even though they no longer share their scruples. Formerly, they themselves had been in the state in which the weak now were. But they had grown in knowledge and no longer had any of the scruples of the weak. Yet for the sake of the weak, they were expected to be like (as) the weak again.

Secondly, Paul moves in the second example to a harder one. While in 9:20a he speaks of becoming culturally and socially as a Jew to his own people, now in 9:20b he writes about becoming under something which governs one's behaviour, the law. Surely, it may be argued that the law

---

339 Fee, *The First Epistle*, 428.
340 Cf. Stephen Barton, "Was Paul a Relativist?" in *Int.* 19 (1976) 164-92, esp. 165.

might have governed the cultural and social appearance or behaviour of the Jews (9:20a). But becoming as one under the law was certainly harder than just appearing as culturally and socially a Jew. Paul is talking about his becoming under a system the holders of which see as being divine and determining of one's behaviour. It is precisely because of this that, unlike in 9:20a where Paul does not qualify with μὴ ὤν, Paul qualifies his becoming 'as under the law' with μὴ ὢν αὐτὸς ὑπὸ νομου.[341] He is not prepared to state that he *is* under the law. His statement 'as under the law' has to be qualified with ὢν αὐτὸς ὑπὸ νομου, undoubtedly because he no longer acknowledges the legacy of the law.

We are not sure whether or not at this point the Corinthian Christians had already been as aware of the question of the role of the law in churches founded by Paul and his associates as scholars of Paul's view of the law have been. Even if they had been, we still do not know what the law constituted in the mindset of Corinthian Christians. Nor do we know whether Paul had coached them during his stay in Corinth about the role of the law in their salvation. Throughout 1 Corinthians he uses the law in a positive sense. He does not discuss here the controversial issue of the role of the law in Christian faith as he does in other letters,[342] not because he had not yet possessed or developed his own view of the law, but because the context did not demand an exposition of his view of the law.

None the less, the fact that he qualifies his statement of becoming 'as under the law' with μὴ ὢν αὐτὸς ὑπὸ νόμου[343] does indicate, at least in his mind, that his readers are or should be made aware of the decreasing role of the law in his soteriology. This is so particularly because he is trying to help his readers see how they should act contrary to their position on the issue of food offered to idols. Paul's implied message would have been heard if they were aware of the decreasing role of the law. Paul wants to let them know that he became as 'under the law' even though he knew that the status of the law was no longer supreme in his life. There is a high degree of consciousness on the part of Paul in ensuring that he is not to be misunderstood by his readers. He wants them to know that he has a

---

341 Again, as in 9:20a, some manuscripts omit this phrase, and Tomson, *Paul* 277-79, regards it as a later interpolation because of the development of the anti-Judaism. However, Paul's point in the immediate context will be lost without this phrase.

342 Cf. Tomson, *Paul,* 70-71, who argues that at the time of the writing of 1 Corinthians the Jewish Law was not a problem in the Corinthian church. There is in this letter an uncomplicated appeal to the law (see 1 Cor. 1:30, 4:4, 6:11,6:18, 10:1-4), although in 7:18, 9:20 and 15:54-56 the theology of justification exists. This causes Tomson to conclude that: "indeed the theology of the law and justification was not the essential core of Paul's thought but could be applied or not, just as the situation required" (71-72).

343 The omission of this clause by some manuscripts may be caused by the absence of μὴ ὢν Ἰουδαῖος in 9:20a.

reservation about the role of the law. He wants to be seen that he is no longer under the law.

This is despite our difficulty in understanding Paul's view of the function of the law, which has been an endless issue in the New Testament studies,[344] and in determining what part of the law Paul has in mind in the context of our passage. 1 Corinthians 9:20b has been read in the light of the wider debate on Paul's view of the law. It is argued that ὑπὸ νόμον describes those who regard the Torah as a way of salvation[345] or "a right standing with God"[346] or as a 'marker' of salvation[347] or a means to stay in the covenant.[348] In fact, scholars have tried to be more specific in their understanding of the νόμος in 9:20b. Frank Thielman argues that the νόμος here is not the Rabbinic 'yoke of the Torah' as suggested by Westerholm,[349] nor law in its entirety (the Torah) but those parts which distinguish the Jews from the Gentiles, namely food or dietary laws. Thielman thinks that the immediate context of 1 Corinthians 9, which discusses the possibility of eating food offered to idols, confirms this reading.[350] However, since Paul is speaking of his past experience, the meaning of the law here cannot be confined to the present context. Paul might have become as one under the law in a sense wider than Thielmann's suggestion. If Paul had food and dietary laws in mind, he would have said so. In view of the importance of this example for his whole discourse of convincing some not to be worried about their freedom status, we should do well to assume that Paul has in mind something more substantial than just food and dietary laws.[351] He is speaking about the source of these laws. Indeed, the fact that Paul does not describe the ethnic identities of those in 9:20b as he will in 10:32 (i.e., Jews and Greeks), does not allow us to see the law here as referring to food and dietary laws alone. If those under the law include Jewish proselytes, God-fearers or God-worshippers, it is difficult to assume that Jewish food and dietary laws are meant here, because these people have some reservation about those laws. They are attracted to the Jewish monotheistic God and religion which is known to have centered on the Torah of God. They are not attracted to the food and dietary laws.

What is of utmost importance for us is to realize that Paul wants to show

---

344 See Calvin J. Roetzel, "Paul and the Law: Whence and Wither?" in *CBR* 3 (1995) 249-75, for a review of the scholarship on Paul's view of the law.
345 Conzelmann, *1 Corinthians*, 160.
346 Fee, *The First Epistle*, 428.
347 Gardner, *The Gifts of God*, 101 -02.
348 E. P. Sanders, *Paul and Palestinian Judaism* (Philadelphia: Fortress, 1977) 180.
349 S. Westerholm, *Israel's Law and the Church's Faith* (Grand Rapids: Eerdmans, 1988) 205-09.
350 Thielman, "The Coherence of Paul's View of the Law," 245-48.
351 Bruce, *1 and 2 Corinthians*, 87, thinks that the νόμος here is the Jewish law which comprises the 613 written precepts and their oral amplification.

them that although the law is no longer important in his eyes, he still became 'as one under the law' when he was dealing with or bringing the gospel to those under the law, in order to win those under the law. He wants to show his readers an example of one acting contrary to what is right in one's mind. He wishes to help them realize that although their refusal to forgo their right to eat food offered to idols for the sake of the weak means acting against their cherished freedom status, it does not mean that they are not free. Just as Paul's becoming 'as under the law' required courage on his part, for by so doing he acted as if he was not free from the law, so will their willingness to accommodate the scruple of the weak and refrain from exercising their right to eat food offered to idols, for by so doing they would act as if they were not free from the scruple of the weak and acted against their freedom status.

Thirdly, when describing his becoming ὡς ἄνομος to τοῖς ἀνόμοις Paul quickly qualifies it with μὴ ἄνομος θεοῦ. Not only that, and unlike his qualification of his becoming ὡς ὑπὸ νόμον 9:20b), Paul moreover adds ἀλλ᾽ ἔννομος Χριστοῦ. Not insignificantly, he uses κερδαίνω rather than κερδήσω in 9:20 and 9:22a. According to Paul, the fact that he became as one of those without the law does not mean that he is without the law of God. On the contrary, it means that he is in or within the law of Christ. Those whose background was without the law would have no difficulty in remembering this action in Paul's missionary activity among them.

It is important to ask why Paul inserts θεοῦ in 9:21. He could have simply said μὴ ὢν ἄνομος, just like in 9:20b where he only says μὴ ὢν ἄνομος. The answer may be found in the fact that Paul is here talking about his becoming as the radical opposite of those under the law. 'Those without the law' is a terminus technicus for people who were not like 'those under the law,' that is to say, those who were not living according to 'the law.' Their identities were not determined by their ethnicity. According to Clarence E. Glad, the term ἄνομος and its cognates in Jewish literature before A.D. 70 mean 'evil,' 'wicked,' 'sinful' and do not refer to Gentiles but Jews or the wicked in general.[352] Since those under the law considered themselves to be acting according to what God willed, those without the law were certainly seen as acting against God.

And so, when he became as 'those without the law' Paul would logically have been seen by 'those under the law' as acting against God. This is what he wants his readers to know. But he also wants them to know that such was not the case. Although he did not live under the precepts of the Torah, he was not without the law of God. To him, the law of God is not to be restricted to what those under the law see as the law of God, namely the Torah. Even though he acted not as the Torah demanded, what he did was not without the law of God. He did it 'in or by the law' (ἔννομος) of Christ.

---

352 Glad, *Paul and Philodemus*, 257.

Dodd captures this thought well when he writes: "At one stage and on one level this law of God is represented by the Torah, and on that level a man's response to the Torah is, quite genuinely, a response to the law of God...At another stage and upon a different level the law of God may be mediated in some other, perhaps some more adequate form, in which it may be obeyed by one who is no longer subject to Torah."[353] My only reservation about Dodd's position is his assumption that Paul is facing his opponents. Hence with an offensive tone, Dodd paraphrases Paul's message: "you are assuming an unwarranted identity of the Torah with the ultimate law of God. A man may be free from Torah and yet be loyal to the law of God, as it is represented or expressed in the law of Christ."[354] There is no need to see Paul's statement as a counter argument against his opponents. Rather, his qualification 'μὴ ὢν ἄνομος θεοῦ' is intended to encourage his readers to embrace the idea that even though their willingness to refrain from eating food offered to idols contradicts their freedom, it does not mean that they are acting against God. Rather, it benefits the weak and fulfils the law of Christ.

Paul does not feel the need to elaborate what he means by the law of Christ. The cotext shows that it refers to the act of becoming as others in order to save them. But some scholars want to be more specific than that. For instance, it is seen by Dodd as "the precepts which Jesus Christ was believed to have given to his disciples,"[355] a view which is rejected by some simply because it is too restrictive.[356] Gardner refers it to a broad sense, namely the obedience to Christ in preaching the gospel as a necessity. This obedience is evidenced in love.[357] But what R.B. Hays thinks is more likely to be the case. He rightly points out that the law of Christ does not refer to a new legal code. To Paul "the pattern of Christ's self-sacrificial death on a cross has now become the normative pattern for his own existence."[358]

In view of the likelihood that his intended audience, those who want to eat food offered to idols, might have known that the strong opposition by the Jews in the *diaspora* (non-Christian and Christians alike) against Paul was mainly caused by his liberal assimilation to cultural practices of the people other than that of the Jews (those under the law),[359] his speech of his

---

353 Dodd, "Ἔννομος Χριστοῦ," 137.
354 Dodd, "Ἔννομος Χριστοῦ, 353.
355 Dodd, "Ἔννομος Χριστοῦ, 138.
356 Conzelmann, *First Epistle*, 161 n. 27; Fee, *The First Epistle*, 430 n. 44.
357 Gardner, *The Gift of God*, 102-03.
358 Hays, *1 Corinthians*, 154.
359 J.M.S. Barclay, "Paul among Diaspora Jews: Anomaly or Apostate?" in *JSNT* 60 (1995) 89-120, esp. 104, argues that Paul's "tactical abandonment of key Jewish practices in the course of his mission, and his particularly close associations with Gentile believers, made him dangerously assimilated in the eyes of many...The intimate associations which Paul enjoyed with Gentiles who were not, in Jewish

becoming as 'those without the law' must have sent a strong message. He had to do it to win those outside the law. He is telling them that even though the Jews opposed him for doing so, he did it none the less because in so doing he did not become as outside the law "of God." On the contrary, it was done under "the law of Christ." This message is very compelling to those who are afraid that by accommodating the view of the weak they act against God. Paul tells them: that is not the case! On the contrary, they act according to the law of Christ.

Fourthly, in describing his identification or accommodation with the weak in verse 22a Paul significantly omits the ὡς which he uses consistently in verses 20-21, despite the attempts by some scribes to insert a ὡς.[360] This is more than just a stylistic repetition as suggested by G.D. Fee,[361] and should not prevent us from seeing its significance.[362] Paul never put himself under the law nor broke the law of God and of Christ in his 'becoming' as a Jew and as those under and without the law. But to the weak he *became* "not *as*" but "*weak.*" Here, there was no need for μὴ ὤν. Greek speaking audiences could not have missed the absence of ὡς and μὴ ὤν, and in the light of 1 Corinthians 8:9 Paul's reference to his becoming weak in the past must have been well understood. Victor P. Furnish rightly says that verse 22a "seems both out of place...and unneeded...With its addition, however, Paul has gotten to the point of his whole chapter: that the Corinthians should find in his conduct an example for their own (note 8:13). Instead of disdaining or remaining indifferent to the weak, they are to accept them as sisters and brothers in Christ, even when that means giving up the right they have, in principle, to eat any kind of meat."[363]

It is not yet clear, however, who were the 'weak' to whom Paul became weak. What kind of 'weak' does he mean by 'weak' in 9:22a? Does Paul have in mind the weak in conscience[364] (8:7, 9-11 cf. 10:28b-29a) because

---

terms, law-observant set him high on the scale, not indeed fully assimilated, but certainly higher than Philo." Moreover, he states: "Paul's preaching of the crucified Christ clearly caused offence (1 Cor. 1.23), but other Christian Jews who did the same seem to have run into fewer problems. Perhaps Paul's social practices made explicit the potential of this message to question the validity of the law (Gal. 2.19; 3.13; 5.15)" (112).

360 Thus Malherbe, "Determinism and Free Will," 252. It is noteworthy that although some manuscripts such as ἀ C D F G ψ include ὡς, the omission of ὡς is strongly supported by older texts such as P46.

361 Fee, *First Epistle*, 430 n.46

362 Pace Barrett, *The First Epistle*, 215, warns against any attempt to overemphasize this omission of ὡς by Paul.

363 Furnish, "Belonging to Christ," 155.

364 There is a considerable debate on the meaning of συνείδησις. See C.A. Pierce, *Conscience in the New Testament* (London: SCM Press, 1955) 42-43, who says that "it is not concerned with the acts, attitudes or characters of others." But it is

throughout his discourse in 1 Corinthians 8:1 - 11:1 he is concerned about the weak in this sense,[365] covering both the weak or superstitious believers and unconverted Jews and Gentiles?[366] Or rather, does it refer to the weak in a social sense (1 Cor. 1:27, 4:10)[367] and in a physical sense (1 Cor. 2:3) because there is nothing to fear on the part of Paul in this sense, as there is in his 'becoming as' under the law and outside the law (9:20-21)? The ambiguity of the case causes G.D. Fee not to opt for one or the other, but resorts to a general meaning which, he argues, is provided by 9:22b.[368]

If the former is the case and given that κερδαίνω is a technical missionary term which means 'to win an unbeliever to your faith,'[369] it implies that Paul ate food offered to idols when he preached the gospel to the Corinthians. If this was the case, however, we would expect him to use ὡς and μὴ ὤν in 9:22a because he has some reservations about the claim of the existence of idols (see 1 Cor. 8:4-6, 10:20) and calls for his readers to flee from idolatry (10:14).[370] In addition, given that the meaning of κερδαίνω includes winning back believers who have strayed away[371] and gaining converts, strengthening "their adherence to the community" and helping them "along the path to salvation,"[372] it is difficult for us to figure

---

concerned with past acts. M. Thrall, "The Pauline Use of συνείδησις" in *NTS* 14 (1967-68) 118-129, regards its functions like that of the Law for the Jews, a guidance for future and moral function. Horsley, "Consciousness and Freedom among the Corinthians: 1 Corinthians 8-10," 581, equates it with one's inner consciousness and awareness. P.W. Gooch, "'Conscience' in 1 Corinthians 8 and 10" in *NTS* 33 (1987) 250-51, differentiates the use of the word in 1 Corinthians 8 as a sense of self-awareness and in 1 Corinthians 10 as bad feelings.

365 Thus Dodd, "Ἔννομος Χριστοῦ," 134, for instance argues that the weak are non-Christians of Jewish religion who cherish similar scruples as that in 8:9-13. Also Thielmann, "Paul's View of the Law: 1 Corinthians," 244. To do so Thielman unjustifiably takes the ἐγενόμην of 9:22 to describe Paul's *present* ministry among the 'weak.' Ellison, "Paul and the Law," 196, argues that they are converts who adopted rigorous attitudes. They were Gentiles who, prior to becoming Christians, were trying to keep the Law without becoming proselytes. They adopted the views of Judaizers. Lenski, *The Interpretation,* 379, argues that the weak are Christians.

366 D.A. Black, "A Note on 'the Weak' in I Corinthians 9, 22" in *Bib* 64 (1983) 240-42, argues that it refers to a broad group of people who do not have the capacity or ability to work out any righteousness for themselves.

367 Cf. Sisson, *The Apostle As Athlete,* 168.

368 Fee, *The First Epistle,* 431.

369 See H. Schlier, "κέρδος, κερδαίνω" in G. Kittel (ed.),*Theological Dictionary of the New Testament* Vol III (Grand Rapids: Eerdmans, 1965) 672-73, esp. 673.

370 Tomson, *Paul,* 276.

371 Daube, *The New Testament and Rabbinic Judaism,* 359-61. Cf. earlier Meyer, *Epistles to the Corinthians,* 273.

372 Hays, *1 Corinthians,* 154-55. Apparently, Hays argues that both meanings are present. Morris, *The First Epistle,* 136. Also Blomberg, *1 Corinthians,* 184, goes

out when Paul ever had a chance of winning back the Corinthian Christians before the writing of 1 Corinthians.[373] If the identity of the weak in 9:22a is confined to that of 8:7-12, we would end up distinguishing Paul's weakness from that of his readers as suggested by Neller who argues that the weak of the former is "self-created because of spiritual maturity" but that of the latter is "due to a lack of knowledge and spiritual maturity."[374]

In becoming weak to the weak, there was nothing inherent in the weak which would cause a degree of hesitancy on the part of Paul. Unlike in his becoming as a Jew, under the law and outside the law, there is nothing here that would cause Paul to conduct a careful accommodation. This observation warns us against the danger of reading the 'weak' here similar to that of 8:9-12 even though Paul's purpose is to encourage some Corinthian Christians to care for the weak in that sense in their dispute over food offered to idols. We should also be wary of seeing Paul's aim here in the light of Theissen's characterising of the dispute as between the strong/rich and the weak/poor, which has been followed by D.B. Martin and D.G. Horrell, arguing that the reason Paul does not speak of his becoming the strong is precisely because it is the strong that Paul tries to persuade not to destroy the weak.[375]

It is more likely that in 9:22a Paul speaks of his becoming physically, socially and economically weak to win the weak in this sense (1:27, cf. 4:10). His weakness in this sense made him weak physically, a condition that caused him to experience living in fear and great trembling (2:3). This may be granted but none the less, the meaning of weak in this sense does not negate the likelihood that, even though Paul has in mind his past experience of becoming weak in a social and physical sense, he now wants his readers to draw a lesson from it for their immediate context of dealing with their brother who is weak in conscience in matters of food offered to idols.

---

so far as to see the parallelism between the groups mentioned in 9:20-22a with those in 10:32, thus saying that the winning is in the sense of "winning to a more mature form of Christian faith." Cf. also Gardner, *The Gifts of God,* 99, who argues that "κερδαίνω can be understood to refer *both* to initial entrance into the community (conversion), *and* to the continuing process of winning people from inadequate ideas to a deeper Christian consciousness."

373 Robertson and Plummer, *Critical Commentary,* 192, argues that it is the overscrupulous that Paul became as.
374 Neller, "1 Corinthians 9:19-23," 138-39, who goes so far as to say: "Perhaps it means not only to win one **outside** Christ **to** Christ and one who has **strayed from** Christ **back to**, Christ, but also to win one **in** Christ (nominally) to a closer walk with Christ"; cf. D.A. Black, "A note on 'the Weak,'" 240-42.
375 D.B. Martin, *Slavery As Salvation,* 123; Horrell, *Social Ethos,* 209, 216.

3.3.5 Historical Reconstruction of Paul's Accommodation in Corinth

Having analyzed Paul's various acts of 'becoming as,' our task now is to reconstruct their historical contexts when Paul was in Corinth. This reconstruction is important for our desire to know the strength of Paul's intended message. Much of our reconstruction depends on Acts which, apparently, is congruous with Paul's correspondence with Corinthian Christians (see e.g., Acts 18:3 and 1 Cor. 4:12, 9:5, 18b, 2 Cor. 11:7, 27).

Before preaching to the Gentiles Paul preached first to the Jews in the synagogue (Acts 18:4; 1 Cor. 1:14). Paul could have had in mind his experience of preaching to the Jews and his living with them. To them Paul became as a Jew. By way of outward appearance, he would have appeared in the synagogue as a Jew (1 Cor. 9:20a). Moreover, he would have behaved as under the law to those who lived under the law (1 Cor. 9:20b). This must not be limited to Paul's experience in the Jewish synagogue alone where he preached. It must include the very way of life of the Jews which he practiced during his stay in Corinth. While staying in the house of Prisca and Aquila (Acts 18:2-3) and preaching in the synagogue (Acts 18:4) he could have practiced Jewish customs in his social relationship with them. According to Acts 18:18 before leaving Corinth Paul in fact cut his hair because he had made a vow. Similarly, after being rejected by the Jews (Acts 18:6; 1 Cor. 1:22) he preached in the houses of Titius Justus and Gaius (Acts 18:7 and Rom. 16:23 cf. 1 Cor. 1:14). While preaching to them, Paul would have lived according to their customs which might not have been controlled by the law of the Jews (1 Cor. 9:21). They lived according to their own customs. In a city where transparency was very strong, what Paul did while among those outside the law must have been watched by the Jews and those under the law of the city. To the *diaspora* Jews of Corinth who, like other Jews in other cities in the *diaspora*, regarded their Jewishness and lawfulness very strongly, the very activity of Paul among those outside the law must have been shocking. And it was not without risk. Based on the report of Acts, the pressure from the Jews of the city was such that a united attack was launched against him by the Jews who brought him before the tribunal, accusing him of "persuading men to worship God *contrary to the law*" (Acts 18:13).

To those without the law, what Paul did among them must have been seen as something very radical. They must have witnessed in Corinth how the Jews drew a clear line in their relationship with the rest of the population, socially and religiously. Their awareness of the radicality of Paul's action during 18 months of his stay in Corinth could also have been precipitated by their knowledge of how Paul had mingled previously with the Jews of the city.[376] And so, when Paul speaks of his past experience now, he is consciously trying to invite the Corinthians to learn from his past actions among them. The principle he kept in living and associating with them was the law of Christ, namely "love" which allowed, or rather, encouraged him to relate to those without the law without first of all considering their ethnic or religious backgrounds and which, in his eyes, never violated but in fact fulfilled the law of God. Unlike other Jews living outside the law of Christ, Paul did not have any obstacle in relating to the non-Jews. The law of Christ (1 Cor. 9:21) determined his living with the Corinthians. But he did it all to win them to Christ. Then from Titius Justus' and Gaius', and probably their colleagues' houses, Paul advanced his preaching to the weak (1 Cor. 9:22a), those in the city and perhaps also in the outskirts of the city (cf. his address in 2 Corinthians 1:1: to all the saints in the region of Achaia), to those economically and socially weak people. To them Paul became not as a weak person but weak. He really became weak in his life. He did not just identify or sympathize with the weak, but really became weak even though he was from a high status by virtue of his status as an apostle. His physical condition was probably weak because he worked to support his mission (1 Cor. 2:3). He endured anything (1 Cor. 9:12b). It was the only way that he could reach, win and save some of the weak (1 Cor. 1:27-28). What he did to the weak was more than just an act of *solidarity*[377] as such, or accommodation with the style of living of the weak, but he *became one of them* in order to bring the gospel to them. Perhaps, Paul's action in becoming weak was as real as Jesus' becoming flesh to save mankind. Paul imitated it from Christ himself (cf. 11:1 and Phil. 2).

We can infer therefore that at some point in Corinth Paul became weak economically by working as a tent-maker in Corinth to win those who were socially and economically weak. In fact at the time of the writing of 1 Corinthians Paul was still weak and the Corinthians had become strong (cf. 4:10). He was still working with his hands in Ephesus (4:12a, cf. Acts 20:34). Similarly, in his preaching as a whole Paul was in 'weakness,' 'fear,' and 'trembling.' This physical, psychological and emotional state of appearance was made clear in his method of speech, namely 'not in plausible words of wisdom' (2:3-4). Both the weak and the strong (1 Cor. 1:26) accepted his gospel, despite his weak appearance. Perhaps, it was precisely his weak appearance that appealed to the weak. When Paul was among them most of them were weak (1 Cor. 1:26-27). By reminding them now of what he did to them while in Corinth when they were weak, Paul

---

376 Barton's view (see "Was Paul a Relativist?," 167) that Paul has in mind here Jewish Christians who still observed the law of Moses is not supported by the purpose of Paul's accommodation, namely to win those outside the law.

377 Thus Bornkamm, "Missionary Stance," 202-03.

expects them to do the same to their weak-conscienced brother in the issue of εἰδωλοθύτων.³⁷⁸ The principle is becoming weak. But the form it takes is different. The Corinthians are now asked to accommodate their weak-conscienced brothers. Paul became weak to the weak in Corinthian society when he was in Corinth. Though he became weak among them they received his gospel. They were saved. The principle with which they can now do what Paul did to them is to be under the law of Christ. If they do it, they will reverse the negative effect of insisting on using their 'right' to eat food offered to idols (i.e., destroying their weak brother, see 1 Cor. 8:11-12). In this sense, D.A. Black's attempt to spiritualize the text and Hurd's suggestion that it is a hypothetical sentence³⁷⁹ as well as Malherbe's attempt to see the word in the light of the moral philosophers' description of some people as weak,³⁸⁰ do not do justice either to the text and or to Paul's historical activity in Corinth.³⁸¹

The form of Paul's accommodating experience is different from that which he expects his readers to do. But the principle is the same. His accommodating experience is in his apostolic ministry of preaching the gospel among the people. He is not calling his readers to imitate the details of his experience. Rather, he is calling them to imitate the spirit that enabled him to carry out his accommodating praxis. He is calling them to do it to their weak conscienced brother whose view they cannot accept and whom they are likely to harm should they insist on their right to eat food offered to idols. It is in this light that we can see the relevance of Paul's closing and yet emphatic statement in 1 Corinthians 9:22b-23: "I have become all things to all, that I might by all means save some. I do it all for the sake of the gospel, that I may become a sharer of its blessings."

Therefore I submit that, so far as the Corinthian Christians are concerned, Paul's language in 9:19-23 is best understood in the context of Paul's initial missionary activity in Corinth. This is confirmed by the use of ἐγενόμην. One may want to read this in the wider context of his apostolic practice and point to Paul's chameleon behavior. This is made possible by 9:19 and 9:22b-23 where Paul uses ἐδούλωσα and γέγονα respectively, as well as by 9:12b and 9:15a where ἐρχησάμεθα and κέχρημαι are used,

---

378 Fee, *The First Epistle,* 431, sees the act of becoming weak as being done by Paul to the Corinthians not before but after they became Christians.
379 Hurd, *The Origins,* 125.
380 Malherbe, "Determinism and Free Will," 233 n. 4 who argues that Paul's argument has in view "matters cognitive rather than social." Philosophers of all sorts "described certain persons as morally and intellectually weak." Again he says: "The weak were generally identified as people who found it difficult to live up to the demands of the virtuous life. Weakness was frequently described as a condition that accompanies moral illness and as a condition or disposition of the self-indulgent (Diogenes Laertius 7.115; Cicero, *Tusc. Disp.* 4.29, 42)." (234).
381 Black, "A Note on 'the Weak,'" 240-242.

covering his whole mission activities up to the time when 1 Corinthians was written from Ephesus. The fact that in his treatment Paul allows his apostolic example to be seen beyond the context of Corinth, explains why, as reported by Acts 21:17-26, Paul permitted Timothy to be circumcised, why he was willing to undertake Jewish rituals just before he was arrested (Acts 21:17-26), and why, according to Galatians 2:11-14, he criticizes the inconsistency of Peter on the matter of eating with the Gentiles. Nevertheless, so far as his purpose of encouraging his readers not to be too worried about their freedom status is concerned, it is more likely that Paul would have in mind his past experiences of accommodating to the position of others which were known to his readers, namely those he carried out in Corinth itself.

We may conclude that Paul's paradigm of not exercising his right in the free-of-charge preaching of the gospel has been supported by another paradigm of self-enslavement and acts of 'becoming as, but not as' (Jews, those under the law and those without the law) and 'becoming weak.' But all these paradigms are designed to address the insistence on the part of some Corinthian Christians to exercise their 'right' and their justification of it by theological knowledge, freedom status and aphoristic saying that 'everything is permitted.'

3.4 The Third Paradigm: The Importance of Self-control (1 Corinthians 9:24-27)

Paul knows that the things he has exhorted in 8:1 (love) and 8:9-9:23 (renunciation of his right for the sake of the gospel and his self-enslavement in order to win or save the more) are by no means easy to undertake either by Paul himself or by the Corinthians. He is a realistic apostle. It is possible that there may be some people who are being complacent[382] about the danger of idolatry because of their belief that their initiation by Christ's sacrament enables them to be immune to all powers,[383] or some who shrug off any fear of the danger of idolatry because of their wish to be in touch with their pagan friends. However, Paul's motivation here is caused more by his awareness of the difficulty faced by his readers in carrying out what he has exhorted earlier, especially because of their theologically legitimate arguments and understandable social reasons, than by his suspicion that they will still be complacent. It is motivated by his desire to help them to carry out his exhortation. To this end, from 1 Corinthians 9:24 following we see Paul speaking not only of the eschatological loss (9:24-27), but also of the present negative consequence to be experienced by those who ignore

---

382 Lawson, *First Corinthians 9:24-10:22*, 106, 119, 143-144.
383 As suggested by H.F. von Soden, "Sacrament and Ethics in Paul" in W.A. Meeks (ed.), *The Writings of St. Paul* (New York: W.W. Norton, 1972) 261.

the danger of idolatry (10:1-22).[384] In 1 Corinthians 9:24-27 he speaks of a point with which he can (a) encourage his church members to carry out his exhortation (vv. 24-25) and (b) express how he himself does it (vv. 26-27).

In verse 24a he directs their attention to what was common to the people of the time.[385] None of them would have been ignorant of the Isthmian games, for instance, in which the competition was intense and the prize was only granted to a sole victor. Paul writes to them: "Do you not know[386] that in a stadium all runners run, but only one receives the prize?" Following this, he admonishes them to do what he has mentioned in 8:9 - 9:23. Speaking in athletic terms he pushes them to do so. He writes: "οὕτως τρέχετε ἵνα καταλάβητε" (likewise run that you obtain).

Even though Paul speaks in athletic terms, his readers will have known that he is not asking them to run literally in athletic contests in the city, but he is speaking about something else: doing what he has thus far exhorted them to do. He is pushing them to do it. The danger of reading verse 24b as encouraging Christians to do rigorous bodily exercise to obtain salvation has caused V.C. Pfitzner to read τρέχετε not as a present active imperative but as an indicative. The argument he uses to support this is that no

---

384 I agree with the view of Jerry L. Sumney, "The Place of 1 Corinthians 9:24-27 in Paul's Argument" in *JBL* 119 (2000) 329-33, that sees 9:24-27 as an introduction to stories in chapter 10, rather than conclusion to 9:1-23. But it has to be said that its role to strengthen 9:1-23 should not be overlooked.

385 As the fame of the Isthmian Games was widespread in the era, it is not necessary for us to decide whether or not Paul might have witnessed the games while he was in Corinth. Some have suggested that Paul's successful strategy of depending on his manual work in order to carry out his mission without any hindrance might have been related to the need of the games' spectator to have tents. He could have known it without having to go to the sites of the games. The Corinthians were host to the Isthmian Games held at a distance of 7 miles from Corinth, at the sanctuary of Poseidon at Isthmia. Cf. O. Broneer, "The Apostle Paul and the Isthmian Games" in *BA* 25 (1962) 2-31, here 5 and 20, conjectures that since Paul abode in Corinth for 18 months (Acts 18:11) during Gallio's proconsulship Paul might have been in Corinth when the spring AD 51 Games were held and had ample opportunity to carry out his tent-making activity and share the gospel to the crowds attending the games. In fact, O. Broneer in his later essay, "Paul and the Pagan Cults at Isthmia" in *HTR* 64 (1971) 169-87, see esp. 169-70,187, argues that Paul's choice of Corinth as the chief base of his missionary work in Greece was due to the importance of the biennial Isthmian festival. This gave Paul ample opportunity to be familiar not only with the pagan rites integral to the festival but also to know the spirit of the game itself. Murphy – O'Connor, *St. Paul's Corinth*, 17, speculates that Paul himself may have attended the games, especially as Paul's self-made tents might have been sold to the visitors.

386 Wuellner, "Paul as Pastor: the function of Rhetorical Questions in First Corinthians," 60, argues that the formula "Do you not know" functions to increase adherence to what is already accepted.

individual part of the image can be given any weight in the argument. To him, the images used in verse 24 are supportive of that in verse 25, namely the idea of 'self-restriction' (ἐγκρατεύεται).[387] This central thought takes up the catchword mentioned in verses 12b,18,19,20-22b, and 23 and "provides an illustration of the Apostle's principle: everything for the sake of the Gospel - including the right use of his liberty in the renunciation of his rights."[388] Fee and Conzelmann disagree, and rightly so. Although sharing Pfitzner's rejection of using the passage to propagate the idea of asceticism, Fee reads verse 24 as imperative. In fact, he considers verse 24 as the center point of the whole paragraph.[389]

To push them further, Paul adds another example from the practice of athletes long before the competition begins and the reward for it (v. 25). For this he speaks of the importance of every athlete πάντα ἐγκρατεύεται (exercising self-control in all things) and of the sole purpose of such an action, namely 'in order to receive φθαρτὸν στέφανον (a perishable wreath).' It is important to note that Paul carries on without repeating here as he does in verse 24 (τρέχοντες...τρέχετε) the verb ἐγκρατεύεται or the noun στέφανον. Rather, he goes on with ἡμεῖς δὲ ἄφθαρτον (but we an imperishable). This means that by implication Paul expects his readers to exercise self-restriction or self-control, as every athlete does even though he does not use the imperative here. The thought of the imperishable would certainly have guided those he expects to forgo their right to eat food offered to idols to think of what they are admonished to do as more important than the perishable wreath for which the exercise of self-control in all things by the athletes is rewarded. Paul expects them to grasp the intended meaning: if every athlete has to exercise self-control in 'all things' for the perishable wreath, how much more should those who expect to obtain the imperishable wreath. Moreover, given the fact that exercising their right to eat food offered to idols must have been a desirable thing to do and the thought of forgoing it would be seen as creating a real disadvantage, Paul's choice of every athlete practicing self-control would have been very striking in terms of encouraging them to forgo their right. Everyone of them would have been aware of the fact that exercising 'self-control in all things' was demanding, but Paul wants them to embrace the idea that receiving the imperishable wreath was even more rewarding.[390] This really reveals Paul's

---

387 V.C. Pfitzner, *Paul and the Agon Motif. Traditional Athletic Imagery in the Pauline Literature* (Leiden: E.J. Brill, 1967) 85-87.
388 Pfitzner, *Paul and the Agon Motif*, 87-88, esp. 88.
389 Fee, *First Epistle*, 435-36, esp. 436 n.13; Conzelmann, *First Epistle*, 162. n. 35; Lawson, *First Corinthians 9:24-10.22*, 116.
390 In view of the fact that from the early times (c. 473 BC) the prize given to the victors of the Isthmian Games was a wreath of withered celery rather than a fresh celery wreaths granted to the victors of the Nemean Games, Paul's contrasting the

genius in trying to win his readers over to carry out his exhortation. *The testing ground of this imperishable wreath in the context of 1 Corinthians 8:1 - 11:1 is no other than the attitude toward the weak-conscienced brother. No one who destroys a brother for whom Christ died, and thereby sins against Christ, will ever obtain the imperishable wreath. So important is the avoidance of destroying one's weak brother to Paul that he is prepared to indicate in 9:24-25 that the obtaining of the imperishable wreath is not to be dissociated from the treatment of the weak brother.*

In verses 26-27 Paul tries to help his readers to understand his point by speaking about himself. Still using athletic terms he seems to be saying that what he has done is not without a purpose. In verse 26, he quite clearly says in a negative sense: "Well, I do not run *aimlessly*, I do not box *as one beating the air*" and he carries on in verse 27 with a positive sense, contradicting verse 26 "but I pommel my body and subdue it, lest after preaching to others, I myself will be disqualified." This must be another way of saying ἐγκρατεύεται (verse 25). Athletes would do such kind of activities (pommelling and subduing the body) to avoid being disqualified. Disqualification was dreaded by every athlete. The idea of failure before starting the contest was the reason why 'self control in all things' had to be undertaken seriously. Paul is speaking metaphorically. He is trying to prevent his readers from doing things at present which will lead them to being disqualified. In the context of the immediate discussion this would be the case if they carried on exercising their right to eat food offered to idols. In fact he uses ἀδόκιμος and κηρύξας. Both would have reminded them of the role of the herald at the public athletic games. The herald called out the athletes before the competition began, announcing the laws or rules of the games which were used to determine the qualification of the competitors. Unlike the herald who did not qualify for the competition, Paul does not want to be disqualified. Hence his apostolic practice of forgoing his right and enslaving himself for the sake of the gospel that he might share in it (9:23).

It is not necessary in this regard to infer as Pfitzner does that Paul does not have the meaning of the traditional setting of the games here in verse 27. According to Pfitzner, Paul changes it to the theological context of his preaching of the gospel[391] because when the *agon* motif was used in a different context, namely out of the public games, the meaning could change from competition and the show of strength to a new context in which the motif was used. Hence he writes: "wherever these terms are to be

---

'perishable' and the 'imperishable' prize must have been well understood by the Corinthians. This is noted by Mark Harding, "Church and Gentile Cults at Corinth" in *GTJ* 10 (1989) 203-23, who reads O. Broneer, "Paul and the Pagan Cults at Isthmia," 186.

391 Pfitzner, *Paul and the Agon Motif*, 92-96.

found isolated and outside of complexes where the occurrence of other terms clearly suggest the athletic image, it is quite possible that the original reference to the games has been lost."[392] However, it must be said that the terms used in verses 24-27 would not have failed to direct the attention of his readers to the athletic context with which they were all very familiar. Their familiarity with the things of the games would have helped them to perceive Paul's intended meaning. Paul uses the language of his readers to assist him in conveying his message.

It is not clear whether Paul's disqualification is that from salvation or from the ministry of apostleship. Judith M. Gundry Volf rightly argues for the latter.[393] Indeed, 9:18 and 23 seems to support this, especially in view of the fact that his apostleship is being examined (9:1-3). Likewise, for the Corinthians to do what Paul has exhorted in 1 Corinthians 8:9-9:23 will not only prevent them from harming their weak conscienced brother and destroying themselves (10:1-22), but it will also prevent them from being disqualified from obtaining the imperishable wreath. *The imperishable prize will not be won by those who, because of eating food offered to idols, injure the weak brother and thereby sin against Christ (8:10-12).* Paul would not have gone so far as to argue this were it not because of his strong desire to prevent them from eating food offered to idols and destroying the weak. It is in this light that Paul's next discourse in chapter 10:1-22 is needed to make them aware of the present danger that exists in participating in idolatry and immorality which will not just disqualify them from gaining the imperishable wreath, but will also provoke God to anger, something which the Israelites' indulgence in immorality did in the past, causing twenty-three thousand people to fall in a single day (10:8).

3.5. Concluding Remarks

In line with what we have concluded in chapter 2 above, we have argued in our interpretation of 1 Corinthians 9 that this chapter is better read as part and parcel of a unified attempt on the part of Paul to convince some of his readers of the importance of abandoning their insistence on exercising their right to eat food offered to idols and, in relation to it, of not being afraid of losing the ground upon which their right is based, namely their freedom status. Our interpretation of 1 Corinthian 9 has come up with the following observations.

Firstly, we have seen that the reason for Paul's having to defend his apostolic status in 1 Corinthians 9:1-3 is precisely that the strength of his apostolic practices described in 9:4-27 depends on it. *Secondly,* we have

---

392 Pfitzner, *Paul and the Agon* Motif, 6-7, here 6.
393 Judith M. Gundry Volf, *Paul and Perseverance: Staying in and falling away* (Tübingen: Mohr, 1990) 233-47, esp. 247.

also suggested that the reason for Paul to speak of his rights to be supported financially in such a comprehensive argument in 9:4-12a, 13-14 and in a language well understood by his readers, only to be juxtaposed with their renunciation in 9:12b and 15-18, is precisely because of his acknowledgement of the legality of their right. The centrality of this right is such that various arguments (i.e., knowledge of God's existence, idol's non-existence, of the neutrality of food before God, freedom status and the aphoristic saying that 'everything is permitted') are garnered by some Corinthian Christians in order to justify not only their insistence on exercising it, but also to express their reluctance to forgo it. Hence, we have also suggested that the high regard for the rights of Roman citizens during the reign of Claudius may be considered as a contributory factor to such an insistence. This right is not as specific as that suggested by Bruce W. Winter (i.e., the right to be invited by the president of the Isthmian Games to a banquet), but a more general one, that which came intrinsically with Roman citizenship status.

In response, Paul argues that just as their right to eat food offered to idols is legitimate, so is his right to financial support. Paul does not fall short of saying, however, that he expects them to know that just as he forgoes his right to financial support to the point that he is willing to act against the command of the Lord (9:14), an action which has been used by some to examine his apostolic status, so are they to forgo their right to eat food offered to idols even though by so doing they would be seen to be acting against their right. Just as Paul's renunciation of his right has been to avoid being a stumbling block to the way of the gospel, so will their forgoing of their right to eat food offered to idols prevent them from being a stumbling block to their weak conscienced brothers.

Thirdly, Paul's desire for them to forgo their right is described in 1 Corinthians 9:12b and 15-18 where he makes it very clear that he would rather die than receive financial support. In fact, he even goes so far as to say that his endurance caused by his refusal to financial support is something about which he boasts, and that he does not allow anyone to empty him of this boasting. Moreover, the likelihood of him receiving pay from his preaching of the gospel is alleviated by speaking in 9:16-18 of his preaching as a necessity and, therefore, that which deserves no pay. Paul would not have spoken such very strong language, were it not because of his desire to prevent some Corinthian Christians from exercising their right to eat food offered to idols.

Fourthly, our close investigation of 1 Corinthian 9 has enabled us to propose that the reason for Paul to consider receiving financial support as constituting an ἐγκοπή to the gospel is not because of his desire to distance himself from the other missionaries or philosophers, or to be independent of the Corinthian Christians themselves, as has been argued by many recent scholars, but basically because of his own perception of the gospel of Christ crucified itself which he preaches free of charge (9:18). This is what caused him to endure hardship. Given that some people have already criticized his apostolic status because of his refusal to accept financial support, it is understandable that Paul boasts about his refusal to receive support and about his endurance therein. In other words, he is attempting to bring about a paradigm shift.

Fifthly, even though 1 Corinthians 9 is meant primarily as an example, it is however not difficult to imagine that - upon reading 1 Corinthians 9 - the other missionaries would see Paul's discourse on the importance of the renunciation of his right to win many as an attack against them and against their practice, even though there is no indication whatsoever in 1 Corinthians 9 that Paul repudiates their practice. Hence, it would also be natural that, as is shown in 2 Corinthians, these missionaries intensified their criticism of Paul, and to Paul's surprise, they managed to convince the Corinthian Christians of the legality of their position, probably partly because of their refusal to heed Paul's exhortation. Although in 1 Corinthians 9 Paul does not attack them, in 2 Corinthians such will no longer be the case. An attack on them will be necessary as his apostolic authority will be at stake.

Next, we have also established that the best way of reading 1 Corinthians 9:19-23 is to see it as an attempt on the part of Paul to address the Corinthian Christians' reluctance to downgrade their freedom status and their belief in the aphoristic saying that 'everything is permitted.' They argue that both are downgraded if they cannot exercise their right to eat food offered to idols. We can paraphrase their reluctance with the following: "What's the point of being free if exercising our right to eat food offered to idols, one which has valid theological grounds and sits well with the importance of our rights as Roman citizens, is being curbed?" It is in this light that we have argued that Paul's elaboration of his self-enslavement (9:20-22a) should not be seen as hyperbolic or the like, but as being derived from historical praxis. Paul's accommodation is meant to convince his readers in such a way that they would be willing to set aside this freedom which constitutes one of the arguments they use to justify their right to eat food offered to idols. Instead, they are asked to prioritize the interest of their weak conscienced brother whose opinion on the issue of food offered to idols they do not share.

He became as a Jew even though he no longer saw himself as being controlled by his Jewishness. He became as under the law, even though he was no longer under the law. He became as without the law, yet in so doing he did not act against God. Rather, he acted within the law of Christ. Lastly, he became weak to the weak. All these accommodating experiences were aimed at winning more. In other words, Paul could still win over and save people even without enslaving himself. But he would win even more when he enslaved himself. In terms of encouraging his readers to be willing to forgo their right to eat food offered to idols and thereby act against their freedom status, as if they were not free from the scruple of the weak, such a language is very compelling indeed. It is in this sense that we can substantiate our view that 1 Corinthians 9:19-23 is more and primarily an example to be imitated by some Corinthian Christians than a defence against those alleged to have criticized his changeable behaviour.

Lastly, Paul realizes that his exhortations in 8:9 - 9:23 are difficult to carry out. It can only be done with the aid of self-control. Hence, we have argued that Paul's elaboration on self-control in 9:24-27 is motivated more by both his acknowledgement of the difficulty that would be faced by his readers in carrying out his exhortation and his desire to help them to overcome that difficulty, than by his suspicion of their hesitancy to carry out his exhortation, even though the latter is also possible. It is in this light that we can see why Paul is willing to introduce the idea of self-control which is linked to the eschatological wreath to the extent that many scholars have been led to conclude that he is propagating the idea of ascetism or rigorous work to achieve salvation, something which is not present in Paul's theology of salvation. Yet such a conclusion would not be reached if we took into account the fact that Paul has gone to that extent because of his desire to prevent some members of Corinthian church from destroying their weak conscienced fellows, and thereby sin against Christ, and from destroying themselves. All these negative effects will certainly occur if they insist on exercising their right to eat food offered to idols. *Apparently, for Paul, one's present and future salvation is not to be separated from one's action against one's own brother for whom Christ died even on the cultural issue of food offered to idols.* This must be known by those who insist on exercising their right to eat food offered to idols. This is what an apostle thinks he has to say in order to accomplish his goal of convincing those who want to eat food offered to idols on the basis of their right which is supported by sound theological and popular arguments related to idols and food offered to idols.

CHAPTER 4

Some Implications

Our exegesis of 1 Corinthians 9 in the context of Paul's discourse on the Corinthian dispute over food offered to idols has some major implications for Corinthian studies and for attempts to resolve conflict or dispute within the church today.

4.1 On the Emergence of the Dispute over εἰδωλοθύτων and the Unity of Paul's Discourse in 1 Corinthians 8:1 - 11:1

Although Winter once argued that "it is not possible to ascertain precisely why some Corinthian Christians wanted to eat food in the idol temple, for no clear indication is given from the text,"[1] our study of the context of the interpretation of 1 Corinthians 9 throws some light on our understanding of the emergence of the dispute over the issue of food offered to idols in the Corinthian church. We have been able to show that the answer to the question of why other churches founded by Paul and his colleagues did not face the same issue lies in the uniqueness of the Corinthian case.

We have argued that, judging from Paul's discourse, the issue of food offered to idols was a normal one for those coming from a Gentile background. This is clear from Paul's mention of the meat market as the place and the invitation of an unbeliever as the occasion where food related or sacrificed to idols is consumed. We have also suggested, however, that it was a cultural issue which imposed a strong social pressure on the Corinthian Christians to go along with what was popular in their society. The Corinthian dispute over the issue was exacerbated by the desire on the part of their contemporaries to seek the favour of the emperor, the imperial family and authorities toward their city by popularizing the Imperial Cult which was celebrated alongside the Isthmian Games and related to the formation of the Federal Imperial Cult in A.D. 54 when Nero became the emperor. It was during the worship of the imperial cult and the celebration of the Isthmian Games that food offered to idols was consumed. Were it not for this reason, it would be difficult to imagine why other churches founded by Paul and his colleagues did not face the same issue. As they came from a Gentile background, most early Christians would have dealt with the issue

---

[1] Bruce W. Winter, "Theological and Ethical Response to Religious Pluralism Corinthians 8 – 10" in *TynBul 41* (1990) 209-26, here 222.

of food offered to idols after their conversion. With the exception of Christians in Rome (see Rom. 14-15), what was faced by Corinthian Christians in relation to food offered to idols was unique. Some of them wanted to have a full engagement with whatever their contemporaries did with regard to the Imperial cult, but others refused to do so. Hence, they differed on the issue of food offered to idols.

Set within this context, we have also been able to suggest that the issue of ἐξουσία (right) was very central in Paul's treatment of the case not only because it was seen by some of his readers as having grounds in the valid knowledge of God's existence, non-existence of idols and of the neutrality of food before God, but also because of their desire to go along with the mood of their contemporaries to exercise their rights as Roman citizens. Indeed, their insistence on exercising their right to eat food offered to idols was harmonious with their freedom status and went along with their belief in the aphoristic saying that 'everything is permitted.'

What remains to be pursued by further research is the question of whether or not the weak (i.e., those who were likely to be influenced by others who insisted on their right to eat food offered to idols) were people who aligned with Paul, and those who wanted to exercise their right to eat food offered to idols were people who aligned with leading figures other than Paul. The following are some observations that have to be taken into account in pursuing this inquiry.

It is very tempting to argue, as Theissen and his followers have done, that those who wanted to eat food offered to idols were the rich and those who refused to eat it are the poor. However, as we have argued in chapter 2 above, it is unlikely that the dispute was between the rich and the poor. The weak could also have come from high status background. The issue was more religious than social. It is even more tempting to assume those who are encouraged by Paul not to eat food offered to idols to be the same as those who criticize him for failing to show eloquent wisdom (1:17 - 3:16) and return to Corinth (4:18-19). However, this is not likely because it is not possible to argue that those who align with Paul in 1 Corinthians 1:12 - 4:21 are poor and those who align with others are rich. There is reason to argue that those of whom Paul speaks favourably (see 1:14-16; 16:15-18) are likely to be people of some means. Both lenient and strict views on the issue could have been propagated by the leaders of the Corinthian church. Whether these leaders were the same as those who were involved in leadership alignment in 1:12 - 4:21 is difficult to determine.

What we can infer is that the issue of food offered to idols constituted one of the conditions of the Corinthian church which encouraged Paul at the beginning of his letter to call for their unity, including their unity of mind (1:10). Their internal conflict was such that not only was there a leadership alignment among them, but there also existed various views on the issue of food offered to idols and on other issues as found in 1 Corinthians 7:1 -

16:4. This indicates the complex nature of the conditions of the Corinthian church. Arguing for the existence of complexity and ambiguity of the issue, Derek Newton rightly emphasizes the social and spiritual variety of the Corinthian Christians.[2] The complexity "was further compounded by the wide range of personalities, positions and attitudes represented within that church at Corinth."[3] It may be argued that their leadership alignment might have affected or intensified their dispute over food offered to idols. However, we cannot ascertain whether there was a cause and effect relation between leadership alignment on the one hand, and the emergence and exacerbation of their dispute over issues as described in 1 Corinthians 7:1 - 16:4, on the other.

Hence, it can no longer be argued that on issues addressed in 1 Corinthians 7:1 - 16:4 Paul is responding to his opponents, as has long been suggested by the proponents of the quest for Paul's opponents in 1 Corinthians. In other words, Paul can no longer be held responsible for the Corinthian Christians' questioning of the issue of food offered to idols (1 Cor. 8:1), as suggested by Hurd, Fee, Gooch, Yamsat and Cheung. Nor can we argue that it is foreign teachings that are to blame for the emergence of the issue.

If the dispute among Corinthian Christians over an issue which was directly related to the social and political context of their city was not quickly solved, then the likelihood for them being divided along issue lines would have been very strong. It is in this light that in Paul's answer we see that he does not opt for 'right' or 'wrong' approach. Rather, he uses a method whereby he can lead his readers to choose an action which, though contrary to their legitimate arguments, is beneficial not only for their fellow Christians, but also for themselves.

In this light, we have been able to suggest that the intended message Paul conveyed to those who wanted to eat food offered to idols was that they should not eat it, neither because they had no reason to eat, nor because their reasons for eating it were illegitimate. Rather, in the context of their intense dispute, they had better not eat it because of the negative effect it would have on their counterparts, those who did not want to eat food offered to idols. In this sense, we have been able to see that Paul does not contradict himself in his discourse on food offered to idols (1 Cor. 8:1 - 11:1).

To achieve his goal of preventing some Corinthian Christians from eating food offered to idols and thereby destroying their weak-consciences brothers and themselves, Paul uses various arguments from chapter 8 through to 11:1. He begins by addressing their use of theological knowledge with 'love' (8:1-6,8). He then warns them not to be careless

---

2 Newton, "Food Offered to Idols," 284-285.
3 Newton, "Food Offered to Idols," 285.

with the use of their right to eat food offered to idols, lest they become a stumbling block to, and destroy their weak conscienced brother for whom Christ died (8:7, 9-12). This warning would have been seen by his readers as a clear indication that Paul, as rightly argued by Newton, "was not in fact happy for them to eat."[4] To support this, Paul argues that he himself would never eat meat if it was to cause his brother to fall (8:13). In order to strengthen this further, he uses his apostolic example of not exercising the apostolic right to financial support in order not to cause a stumbling block to the gospel of Jesus (8:4-18). This he does after defending his apostolic status which had been criticized by other missionaries because of his refusal to accept financial support (9:1-3). Moreover, to help his readers not to be too worried about acting against their freedom status and their belief in the aphoristic saying that 'everything is permitted,' Paul speaks of his past self-enslavement which he did in order to win more people. Aware of the difficulty faced by his readers in carrying out his exhortations to forgo their right and act against their freedom status in order to win the weak, Paul speaks of the importance of self control. He does so in a way that would give the impression to his readers that their failure to heed his exhortations would cost them their eternal prize or disqualify them from eschatological reward. In 10:1-22 and 10:13-14, 27-29a Paul continues his discourse by warning his readers of the danger of insisting on exercising their right. They would destroy themselves. Hence, they are asked to shun the worship of idols (10:14). Even in a context in which there is every reason for them to eat, namely at the invitation of an unbeliever, so long as the voice of the weak is made known, they should not eat food sacrificed to idols (10:27-29a).

Paul's concentration on preventing some of his readers from eating food offered to idols is done, however, not at the expense of acknowledging the position of those who want to have a total disengagement with the world because to them idols do exist. Hence in 8:6 he expresses his qualification of the existence of idols (8:5) and, by implication, denies their existence in 10:19. Moreover, in 10:25-26 and 29b-30 he gives strong reasons for rejecting any total disengagement with the world and the earth.

We would not have achieved this without our appreciation of the importance of 1 Corinthians 9 in the whole discourse. It is part of Paul's attempt to convince some of his readers of the need to care for the weak who are their counterparts in the dispute. Paul would neither have resorted to the use of his apostolic example of renouncing his right to financial support, especially as it had been examined by some missionaries and Corinthian Christians, were it not because of his realization of the importance of their right to eat food offered to idols. Nor would he have written about his self-enslavement, were it not because of his

---

4   Newton, "Food Offered to Idols," 288.

acknowledgement that by forgoing their right the Corinthian Christians would have acted against their freedom status and the aphoristic saying that 'everything is permitted.' He would not have presented to his readers the importance of self-control in a language familiar to them were it not because of his awareness that to imitate him in forgoing their right and accepting the position of the weak by not eating food offered to idols would have been very difficult to carry out in practice, given the strength of their reasons and the weight of the social and political nature of the issue. Nor would he have spoken of the eternal wreath to the extent that gives the impression that one's action to the weak conscienced brother would cause one's disqualification from obtaining the eternal wreath, were it not in order to provide the strongest warning against insistence to use their right to eat food offered to idols. Above all, Paul had to resort to what he described in 1 Corinthians 9 not because of the weak alone, but also because of his desire that those who wanted to eat should also be saved from the danger of falling into idolatry. This he did by speaking also of the benefit he gains for himself in waiving his right, enslaving himself, and exercising self-control. It is now high time to leave behind us all the controversies surrounding the unity of 1 Corinthians 8-10 and the view that Paul is inconsistent in 1 Corinthians 8:1-13, 10:23 - 11:1 and 10:1-22.

4.2 On the Question of Paul's Defence

Our study has also established that in order to make his use of the apostolic paradigm credible in the eyes of his readers, Paul has to defend his apostolic status which has been examined by some people because his apostolic practice itself is not in harmony with that of others. We have established that it was the other missionaries who initially questioned Paul's apostolic status. They did so because some Corinthian Christians asked them why, unlike Paul, they accepted financial support in Corinth and elsewhere. In the course of time and due to the existence of factionalism amongst Corinthian Christians, it was natural that some of the Corinthian Christians who aligned themselves with leading figures other than Paul made use of Paul's reluctance to accept financial support in order to undermine his apostleship and those who aligned with him.

We have also established that in his use of apostolic practice as a paradigm to be imitated by some Corinthian Christians in their dispute over food offered to idols (11:1), there is no indication that Paul refutes those who accept financial support. This is in spite of the fact that they were probably the initiators of the criticism of Paul's apostolic status. On the contrary, Paul uses the ground upon which their practice is based, namely the command of the Lord (9:14) as one of his arguments to legitimize his right to financial support.

None the less, we have also shown that the way Paul describes his reasons for refusing to accept financial support (9:12b, 15-18: that accepting financial support would create a stumbling block to the way of the gospel to such an extent that he would rather die than receive it, and that he considered it as his boasting which no one would empty him of) is prone to be seen differently by his initial examiners, the other missionaries. They perceived his answers as an attack on their practice of receiving financial support and, therefore, on their missionary status. It is in this light that we can see why later on, as is evident in 2 Corinthians, these missionaries intensified their attack on Paul's apostolic status. The implication is that, although we cannot determine their identity, those who examined Paul's apostolic status because of his practice of renouncing his right to financial support are the missionaries spoken of by Paul in 2 Corinthians 10-12.

Our exegesis on 1 Corinthians 9 has therefore enabled us to solve two problems. First, it enables us to see why Paul has to defend his apostolic status (9:1-3) before proceeding to describe his apostolic practices which, in the context of 1 Corinthians 8:1 - 11:1, are used to encourage some Corinthian Christians not to use their right to eat food offered to idols. Secondly, it enables us to see why in the first place some missionaries questioned Paul's apostolic status and continued to do so after the arrival of 1 Corinthians. In other words, it explains why 2 Corinthians 10-12 still deals with the same issue and why Paul is so strong in attacking them in 2 Corinthians. It follows that the view that no missionaries had been in Corinth before 1 Corinthians was sent can no longer be defended. The strong argument in favour of their presence is supported by 1 Corinthians 9, especially the information it provides on the practice of financial support enjoyed by them (9: 12a) and on the grounds for doing so (9:14).

From Paul's answers in 1 Corinthians 9, we may infer that these missionaries might not initially have come to Corinth in order to attack Paul or destroy his work in Corinth, as J. Murphy O'Connor postulates. Had Paul been aware of the systematic attack launched by them against his apostolic status, it is difficult to imagine why he did not attack them strongly in 1 Corinthians 9. Rather, their examination of Paul's apostolic practice occurred because they themselves were asked by some Corinthian Christians why they, unlike Paul, received financial support. Hence, it is logical that Paul would later be surprised to know that the good apostolic intentions he had in writing 1 Corinthians 9 would be seen by these missionaries as an attack on them. Paul's intention was to safeguard his converts from falling into the sin of destroying their fellow Christians and themselves by falling into idolatry. He wanted to prevent the church from disintegrating further. The failure of these missionaries to see this point and the probability that they felt offended by Paul's explanation of the renunciation of his right to financial support in 9:12b, 15-18 might have constituted some of the reasons why they began to intensify their attack on Paul's apostolic status to such an extent that, in response, Paul attacked them and considered them "false apostles, deceitful workmen" and people who "disguised themselves as apostles of Christ" (2 Cor. 11:13).

4.3 On the Use of Paul's Refusal to Live off the Gospel as a Paradigm

Whilst interpreting Paul's practice of renouncing his right itself, our exegesis has thrown some light on the question of why in his missionary work Paul refused to live off the gospel. Our proposal that sees the gospel and its proclamation as the primary reason for Paul's refusal of financial support gives us a strong reason to reassess various proposals previously made by some scholars regarding this issue.

As we have shown, scholars have argued that Paul's decision to forgo his right was caused by various circumstances. Some look to his Rabbinic tradition of combining the study of Torah with the practice of trade for independence (Hengel and Harvey). Others relate it to his desire not to be associated with itinerant missionaries (either Palestinian [G. Theissen and Horsley] or Gentile) and itinerant philosophers (either Stoic [R.F. Hock] or Sophist [Bruce W. Winter]). Hock's view has been developed by some scholars who relate it to the Corinthians' inherited patronage system in which the giving and acceptance of pay was seen not only as normal custom (Carter) but also as an expression of friendship (P. Marshall and J.K. Chow). Its refusal is considered to be a declaration of enmity.

However, the scholars' reliance on the study of those suggested circumstances is such that they have overlooked what the text says. We have shown that it is Paul's own perception of the gospel that motivates his refusal of financial support. He sees that accepting pay, even though it is his right, will create a stumbling block to the way of the gospel. His insistence on not accepting that support from Corinthian Christians is such that he boasts about it (1 Cor. 9:15b; 2 Cor. 11:10) and goes so far as to tell them that he is their father and therefore is the one who should give to them (2 Cor. 12:14). Paul was not willing to become a burden to his Corinthian converts, not because they were less capable than those of Macedonian churches (see 2 Cor. 8:2) or gave a different kind of support or had a motive different from that of the latter in supplying Paul's need. He emphasizes this notion not only because it is needed in his discourse as an attempt to encourage some of his readers not to exercise their right to eat food offered to idols, but also because the gospel itself is to him that of Christ crucified which characterizes his preaching activity. It is this reason that encouraged Paul to work with his hands and endure hardship in order to support himself and his team.

A more pressing question that comes out of this observation, none the less, is that of how we can square it with his acceptance of money from other churches. Apparently, Paul admits that he was once refreshed by the Corinthian delegation sometime after his departure from Corinth (1 Cor.

16:5-6), and expects them to speed him on his next journey from his intended visit to Corinth (16:6) and Timothy on his way back to Paul (16:11b). Indeed, he acknowledges that when he was in Corinth he accepted financial support from Macedonian churches (2 Cor. 11:7-11). He explains that he did so in order not to burden Corinthian Christians (2 Cor. 11:7-10; 12:11-13, 16-18). Similarly, to the Thessalonian Christians he wrote that in labour he worked night and day (2 Thess. 3:8-9 cf. 1 Thess. 2:9) and used what he did among them as a paradigm for those who did not want to work, even though he received or expected some kind of help from Philippian Christians when he was in Thessalonica (Phil. 4:15-16) and in prison (Phil. 4:18). While he was in Ephesus he worked with his hands (1 Cor. 4:12a; Acts 20:34-35) and used this as a paradigm for them to help the weak, even though he was refreshed by the Corinthian delegation (1 Cor. 16:15-18).

It may be said that Paul accepts support from churches because he does not see it as causing a stumbling block to the gospel. Therefore we must ask the following: What is it that Paul regards as constituting a stumbling block to the gospel? Scholars have argued the circumstances of the gifts or of the givers to answer this question. It follows that when it comes to praxis Paul's policy of putting the preaching of the gospel free of charge above everything else makes room for a dialogue with the circumstances. The weakness of this proposal, however, is that it leads us to infer that Paul exercises his right when he receives money from the churches. He does so because he does not see any stumbling block to the gospel being created by it. Conversely, it implies that Paul refuses to exercise his right because the circumstances make it necessary for him to do so. Clearly, however, this inference cannot be squared with 1 Corinthians 9:12b, where Paul states very strongly that he has never made use of his right. It is also weakened by the difficulty we have in ascertaining which are the circumstances that made Paul decide to forgo his right when working with Barnabas (1 Cor. 9:6) and when he was in Thessalonica, Corinth and Ephesus, and which are the ones that led him to receiving support from Philippi when he was in Thessalonica (Phil. 4:15-16) and in prison (Phil. 4:18), from Macedonian churches when he was in Corinth (2 Cor. 11:7-11), and from Corinthian Christians when he was in Ephesus (1 Cor. 16:17-18) and when he requested them in his letter to speed him on his journey from Corinth to his next destination (1 Cor. 16:6). Furthermore, the different proposals made by scholars to explain these circumstances strengthen our reservation.

A more plausible explanation is therefore needed: It is provided by our appreciation of Paul's strong statement in 1 Cor. 9:4-18 on his refusal to exercise the right to live off the gospel. In this light we may infer that, for Paul, being refreshed by the Corinthian delegation (1 Cor. 16:15-18) and expecting them to speed him on his missionary journey (16:5-6) or Timothy back to him (15:11b) did not amount to 'living off the gospel.' Hence his strong statement in 9:12b. The support from Macedonian churches while he was in Corinth was important to his work. It was none the less supplementary to his desire to avoid being a burden to the Corinthian Christians. It did not constitute what was termed as 'living off the gospel' or exercising his right to financial support. What he received from Philippian Christians when he was in Thessalonica and in prison may also have been of the same nature. He did not want his daily needs to be met by the support of the churches, even if he had the right to their support. Even if they had wanted to meet his daily needs, Paul would have refused mainly because of his view of the gospel of Christ crucified which had to be preached free of charge. Hence, the necessity and constancy of working with his hands, and the frustration of Corinthian Christians. They were frustrated because they wanted to give Paul what they gave the other apostles, namely the gift not of the kind that they gave him through their delegates (16:17-18), nor of that which he would expect them to offer him when he would travel from their city to his next destination (16:6), but of that which amounted to 'living off the gospel.'

We may therefore conclude that what is used by Paul as a weight against which he measures the circumstances is neither the gift itself, nor the motivation of the giver. Rather, it is what constitutes 'living off the gospel' itself. Hence, if the gift does not amount to 'living off the gospel' and therefore creates no stumbling block to the gospel, Paul sees no reason to reject it. But if it does, he forgoes his right to receiving it. It is this understanding that enables us to see why Paul claims in his first letter to the Corinthians that he has never made use of his right to financial support (1 Cor. 9:12b), but at the same time receives support from them and other churches.

From the above observations we can draw two major implications. First, it demands a careful use of social history for interpreting our text. It is true that our knowledge of the historical background of a particular text is crucial in interpreting any biblical text. We have seen this to be the case in our study of the background of the Corinthian Christians' insistence on exercising their right. The text clearly indicates that their right is based on a solid theological knowledge of God's existence, idols' non-existence and of the neutrality of food before God. It is also supported by two further arguments, namely freedom status and the aphoristic saying that 'everything is permitted.' Yet, it is when we read it against the background of the importance of Roman citizenship under the reign of Claudius that we understand better than otherwise why Paul does not negate the legitimacy of their right but, instead, presents his example of waiving his right to live off the gospel to be imitated by them. We can then see that just as Paul's refusal to exercise his right to financial support has caused him to exercise endurance in all things and yet prevented him from creating a stumbling block to the gospel, so will their refusal to exercise their right to eat food offered to idols cause them to exercise endurance, especially because the context of eating food offered to idols is related to the Imperial cult, and yet prevent them from being a stumbling block to, and from destroying, their brother.

Nevertheless, we have shown that our study of the historical background of the issue of food offered to idols must not be done at the expense of the text of 1 Corinthians 8:1 - 11:1 in which we can see that the context of the issue goes beyond the imperial cult. It is a normal issue which is present in the meat market and at a meal presented by an unbeliever, most probably in his house. Hence, we are able to build a comprehensive picture: the issue of food offered to idols was a normal issue for any Christian coming from a Gentile background, but it became a major issue for Corinthian Christians, one that caused a division among them, because of its relation to the propagation of the Imperial cult in the city.

Our suggestion that the text cannot be dispensed with in any investigation of its background[5] finds more support in our study of the reason for Paul's refusal to accept financial support. Our study of his own explanation in 1 Corinthians 9:14-18 tells us that what he says is even more significant than our inconclusive knowledge of the historical background against which his conduct of refusing to accept financial support has been read by some scholars. At least it must be stated that in interpreting the biblical text we must see what is obvious in the text as a primary source of information assisting us to answer the questions we raise concerning a particular text. In this regard, we should not allow our certain knowledge of the means of support of philosophers in the first century AD to determine the reason why Paul refused to accept financial support. Paul's practice differed even from other Christian missionaries contemporaneous with him. It was neither because they were doing what other popular and greedy philosophers did, nor acting contrary to the proper tradition of the church, for according to 1 Corinthians 9:14 there was a tradition legitimating people to live off the gospel. It was not because Paul considered their practice to have an illegitimate ground. Rather, it was because of his own specific perception of the gospel of Christ crucified itself. This is what caused him to see preaching the gospel as a necessity and free of charge. Hence, there is justification for a cause to call for the primacy of the text and the secondary function of our attentive knowledge of the social and historical conditions that we think might have shaped the formation of a biblical text.

Secondly, what is more significant to draw from Paul's discourse in 1 Corinthians 9 is his courage not only to forgo his right to live off the gospel for the sake of the gospel and salvation of many, even though by so doing

---

5 Cf. P.J. Hartin and J.H. Petzer, "Introduction" in P.J. Hartin and J. H. Petzer (eds), *Text and Interpretation. New Approaches in the Criticism of the New Testament* (Leiden: Brill, 1991) 1-11, esp. 4: "The Text remains the starting point for any form of interpretation and without an established text all interpretation is fruitless."

he acts against the command of the Lord (9:14) and sets a new practice which was not in harmony with the practice of other missionaries, but also to use it in his discourse even though he knows that it is being used by some to examine his apostolic status.

D.G. Horrell has developed the first paradigm, that is to say Paul's practice of acting against the command of the Lord, for modern hermeneutical enterprise in addressing conflicting issues of our time, such as sexuality or the ordination of women. Horrell writes: "Paul's example may certainly instruct us, however, that in the midst of heated debates on sexuality or women's ordination, as in the early Church on the question of support for missionaries, to adopt such an interpretative strategy is certainly not conducive to consensus. Criticism and rejection may be expected of those who dare to set aside a word of the Lord in order to do what they believe that following Christ demands. This, Paul might warn us, is nothing new."[6]

However, it must also be emphasized that attempts to develop Paul's courage to act against the command of the Lord must not be separated from his purpose of using this action as an example in his discourse in 1 Corinthians 8:1 - 11:1. For, even though it is true that Paul's conscious action to act against the command of the Lord naturally caused him and his colleagues to distance themselves from other missionaries and, thereby, eventually creating confusion amongst Corinthian Christians, *the retelling of it* in the present discourse is aimed at preventing some Corinthian Christians from exercising their right to eat food offered to idols. It is used to encourage them to act against their theological knowledge which is used to justify that right, and to prevent the disintegration of the Corinthian church. They were exhorted to give up their right for the sake of those who do not have advanced knowledge of God's existence, idols' non-existence, neutrality of food, freedom status and slogan that 'everything is permitted' (8:4-6,8; 10:23). The forgoing of legitimate and justified right for the sake of others for whom Christ died is Paul's message for them, and for us today. He hopes that if imitated by the Corinthian Christians (1 Cor. 11:1) his apostolic example will not only benefit the weak conscienced brothers, but will also prevent those who want to eat food offered to idols from falling into the sins of idolatry and of provoking God to anger. In fact, it will eventually serve Paul's call for them to be united (1 Cor 1:10). There is no indication whatsoever that Paul's act against the Jesus tradition is intended for the destruction of others. On the contrary, it is for the salvation of many. Therefore, there is no reason to suggest that Paul would still ask his Corinthian Christians to imitate him in not exercising his right if he knew that it would cause the Corinthian church to be divided further. It is against this insight that we must measure any attempt to seek the relevance

---

6 Horrell, "The Lord Commanded," 603.

of Paul's courageous action against the command of the Lord for our hermeneutical enterprise today.

Hence, in attempting to solve a dispute amongst believers over a delicate issue such as eating food offered to idols,[7] one's approach should not resort to the method of pronouncing which view is right or wrong. Nor should he or she resort to the method whereby one party is allowed to insist on what it thinks best or what it thinks the will of God is and no criticism can therefore stop it from doing so, as Horrell seems to propagate, however legitimate its position may be. Rather, like Paul, one should use the method of emphasizing the importance of 'forgoing' even of one's right and its legitimate arguments, for the sake of the well-being of one's counterparts.

In a world in which the spirit of negative competition, that is the idea of defeating one's counterpart in order to gain one's own interest, is still prevalent and very influential in all aspects of life in our time, such a message is very significant. It is this method that we should use in addressing other issues which separate Christians today. Paul's method of preventing those involved in a dispute from committing an action which leads to the destruction of others by conducting a passionate discourse is certainly needed in our time, particularly because of the fact that we are dealing with issues which are divisive in nature and which have no conclusive answers.

Our time has shown that values change. Old values are challenged by

---

[7] The issue of food offered to idols is still relevant in some parts of the world today. See Yeo, *Interaction*, 294-311, for Chinese ancestral worship; Yamsat, "The Ekklesia," 14, for African traditional religions; Derek Newton, "Food Offered to Idols," 15-45, 290-91, uses the dispute amongst Torajan Christians in Indonesia over ancestor worship in order to support his thesis that the issue of food offered to idols in the Corinthian church was complex, and it was because of its complexity that Paul resorted to the idea of community and care for the weak as the solution to their dispute. Thus he argues that it is an issue of timeless dilemma and has no universal solution. Delobel, "Coherence," 187 writes: "The Corinthian Sitz-im-Leben was unique and is, as such, over. But in countries where Christians are constantly confronted with non-Christian religions and non-Christian worship with food offerings and cultic meals, the close analogy with the Corinthian situation becomes striking." Moreover, he says that these Christians are confronted with questions of "religious corroboration, integration, syncretism, apartheid and social obligations towards non-Christians concerning some form of cultic involvement" (190). Hays, *1 Corinthians*, 145, suggests that in the framing of analogies "only to those situations in which the boundary-defying actions of the "strong" might actually jeopardize the faith and salvation of others by leading the weak to emulate high-risk behaviours." He rejects any attempt to seek the relevance of the passage in a way that made the church "hostage to the standards of the most narrow-minded and legalistic members of the church" such as the "drinking alcohol and dancing or dressing in certain ways might cause offence to more scrupulous church members." But Hays regards idolatry as still real now: the gods of wealth, military power, and self-gratification. (146).

new ones. In fact, new values can be quickly considered to be redundant. This change of values is present in all aspects of life and in any part of the world. Sometimes, it is promoted by some agencies or schools of thought which have their own interests, but sometimes it is a natural phenomenon. Amidst this value-changing phenomenon, Christians are therefore placed in the formidable position of having to choose which value/s is/are acceptable and which are not. This is particularly so when we have neither explicit nor implicit answer in the Scripture. In such a circumstance, a method of justifying the position of one and rejecting the other does not help. If we insist on keeping one, either old or new, and abandoning the other on the basis of the principles of 'right' or 'wrong,' it is very likely that Christians and churches will continue to fight against each other and many more may be destroyed. As Paul did, we must seek to address the interests and fears of those involved in dispute or conflict.[8]

Paul's answers in 1 Corinthians 9 offers, on the one hand, a paradigm of the need to be mindful of those who are likely to be negatively affected by our decisions or actions, and to do something to prevent it from happening. On the other hand, his answers challenge us to think of the need to take some necessary and proactive action which will have a positive effect on others. Forgoing right, self-enslavement and self-control are three manifestations of such action. These principles are still valid for us today: on the one hand, how we propagate the idea of not destroying others and, on the other hand, how we forgo our right, enslave ourselves and practice self-control in order to do good to others. This insight gives us some cause to see the relevance of Paul's answer to the Corinthian Christians dispute over the issue of food offered to idols not just for the same issue, but also for other issues faced by churches today.

A cursory reading of church history informs us that church division occurs whenever churches or Christians fail to solve dispute or conflict over various issues, either doctrinal or organizational. It has been considered axiomatic that whenever Christians differ it always leads to formal and incurable separation or division. Our studies of 1 Corinthians 9 gives us an apostolic example of how to prevent a dispute over certain issues from causing a formal separation. 1 Corinthians 9 speaks of an example of how Paul puts into practice his call to unity which he expresses at the beginning of his letter to the conflict-ridden church of Corinth (1 Cor. 1:10). Whether or not his Corinthian readers gave heed to his suggested solution is another

---

8 See Marc Howard Ross, *The Culture of Conflict. Interpretations and Interests in Comparative Perspectives* (New Haven and London: Yale University Press, 1993) 1 and his *Management of Conflict. Interpretations and Interests in Comparative Perspectives* (New Haven and London: Yale University Press, 1993) 191-94, for the importance of realizing and interpreting the deeper concerns of those involved in conflicts for conflict management.

Some Implications 213

matter.[9] None the less, so far as our understanding of the emergence of the issue is concerned, it is perceivable that Paul's suggested solution is effective and, therefore, worthy of being imitated.

In the next chapter, we will endeavour to see how the Batak Christian Protestant Church (the HKBP) in Indonesia solved its crisis. It will be shown that Paul's suggested solution to the Corinthian Christians' dispute over food offered to idols has some relevance in the HKBP's success in bringing its crisis to an end. Even though two leaderships had existed since the crisis erupted on 23 December 1992 and the consequence of the crisis was such that there was a wall of division between both parties involved, a joint synod was held on 18-20 December 1998 to begin to end the crisis and safeguard the unity of the church. Previous efforts to solve the crisis failed when the parties involved were not prepared to accept the other's position. However, when all were willing to forgo their positions, the solution to the crisis was widely open and the opportunity to reunite was not wasted.

---

9 See Brunt, "Rejected, Ignored, or Misunderstood?" 113-24, shows that the early Church did not appreciate Paul's unique position on the issue of food offered to idols.

CHAPTER 5

1 Corinthians 9 and the Solution of the Crisis of the HKBP: A Case Study[1]

5.1. Introductory Remarks

Dispute and conflict within a church is nothing new in the history of the church. The nature, intensity and effect of the conflict vary from place to place and era to era. The history of the Batak Christian Protestant Church (the HKBP) in Indonesia, both at congregational level and as a whole, is no exception. Since it was founded in 1861 this church has undergone various conflicts and, as a result, a number of sister churches have been formed out of it. Various reasons have been given to explain the emergence of these conflicts. Social, cultural and political factors are contributory to them.[2] Starting from 1986 this church of approximately three million members experienced another conflict which exploded in 1992 through the intervention of an external power, the military, and thereupon turned it into a crisis that brought it on the brink of a split. The effect of the crisis was devastating. However, unlike previous conflicts, it was eventually solved in 1998 when both parties involved agreed to hold a joint synod at which a new leadership was elected.

---

1 See pages 234-35 for a *dramatis personae* which is arranged alphabetically.
2 For a brief account of the various conflicts which have been experienced by the HKBP since 1917 until 1992, see Paul B. Pedersen, *Batak Blood and Protestant Soul: the Development of national Batak Churches in North Sumatra* (Grand Rapids: Eerdmans, 1970) 73-118, 149-5, 173-78; Jan S. Aritonang, *Mission Schools in Batak Land (Indonesia) 1861-1940*. ET. by Robert R. Boehike (Leiden: E.J. Brill, 1994) 231-47, 304-09; Bungaran A. Simanjuntak, "Konflik Status dan Kekuasaan Orang Batak Toba." Unpublished PhD. Dissertation (Gajah Mada University: Jogyakarta,1994) esp. 534-615. Pedersen views the formation of independent churches from the perspective of the nationalistic influence and tribal desire of the Bataks. Aritonang shows that the conflict between Batak Christians and RMG missionaries and Dutch government was motivated by the desires of the Toba Bataks to be independent. This was the fruit of their education brought by the missionaries and by their openness to new development happening around them such as nationalistic movement. Simanjuntak argues that much of the Toba Batak Conflicts are caused by their philosophical purpose of life (i.e. to gain riches, many children and honour) which, in practice, has often been in conflict with their ideological knowledge gained from Christianity and from their encounter with others in their migrated areas. The Christian values are exercised in times of peace. When there is conflict, the Toba Bataks will exercise their unchristianized characteristics. Hence the Toba Bataks conflicts are naturalistic.

What caused the conflict and how it was finally solved are two questions which need to be addressed. We will see that there were many attempts made to solve the crisis since it erupted. Some failed, others succeeded. The main reason for their failure was the determination of each party involved in the crisis to justify its position, rightly or wrongly. Conversely, in terms of finding a solution to the crisis, the willingness to accept the position of each party in the crisis is one of the most important factors that made what looked impossible possible. Of course, the historical conditions surrounding the crisis were also important factors in finding a solution to it. Indeed, as we shall see, the solution to the crisis could not be separated from the social, economical and political conditions in Indonesia. Just as the intervention of the military turned an internal conflict into a serious crisis and brought it on the brink of a split, so the withdrawal of the military support of one party in the dispute provided ample opportunity for both parties to be reunited.[3] None the less, it was the willingness to recognize the position of each other that enabled the HKBP to use these situations effectively for its reunification.

It must be acknowledged that I have been personally involved in the crisis. This means, on the one hand, that as an insider I am in a better position than otherwise to describe the nature and development of the crisis. On the other hand, there exists the danger of subjectivity, because I support one party involved in the crisis. I have endeavoured to overcome this danger by informing myself of the position of the other side through reading their publications.

5.2 Sustained Attempts to Oust the Top Leadership of the Church

What began in 1987 at the church's 47th synod as a dispute over the question of who should lead the church, developed into a dispute over the question of whether or not the government, in this regard the military, could intervene in the church's internal affairs. The issue of who should lead the church was crucial because the survey carried out by the church prior to the celebration of its 125th anniversary in 1986 had discovered some frightening prospects of the life and witness of the church, and recommended some steps to be taken by the church to avoid those

---

3 Thus, Hotman A. Siahaan, "Konflik HKBP di Pentas Politik Indonesia" in Einar M Sitompul and Rainy M.P. Hutabarat (eds), *Gereja di Pentas Politik* (Jakarta: PT. Anem Kosong Anem, 1997) 1-40, rightly argues that the recent HKBP conflict is related to the political system in the country. It is both organismic/naturalistic and systemic/structuralistic. The political system in Indonesia plays a role. Also Wirodono, *Gerakan Politik di Indonesia: Catatan 1994* (Jakarta: Puspa Swara 1994). Gomar Gultom, et al., *Keyakinan dalam Pencobaan, Studi Kasus Gereja HKBP* (Jakarta: Pustaka Sopo Metmet, 1993).

frightening prospects. The question of who could lead the church to face such difficult challenges was, therefore, very much in the mind of many decision makers within the church.

Since elected at this synod in April 1987, the new top leadership of the church, the Ephorus, Rev Dr S.A.E. Nababan, was sustainably discredited by the one who lost the leadership contest, Rev P.M. Sihombing, and 37 supporters who were later called the *Parritrit*, meaning those who had a retreat to meditate. Their failure to garner widespread support from church members and the fact that, as a result of their insistence and the inability of the church leadership to appease them completely, 19 pastors from among them were relieved of their duties and their priesthood revoked, left them with no choice but to seek the help of the authorities outside the church. The authorities themselves, whose interests had been threatened by the programmes of the church, especially ones related to the issues of justice, peace and integrity of creation, were more than willing to lend support to the *Parritrit*. They used as a justification for their help the fact that the leadership of the church was not able to solve completely the problem caused by the *Parritrit*.

The support given by the authorities to the Parritrit was no small deal. At first, they tried to give the impression that the leadership of Ephorus Nababan was not supported by the government. The clearest evidence of this was the refusal to give permission for the church to hold its 50th synod on 1-7 August 1990 in Pematangsiantar, North Sumatra, only hours before the opening ceremony. Among others, as stated in item four of his letter, the reason given by the Chief of Indonesian Police for the refusal was that "there are some activities carried out by the HKBP or its leadership which are political in nature and which are felt to have caused nervousness and unease to the society in general..."[4]

This kind of strategy was intensified by indirect intervention in the affairs of the church. For instance, by means of a confidential memo dated 9 September 1990,[5] the Minister of Religion gave a mandate to the Chairman of the Supreme Advisory Council, General (retired) M. Panggabean who happened to be a member of the HKBP, to deal with the HKBP problem. The latter then formed a Peace Team, the membership of which consisted of high ranking government officials. This team held meetings in various towns. At the meetings, among other things, General Panggabean informed the audience that he was not to blame for the refusal of the government to issue a permit for the holding of the 50th synod. It was

---

4 See doc. no. 01. This explanation was given in response to the question raised to the police by the General Secretary (see doc. no. 02.). When asked by Ephorus Nababan in a letter dated 21 September 1990 (see doc. no. 03) about which activities and by whom, the government did not reply.

5 No MA/132/1990. See doc. no.04.

because of the unresolved internal problem of the HKBP.[6] He also stated that the leadership of Ephorus Nababan was bad and should therefore be 'terminated.'[7]

It was ironic that, rather than ending the problem, this team caused a gradual split in the leadership of the church over its legality, necessity and effectiveness. Some supported it, due partly to their increasing dislike of the way in which Ephorus Nababan had led the church, partly also to their reluctance to oppose the authorities who themselves disliked the concern shown by the church over the issues of Justice, Peace and Integrity of creation. They were led by the General Secretary, Rev O.P.T. Simorangkir, who set out to oppose Ephorus Nababan openly in the media and then at the 50th synod in April 1991 accused him, among other things, of being authoritarian and of relieving him of his duties. Others, however, rejected the team due partly to the strong support they received from the majority of church members because of the programmes carried out throughout the church, and to their reluctance to allow outside powers to intervene in the church internal affairs. They were led by Ephorus Nababan.

Set within the context of Indonesia during this time when, on the one hand, the power of the government was very strong in stifling the power of social and religious institutions and, on the other hand, the support given by the people to those daring to oppose the power of the government was equally strong, it was inevitable that the above opposing groups could not come together. Indeed, the internal forces opposing Ephorus Nababan and his programmes then corroborated with the authorities, firstly in order to discredit his leadership and, secondly, to campaign against his reelection. This was particularly because the likelihood of his reelection was very high.

So, even though the 19 pastors were reaccepted by the 50th synod in April 1991 and the strained relationship between the Ephorus and the General Secretary was restored at this synod, their differences resurfaced after the synod. The 19 pastors refused to abide by the procedures of their reacceptance as formulated by the Central Church Board, and the relationship between Ephorus Nababan and Rev O.P.T. Simorangkir worsened. Before, during and after the election synod held on 23-28 November 1992, the General Secretary and the government worked together to make the synod fail in its task of electing a new leadership. Even after the synod being constitutionally adjourned by Ephorus Nababan two hours before the expiry of its permission until an uncertain time and in his absence, they also attempted to make the adjourned synod either elect five caretakers to lead the church until the next synod or hand over the

---

6 See General M. Panggabean's own explanation written to Ephorus Nababan which he asked him to distribute to all congregations. (doc. no.05)

7 See Moxa Nadeak, et.al, *Krisis HKBP: Ujian Bagi Iman dan Pengamalan Pancasila* (Biro Informasi HKBP, Oktober 1995) 70.

problem of the church to the government. Indeed, when this attempt was unanimously and totally rejected by the synod and aware of the fact that, constitutionally, the incumbent leader would continue to lead the church, they used a military decree to oust Ephorus Nababan, an action which instantly sparked protest and immediately divided the church up to the congregational level.

The military decree was issued on 23 December 1992 by the head of the Northern Sumatra Agency for the Co-ordination of Support for National Stability, Major General H.R. Pramono.[8] It appointed Rev Dr S.M. Siahaan as Acting Ephorus with the task of convening an Extraordinary Synod. By this decree, General Pramono and those opposing Nababan from within the church thought that he had been ousted once and for all. However, this was not what Nababan and the majority of the church members and pastors thought. On the contrary, rather than ousting Nababan, the decree caused him to stand up longer than might have been otherwise, and resulted in a much more dangerous and large scale division of the church, as we shall see below.

5.3 Dispute Over the Intervention of the Military Decree

Before and after the extraordinary synod was held at Tiara Convention Hall on 11-13 February 1993, at which Dr P.W.T. Simanjuntak and Dr S.M. Siahaan were elected the Ephorus and the General Secretary respectively, the church was divided into two factions: a) those who supported the military decree, the synod convened by the Acting Ephorus, and the leadership elected there, and b) those who rejected the decree and its results. The former was then known as the Extraordinary Synod faction (the SAI-HKBP) and the latter as the HKBP Constitution (the AP-HKBP) or the SSA-HKBP. Both claimed to be the legitimate HKBP and to have the right to own and use its assets. It is instructive to see how both factions justified their positions on the military decree, for it was their justifications that caused the church to divide in an unprecedented manner and made it difficult for it to reunite.

5.3.1 The Justification for the Support of the Military Decree

As we hinted above, it is clear that both internal and external forces had thought that the military decree was the only way to prevent Ephorus Nababan from being re-elected. Both the government and the SAI faction were therefore of one mind in justifying the decree. For instance, after issuing the decree, General Pramono argued in his press release that he

---

8 See doc. no. 06.

would not have done so without the HKBP prompting,[9] and if not for the sake of national security. To justify this assertion, he referred to the failure of the church's 51st grand synod in November 1992 to elect a new leadership, which he thought "might lead to disorder, which could have an effect on the general session of the People's Consultative Assembly in March"[10] (1993). When asked about why he was willing to be the military appointee, Dr S.M. Siahaan argued that the decree was the hand of God to save the church from disaster and that his appointment was not a government attempt to intervene in the internal affairs of religion. To him, there was no need to be afraid of it setting a precedent for the future. He said: "What the government does is to avoid factionalism."[11] He wrote to the congregations that he had no ambition to become the Ephorus and would return to the seminary after completing his task.[12] His view was later reiterated by those of his faction.

For instance, as expressed in its magazine, the SAI-HKBP faction[13] argues that since Indonesia is neither a religious state nor a secular one, there is no absolute separation between religion and state. Hence "the government intervention in religious context, is greatly needed by the Indonesian society and nation...The freedom of religion is not lessened by the government intervention."[14] Similarly, in the opening speech of his faction's synod on 29 September-1 October 1994, which was held after widespread occurrence of violence and which was attended by many high ranking government officials, as the Ephorus of his faction P.W.T. Simanjuntak stated: "...The Government has never intervened in the internal affairs of the HKBP. What has been done by the Government to the HKBP is still in their capacity as the Protector and Builder of organization.

---

9 Cf. The analysis of Dr. A.A. Sitompul of the reason for the existence of two factions among the HKBP members. In his report to the Pastors' Meeting organised by the SAI-HKBP leadership in Sipoholon on 26-28 September 1994 (See doc. no. 07 on *Immanuel* 11 (1994) 22, Sitompul said that some members of the 51st synod verbally handed over the solution to the leadership election to the government.
10 See the editorial of *The Jakarta Post* on Thursday, 7 January 1993, "Of Church and State." See doc. no. 08.
11 Daily News *Kompas* 12 January 1993, see doc. no. 09; see also the letter of Siahaan on 16 January 1993 written as a response to the statement of the Communion of Churches in Indonesia (CCI) against the decree. See doc. no. 10.
12 See doc. no. 11.
13 See J.R. Hutauruk and N. Manurung, "HKBP in Indonesia: Suatu Upaya Meluruskan Informasi" in the SAI-HKBP *Immanuel* 5 (1994) 10-13 and *Immanuel* 6 (1994) 7-10. Doc. no.12.
14 The SAI-HKBP *Immanuel* 6 (1994) 8. This same view was also articulated by J.R. Hutauruk to the officers of World Council of Churches in Geneva. See the letter of Dr. Clement John to Dr. Konrad Raiser, the General Secretary of WCC, dated 10 March 1995 page 1. Doc. no. 13.

Therefore, we always have to build and improve dialogical relation with the government."[15] Yet at the same time he explained: "We have to acknowledge, that if the problem we faced was still in the stage of difference of perceptions, the Government would never intervene, but because it has escalated to physical conflict, which can disturb public order and security, the government cannot close its eyes, but has to intervene because, if not, this will disturb stability, which in turn will also hamper development."[16]

It was this justification that caused the government to confidently and consistently recognize the leadership of the SAI-HKBP faction throughout the crisis. Had this not been the case, the military would not have occupied the headquarters of the church with combat troops in the early morning of 16 January 1993, arresting and torturing church members and pastors who had been there since 24 December 1992 to prevent it from being taken over by the military.[17] Were it not for this belief, the military would not have forced some legitimate synod members to come to the extraordinary synod in order that there should be a quorum.[18] Nor would they have arrested without letter of arrest and then tortured 49 HKBP pastors and church members who welcomed Ephorus Nababan at the Medan airport on 17 January 1993. Seventeen of them were not released until 23 January 1993. Together with those arrested at the church headquarters, they were detained and tortured in the detention centre of the Regional Military Command in Jln Gaperta Medan.[19]

If it had not been for this belief, Dr Tarmizi Taher, the Minister of Religion would not have written to the chairman of the Community of Churches (CCI) in Indonesia on 7 May 1993,[20] stating that the leadership of HKBP elected at this synod was final, and reiterated it at the meeting of the Full Board of CCI in Bandung[21] by asking in his address that the issue of the HKBP should not be discussed there. What his subordinate, Jan Kawatu,[22] said to the delegates of the CCI-XII General Assembly in Jayapura-Irian Jaya on 21-30 October 1994 for which he was spontaneously

---

15 The SAI *Immanuel* 11 (1994) 75. Doc. no.14.
16 The SAI *Immanuel* 11 (1994) 75.
17 This action was in line with the policy set out in the letter of Bakorstanasda Sumbagut dated 13 January 1993, which was sent to its subordinates, stating that the court decision did not have legal power. Doc. no. 15.
18 See Nadeak, *Krisis HKBP* 84.
19 See doc. no.16. *Warta HKBP* 18 (25 Jan 1993) 1-4.
20 No MA/114/1993. See doc. no. 17.
21 On 7-13 May 1993. See Nadeak, *Krisis HKBP*, 97.
22 Jan Kawatu is the Director General of Christian Protestant Society Guidance.

and unanimously booed by the audience,[23] and wrote to the head of the Central Agency for the Coordination of Support for National Stability[24] followed the same lines.

Had the government not recognized the SAI leadership, there would have been no reason for the Minister of Defence and Security, General Edi Sudradjat, to receive the leaders of the SAI-HKBP faction in his office, and for President Soeharto to do likewise in the state palace on 22 March 1994.[25] This is despite the fact that later, after knowing that hundreds of the pastors and church members of the AP-HKBP faction visited the House of People's Representatives to lodge their protest at the involvement of the military in the violence and torture committed against them, the Commander in Chief of the Armed Forces, General Faisal Tanjung denied that the government had issued a recognition of the HKBP leadership.[26] He said that "if the President previously received Simanjuntak group, it does not mean that the government acknowledges Simanjuntak's leadership."[27] If the government had not been partial, Ephorus Nababan's request[28] to meet General Tanjung in his office to explain the HKBP case would not have been rejected.[29] Nor would the head of the Northern Sumatra Agency for the Coordination of Support for National Stability have sent a telegram to his subordinates, stating that the leadership elected at the Tiara convention centre was legitimate.[30] Nor would the Governor of North Sumatra, Major General (retired) Raja Inal Siregar, have done the same,[31] instructing the heads of the regencies and Majors of towns in North Sumatra to support the SAI-HKBP leadership, and prohibiting those rejecting the military decree to carry out any activity inside and outside the church without the knowledge of the SAI-HKBP leadership.[32] As a result, both civil and military leaders in all the regencies of North Sumatra constantly and forcefully forbade

---

23 The youth and intellectual Christian mass-organizations (GMKI, PIKI and GAMKI) issued an open letter to the assembly participants rejecting any recognition by the state of the leadership of the church. Doc. no. 18.
24 Doc. no. 19.
25 Doc. no. 20 on the request of the SAI-HKBP leadership to meet the president on 1 February 1994, and doc no. 21, the Daily *Jakarta Post*, 23 March 1994, on news of the visit.
26 In the hearing of the Indonesian Parliament on 7 June 1994. See doc. no. 22.
27 See doc. no. 23a and b.
28 Doc. no. 24 on the letter of Nababan to General Faisal Tanjung dated 14 May 1994.
29 See doc. no. 25 on the letter of Major General Hari Sabarno to Nababan dated 7 July 1994.
30 Doc. no. 26.
31 Dated on 2 September 1993 and 24 September 1993. Doc. no. 27 and 28.
32 As a result, the church members who did not recognize the SAI-HKBP leadership were denied the right to have letters of certification from the leaders of sub-regency in North Tapanuli. Doc. no. 29.

Nababan to preach in their areas.[33] The government never refused any request of the SAI-HKBP faction for permission to hold their gatherings in most provinces. They tried very hard to prevent those who opposed the decree from holding their gatherings, small and large. Indeed, the military and the police were not hesitant to arrest and torture some church members and pastors of the AP-HKBP faction in detention.

It was this belief in the rightness of the military decree that caused the leadership of the SAI-HKBP faction and its followers to impose the decision of the extraordinary synod and other decision making meetings of their own on the life of the church. They did not hesitate to resort to using force leading to the occurrence of violence in installing their personnel in the congregations and trying to take over the HKBP assets especially when facing opposition from the other faction. In imposing their decisions, they were first assisted by the military, police and also paid thugs. Then, when the House of People's Representatives, the National Commission on Human Rights and the Central Government were informed by the AP-HKBP faction about the violence committed by the military and police against church members and pastors, the SAI-HKBP formed their own Task Force, whose members were trained by retired military officers. When this failed, the faction formed a Special Commission called Special Commission (*Komsus*) to persuade those who opposed the decree to accept the SAI-HKBP installations of its personnel and hand over the HKBP assets and, if necessary, to use force to achieve its tasks. This use of force injured many and, in fact, killed some people. It was apparent that the police did not investigate further any report of violent action committed by the SAI-HKBP faction against their opponents, even that which caused casualties. To propagate their own version of the story of events, they continued publishing the church monthly magazine called Immanuel and were supported by one local daily news in North Sumatra, *Sinar Indonesia Baru*.

5.3.2 The Justification for the Opposition of the Military Decree

Though acknowledging the existence of the HKBP unresolved internal conflict, many people rejected the legitimacy and necessity of the decree because it was seen as a blatant attempt to rid the church of its religious freedom as guaranteed by chapter 29 of the Basic Constitution 1945 of the Indonesian State, and as the trigger of a widespread division. They strongly argued that the core of this chapter had been rightly and repeatedly emphasized by President Soeharto in his public address at various religious festivals. For instance, in his address to the Buddhist Darma Canti Nyepi Evening Festival on 9 April 1992 Soeharto clearly remarked that: "...for us the freedom of religion is one of the most fundamental rights and comes

---

33 Doc. no. 30a-c.

from God himself, and does not come from the state at all. Therefore the state, much less the government has no right to intervene in the internal affairs of religion, both in its doctrine and institutions."[34] Since the office of Ephorus is religious in nature, it was argued that there was no ground for any authority outside the church, much less the military, to appoint anyone to be head of the church. Hence, the appointment of Ephorus by the military was seen as an insult to religious rights.[35]

It was also argued that even under Regulation No. 8/1985, in which the HKBP is considered to be a mass organization, and the government as its Protector and Builder, there is no justification for the central government, far less the provincial government, to replace or elect the head of social and religious organizations. The only right the central government has is to disperse a social or religious organization which is considered to have threatened the security of the country. Yet even this action can only be done after consultation with the Supreme Court. According to Presidential Decision No. 29, 1988 - upon which this agency was formed and in which it is described as a coordinating rather than an operational agency - the decree issued by General Pramono was operational in nature and therefore went beyond its function.[36]

Moreover, the decree was also seen as contradictory to the church belief as stated in its constitution and the book of confession. The constitution of the church states that the right to elect the leadership of the church lies in the hands of the synod. This position is supported by the statement in chapter 12 of the HKBP book of confession which rejects any idea that 'the State is a religious state.' This is because "the State and Church each have their own scope (Matthew 22:21 b)."[37]

Were it not on these grounds, Ephorus Nababan would neither have filed a suit against Major General H.R. Pramono in the State Administrative Court (PTUN) on 29 December 1992 in Medan for appointing a shadow Ephorus,[38] nor written to President Soeharto, asking him to cancel the extraordinary synod,[39] nor announced that it was illegal.[40] Were it not for this conviction, the PTUN Judge, Lintong Oloan Siahaan, would not have ruled against the decree on 11 January 1993, ordering the General to

---

34 Doc. no. 31; cf. also his address at the Maulid Remembrance of Prophet Muhammad. Doc. no. 32.
35 Cf. Hilman Hadikusuma, *Anthropologi Agama* (Bandung: PT. Citra Aditya Bakti, 1992) 290-91.
36 See Nadeak, *Krisis HKBP*, 93-94.
37 Doc. no . 33.
38 See *Forum Keadilan* 21, 4 February 1993. Doc. no. 34.
39 See doc. no. 35 on the letter of Nababan to President Soeharto dated on 8 February 1993.
40 See doc. no. 36 on the press release of Ephorus Nababan and the HKBP Information Bureau.

postpone its execution,[41] nor would the attorneys of either party have accepted his ruling. The Judge argued that the verdict was aimed at safeguarding the unity of the church and ensuring administrative accountability of all assets of the church. He also argued that he reached the verdict because of the fact that the Minister of Home Affairs had sent a telegram dated 23 December 1992 to all civil and military officials, stating that due to the People's Consultative Assembly in March 1993 there must not be any political, social and religious conference, congress or assembly.[42] Judge Siahaan stood up for his ruling even though he was terrorized in the days following the verdict to the extent that stones, blood and rotten meat were thrown into his house, breaking the window of his bedroom. He stood up despite the fact that General Pramono ignored this ruling by his office sending guidelines to all commanders of military districts in his constituency to explain that the court decision did not have any legal power.[43] The judge never changed his mind even though the appeal made by the Justice Minister, Ismail Saleh, and by the head of the Indonesian Supreme Court pleading for his protection, went unheeded.[44] He upheld his decision, even though as a result he was replaced by his deputy, Soebechi who, based on the letter of the assistant of the Coordinating Minister of Politics and Security, then ruled against the suit and gave the General a "dispensation" to carry out the decree.[45] If not for this conviction, Ephorus Nababan would not have appealed to the High Administrative Court (PTTUN), and then to the Supreme Court, against Soebechi's ruling.

Indeed, were it not for this belief, thousands of HKBP members, accompanied by their pastors, would not have gone out onto the streets, government offices and provincial and central parliament to lodge their protests and demand that the decree should be revoked. Nor would 230 pastors have met on 1-4 June 1994 in a Catholic House of Meditation, Jakarta, to formulate and express their declaration of faith rejecting the decree and violence in and by the church,[46] and then, on 5-7 June 1994, gone to the House of People's Representatives, wearing their priest's robes, to demand the House revoke the decree. The same belief was held by many churches, social-religious organizations and individual intellectuals in

---

41 See doc. no. 37a-f on the announcement of the verdict by the HKBP lawyers, and no 379 on the verdict.
42 Daily News *Kompas*, 12 January 1993 (doc. no. 38) and telegram of Rudini (doc. no. 39).
43 See *Forum Keadilan* no. 21, 4 February 1993, doc. no. 34; also Press Release of Indonesian Legal Aid Institution on 19 January 1993 signed by Hendardi. Doc. no. 40.
44 See *Forum Keadilan*, 21, Doc. no. 41.
45 See doc. no. 42 on the court decision taken on 6 February 1993.
46 See doc. no. 43.

Indonesia, who issued statements attacking the decree and sending letters of protest to the government,[47] and by international communities who sent letters of inquiry and protest to Indonesian government ambassadors and to President Soeharto.[48] In particular, the Community of Churches in Indonesia lodged a strong protest against the appointment,[49] and complained to the Minister of Religious Affairs, Munawir Sjadzali.

Even when the government continuously supported the SAI-HKBP faction in imposing its decision on them, the pastors and church members of the AP-HKBP faction continued to reject the legitimacy of the military decree and its results. In the event of their losing their church buildings and facing prohibition to use them in turn, they worshipped in open places such as graveyards, schools and their own houses. Indeed, when the military forbade them to worship together in the houses, they used cassettes and leaflets of liturgies to be used in their own individual houses. Their confidence did not wane. On the contrary, they continuously organized mass worship led by Ephorus Nababan, aiming at strengthening their resistance, even though the SAI-HKBP faction and the military tried not only to prevent it from taking place, but also to block the church members and Ephorus Nababan from entering into the area where the worship was to take place.

Were it not for this belief, a communication forum of church members, aiming to defend themselves against the attempt to take over their assets by the SAI-HKBP faction who always came with the assistance of the military, would not have been born. This forum organized and sent delegates to the House of People's Representatives and Central Government Offices as well

---

47 See doc. no. 44a-m for letters of protest against the decree.
48 See doc. no. 45a-b (from the LWF) and no 46a-p (from the councils of churches in Japan, Namibia, Britain and Ireland, India, Holland, Thailand, USA, Australia, Switzerland and Germany).
49 On 4 January 1993 the Executive Committee of CCI issued a statement (See doc. no. 47). There are three important grounds described in the statement for rejecting the decree: a) as a religious institution the church possesses full authority, in matters related to religious affairs such as doctrine, worship and church leadership; b) according to Pancasila ideology, the state has the task and responsibility to support to the development of lively religious life by upholding the basis/identity/nature of the religion itself; c) the decree marks a direct intervention in the internal affairs of the church, against the constitution of the church and could create a new problem in the body of the HKBP and also set a bad precedent in relations between the state and the church. Previously, in its letter of 28 Dec 1992, the CCI Executive Committee asked Siahaan not to accept the decree (see doc. no. 48). Furthermore, on 10 Feb 1993 the CCI asked President Soeharto to cancel the synod convened by Dr. S.M. Siahaan on 11-13 February 1993 (see. doc. no. 49). After Siahaan carried out his task set out by the decree (see doc. no. 50) the CCI statement on 4 January 1993 was reaffirmed on 2-5 March 1993.

as the National Commission on Human Rights to report the violence committed against them by the SAI-HKBP faction and the military. Indeed, knowing that the government did not allow the local and national daily news and magazines to print their side of the story of events, the AP-HKBP faction continued to publish the weekly News of the HKBP and the monthly Immanuel magazine,[50] and created weekly District News.[51] They were also helped by a Jakarta based Weekly Tabloid, *Sentana*. They even developed various slogans in their struggle, such as Hot di Kristus Hot di Aturan (= Firm in Christ, Firm in the Constitution), Aturan/Peraturan (= Constitution), Setia Sampai Akhir (SSA = Faithful To the End, a slogan derived from Rev 2:10). Over a period of time, the latter became the best known and most loved slogan which they always sang on various occasions when they met, such as in mass worship and on social occasions.[52] This slogan had the gradual effect of creating a sense of group belonging and separated the AP-HKBP faction further from those supporting the SAI leadership.

5.4 The Effect of the Disagreement over the Military Decree

What was predicted by the Jakarta Post editorial on 7 January 1993, soon after the Communion of Churches in Indonesia (CCI) had lodged its strongest protest against the decree on 4 January 1993, held true. The editor warned that "the act of interfering in the internal affairs of an influential religious institution might have a lasting unfavourable impact on at least a certain section of our society."[53] A similar prediction was expressed by an International Human Right activist, Sidney Jones, who said that the military support for the anti-Nababan forces within the HKBP before the 51st synod had helped polarize the two sides in an internal conflict: "the use of troops to close down the synod and appoint a new Ephorus transformed that conflict into a situation of serious civil strife, often involving violence, that will take years, perhaps generations, to heal. Active government support of one side and severe military abuses against what has become known as the AP-SSA faction have placed the conflict far beyond the bounds of a leadership struggle and removed the possibility that anyone associated in any way with the government can play a mediatory role."[54]

---

50 The *Immanuel* magazine was first published in 1890. The weekly *News of the HKBP* was published in 1992.
51 See doc. no. 51, "Suara Jemaat 'Na Lambok Malilung' - Silindung North Tapanuli," No 10, 1996.
52 Such as at marriages, during the periods of mourning and at funerals.
53 The *Jakarta Post*, 7 January 1993. See doc. no. 08.
54 Sidney Jones, *Human Rights in Indonesia and East Timor: The Limits of Openness* (New York, September 1994) 99.

Society itself became divided. This had a massive effect on the relationship between church members in their daily lives. In villages, for instance, some coffee shops lost their customers who happened to be on the other side in the crisis. Family relationship of the HKBP members was also affected. Sometimes, marriage plans between members of different factions had to be cancelled. Decisions on where the wedding ceremony was to be conducted have become problematic. Families stopped greeting or visiting each other. The so called Batak social relationship system of *Dalihan Natolu*[55] was badly affected.

The Batak church has all but disintegrated. The dividing wall separating members and pastors of the church became higher and higher. Since the military decree was issued, its destructive effect on the church had been felt by Christians in Indonesia, and more specifically by the HKBP members and pastors. The task of the church was not carried out. The previous achievements of the church were virtually destroyed. The position of the Bataks in society at large was greatly affected. Rumours had it that it was difficult for members of the church to be promoted in their professions. Batak of working age seeking further education and jobs experienced difficulty. The good image of the Church and Christianity in Indonesia had been destroyed.

5.5 Efforts of Reconciliation: The Relevance of 1 Corinthians 9

As we pointed out at the end of chapter 4, Paul's intended message on the Corinthian dispute over food offered to idols is to expect one party in the dispute to be wiling to forgo their right to eat food offered to idols, together with its theological and civil justifications, for the sake of their counterparts who are likely to be negatively affected and, in fact, destroyed if they insist on eating food offered to idols. Indeed, Paul argues that by not insisting on their right, they will also safeguard themselves from falling into the sins of idolatry and of provoking God to anger, and thereby destroying themselves. In fact, like Paul they will be able to do something good for their counterparts. They will safeguard the unity of the church.

The relevance of this message may be observed in the failure or success of efforts to end the crisis of the HKBP. Whenever any party involved in the dispute insisted on justifying its position, there was no prospect of resolving the crisis. This applies to both parties within the church and to the government. Our exegesis shows that it is those who were thought to have legitimate reasons that were expected by Paul to forgo their right for the sake of those whose views are thought to have no legitimacy. Paul's message reverses the normal practice that those in a better position would

---

55 This is a system of relationship between the Bataks which has been inherited from their ancestors.

always expect their counterparts to comply with their demands. Paul's message expects accommodation on the part of those with legitimate position for the sake of the illegitimate one. Whenever this message failed to be implemented in the crisis of the HKBP, there was no solution to the crisis. As we described above, none of the internal and external parties involved in the crisis of the HKBP thought itself illegitimate. They all considered their position and actions to be legitimate. Whenever any of them insisted on its position, no reconciliatory efforts would succeed, and the effect was fatal, as we have shown above. Conversely, whenever those thought to have a better position agreed to forgo their demands and thought, instead, of the welfare of the HKBP as a whole, the solution to the crisis was widely open.

5.5.1 Failure after Failure

It was the insistence on the rightness of his decree that caused Major General H.R. Pramono to reject the suggestion made by the Judge of the State Administrative Court to reconcile with Ephorus Nababan. The Ephorus was willing, but the General refused. Then, later in the course of the crisis, after the frequent occurrence of violence and after many people felt its negative effect, the leaders of both factions signed a Joint Statement on 14 June 1993. This reconciliation was mediated by the State Minister of the Utilization of the State Apparatus, Major General (retired) T.B. Silalahi. Nababan was willing to support the policy of the government by recognizing the leadership of P.W.T. Simanjuntak and thereby allowing him to lead the church until the next synod, with the condition that all violent action was stopped, all church members could worship freely in the church and the general synod could be held immediately in order to end the problem of the HKBP.[56] However, he was then accused of violating the agreement because he explained to the church members that he would only hand over his *ephoruship* at the next synod and that Simanjuntak was only

---

56 The statements reads 1) We, Rev. Dr. P.W.T. Simanjuntak and Rev. Dr. S.A.E. Nababan based on Christian faith, are willing to work towards reconciliation for the sake of the wholeness, unity and integrity of the HKBP with its congregations; 2) Rev. Dr. S.A.E Nababan supports the decision of the Government by recognizing Rev. Dr. P.W.T. Simanjuntak as Ephorus of the HKBP and gives him the opportunity to lead the HKBP harmoniously and peacefully; 3) This leadership will be reviewed in the next General Synod according to the Constitution of the HKBP; 4) The transfer of office which has not taken place is halted for the time being in order to speed up the process of re-unifying the congregations; 5) In all divided congregations, an opportunity is given to the church members to facilitate worship in the church building in turn; 6) The bringing to an end of problems arising in the congregations case per case by deliberation and consensus is to be carried out by both sides and, if necessary, directly in the area where the problem exists.

functioning as the Ephorus. Similarly, Simanjuntak was seen to have failed to comply with the conditions stated in the agreement. This agreement lasted for two weeks. Silalahi handed over the case to the Minister of Religion to whom he conveyed in a memorandum the idea of convening a joint synod as the best solution to the crisis. Since then there had been no attempt by the Ministry of Religion to unite the parties. On the contrary, it had only acknowledged one party, the SAI-HKBP faction. In fact, it tried to divide the church officially, an attempt which was totally rejected by Ephorus Nababan.[57]

After this joint statement failed to reunite the church, the Indonesian Council of Churches approached both parties and persuaded them to have a tripartite meeting in Jakarta on 15-16 September 1994 and to attend the CCI General Assembly in Jayapura, Irian Jaya, in October 1994. The main difficulty faced by the CCI was the demand made by the SAI leadership for the CCI to recognize its status, something which could not be done.[58] And so, at the assembly, the SAI faction withdrew mainly because their leader was not introduced to the Assembly as the Ephorus of the HKBP. All efforts of the CCI after the assembly failed, with the effect that in June 1995 the HKBP's participation in the CCI was suspended until both parties were reconciled.[59] The World Council of Churches and the Lutheran World Federation as well as the United in Mission tried to mediate between both parties by sending their Fact Finding teams. However, their earlier and constant rejection of the military decree, their refusal to acknowledge the leadership of the church resulting from this decree, and their acknowledgement of the legality of the leadership of the AP-HKBP faction caused both the Indonesian Government and the SAI-HKBP faction to reject their efforts at the outset.[60]

After all these major attempts failed, attempts to reconcile by both internal parties experienced the same fate. The Special Commission created by the SAI-HKBP faction, for instance, failed to make any progress in encouraging the HKBP faction to recognize the legality of its leadership and join its ranks. The initiative of the chairman of the Pastors' Meeting of the church, Rev Dr A.A. Sitompul, failed simply because he was seen as taking sides with the leader of the SAI-HKBP faction, as was seen in his co-signing the invitation letter to the meeting with Dr P.W.T. Simanjuntak.

Conversely, attempts by the AP-HKBP faction to approach the government and the SAI-HKBP faction failed to bear fruit simply because they were always expected to recognize the leadership of the SAI-HKBP

---

57 See doc. no. 52.
58 According to the CCI General Secretary. See doc. no. 53.
59 See doc. no. 54 page 6.
60 See doc 55.

faction as a prerequisite for any talk of reconciliation.[61] Similarly, the AP-HKBP faction had always held that it was the only legitimate HKBP and would never recognize the legality of the SAI-HKBP faction. It constantly proposed a joint synod, that is a synod which is organized, facilitated and attended by all to elect a new leadership. However, this was totally rejected by the SAI-HKBP leadership.[62]

5.5.2 Re-united at Last: A Joint Synod.

While both parties were still trying to find other ways of reconciliation, something happened in the political context of the country. The president of Indonesia, Soeharto, was forced to step down by popular protests led by the students. The economic prosperity which had always been used by Soeharto to clamp down any dissent throughout his 32 years rule in Indonesia backfired. The region was hit by an economic crisis, and Indonesia was the worst hit. The value of its currency fell sharply. Following Soeharto's fall, the image of the military was tarnished by the revelation of tortures and killings it committed during his rule. The people of Indonesia demanded total reformation in the country.

This change of political and economic context in Indonesia played an important role in the finding of a solution to the crisis of the HKBP. This political situation cannot be set aside when we ask the question of why, after the fall of Soeharto, the HKBP church members began to demand an end to the crisis of the HKBP which was seen, at least by some, as being basically caused by the Soeharto's government intervention. The absence of any solution to the crisis was also caused by government support of the military decree. Before his fall, it was evident that so long as the support of the government of the New Order was enjoyed by the SAI-HKBP faction, all attempts to end the crisis of the HKBP failed. Therefore, after Soeharto's fall and when the government support could no longer be relied on by the SAI-HKBP faction, the way to end the crisis of the HKBP opened widely.

With the exception of some congregations, the members of the HKBP from both factions became more willing to reconcile with each other than they had been. For instance, the people of the Tarutung, North Tapanuli, where the headquarters of the church is situated, pleaded that their town

---

61 See P.W.T. Simanjuntak's report to the synod of his faction on 17-22 Nov 1996, page 6. Doc. no. 56 and S.M. Siahaan's report of the same synod, page 5. Doc. no. 57.
62 The SAI-HKBP Elders' Consultation held in the campus of Satya Negara Indonesia University (USNI) on 1-4 August 1996 rejected a joint synod. See "Hasil Mubes Sintua HKBP 1-4 August 1996," which was reported to the synod of SAI on 17-22 November 1996, 2. See doc. no. 58 page 2.

should no longer be used as a combat arena for both parties.[63] They were no longer willing to listen to, far less to support, any of their leaders who did not want to make the reconciliation succeed. This was evident when the SAI-HKBP leadership failed to collect funds needed to protect the headquarters of the church from an attempted take over by the members of the AP-HKBP faction on 3 and 13 June 1998.[64] Nor could the government offer any hand to the SAI-HKBP side, for the nation was in crisis. Hence, when Simanjuntak and his team met Soeharto's successor, B.J. Habibie, in Jakarta on 5 June 1998, and the Commander in Chief of the Regional Military Bukit Barisan in Medan on 16 June 1998 to ask for help, they were advised to solve the crisis internally.[65]

Some churches which had been separated and worshipped in separate church buildings began to worship together (eg. Sudirman Medan and Kampung Kristen Pematangsiantar in North Sumatra), or to use the church in turn (e.g., Bandung, West Java), despite the fact that the previous synod of the SAI-HKBP faction had decided that no use of church buildings in turn was allowed.[66] Ninety four pastors of both factions held a joint retreat on 25-26 August 1998 in Caringin West Java. Churches, which in the past were taken over by force, were retaken by the AP-HKBP faction without any difficulty.[67]

Talks of reconciliation were then conducted by the representatives of both sides with a more serious intent than the previous ones. Pressures from the AP-HKBP faction and the call for an end to the crisis prompted the leader of the SAI-HKBP faction, Dr P.W.T. Simanjuntak, to hold an extraordinary synod on 09-12 July 1998 in Pematangsiantar. This synod was aimed at addressing the question of how open should this faction be in relating to the other faction which, to him, was threatening to take over the assets of the HKBP. It was also aimed at seeking a mandate from the synod to give more power to the members of team 9 of reconciliation to carry out their negotiating task further. Simanjuntak convened this synod, even though the General Secretary of his faction, Dr S.M. Siahaan, and some district leaders did not attend.[68] This synod decided to hold another synod in October 1998 to which pastors of the other faction would be invited.[69]

---

63 See P.W.T. Simanjuntak's report to the extra-ordinary synod of the SAI faction in Pematangsiantar on 09-12 July 1998, 7. Doc. no. 59.
64 In his report to the extraordinary synod Simanjuntak reported that the leadership of the SAI-HKBP faction had to spend one hundred million rupiah which was taken from different fund because the church members contributed only 15 million rupiah. See Simanjuntak's report (1998), 4.
65 See Simanjuntak's report (1998) 7.
66 See Simanjuntak's report (1998) 8.
67 See Simanjuntak's report (1998) 3.
68 See Daily News, *Sinar Indonesia Baru,* 11 July 1998. Doc. no. 60.
69 See Daily News, *Sinar Indonesia Baru,* 12 July 1998. Doc. no. 61.

In the process of negotiation between the representatives of both factions, when the members of the AP-HKBP faction realized on 9 October 1998 that there was a deadlock in the negotiations and that the SAI-HKBP faction refused to sign a letter of agreement needed for holding a joint synod, they took over the headquarters of the church on 9 November 1998 without much difficulty and demanded that the leader of the SAI-HKBP faction hold a joint synod. They made it very clear that their occupation of the headquarters was not the aim in itself. They wanted to push forward the talks of reconciliation. Hence they insisted that they would not leave the headquarters of the church before the joint synod was held. Attempt to reclaim the headquarters of the church by SAI-HKBP faction on 10-11 October 1998, an action which caused the death of the Rev. M. Rajagukguk and injured some people, failed. The military no longer offered them any assistance as it had done.

The occupation of the headquarters by the HKBP faction was seen by some as a setback as far as the reconciliation process was concerned. In spite of this situation, the talk of reconciliation continued. The representatives of both factions held talks in the headquarters of the church on 23 October 1998.

When reconciliation was again hampered by the plan of SAI-HKBP faction to have a synod of its own in Pematangsiantar, North Sumatra on 26-28 October 1998, thousands of the HKBP faction's members prevented it from being officially opened by breaking into the venue and forcing the members of the synod to leave. The insistence of the church members to reject any synod attended by one party was such that when it was eventually moved to the military headquarters, they tried to enter the venue, albeit without success. Perhaps, it was because of pressure from these church members that this synod did not appoint new leaders. Instead, it appointed Rev Dr J.R. Hutauruk, the Chairman of Pastor's Meeting of this faction, to be the Acting Ephorus and gave him the task of convening a joint synod within three to six months.

After being inaugurated on 1 November 1998 in Balige, North Sumatra, and with the mandate given by his faction's synod, Hutauruk met Nababan. Then on 17 November 1998, witnessed by around 250 people including the officials of both parties and without much publicity, both signed a historic agreement in the HKBP Sudirman, Medan, North Sumatra. They agreed to work toward the end of the crisis and safeguard the unity of the church by holding a joint synod in Pematangsiantar on 18-20 December 1998 to elect a new leadership of the church consisting of the Ephorus, the General Secretary, the members of the Central Church Board and the leaders of the HKBP districts.[70]

Unlike the Joint-Statement made in June 1993, this agreement did not

---

70 See Daily News *Suara Pembaruan*, 18 November 1998, 1. Doc. no. 62.

elaborate any conditions or details that both sides had to abide by in order to achieve the goal of the agreement. Rather, it left the technicality of the synod preparation to be worked out later by a joint synod committee which was formed the next day in Medan. They asked all church members to pray and support the preparations of the synod in the spirit of acceptance and forgiveness. The invitation to the synod, which was attended by 1098 delegates of both sides, was signed by Dr Hutauruk and Dr Nababan as the Acting Ephorus and the Ephorus respectively. Both called for the interest of all to be prioritized for the future of all. They both opened the synod and handed over its leadership to Rev M. Lumbangaol and Rev. T.P. Simorangkir, both of whom are the eldest pastors of each faction. The number of delegates for a normal synod is around 600. Just as stated by the joint committee of the synod in its press release on 11 December 1998, the synod elected a new leadership, the composition of which reflects equal representation of both parties. Before the synod, delegates of both parties held a joint worship at the HKBP Martoba Pematangsiantar on 17 December 1998, to prepare them wholly for the long awaited joint synod and the beginning of an end to their painful six year long crisis.

5.6 Concluding Remarks

In conclusion, it is clear that the crisis of the HKBP erupted when the military intervened. As a result, the HKBP could no longer solve its own internal bickering. In fact, it experienced a full scale, widespread and devastating effect. For 6 years the church was divided. At times, it was tempting for each faction to formally break up by forming a new name and organization, as is often the case in church history. The SAI-HKBP faction and the government had thought that separation might be the easiest way to end the conflict, but the AP-HKBP faction rejected the idea and constantly tried to convince their counterparts that a joint synod was the only viable solution. Then for some reasons, the former changed its mind, and the latter responded with joy to the fulfilment of their long awaited demand for both to have a joint synod.

It is true that favourable external and internal conditions were needed for the reunification to take place. The fall of Soeharto, the spirit of reform of the political system running throughout Indonesia and the pressure from the church members played an important role in this regard. As a result, it was no longer possible for the SAI-HKBP faction to seek the help of the military, which was struggling to repair its battered image in the country, and to garner support from the church members. The government had a more important task to handle: to save the economy of the country and to deal with the strong demand for total political and economic reforms, and for the withdrawal of the military from Indonesian politics. This time, the government had no time to continue meddling in the internal affairs of the

HKBP. However, the willingness of Dr J.R. Hutauruk to carry out the mandate assigned him by his faction synod and to regard Dr S.A.E. Nababan as Ephorus of the HKBP as was evident in their agreement, something which he and his faction would never have done before, was very significant. Conversely the willingness of Nababan to regard Hutauruk as the Acting Ephorus of a faction that he had never before legally recognized is equally crucial. They both made use of the conditions. The willingness of both parties to be reunited was also made clear in the composition of the top leadership of the church elected at the joint synod, Rev. Dr. J.R. Hutauruk of the SAI-HKBP faction, and Rev Willem T.P. Simarmata MA of the AP-HKBP faction as the new Ephorus and General Secretary respectively. Hence, the willingness of each party to forgo its 'justification' of its position in the dispute over the legality of the military decree, and to think, instead, of the welfare of the HKBP as a whole, were the principles that were taken by all parties in the dispute, including the military. The HKBP case may therefore provide justification for a cause to call for the need to consider seriously Paul's suggested solution to the first century Corinthian dispute over food offered to idols in our attempt to address issues of conflict that are threatening the unity of the church today.

Dramatis Personae

Hutauruk, J.R., Rev Dr: Prior to his election as a member of the Central Church Board of the SAI-HKBP faction at the Tiara extraordinary synod, he lectured in Church History at the HKBP-Theological Seminary Pematangsiantar. Later, he was elected as the Chairman of the Pastors' Meeting and then as the acting Ephorus of the SAI-HKBP faction. On 18 November 1998, he co-signed a joint agreement with Ephorus Dr S.A.E. Nababan to hold a joint synod on 18-20 December 1998, at which he was elected as the Ephorus of the HKBP.

Munawir Sjadzali, MA: The Minister of Religion who gave a memo to General (retired) M. Panggabean, a member of the HKBP and the Chairman of the Supreme Advisory Council, to try to solve the internal problem of the HKBP.

Nababan, S.A.E., Rev Dr: The Ephorus of the HKBP (1987-92) who continued to exercise as the legal and constitutional Ephorus of the HKBP (1992-1998) even though the government and the other faction did not recognize him as such after the military decree.

Panggabean, M., General (retired): Chairman of the Indonesian Supreme Advisory Council and a member of the HKBP. He formed and dismissed the Peace Team which, though aiming to help solve the internal problem of the HKBP, proved to have caused deeper polarisation within the leadership of the HKBP.

Pramono, H.R., Major General: The Head of the Northern Sumatra Agency for the Co-ordination of Support for National Stability who issued a military decree on 23 December 1992, appointing Rev. Dr. S.M. Siahaan as the acting Ephorus of the HKBP.

Siahaan, L.O.: The Chief Judge of the State Administrative Court in Medan who presided the litigation filed by Ephorus Nababan against Major General H.R. Pramono. After deciding in favour of Ephorus Nababan, his house was terrorised, and he himself was replaced by his deputy, Judge Soebechi.

Siahaan, S.M., Rev Dr: Before being appointed by Major General H.R. Pramono as the acting Ephorus of the HKBP, he was a lecturer in the Old Testament Studies at the HKBP Theological Seminary and a member of the HKBP Central Church Board. Based on the military decree, he called the extraordinary synod at Tiara Convention Center, Medan, on 11-13 February 1993 where he was elected as the General Secretary of the SAI-HKBP faction.

Sihombing MTh, P.M., Rev: The General Secretary of the Church (1978-1986) who failed the leadership contest at the HKBP Synod in 1987. He led a group of 19 pastors called as the Parritrit to campaign against the leadership of Ephorus Nababan and his possible reelection.

Silalahi, T.B., Major General (Retired): The State Minister of the Utilization of the State Apparatus who initiated, helped to bring about, but also, brought to a halt the Joint Statement signed by Dr. S.A.E. Nababan and Dr. P.W.T Simanjuntak in June 1993 aimed at ending the crisis of the church.

Simanjuntak, P.W.T., Rev Dr: Before being elected as the Ephorus of the SAI-HKBP faction at the extraordinary synod held at Tiara Convention Hall in 1993, he lectured in Practical Theology at the HKBP-Theological Seminary, Pematangsiantar.

Simorangkir, O.P.T., Rev: The General Secretary of the HKBP (1987-1992) who, after accusing Ephorus Nababan of being authoritarian, was involved in a campaign against his leadership and reelection.

Soeharto, General (retired): President of Indonesia who, although he continuously spoke of the freedom of religion in Indonesia through his address at national religious celebrations, did nothing to prevent Major General Pramono from implementing his military decree. In fact, he had an audience with the leadership of the SAI-HKBP faction at the State Palace, an action which was seen by many as indication of his approval of the leadership of this faction.

Chapter 6

Conclusions

By arguing that Paul is not to be held responsible for the emergence and intensification of the dispute among Corinthian Christians over food offered to idols, and by inferring, instead, that the mood of the city to propagate the worship of the imperial cult was the trigger of what was otherwise a normal issue in the early Church, we have been able to see the centrality of 'right' (ἐξουσία) in the minds of some Corinthian Christians who wanted to participate fully in the social, political and religious life of the city by eating food offered to idols. Given that other Corinthian Christians did not want to follow this total participation, it was natural that those who wanted to eat food offered to idols justified their 'right' with theological arguments based on their knowledge of the existence of a monotheistic God, non-existence of idols, neutrality of food before God and of the aphoristic saying that 'everything is permitted.'

It is this background that caused Paul to emphasize the importance of forgoing his right in 1 Corinthians 8:9 - 9:18. The various arguments used in 1 Corinthians 9:4 - 12a, 13-14 to legitimize his own right to financial support betray the centrality of right in the minds of those who wanted to eat food offered to idols. We have shown that, indeed, Paul's elaboration of his right is best read against the background of the economic life of his readers. In choosing some examples of right and in using rhetorical questions expecting positive answers Paul helps his readers to know that he too respects his own right to financial support very highly. At the same time, however, he makes it very clear that it is this right that must be set aside for the sake of the gospel. Paul would not have resorted to this kind of powerful discourse were it not because of his recognition of the importance of right for his intended readers who viewed their Roman citizenship very highly and who, should they forgo their right to eat food offered to idols, would be afraid of acting against their freedom status and their aphoristic saying that 'everything is permitted.' Nor would Paul have continued in 1 Corinthians 9:19-23 to write on his experience of enslaving himself in order to win more people, if it had not been because of his awareness of the importance of freedom status to most of them. Nor would he have gone on to speak of the importance of self-control in 9:24-27, were it not because of his awareness of the difficulty that might be faced by his readers in forgoing their right, acting against their freedom status, and accommodating the view of the weak on the issue of food offered to idols. All in all, Paul speaks of his personal example, not because he wants to reassert his authority, but because he wants to help his readers to know how they can imitate Christ in their treatment of others in their community and outside it, even in the case of food offered to idols (11:1). Therefore, the elaboration of the reason for his refusal to live off the gospel in 9:12b, 14-18 is meant to enable his readers to see not only the consequence, but also the benefit of forgoing their right for the sake of the weak and others.

To strengthen this exhortation further, in 1 Corinthians 10:1-22 Paul introduces into his discourse the warning against idolatry and the calling to flee from it. We have shown that by so doing Paul wants to make those who want to eat food offered to idols aware of the fact that their insistence on eating such food will not only jeopardize their counterparts (8:9-13), but it will also destroy themselves. Paul's exhortation for them to care for the weak and flee from idolatry was such that even eating food associated with idols at the invitation of an unbeliever, that is to say, in a venue quite far away from the public temple, is not advisable when the scruple of the weak is made known to them (10:27-29b). In fact, Paul develops the idea of caring for the weak on the issue of food offered to idols. In 1 Corinthians 10:23-24, 10:31 - 11:1 he speaks of the importance of seeking the good of others for the glory of God, and of avoiding giving offence to the Jews, Greeks and the church of God. This is not to say, however, that Paul justifies the position of those who, because of their familiarity with idolatry, want to abstain from food associated with idols even that sold in the meat market. What he writes in 1 Corinthians 10:19-20, 25-26, 30b is an implicit rejection of their position.

It is this reading of the overall discourse of Paul that has enabled us to argue that 1 Corinthians 9 functions primarily as an example. It is meant to give an example to one party in the dispute of the importance of waiving their right to eat food offered to idols for the sake of the weak. However, there is also an element of defence in 1 Corinthians 9 on the part of Paul. Given the presence of some missionaries who had visited Corinth and reaped material benefit from Corinthian Christians, and in the light of the existence of a leadership alignment among Corinthian Christians (1 Cor. 1:10 - 4:21), we have argued that Paul defends his apostolic example of renouncing his right to financial support because it has been used by some to criticize his apostolic status. Hence, content-wise, there is a close relationship between 1 Corinthians 1 - 4 and 1 Corinthians 9.

Though short, Paul's defence in 1 Corinthians 9:1-3 is stronger than that in 1 Corinthians 4:1-5. This is not entirely because the criticism of his apostolic status in the former is more substantial than in the latter. (It may be argued that the criticism of his having not witnessed the resurrection of Jesus is fiercer than that of his weakness in terms of preaching capability by means of eloquent wisdom). Rather, his defence here is stronger because of his belief that it is his apostolic practice of renouncing his apostolic right that may convince some Corinthian Christians not to insist on exercising their right to eat food offered to idols (9:4-18). Were this not the case, Paul would not have retold his experience of having to act against the command of the Lord (9:4-14), enslave himself (9:19-23) and exercise self-control (9:24-27). We have also suggested that his refusal to accept financial support was not influenced by anything but his own perception of the gospel of Christ crucified which requires him to avoid creating a stumbling block to the preaching of the gospel freely and to the salvation of others. It is an enterprise which has nothing to do with, as many scholars have alleged, his desire to differ from the practice of many itinerant and popular philosophers of the time. It is precisely because of his confidence in this reason for the refusal of his right to live off the gospel that encourages Paul to bring it to the attention of those who wanted to eat food offered to idols on the basis of their right, so that they can imitate it in their attitude towards those with whom they disagreed. Indeed, Paul's attempt to get his message across is made clear by his assertion that the refusal to accept financial support, self-enslavement and self control does not just benefit others but also himself (9:15b, 23, 27). He would not have done this were it not in order to convince those who wanted to exercise their right in the case of food offered to idols of the importance of prioritizing the welfare of others as opposed to insisting on exercising their right.

Our exegesis of 1 Corinthians 9 as an integral part of Paul's overall discourse has also thrown some light on conflict resolution in our church today. Paul's method of encouraging one party in the dispute to give up their position without negating their theologically, socially and politically legitimate arguments, on the one hand, and of caring for the weak without justifying their theologically illegitimate position, on the other hand, is very much needed by anyone called to mediate in any form of conflict within the church today. Paul's acknowledgement of what those involved in the dispute over food offered to idols had in mind and his desire to prevent the church from falling apart caused him to write the way he did in 1 Corinthians 8:1 - 11:1. The use of various materials in his discourse was meant to help his readers to act not according to their legitimate arguments, but according to Christological praxis which he himself had shown in his missionary work.

In facing a delicate and intense dispute such as the issue of food offered to idols which emerged because of the desire among the people of Corinth to propagate the Imperial cult in order to gain favour from the Roman authorities, such a method would not only prevent the church from disintegrating, but it would also help Corinthian Christians to act in imitation of Christ. In an era where the likelihood of the church having to face various conflicting issues is very high, the legitimacy of such a method should therefore not be undermined, if we are to follow Christ and safeguard the unity of the church today. In essence, on disputed issues which have exhausted all efforts to reach a possible consensus and pointed to a remote possibility of finding a consensus – despite an extended discussion and constant interaction between holders of opposing views, Paul's counsel is not to resort to consensus, but to ask those who think that they have legitimate rights to do certain disputed actions based on legitimate reasons to refrain from doing so for the sake of 'others' in the same community - whose opinion on the matter of discussion is thought to be based on unclear or even unjustified reasons, yet for whom Christ has died – and consequently for the sake of 'themselves.' That act of refraining is entirely in imitation of Christ who dies for others, not because they are right but precisely because they are not righteous. The reunification of the Batak Christian Protestant Church, which was in crisis for 6 years because of the dispute over the question of, first who should lead the church, then of how the church should be led, what it should do in Indonesian context, and finally over the legality of the government intervention in its internal affairs, is the result of the willingness of each party to renounce their position not only for the sake of others in the community, but also and ultimately for the sake of the community itself for which Christ has died. Certainly, a united Batak Church would serve God and the nation much better than a divided one.

Bibliography

I. Literature Consulted for Chapters 1-4

Abbott, F.F. and Johnson, A.C., *Municipal Administration in the Roman Empire* (Princeton: Princeton University Press, 1926).

Achtemeier Paul J., "Gods made with hands: The New Testament and the Problem of Idolatry" in *Ex Auditu* 15 (1999) 43-61.

Agrell, G., *Work, Toil and Sustenance: An Examination of the View of Work in The New Testament* (Lund: Verbum-Haken Ohissons, 1976).

Allison, D.C., "The Pauline Epistles and the Synoptic Gospels: The Pattern of the Parallels" in *New Testament Studie* 28 (1992) 1-32.

Andrews, Mary E., "The party of Christ in Corinth" in *Anglican Theological Review* 19 (1937) 17-29.

Applebaum, S., *Jews and Greeks in Ancient Cyrene* (Leiden: E.J. Brill, 1979).

Arafat, K.W., *Pausanias' Greece. Ancient Artists and Roman Rulers* (Cambridge: Cambridge University Press, 1996).

Auguet, R., *Cruelty and Civilization: The Roman Games*. ET. (London: George Allen and Unwin, 1972).

Badian, E., *Publicans and Sinners: Private Enterprise in the Service of the Roman Republic* (Oxford: Blackwell, 1972).

Baird, W., "One Against Another: Intra-Church Conflict in 1 Corinthians" in Robert T. Fortna and Beverly R. Gaventa (eds.), *The Conversation Continues Studies in Paul and John in honor of J. Louis Martyn* (Nashville: Abingdon Press, 1990) 116-36.

Barclay, J.M.S., "'Thessalonica and Corinth': Social Contrast in Pauline Christianity" in *Journal for the Study of New Testament* 47 (1992) 49-74.

— "Paul among Diaspora Jews: Anomaly or Apostate?" in *Journal for the Study of the New Testament* 60 (1995) 89-120.

Barrett, C.K., "Christianity at Corinth" in *Bulletin of the John Rylands Library* 46 (1964) 269-97.

— *The First Epistle to the Corinthians*. HNTC (New York/Evanston: Harver and Row, 1968).

— "Boasting (καυχασθαι, κτλ) in the Pauline Epistles" in A. Vanhoye (ed.), *L'Apôtre Paul Personalité; style et conception du ministère* (Bibliotheca Ephemeridum theologicarum Lovaniensium, 73; Leuven: University Press, 1986) 363-68.

— "Cephas and Corinth" in *Essays on Paul* (London: SPCK, 1982) 28-39.

— "Things Sacrificed to Idols" in *New Testament Studies* 11 (1965) 138-153.

— *On Paul: Aspects of His Life, Work and Influence in the Early Church* (London and New York: T and T Clark, 2003).

Bartchy, S. Scott, *Mallon Chresai: First Century Slavery and the Interpretation of 1 Corinthians 7:21*. SBLDS 11 (Missoula, Mont: SBL, 1973).

Barton, Stephen, "'All Things to All Men' (1 Corinthians 9:22): The Principle of Accommodation in the Mission of Paul," Unpublished BA. Hons. Thesis, Macquire

University, 1975.
— "Was Paul a Relativist?" in *Interpretation* 19 (1976) 164-192.
— "'All Things to all people.' Paul and the law in the light of 1 Corinthians 9:19-23" in James D.G. Dunn (ed.), *Paul and the Mosaic Law* (Tübingen: Mohr, 1996) 271-285.
— *Invitation to the Bible* (London: SPCK, 1997).
Baur, F.C., "Die Christuspartei in der korinthischen Gemeinde, der Gegensatz des paulinischen und petrinishen Christentums in der altesten Kirche, der Apostel Petrus in Rom" in Klaus Scholder (ed.), *Ausgewahite Werke in Einzelausgaben* (Stuttgart- and Bad Cannstatt: Ffrommann, 1963) 1-146. Originally, "Die Christuspartei in der korinthischen Gemeinde" in *Tübinger Zeitschrift für Theologie* 5 (1831) 61-206.
— *Paul, The Apostle of Jesus Christ. His Life and Work, His Epistles and His Doctrine. A Contribution to a critical history of primitive Christianity.* ET By Eduard Zeller (London: Williams and Norgate 1876).
— *Paulus der Apostel Jesu Christi.* Vol. 1. (Osabruck: Otto Zaller, 1968).
Best, E., "Paul's Apostolic Authority" in *Journal for the Study of the New Testament* 27 (1986) 3-25.
— *Paul and His Converts. The Spurnt Lectures 1985* (Edinburgh: T and T Clark, 1988).
Black, D.A., "A Note on 'the Weak' in I Corinthians 9,22" in *Biblica* 64 (1983) 240-242.
Blasi, A.J., *Early Christianity as a Social Movement.* Toronto Studies in Religion, 5 (New York: Peter Lang, 1988).
Blomberg, C. *1 Corinthians*. NIV Application Commentary (Grand Rapids: Zondervan, 1994).
Bookidis, N., "Ritual Dining in the Sanctuary of Demeter and Kore at Corinth: Some Questions," Ch. 5 in Sympotica: *A Symposium on the symposium.* Oswyn Murray (Oxford: Clarendon Press, 1990) 86-94.
Bookidis, N. and Fisher, J.E., "Preliminary Report on Demeter and Kore" in *Hesperia* 41 (1972) 283-331.
Borgen, Peder, "Catalogues of Vices: The Apostolic Decree and the Jerusalem Meeting" in J. Neusner et. al., (eds.), *The Social World of Formative Christianity and Judaism* (Philadelphia: Fortress Press, 1988) 126-141.
— "'Yes,' 'No,' 'How Far?': The Participation of Jews and Christians in Pagan Cults" in Troels Engberg-Pedersen (ed.), *Paul in His Hellenistic Context* (Edinburgh: Tand T Clark, 1994) 30-59.
Bornkamm, G., "The Missionary Stance of Paul in 1 Corinthians and Acts" in L.E. Keck and J.L Martyn (eds.) *Studies in Luke-Acts* (London, 1968) 194-207.
— *Paul* (London: Hodder and Stoughton, 1971).
Bradley, Keith, *Slaves and Masters in the Roman Empire: A Study in Social Control* (Oxford: Oxford University Press, 1987).
— *Slavery and Society at Rome* (Cambridge: Cambridge University Press, 1994).
Braudel, F., *The Mediterranean and the Mediterranean World in the Age of Philip II.* ET. by S. Reynolds (London: Collins, 1972).
Braund, David C., *Augustus to Nero: A Sourcebook on Roman History. 31 BC-AD 68* (London, Sydney: Croom Helm, 1985).
Breadslee, William A., *First Corinthians. A Commentary for Today* (St. Louis: Chalice Press, 1994).
Brewer, D. Instone, "1 Cor 9.9-11: 'Do not muzzle the ox'" in *New Testament Studies* 38 (1992) 554-565.

Broneer, O., "Hero Cults in the Corinthian Agora" in *Hesperia 11* (1942) 128-61.
— "Corinth - Center of St. Paul's Missionary Work in Greece" in *BA* 14 (1952) 78-96.
— "The Apostle Paul and the Isthmian Games" in *Biblical Archaeologist* 25 (1962) 2-31.
— "Paul and the Pagan Cults at Isthmia" in *HTR* 64 (1971) 169-187.
Broughton, T.R.S., *The Magistrate of the Roman Republic.* Vol.1 (Atlanta, Georgia: Scholars Press, 1986).
Bruce, F.F., *1 and 2 Corinthians.* NCBC (Grand Rapids, Ml.,: Eerdmans, 1971).
— *Paul and Jesus* (Grand Rapids, MI: Baker Book House, 1974).
Brunt, John C., "Rejected, Ignored, or Misunderstood? The Fate of Paul's Approach to the problem of Food Offered to Idols in Early Christianity" in *New Testament Studies* 31 (1985) 113-124.
Brunt, P.A., *Italian Manpower. 225 B.C.- A.D. 14* (Oxford: Clarendon Press,1987).
Byron, John, *Slavery Metaphors in Early Judaism and Pauline Christianity* (Tübingen: Mohr Siebeck, 2003).
Cadbury, H., "Erastus of Corinth" in *Journal of Biblical Literature* 50 (1931) 42-58.
— "The Macellum of Corinth" in *Journal of Biblical Literature* 53 (1934) 134-141.
Campbell, J.P., *The Roman Emperor and the Roman Army. 31 BC - AD 235* (Oxford: Clarendon Press, 1984).
Carson, D., "Paul's Inconsistency: Reflections on I Corinthians 9.19-23 and Galatians 2.11 -14" in *Churchman* 100 (1986) 7-45.
Carter, Philippa, *The Servant-Ethic in the New Testament* (New York: Peter Lang, 1997).
Carter, Timothy L., "'Big Men' in Corinth" in *Journal for the Study of the New Testament* 66 (1997) 45-67.
Castelli, E.A., *Imitating Paul: A Discourse of Power. Literary Currents in Biblical Interpretation* (Westminster: Louisville, 1991).
Catchpole, D., "Paul, James, and the Apostolic Decree" in *New Testament Studies* 23 (1977) 428-44.
Cha, Young-Gil, "The Function of Peculium in Roman Slavery during the First Two Centuries A.D" in T. Youge and M. Doi (eds.), *Forms of Control and Subordination in Antiquity. Tokyo: The Society for Studies on Resistance Movements in Antiquity* (Leiden: E.J. Brill, 1988) 433-36.
Chadwick, H., "All Things to All Men (1 Cor. IX.22)" in *New Testament Studies* 1 (1954-5) 261-75; Heresy and Orthodoxy in the Early Church (Aldershot: Variorum, 1991).
Chapple, A.E., "Local Leadership in the Pauline Churches: Theological and Social Factors in its Development. A Study Based on 1 Thessalonians, 1 Corinthians and Philippians." Unpublished PhD Thesis (Durham Univ. 1984).
Cheung, Alex T., *Idol Food in Corinth: Jewish Background and Pauline Legacy.* JSNT Suplement Series 176 (Sheffield: Sheffield Academic Press, 1999).
Chow, J.K., *Patronage and Power: A Study of Social Networks in Corinth* (Sheffield: JSOT, 1992).
— "Patronage in Roman Corinth" in R.A. Horsley (ed.), *Paul and Empire. Religion in Roman Imperial Society* (Pennsylvania: Trinity Press International, 1997) 104-25.
Clarke, A.D., *Secular and Christian Leadership in Corinth: A Socio-Historical and Exegetical Study of 1 Corinthians 1-6* (Leiden: Brill, 1993).
— "'Be Imitators of Me': Paul's Model of Leadership" in *Tyndale Bulletin* 49 (1998)

327-360.
Clarke, G.W., "The Origins and Spread of Christianity" in A.K. Bowmann, et.al., (eds.), *The Cambridge Ancient History. 2nd ed. Vol. X. The Augustan Empire. 43 B.C. - A.D. 69* (Cambridge: Cambridge University Press, 1996) 848-872.
Conzelmann, H., *A Commentary on the First Epistle to the Corinthians* (Philadelphia: Fortress, 1975).
Corbier, M., "The Ambiguous Status of Meat in Ancient Rome" in *Food and Foodways* 3 (1989) 223-264.
Coye Still III, E, "The Meaning and Uses of ΕΙΔΩΛΟΘΥΤΟΝ in First Century Non-Pauline Literature and 1 Cor 8:1-11:1: Toward Resolution of the Debate" in *Trinity Journal* 23 (2002) 225-234.
— "Paul's Aims Regarding ειδωλόθυτα: A New Proposal for Interpreting 1 Cor 8:1-11:1" in *Novum Testamentum* 44 (2002) 333-43.
Crafton, Jeffrey A., *The Agency of the Apostle: A Dramatic Analysis of Paul's Responses to Conflict in 2 Corinthians* (Sheffield: Academic Press, 1991).
Crook, J.A., *Legal Advocacy in the Roman World* (London: Duckworth, 1995).
Dahl, N.A., "Paul and the Church at Corinth According to 1 Corinthians" in W.R. Farmer, et.al., (eds.), *Christian History and Interpretation. Studies Presented to John Knox* (Cambridge: Cambridge University Press, 1967) 313-35.
Daube, D., *The New Testament and Rabbinic Judaism* (London: The Athlone Press, 1956).
Davies, James A., "The Interaction Between Individual Ethical Conscience and Community Ethical Consciousness in 1 Corinthians" in *Horizons in Biblical Theology* 10 (1988) 1-18.
Davies, W.D. and Allison, D.C., *The Gospel According to Saint Matthew*, vol. II (ICC, Edinburgh: T and T Clarke, 1991)
De Boer, Martinus, *The Defeat of Death: Apocalyptic Eschatology in 1 Corinthians 15 and 5* (Sheffield: JSOT Press, 1988).
Deissmann, A., *Light From the Ancient East*. ET. by L.R.M. Strachan (London: Hodder and Stoughton, 1927).
Delobel, J., "Coherence and Relevance of 1 Corinthians 8-10" in R. Bieringer, *The Corinthian Correspondence* (Leuven: University Press, 1996) 177-190.
DeMaris, Richard E., "Corinthian Religion and Baptism for the Dead (1 Corinthians 15:29): Insights from Archaeology and Anthropology" in *Journal of Biblical Literature* 14 (1995) 678-681.
— "Demeter in Roman Corinth: Local Development in a Mediterranean Religion" in *Numen* 42 (1995) 105-17.
Deming, Will, *Paul on Marriage and Celibacy: the Hellenistic Background of 1 Corinthians 7* (Cambridge: Cambridge University Press, 1995).
Denaux, A., "Theology and Christology in 1 Cor 8, 4-6: A Contextual-Redactional Reading" in R. Bieringer (ed.), *Corinthian Correspondence* (Leuven: Leuven University, 1996) 593-606.
Dickson, John P., *Mission Commitment in Ancient Judaism and in the Pauline Communities: The Shape, Extent and Background of Early Christian Mission* (Tübingen: Mohr Siebeck, 2003)
Didier, G., "Le salaire du désintéressement (1 Co. 9.14-27)," in *RecSciRel* 43 (1955) 228f.,
Dixon, Suzanna, The *Roman Family* (Baltimore and London: The John Hopkins

University Press, 1992).
Dodd, C.H., "Εννομος Χριστου" in *More New Testament Studies* (Manchester, 1968) 134-48.
Doubschütz, E., *Christian Life in the Primitive Church* (New York: P.G. Putnam and Sons, 1904).
Douglas, M., *Natural Symbols: Explorations in Cosmology* (New York: Pantheon, 3rd edn. 1982. repr. London: Routledge, 1996).
Downing, F. Gerald, "A Bas Les Aristos. The Relevance of Higher Literature for the Understanding of the Earliest Writings" in *Novum Testamentum* 30 (1988) 212-230.
Drane, J.W., *Paul: Libertine or Legalist? A Study in the Theology of the Major Pauline Epistles* (London: SPCK, 1975).
Duff, A. M., *Freedmen in the Early Empire* (Cambridge: W. Hefner, 1958).
Dumbrell, W.J. *The Search for Order: Biblical Eschatology in Focus* (Michigan: Baker Books, 1994).
— "Law and Grace: The Nature of the Contrast in John 1:17" in *EQ* LVIII (1984) 25-37.
Dungan, D. L., *The Sayings of Jesus in the Churches of Paul: The Use of the Synoptic Tradition in the Regulation of Early Church Life* (Oxford: Basil Blackwell, 1975).
Dunn, J.D.G., *1 Corinthians* (Sheffield: Sheffield University Press, 1995).
— *The Theology of Paul the Apostle* (Edinburgh: T and T Clark, 1998).
Ebner, M., *Leidenslisten und Apostelbrief: Untursuchungen zu Form, Motivik und Funktion der Peristasenkatalogue bei Paulus. Furschung zur Bibel*, Band 66 (Wuryburg, Echter 1991)
Ehrhard, A., "Social Problems in the Early Church" in *The Framework of the New Testament Stories* (Manchester: Manchester University Press, 1964).
Elliott, Neil, "The Anti-Imperial Message of the Cross" in R.A. Horsley (ed.), *Paul. Empire: Religion and Power in Roman Imperial Society* (Pennsylvania: Trinity Press International, 1997) 167-83.
— *Liberating Paul: The Justice of God and the Politics of the Apostle* (Maryknoll: Orbis Books, 1994).
Ellison, H.L., "Paul and the Law – 'All Things to All Men'" in W.W. Gasgue and R.P. Martin (eds.), *Apostolic History and the Gospel* (Exeter: Paternoster Press, 1970) 105-202.
Engberg-Pedersen, T., "The Gospel and Social Practice According to 1 Corinthians" in *NTS* 33 (1987) 269-70.
Engels, D., *Roman Corinth: An Alternative Model for the Classical City* (Chicago: University of Chicago Press, 1990).
Fee, G.D., "II Corinthians VI. 14-VII.1 and Food Offered to Idols" in *New Testament Studies* 23 (1977) 140-161.
— *The First Epistle to the Corinthians.* NIC (Grand Rapids, M.I.,: Eerdmans, 1987).
— "Eidolothyta Once Again: An Interpretation of 1 Corinthians 8-10" in *Biblica* 61 (1980) 172-97.
Ferguson, E., *Backgrounds of Early Christianity* (Grand Rapids: Eerdmans, 1989).
Filson, F.V., "The Significance of the Early House churches" in *Journal of Biblical Literature* 58 (1939) 105-112.
Finley, M.I., *The Ancient Economy* (London: Chatto and Windus, 1973).
Fiore, B., "'Covert Allusion' in 1 Corinthians 1-4" in *Catholic Biblical Quarterly* 47 (1985) 85-102.

Fiorenza, S.E., "Toward a Feminist Model of Historical Reconstruction" in *In Memory of Her. A Feminist Theological Reconstruction of Christian Origins* (New York: Crossroad, 1989).
— "Rhetorical Situation and Historical Reconstruction in 1 Corinthians" in *New Testament Studies* 33 (1987) 386-403.
Fisk, Bruce N., "Eating Meat Offered to Idols: Corinthian Behaviour and Pauline Response in 1 Corinthians 8-10 (A Response to Gordon Fee)" in *Trinity Journal* 10 (1989) 49-70.
Fitzgerald, John T.,*Cracks in an Earthen Vessel. An Examination of the Catalogues of Hardships in the Corinthian Correspondence* (Atlanta, Georgia: Scholars Press, 1988. PhD dissertation, Yale University, 1984)
Fjärstedt, B., *Synoptic Tradition in I Corinthians: Themes and Clusters of Theme Words in I Corinthians 1-4 and 9* (Uppsala: Theologiska Institutionen, 1974).
Foerster, W., "ἔξεστιν, ἐξουσιααν δ ζω, κατεξουσιααν δ ζω" in G. Kittel (ed.), *Theological Dictionary of the New Testament Vol. II* (Grand Rapids: WB. Eerdmans, 1964) 560-575.
Forbes, Clarence A., "The Education and Training of Slaves in Antiquity" in *TAPA* 86 (1955) 321-60.
Fotopoulos, John, *Food Offered to Idols in Roman Corinth* (Tübingen: Mohr Siebeck, 2003).
Frank, Richard I, "Augustus' Legislation on Marriage and Children" in *California Studies in Classical Antiquity* 8 (1976) 41-52.
Furnish, V.P., "What Can Archaeology Tell Us?" in *BAR* 15 (1988) 15-27.
— "Belonging to Christ: A Paradigm for Ethics in First Corinthians" in *Interpretation* 44 (1990) 145-157.
Gager, John G., "Religion and Social Class in the Early Roman Empire" in S. Benko and J.J. O'Rourke (eds.), *Early Church History. The Roman Empire as the Setting of Primitive Christianity* (London: Oliphants, 1971) 99-120.
Galinski, Karl, "Augustus' Legislation on Morals and Marriage" in *Philologus* 125 (1981) 126-44.
Gardner, Jane F., *Leadership and the Cult of Personality* (London, Hahhert, Toronto: J. M. Deut and Sons Ltd, 1974).
— "Proof of Status in the Roman World" in *BICS* 33 (1986) 1-14.
Gardner, P. D., *The Gift of God and the Authentication of a Christian: An Exegetical Study of 1 Corinthians 8-11:1* (Lanham: University Press of America, 1994).
Garnsey, P., *Social Status and Legal Privilege in the Roman Empire* (Oxford: Clarendon Press, 1970).
— "Legal privilege in the Roman Empire" in M.I. Finley (ed.), *Studies in Ancient Society. Past and Present Series* (London and Boston: Routledge and Kegan Paul, 1974).
— *Famine and Food Supply in the Graeco-Roman World* (Cambridge: Cambridge University Press, 1988).
— "Meat Consumption in Antiquity: Towards a Quantitative Account" in P. Garnsey (ed.), *Food, Health and Culture in Classical Antiquity* (Cambridge: Classical Department Working Papers, 1989).
Garnsey P. and Woolf, G., "Patronage of the Rural Poor in the Roman World" in A. Wallace-Hadrill (ed.), *Patronage in Ancient Society* (London and New York: Routledge, 1990) 153-67.

Garrison, Roman, *The Graeco-Roman Context of Early Christian Literature*. Journal for Studies of the New Testament Suppl. Series 137 (Sheffield: Academic Press, 1997).

Garzetti, A., *From Tiberius to the Antonines. A History of the Roman Empire. AD 14-192*. ET. by J. R . Foster (London: Muthuen, 1974).

Geagan, Daniel J., "Notes on the Agonistic Institution of Roman Corinth" in *Greek, Roman and Byzantine Studies* 9 (1968) 75-76.

Gelzer, M., *The Roman Nobility* (Oxford: Basil Blackwell, 1969).

Gill, D.W.J., "The Meat Market at Corinth (1 Corinthians 10:25)" in *TynBul* 43 (1993) 389-393.

— "Corinth a Roman city in Achaea" in *BZ* 37 (1993) 259-264.

— "In Search of the Social Elite in the Corinthian Church" in *Tyndale Bulletin* 44 (1993) 323-337.

— "The Roman Empire as a Context of the New Testament" in Stanley E. Porter (ed.), *Handbook to Exegesis of the New Testament* (Leiden, New York, Koln: E.J. Brill, 1997) 389-406.

Glad, Clarence E., *Paul and Philodemus* (Leiden: E.J. Brill, 1995).

Glancy, J.A., "Obstacles to Slaves' Participation in the Corinthian Church" in *Journal of Biblical Literature* 117 (1998) 481-501.

Godet, F., *Commentary on St Paul's First Epistle to the Corinthians* (Edinburgh: T and T Clark, 1898).

Goguel, M., *Introduction Noveau Testament*. Vol. 4 (Paris: Editions Ernest Leroux, 1926).

Goldstein, J., "Jewish Acceptance and Rejection of Hellenism" in Sanders, Baumgarten, and Mendelson (eds.), *Jewish and Christian Self-Definition. Vol. II: Aspects of Judaism in the Greco-Roman Period* (London: SCM Press, 1981) 64-87.

Gooch, P.D., *Dangerous Food: 1 Corinthians 8-10 in Its Context* (Waterloo: Wilfird Laurier University Press, 1993).

Gooch, P.W., "'Conscience' in 1 Corinthians 8 and 10" in *New Testament Studies* 33 (1987) 244-254.

Goodman, M., *The Roman World. 44 BC-AD 180* (London and New York: Routledge, 1997).

Gordon, J.C., *Sister of Wife: 1 Corinthians 7 and the Cultural Anthropology*. Journal for Studies of the New Testament Suppl. Series 149 (Sheffield: Academic Press, 1997).

Gordon, R., "The Veil of Power: Emperors, Sacrifice and Benefactors" in M. Beard and J. North, *Religion and Power in the Ancient World* (Ithaca: Cornel University, 1990) 201-231.

Goulder, M.D., "Sofia in 1 Corinthians" in *New Testament Studies* 37 (1991) 516-534.

Grant, F.C., *Ancient Rome Religion* (Indianapolis: The Bobbs-Merrill Co, Inc. 1957).

Grant, Robert M., *Paul in the Roman World. The Conflict at Corinth* (Westminster: John Knox Press, 2001)

Grosheide, F.W., *Commentary on the First Epistle to the Corinthians* (Grand Rapids: Eerdmans, 1953).

Hagge, H., "Die übeiden berlieferten Sendschreiben des Apostels Paulus an die Gemeinde zu Korinth," in *Jahrbücher für protestantiche Theologie II* (1876) 481-531.

Hall, B., "All Things to All People: Study of 1 Corinthians 9:19-23" in Robert T. Fortna and Beverly R. Gaventa (eds.), *The Conversation Continues. Studies in Paul and John in honor of J. Louis Martyn* (Nashville: Abingdon Press, 1990) 137-157.

Harding, Mark, "Church and Gentile Cults at Corinth" in *GTJ* 10 (1989) 203-223.
Harrill, J.A., *The Manumission of Slaves in Early Christianity* (Tübingen: J.C.B. Mohr, 1995).
Hartin, P.J. and Petzer, J.H., "Introduction" in P.J. Hartin and J.H. Petzer (eds), *Text and Interpretation. New Approaches in the Criticism of the New Testament* (Leiden: Brill, 1991) 1-11.
Harvey, A.E., "The workman is worthy of his hire: Fortunes of a proverb in the early church" in *Novum Testamentum* 3 (1982) 209-221.
Harvey, Graham, "Synagogues of the Hebrews: 'Good Jews' in the Diaspora" in S. Jones and S. Pearce (eds.), *Jewish Local Patriotism and Self Justification in the Graeco-Roman World* (Sheffield: Academic Press, 1998) 132-147.
Hays, Richard B., "Ecclesiology and Ethics in 1 Corinthians" in *Ex Auditu* 10 (1994) 31-43.
— *First Corinthians*. Interpretation. A Bible Commentary for Teaching and Preaching (Louisville: John Knox Press, 1997).
Héring, J., *The First Epistle of St. Paul to the Corinthians* (London: Epworth, 1961).
Hengel, M., *The Pre-Christian Paul* (London: SCM, 1991).
Hock, R.F., *The Working Apostle: An Examination of Paul's Means of Livelihood*. PhD. Thesis. Yale, 1974 (Ann Arbor: UMI, 1978)
— "Paul's Tentmaking and the problem of his Social Class" in *Journal of Biblical Literature* 92 (1978) 555-564.
— *The Social Context of Paul's Ministry: Tentmaking and* Apostleship (Philadelphia: Fortress Press, 1980).
Holladay, Carl R., "1 Corinthians 13. Paul as an Apostolic paradigm" in D.L. Bach, et. al., (eds.) Greeks, Romans and Christians (Philadelphia: Fortress Press, 1990) 80-98.
Hollander, Harm W., "The meaning of the term 'Law' (Nomos) in 1 Corinthians" in *Novum Testamentum* XL (1998) 117-135.
Holmberg, B., *Sociology of the New Testament*. An appraisal (Minneapolis, MN: Fortress Press, 1990).
— *Paul and Power: The Structure of Authority in the Primitive Church as reflected in the Pauline Churches* (Lund: Coniectanea Biblica, 1978)
Hooker, Morna D., *Paul. A Short Introduction* (Oxford: Oneworld, 2003)
Hooleman, Joost, *Resurrection and Parousia: A Traditio-Historical Study of Paul's Eschatology in 1 Corinthians 15* (Leiden, New York, Koln: E.J. Brill, 1996).
Hopkins, Keith., "Elite Mobility in the Roman Empire" in M.I. Finley (ed.), *Studies in Ancient Society. Past and Present Series* (London and Boston: Routledge and Kegan Paul, 1974) 103-119.
Horrell, D.G.,"The Development of Theological Ideology in Pauline Christianity. A Structuration Theory Perspective" in Philip F. Esler (ed.), *Modelling Early Christianity. Social-Scientific Studies of the New Testament in its Context* (London, New York: Routledge, 1995) 224-236.
— "Review of Peter D. Gooch, Dangerous Food: 1 Corinthians 8-10 in Its Context" in *Journal of Theological Studies* 46 (1995) 279-282.
— "Review of Paul D. Gardner, *The Gifts of God and the Authentication of a Christian: An Exegetical Study of 1 Corinthians 8-11:1*" in *Journal of Theological Studies* 46 (1995) 651-654.
— *The Social Ethos of Pauline Christianity: Interests and Ideology in the Corinthian Correspondence from 1 Corinthians to 1 Clement* (Edinburgh: T and T Clark, 1996).

— "Theological Principle or Christological Praxis? Pauline Ethics in 1 Corinthians 8:1-11:1" in *Journal for Studies of the New Testament* 67 (1997) 83-114.
— "'The Lord Commanded But I Have not Used.' Exegetical and Hermeneutical Reflections on 1 Cor 9.14-15" in *New Testament Studies* 43 (1997) 587-603.
Horsley, R.A., "Consciousness and Freedom among the Corinthians: 1 Corinthians 8-10" in *Catholic Biblical Quarterly* 40 (1978) 574-589.
— "Pneumatikos vs. Psychikos: Distinctions of Spiritual Status among the Corinthians" in *Harvard Theological Review* 69 (1976) 269-288.
— "Wisdom of Word and Words of Wisdom in Corinth" in *Catholic Biblical Quarterly* 39 (1977) 224-229.
— "The Background of the Confessional Formula in 1 Cor. 8.6" in *Zeitschrift für die neutestamentliche Wissenschaft* 69 (1978) 130-135.
— "How Can Some of You Say There is No Resurrection of the Dead: Spiritual Elitism in Corinth" in *Novum Testamentum* 20 (1978) 203-231.
— "Spiritual Marriage with Sophia" in *Vigiliae Christiniae* 33 (1979) 30-45.
— "Gnosis in Corinth" in *New Testament Studies* 27 (1980) 32-51.
— "I Corinthians: A Case Study of Paul's Assembly as an Alternative Society" in R.A. Horsley (ed.), *Paul and Empire. Religion in Roman Imperial Society* (Pennsylvania: Trinity Press International, 1997) 242-252.
— "Building an Alternative Society: Introduction" in R.A. Horsley (ed.), *Paul and Empire. Religion in Roman Imperial Society* (Pennsylvania: Trinity Press International, 1997) 206-214.
— "Patronage, Priesthoods, and Power: Introduction" in R.A. Horsley (ed.), *Paul and Empire. Religion in Roman Imperial Society* (Pennsylvania: Trinity Press International, 1997) 88-95.
Hurd, J.C., *The Origins of 1 Corinthians* (London: SPCK, 1965).
Hyldahl, N., "The Corinthian 'Parties' and the Corinthian Crisis" in *Studia Theologica* 45 (1991) 19-32.
Jeremias, J., "Chiasmus der Paulusbriefen" in *Zeitschrift für die neutestamentliche Wissenschaft* 49 (1958) 145-156.
Jewett, A.R., "The Redaction of 1 Corinthians and the Trajectory of the Pauline School" in *Journal of the American Academy of Religion* 4 Suppl. B. Dec. 1978, 396-404.
Jewett, R., *Paul's Anthropological Terms. A Study of Their Use in Conflict Setting* (Leiden: E.J. Brill, 1971).
— *Christian Tolerance: Paul's Message to the Modern Church* (Philadelphia: Westminster Press, 1982).
Jones, James L, "The Roman Army" in S. Benko and J.J. R'Ourke (eds.), *Early Church History. The Roman Empire as the Setting of Primitive Christianity* (London: Oliphants, 1971) 187-217.
Joubert, Stephen J., "Managing Household. Paul as *paterfamilias* of the Christian household group in Corinth" in Philip F. Esler (ed.), *Modelling Early Christianity: Social-Scientific of the New Testament in Its Context* (London, New York: Routledge, 1995) 213-223.
Judge, E.A., *The Social Patterns of the Christian Groups in the First Century: Some Prolegomena to the Study of New Testament Ideas of Social Obligation* (London: Tyndale Press, 1960).
— "The Early Christians as a Scholastic Community" in *Journal of Religious History* 1 (1960) 4-15, 125-137.

— "St. Paul and Classical Society" in *Jahrbuch für Antike und Christentum* (1972) 19-36.
Kaiser, Walter C., "The Current Crisis in Exegesis and the Apostolic Use of Deuteronomy 25:4 in 1 Corinthians 9:8-10" in *Journal of the Evangelical Theological Society* 21 (1978) 3-18.
Käsemann, E., *New Testament Questions of Today* (Philadelphia: Fortress 1969).
— "A Pauline Version of the 'Amor Fati'" in *New Testament Questions for Today* (Philadelphia: Fortress, 1969) 217-35.
Kee, H.C., "From Jesus Movement toward Institutional Church" in Robert W. Hefner (ed.), *Conversion to Christianity. Historical and Anthropological Perspectives on a Great Transformation* (Berkeley, Los Angeles, Oxford: University of California Press, 1993) 47-63.
Keifer, O., *Sexual Life in Ancient Rome* (London: Constable, 1994).
Kelly, J.M. *Roman Litigation* (Oxford: Clarendon Press, 1966).
Kennedy, C. A, "The Cult of the Dead in Corinth" in John Marks and Robert M. Good (eds.), *Love and Death in the Ancient Near East. Essays in Honor of Marvin H. Pope* (Connecticut: Four Quarters Publishing Company USA, 1987) 227-236.
Kennedy, Charles A., "The Structures of 1 Corinthians 8-10" in *SBL American Academy of Religion Abstracts* No. 426 (1980).
Kim, Seyoon, "Jesus, Sayings of" in Hawthorne, Gerald F. (ed). *Dictionary of Paul and His Letters* (Downers Grove: IVP, 1993) 475-480.
Kling, C.F., *The Epistle of Paul to the Corinthians*. ET. D.W. Poor (New York: Charles Scribner, 1869).
Klutz, Todd E, "Re-Reading 1 Corinthians after *Rethinking 'Gnosticism'*" in *Journal for the Study of the New Testament* 26 (2003) 193-216.
Knox, W.L., *St. Paul and the Church of Jerusalem* (Cambridge: Cambridge University Press, 1925).
Koester, H., *Introduction to the New Testament*. II (New York: de Gruyter, 1982).
Kraabel, A.T., "The Roman Diaspora: Six Questionable Assumptions" in *Journal of Jewish Studies* 33 (1982), *Essays in Honour of Y. Yadin*, 1-2, 445-464.
Kraemer, Ross Shephard, *Her Share of the Blessings: Women's Religions Among Pagans, Jews and Christians in the Greco-Roman World* (New York and Oxford: Oxford University Press, 1992).
Kuck, David W., *Judgement and Community Conflict. Paul's Use of Apocalyptic Judgement Language in 1 Corinthians 3: 5-4:5* (Leiden: Brill, 1992).
Lanci, John R., *A New Temple at Corinth: Rhetorical and Archaeological Approaches to Pauline Imagery* (New York: Peter Lang, 1997).
Laughery, G.J., "Paul: Anti-marriage? Anti-sex? Ascetic? A Dialogue with 1 Corinthians 7:1-40" in *Evangelical Quarterly* 69 (1997) 109-128.
Lawson, W.H., *First Corinthians 9:24-10:22 in Its Contextual Framework*. PhD. Diss. The Southern Baptist Theological Seminary (Ann. Arbor: UMI 1984).
Lee, Clarence L. "Social Unrest and Primitive Christianity" in S. Benko and J.J. O'Rourke (eds), *Early Church History. The Roman Empire as the Setting of Primitive Christianity* (London: Oliphants, 1971) 121-138.
Lenski, R.C.H., *The Interpretation of St Paul's First and Second Epistles to the Corinthians* (Minneapolis: Augsburg Publishing House, 1963).
Lent, John Clayton, Jr., *Luke's Portrait of Paul* (Cambridge: Cambridge University Press, 1993).

Lietzmann, H., *Messe und Herrenmahl. Eine Studie zur Geschichte Liturgie* (Bonn, 1926)
Lieu, Judith, "'Impregnable Ramparts and Walls of Iron: Boundary and Identity in 'Early Judaism' and 'Christianity'" in *New Testament Studies* 48 (2002) 297-313.
Lisle, Robert, "The Cults of Corinth." PhD Diss. John Hopkins University Baltimore, Maryland, 1955.
Liftin, D., *St. Paul's Theology of Proclamation. 1 Cor 1-4 and Greco-Roman Rhetoric* (Cambridge: Cambridge University Press, 1994).
Longenecker, R., *Paul, Apostle of Liberty* (New York: Harper and Row, 1964).
Louw, J.P. and Nida, E.A., *Greek-English Lexicon of the New Testament Based on Semantic Domains.* Vol. II (New York: UBS, 1988, 1989).
Lund, N.W., *Chiasmus in the New Testament: A Study in Formgeschichte* (Chapel Hill: University of North Caroline Press, 1942).
Lüdemann, G., *Opposition to Paul in Jewish Christianity* (Minneapolis: Fortress Press, 1989).
Lütgert, W., *Freiheitspredigt und Schwarmgeister in Korinth: ein Beitrag zur Characteristik der Christus Partei* (Gütersloh: C.Bertelsmann, 1908).
Lyttelton, M. and Forman, W., *The Romans, Their Gods and Their Beliefs* (London: Orbis, 1984).
Mack, Burton L., *Rhetoric and the New Testament* (Minneapolis: Fortress Press, 1990).
McRay, J., *Archaeology and the New Testament* (Grand Rapids: Baker Books House, 1991).
Magee, B.R., "A Rhetorical Analysis of First Corinthians 8:1-11:1 and Romans 14:1 15:13." PhD Dissertation. New Orleans Baptist Theological Seminary, 1988.
Malherbe, A.J., *The Social Aspects of Early Christianity.* 2nd edition (Philadelphia: Fortress Press, 1983).
— "Determinism and Free Will in Paul: The Argument of 1 Corinthians 8 and 9" in Troels Engberg-Pedersen (ed.), *Paul in His Hellenistic Context* (Edinburgh: T and T Clark, 1994) 231-255.
Malina, B.J., "Review of *The First Urban Christians* by Wayne A. Meeks" in *Journal of Biblical Literature* 104 (1985) 46-49.
Manson, T.W., "The Corinthian Correspondence (1) (1941)" in ed. M. Black, *Studies in the Gospels and Epistles* (Manchester: University Press, 1962) 190-209.
Marshall, P., *Enmity in Corinth: Social Conventions in Paul's Relations with the Corinthians* (Tübingen: J.C. B. Mohr, 1987).
— "'The Enigmatic Apostle': Paul and Social Change. Did Paul Seek to transform Graeco-Roman Society?" in T. W. Hillard et. al., (eds.), *Ancient History in a Modern University.* Vol. 2, *Early Christianity, Late Antiquity and Beyond* (Michigan, Cambridge: Eerdmans, 1998) 153-69.
Martin, D.B., "Tongues of Angels and Other Status Indicators" in *Journal of the American Academy of Religion* 59 (1991) 547-89
— *Slavery As Salvation: The Metaphor of Slavery in Pauline Christianity* (New Haven: Yale University Press, 1990).
— *The Corinthian Body* (New Haven and London: Yale University Press, 1995).
Maxey, M., *Occupations of the Lower Classes* (Chicago: University of Chicago, 1938).
Meeks, W.A., "'And Rose Up to Play': Midrash and Paraenesis in 1 Corinthians 10:1-22" in *Journal for the Study of the New Testament* 16 (1982) 64-78.
— *The First Urban Christians - The Social World of the Apostle Paul* (New Haven and

London: Yale University Press, 1983).
— *The Moral World of the First Christians. Library of Early Christianity* (Philadelphia: Westminster Press, 1986).
Meggitt, J.J., "Meat Consumption and Social Conflict in Corinth" in *Journal of Theological Studies* 45 (1994) 137-41.
— "The Social Status of Erastus (Rom. 16:23)" in *Novum Testamentum* 38 (1996) 218-223.
— *Paul, Poverty and Survival* (Edinburgh: T and T Clark, 1998).
--- "Response to Martin and Theissen" in *Journal for the Study of the New Testament* 84 (2001) 85-94.
Meyer, H. A. E., *Critical and Exegetical Handbook to the Epistle to the Corinthians* (Edinburgh:T and T Clark, 1892).
Milleker, E.J., "Three Heads of Serapis from Corinth" in *Hesperia* 54 (1985) 121-35.
Mitchell, M.M., "Concerning ΠΕΡΙ ΔΕ in 1 Corinthians" in *Novum Testamentum* 31 (1989) 229-56.
— *Paul and the Rhetoric of Reconciliation: An Exegetical Investigation of the Language and Composition of 1 Corinthians* (Westminster: John Knox Press 1991).
— "Rhetorical Shorthand in Pauline Argumentation: The Function of the 'gospel' in the Corinthian Correspondence" in L. Ann Jervis and Peter Richardson (eds.), *Gospel in Paul. Studies on Corinthians, Galatians and Romans for Richard N. Longenecker*. Journal for the Study of the New Testament Suppl. Series 108 (Sheffield: Academic Press, 1994) 62-68.
--- "A Variable and Many-sorted Man:" John Chrysostom's Treatment of Pauline Inconsistency" in *Journal of Early Christian Studies* 6 (1998) 93-111
Moffatt, J., *The First Epistle of Paul to the Corinthians*. The Moffat N.T. Commentary (New York, London, 1930).
Momigliano, A, *Claudius. The Emperor and His Achievement*. ET by W.D. Hogart with a new bibliography (Cambridge: W. Heffers and Sons, 1934, 1961).
Morris, L., *The First Epistle of Paul to the Corinthians* (Leicester: IVP, 1985).
Munck, J., "The Church Without Factions.Studies in 1 Corinthians 1-4" in *Paul and the Salvation of Mankind* (London, 1959) 135-167.
Murphy-O'Connor, J., "Freedom or the Ghetto (I Cor 8:1-13; 10:23 - 11:1" in *Revue Biblique* 85 (1978) 543-574.
— *St Paul s Corinth ---Text and Archaeology* (Wilmington, MN: Glazier, 1983).
— "The Corinth that Paul saw" in *Biblical Archaeologist* 47 (1984) 147-159.
— *Paul: A Critical Life* (Oxford: Clarendon Press, 1996).
Moulton, J. H., and Milligan, G., *The Vocabulary of the Greek New Testament from the Papyry and other non-literary sources* (London: Hodder and Stoughton, 1930)
Nakahashi, Osamu, "Idol Meat and Monotheism: A Study of the Church in Corinth (1 Cor. 8-10)." MTh. Diss. Faculty of Divinity, University of Glasgow, 1 992.
Nasuti, Harry, P., "The Woes of the Prophets and the Rights of the Apostle: The Internai Dynamics of 1 Corinthians 9" in *Catholic Biblical Quarterly* 50 (1988) 246-264.
Neirynck, F., "Paul and the Sayings of Jesus" in A. Vanhoye (ed.) *L'apotre Paul Personalite Style et Concept du Ministere*. BTL73 (Leuven: Leuven University Press, 1986) 265-321.
Neller, K.V., "1 Corinthians 9:19-23. A Model for Those Who Seek to Win Souls" in *RQ* 29 (1987) 129-42.
Newton, D, "Food Offered to Idols in 1 Corinthians 8-10: A Study of Conflicting

Viewpoints in the Setting of Religious Pluralism in Corinth." Unpublished Dissertation (Sheffield University, 1995). It has appeared in print under a title: *Deity and diet: The dilemma of sacrificial food at Corinth*, Journal for the study of the New Testament supplement series, 169 (Sheffield: Sheffield, 1998). The unpublished work is used in this book.

Omanson, Roger L., "Some Comments About Style and Meaning: 1 Corinthians 9:15 and 7:10" in *The Bible Translator* 34 (1983) 135-139.

O'Rourke, J. J., "Roman Law and the Early Church" in S. Benko and J.J. O'Rourke, *Early Church History. The Roman Empire as the Setting of Primitive Christianity* (London: Oliphants, 1971) 165-186.

Orr, D.G., "Roman Domestic Religion: the Evidence of the Household Shrines" in *Aufstieg und Niedergang der römischen Welt* 2 (1978) 1557-1591.

Oster, R.E. Jr., "Use, Misuse and Neglect of Archaeological Evidence in Some Modern Works in 1 Corinthians (1 Cor 7, 1-5, 8, 10; 11, 2-16; 12:14-26)" in *Zeitschrift für die neutestamentliche Wissenschaft* 83 (1992) 52-73.

Paige, T.P., "Spirit at Corinth: The Corinthian Concept of Spirit and Paul's Response as Seen in 1 Corinthians." Unpublished PhD. Thesis (Sheffield University, 1993).

Parkins, Helen, "The 'Consumer City' domesticated? The Roman city in elite economic strategies" in Helen M. Parkins (ed.), *Roman Urbanism Beyond the Consumer City* (London, New York: Routledge, 1997) 82-111.

Pearce, S. and Jones, S., "Introduction: Jewish Local Identities and Patriotism in the Graeco-Roman" in S. Jones and S. Pearce, *Jewish Local Patriotism and Self-Identification in the Graeco-Roman World* (Sheffield: Academic Press, 1998) 13-28.

Pearson, B.A., *The Pneumatikos-Psychikos Terminology in 1 Corinthians* (SBLDS 12; Missoula, MT: Scholars Press, 1973).

Pfitzner, V.C., *Paul and the Agon Motif. Traditional Athletic Imagery in the Pauline Literature* (Leiden: E.J. Brill, 1967).

Pickett, Raymond, *The Cross in Corinth: The Social Significance of the Cross of Christ* (Sheffield: Sheffield Academic Press, 1997).

Pierce, C.A., *Conscience in the New Testament* (London: SCM Press, 1955).

Pogoloff, S.M., *Logos and Sophia: The Rhetorical Situation of 1 Corinthians* (SBLDS 12, Missoula: MT Scholars Press, 1992)

Pomeroy, A.J., "Status and Status-Concern in the Greco-Roman Dream Books" in *Ancient Society* 21 (1990) 51-74.

Pomeroy, Sarah B., *Goddesses, Whores, Wives and Slaves* (London: Pimlico, 1975).

Price, S.R.F., "Man and God: Sacrifice in the Roman Imperial Cult" in *Journal of Roman Studies* 70 (1980) 28-43.

— *Rituals and Power - the Roman Imperial Cult in Asia Minor* (Cambridge: Cambridge University Press, 1984).

— "From Nobel Funerals to divine cult: the Consecration of Roman Emperor" in D. Cannadine and S. Price (eds.), *Rituals and Royalty. Power and Ceremonial in Traditional Societies* (Cambridge: Cambridge University Press, 1987) 56-105.

Prior, D., *The Message of 1 Corinthians* (Downers Grove: IVP, 1985).

Rainbow, Paul Andrew, "Monotheism and Christology in I Corinthians 8.4-6." Unpublished D. Phil. Thesis (Oxford University, 1987).

Räisänen, H., *Paul and the Law* (Philadelphia: Fortress, 1983).

Ramsaran, Rollin A., *Liberating Words: Paul's Use of Rhetorical Maxims in 1 Corinthians 1-10* (Pennsylvania: Trinity Press International, 1996).

Ramsay W. and Lanciani, R., *A Manual of Roman Antiquities* (London: Charles Griffin, 1894).

Rauer, M., "Die Schwachen in Korinth und Rom nach den Paulusbriefen" in *Biblische Studien* XXI (1923) 1 -192.

Rawson, Beryl, "Roman Concubinage and Other *de facto* Marriages" in *Transactions of the American Philological Association* 104 (1974) 279-305.

Read-Heimerdinger, J., "Barnabas in Acts: A Study of His Role in the Text of Codex Bezae" in *Journal for the Study of the New Testament* 72 (1998) 23-66.

Rees, W., "Corinth in St. Paul's Time. Part 1. Topography" in *Scripture* 2 (1947) 71-76.

Reitzenstein, R., *Hellenistic Mystery Religions: Their Basic Ideas and Significance* (Pittsburgh: Pickwick Press, 1978).

Richardson, P., "Pauline Inconsistency: I Corinthians 9: 19-23 and Galatians 2:11-14" in *New Testament Studies* 26 (1980) 347-362.

— "Temples, Altars and Living From the Gospel (1 Cor. 9. 12b-18)" in L. Ann Jervis and Peter Richardson (eds.), *Gospel in Paul. Studies on Corinthians, Galatians and Romans for Richard N. Longenecker*. Journal for the Study of the New Testament Suppl. Series 108 (Sheffield: Academic Press, 1994) 89-110.

Richardson, P and Gooch, P.W., "Accommodation Ethics" in *Tyndale Bulletin* 29 (1978) 89-117.

Richter, P.J., "Recent Sociological Approaches to the Study of the New Testament" in *R*14 (1984) 77-90.

Robertson, A. and Plummer, A., *A Critical Commentary on the First Epistle of St Paul to the Corinthians* (Edinburgh: T and T Clark, 1914)

Roebuck, C., *Corinth. Vol 14. The Asclepion and Lerna. ASCSA* (Princeton, 1951).

Roetzel, Calvin J., *Judgement in the Community. A Study of the Relationship Between Eschatology and Ecclesiology in Paul* (Leiden: Brill, 1972).

— "Paul and the Law: Whence and Wither?" in *Current in Biblical Research* 3 (1995) 249-275.

Romano, D.G., "Post-146 B.C. Land Use in Corinth, and Planning of the Roman Colony of 44 BC" in Timothy E. Gregory (ed.), *The Corinthia in the Roman Period* (Ann Arbor: MI, 1993) 9-30.

Rose, F.S., *The Date and Author of the Satyricon* (Leiden: E.J. Brill, 1971).

Rosner, B.S., "Temple Prostitution in 1 Corinthians 6:12-20" in *Novum Tetamentum* XL (1998) 336-51.

Ross, Marc Howard, *The Culture of Conflict. Interpretations and Interests in Comparative Perspectives* (New Haven and London: Yale University Press, 1993).

— *Management of Conflict. Interpretations and Interests in Comparative Perspectives* (New Haven and London: Yale University Press, 1993)

Saller, R.P., "Promotion and Patronage in Equestrian Careers" in *Journal of Roman Studies* 70 (1980) 44-59.

— "Review of Donald Engels, Roman *Corinth: An Alternative Model for the Classical City*" in *Classical Philology* 86 (1991) 351-357.

Salmon, E.T., *Roman Colonization under the Republic* (London: Thames and Hudson, 1969).

Sampley, J. *Paul, Pauline Partnership in Christ* (Philadelphia: Fortress Press, 1980).

Sanders, E.P., *Paul and Palestinian Judaism* (Philadelphia: Fortress Press, 1977).

— *Paul, the Law and the Jewish People* (Philadelphia: Fortress 1983).

Sanders, J.T., *Schismatics, Sectarians, Dissidents, Deviants: The First One Hundred*

Years of Jewish-Christian Relations (Pennsylvania: Trinity Press International, 1993).
— "Paul Between Jews and Gentiles in Corinth" in *Journal for the Study of the New Testament* 65 (1997) 67-83.
Savage, T.B., *Power Through Weakness: An Historical and Exegetical Examinations of Paul's Understanding of the Ministry in 2 Corinthians* (Cambridge: Cambridge University Press, 1996).
Sawyer, W.T., "The Problem of Meat Sacrificed to Idols in the Corinthian Church." DTh. Dissertation (Southern Baptist Theological Seminary, 1968).
Schlatter, A., *Die Korinthische Theologia* (BFCT 18: Gutersloh: C. Bertelsmann, 1914).
Schlier, H., "κεανδ ρδος, κερδαιανδ νω" in G. Kittel (ed.), *Theological Dictionary of the New Testament.* Vol. III (Grand Rapids: Eerdmans, 1965) 672-673.
Schmithals, W., *Gnosticism in Corinth: An Investigation of the Letters to the Corinthians.* ET. (Nashville: Abingdon Press, 1971).
Schrage, W., *The Ethics of the New Testament* (Philadelphia: Fortress Press, 1982).
Schütz, J.H., *Paul and the Anatomy of Apostolic Authority*, SNTS (Cambridge: Cambridge University Press, 1975).
Sellin, G., *Der Streit um die Auferstehung der Toten. Eine religionsgeschichtliche und exegetische untersuchung von 1 Corinther 15.* FRLANT 138 (Göttingen: Vandenhoeck/Ruprecht, 1986).
Sherwin-White, A.N., *The Roman Citizenship.* 2nd ed. ch. IX "The Claudian Problem and Viritane Grants" (Oxford: Clarendon Press, 1973).
Shilington, V. George, "Atonement Texture in 1 Corinthians 5.5" in *Journal for the Study of the New Testament* 71 (1998) 29-50.
Shoe, L., "The Roman Ionic Base at Corinth" in L. Freeman Sandler (ed.), *Essays in Honor of Karl Letimann* (New York, 1964) 300-304.
Sibinga, J.S., "The Composition of 1 Cor. 9 and its Context" in *Novum Testamentum* XL (1998) 132-163.
Sisson, Russell Barrett, *The Apostle as Athlete: A socio-rhetorical interpretation of 1 Corinthians 9.* PhD. Diss. Emory University (Ann. Arbor: UMI, 1994).
Smit, Joop F.M., "The Rhetorical Disposition of First Corinthians 8:7-9:27" in *Catholic Biblical Quarterly* 59 (1997) 476-91.
— *"About the Idol Offering": Rhetoric, Social Context, and Theology of Paul's Discourse in First Corinthians 8: 1-11:1* (Leuven: Peeters, 2000)
Smith, D.E., "The Egyptian Cults at Corinth" in *Harvard Theological Review* 70 (1977) 201-23.
Soden, F.H. von, "Sacrament and Ethics in Paul" in W.A. Meeks (ed.), *The Writings of St. Paul* (New York: W.W. Norton and Company, 1972).
Songer, Harold S., "Problems Arising from the Worship of Idols" in *Review and Expositor* 80 (1983) 363-375.
Spawforth, A.J.S., "Roman Corinth and the Ancient Urban Economy. Review of Donald Engels, *Roman Corinth: An Alternative Model for The Classical City* (Chicago and London: University of Chicago Press, 1990)" in *The Classical Review* 42 (1992) 119-122.
— "Corinth, Argos and the Imperial Cult: Pseudo-Julian, Letters 198" in *Hesperia* 63 (1994) 211-32.
— "The Achaean Federal Cult. Part 1: Pseudo-Julian, Letters 198" in *Tyndale Bulletin* 46 (1995) 151-68.

Spawforth, A and Cartledge, P., *Hellenistic and Roman Sparta: A Tale of Two Cities* (London: Routledge, 1989).
Staumbaugh, J. E., "The Functions of Roman Temples" in *Aufstieg und Niedergang der römischen Welt* 2.16.1 (1978) 554-608.
Ste. Croix, B.E.M. de, *Struggle in the Ancient Greek World* (London: Duckworth, 1981).
Stephen De Vos, Craig, "Stepmothers, Concubines and the Case of Πορνεια in 1 Corinthians 5" in *New Testament Studies* 44 (1998) 104-114.
Stone, M., *Scriptures, Sects and Visions* (Philadelphia: Fortress Press, 1980).
Stowers, Stanley K., "A Debate over Freedom: 1 Corinthians 6:12-20" in Everett Ferguson (ed.), *Christian Teaching. Studies in Honor of LeMoine G. Lewis* (Abilene Christian University Press, 1981) 59-71.
— "Social Status, Public Speaking and Private Teaching: The Circumstances of Paul's Preaching Activity" in *Novum Testamentum* 26 (1984) 59-82.
— "Paul on the Use of Reason" in D. Bach, et. al. (eds.), *Greeks, Romans, and Christians* (Minneapolis: Fortress, 1990) 253-86.
— "Greeks Who Sacrifice and Those Who Do Not: Toward an Anthropology of Greek Religion" in L.M. White and L. Yarbrough (eds.), *The Social World of Early Christians. Essays in Honor of Wayne Meeks* (Minneapolis: Fortress, 1995) 293-333.
Stroud, Ronald S., "The Sanctuary of Demeter on Acrocorinth in the Roman Period" in Timothy E. Gregory (ed.), *The Corinthia in the Roman Period* (Ann Arbor: MI, 1993) 65-77.
Sumney, Jerry L., *Identifying Paul's Opponents: The Question of Method in 2 Corinthians* (Sheffield: Academic Press, 1990).
--- "The Place of 1 Corinthians 9:24-27 in Paul's Argument" in *Journal of Biblical Literature* 119 (2000) 329-333.
Syme, Ronald, *The Roman Revolution* (Oxford: Oxford University Press, 1939).
Tasker, R.V.G.,*The Second Epistle to the Corinthians*. Tyndale NT Commentaries 8 (Grand Rapids: Eerdmans, 1963).
Taylor, N. Paul, *Antioch and Jerusalem. A Study in Relationships and Authority in Earliest Christianity*. JSNT (Sheffield: Academic Press, 1992).
Taylor, Nicholas H., "The Social Nature of Conversion in the Early Christian World," in Philip F. Esler (ed.), *Modelling Early Christianity: Social Scientific Studies of the New Testament in Its Context* (London, New York: Routledge, 1995) 128-136.
Terry, Ralph Bruce, *A Discourse Analysis of First Corinthians* (Dallas: Summer Institute of Linguistics, 1996).
Theissen, G., *Essays on Corinth: The Social Setting of Pauline Christianity* (Edinburgh: T and T Clark, 1982).
— "Gospels and Church Politics in Early Christianity." The Reid Lectures (Westminster College, Cambridge, June 1994).
--- "The Social Structure of Pauline Communities: Some Critical Remarks on J.J. Meggitt, *Paul, Poverty and Survival*" in *Journal for the Study of the New Testament* 84 (2001) 65-84.
--- "Social Conflicts in the Corinthian Community: Further Remarkson J.J. Meggitt, *Paul, Poverty and Survival*" in *Journal for the Study of the New Testament* 25 (2003) 371-391.
Thielman, F., "The Coherence of Paul's View of the Law: The Evidence of First Corinthians" in *New Testament Studies* 38 (1992) 235-53.

— *Paul and the Law* (Illinois: IVP, 1994).
Thiselton, A.C., "Realized Eschatology at Corinth" in *New Testament Studies* 24 (1978) 510-26.
— "Human Being, Relationality and Time in Hebrews, 1 Corinthians and Western Traditions" in *Ex Auditu* 13 (1997) 76-95.
Thompkins, D.P., "Review of D. Engels' Roman Corinth: An Alternative Model for the Classical City" in *Bryn Mawr Classical Review* 1 (1990) 20-33.
Thrall, M., "The Pauline Use of συείδησίς" in *New Testament Studies* 14 (1967-78) 118-129.
Tomlin, Graham, "Christians and Epicureans in 1 Corinthians" in *Journal for the Study of the New Testament* 68 (1997) 51-72.
Tomson, Peter J., *Paul and the Jewish Law: Halakha in the Letters of the Apostle to the Gentiles* (Minneapolis: Fortress Press, 1991).
Trail, Ronald, *An Exegetical Summary of 1 Corinthians 1-9* (Dallas: Summer Institute of Linguistics, 1995).
Trebilco, Paul R., *Jewish Communities in Asia Minor* (Cambridge: Cambridge University Press, 1991).
Treggiari, Susan, "Social Status and Social Legislation" in A.K. Bowmann et.al. (eds.), *The Cambridge Ancient History.* Vol 10. The Augustan Empire 43 B.C. - A.D. 69 (Cambridge: Cambridge University Press, 1996) 873-904.
Tucker, T.G., *Life in the Roman World of Nero and St. Paul* (London: MacMulen 1910).
Tuckett, Christoper, "Jewish Christian Wisdom in 1 Corinthians?" in Stanley E. Porter et. al., (eds.), *Crossing the Boundaries. Essays in Biblical Interpretation in Honor of Michael D. Goulder* (Leiden: E.J. Brill, 1994) 201-19.
Verbrugge, Verlyn D., *Paul's Style of Church Leadership Illustrated by His Instructions to the Corinthians on the Collection* (San Fransisco: Mellen Research University Press, 1992).
Vielhauer, P., "Paulus un die Kephaspartei in Korinth" in *New Testament Studies* 21 (1975) 341-352.
Volf, Judith M Gundry, *Paul and Perseverance: Staying in and falling away* (Tübingen: Mohr, 1990)
Wallace-Hadrill, A., "Elite and trade in the Roman town" in John Rich and A. Wallace Hadrill (eds.), *City and Country in the Ancient World* (London and New York: Routledge, 1991) 241-72.
— *Houses and Society in Pompeii and Herculaneum* (Princeton: 1994).
Wallbank, Mary E. Hopkins, "Pausanias, Octavia and Temple E at Corinth" in *Annual of the British School at Athens* 84 (1989) 361-94.
Wallbank, M.H., Abstract of "The Nature of Early Roman Corinth" in *American Journal of Archaeology* 90 (1986) 220-221.
Watson, A., *The State, Law and Religion. Pagan Rome* (Athens and London: The University of Georgia Press, 1992).
— *Roman Slave Law* (Baltimore and London: The John Hopkins University Press, 1987).
Watson, D.F., "1 Corinthians 10: 23-11:1 in the Light of Graeco-Roman Rhetoric" in *JBL* 108 (1989) 301-318.
Watson, F., Paul, *Judaism and the Gentiles: A Sociological Approach.* SNSMS 56 (Cambridge: Cambridge University Press, 1986).
Weaver, Paul, "Children of Junian Latins" in B. Rawson and P. Weaver (eds.), *The*

Roman Family in Italy. Status, Sentiment, Space (Oxford: Clarendon Press, 1997) 55-72.

Weaver, P.R.C., *Familia Caesaris* (Cambridge: Cambridge University Press, 1972).

— "Social Mobility in the Early Roman Empire: The Evidence of the Imperial Freedmen and Slaves" in M.I. Finley (ed.), *Studies in Ancient Society. Past and Present Series* (London and Boston: Routledge and Kegan Paul, 1974) 121-140.

— "Children of Freedmen (and Freedwomen)" in B. Rawson (ed.), *Marriage, Divorce, and Children in Ancient Rome* (Oxford: Clarendon Press, 1996) 167-190

Weber, M., *The Agrarian Sociology of Ancient Civilizations*. E.T. by R. I. Frank (London and New York, 1988).

Wedderburn, A.J.H., "The Problem of the Denial of the Resurrection in 1 Corinthians XV" in *Novum Testamentum* 23 (1981) 229-241.

Weiss, J., *Der erste Korintherbrief* (Göttingen: Vandenhoeck and Ruprecht, 1910).

Welborn, L.L., "On the Discord in Corinth: 1 Corinthians 1-4 and Ancient Politics" in *Journal of Biblical Literature* 106 (1987) 85-111.

Wenham, D., *Paul: Follower of Jesus or Founder of Christianity?* (Michigan, Cambridge: Eerdmans, 1995).

— "Whatever went wrong in Corinth" in *Expository Times* 108 (1997) 137-41.

West, A.B., *Latin Inscriptions 1896-1926. Corinth: Results, VIII.2* (Cambridge, Mass.: Harvard University Press, 1931).

Westerholm, S., *Israel's Law and the Church's Faith* (Grand Rapids: Eerdmans, 1988).

Westermann, W.L., "Slavery and the Elements of Freedom in Ancient Greece" in *Quarterly Bulletin of the Polish Institute of Arts and Science in America* 1 (1943) 1-14.

White, Joel R., "Baptized on Account of the Dead: The Meaning of 1 Corinthians 15:29 in Its Context" in *Journal of Biblical Literature* 116 (1997) 487-899.

Whittaker, C.R., "The Consumer City Revisited: the vicus and the city" in *Journal of Roman Archaeology* 3 (1990) 110-18.

Wiedemann, Thomas E.J., "The Regularity of Manumission at Rome" in *Classical Quarterly* 35 (1985) 62-75.

Wiedemann, Thomas, *Adults and Children in the Roman Empire* (London: Routledge, 1989).

William II, C.K., "The Refounding of Corinth. Some Roman Religious Attitudes" in S. Macread and F.H. Thomson (eds.), *Roman Architecture in the Greek World* (The Society of Antiquarians of London, 1987) 26-37.

— "A Re-evaluation of Temple E and the West End of the Forum of Corinth" in S. Walker and A. Cameron (eds.), *The Greek Renaissance in the Roman Empire. Suppl. 55. Papers from the 10th British Museum Classical Collegium, Institute of Classical Studies* (London: University of London, 1989) 156-62.

— "Roman Corinth as a Commercial Center" in Timothy E. Gregory, *The Corinthia in the Roman Period. Journal of Roman Archaeology Suppl. 8* (Ann Arbor: MI, 1993) 31-46.

Willis, W., "An Apostolic Apologia? The Form and Function of 1 Cor 9" in *Journal for the Study of the New Testament* 24 (1985) 33-48.

Willis, W., „Corinthusne deletus est?" in *Biblische Zeitschrift* 35 (1991) 233-241.

Willis, W.L., *Idol Meat in Corinth. The Pauline Argument in 1 Corinthians 8 and 10*. SBLDS 6 (Chico, CA: Scholars press, 1985).

Wilson, A.N., *Paul. The Mind of the Apostle* (New York and London: W.W. Norton and

Company, 1997)
Wilson, J.H., "The Corinthians Who Say There is No Resurrection of the Dead" in *Zeitschrift für die Neutestamentliche Wissenschaft NW* 59 (1968) 95-97.
Wilson, R. McI, *Gnosis and the New Testament* (Philadelphia: Fortress Press, 1968).
— "How Gnostics Were the Corinthians" in *New Testament Studies* 19 (1972-73) 65-74.
Windisch, H., *Der Zweite Korintherbrief, Kritisch-Exegetischer Kommentar uber das Neue Testament begrundet von H.A. W. Meyer,* part 6, 9th edition (Göttingen: Vandenhoeck and Ruprecht, 1924).
Winter, Bruce W., "In Public and in Private: Early Christian Interactions with Religious Pluralism" in Andrew D. Clarke and Bruce W. Winter (eds.), *One God, One Lord in a World of Religious Pluralism* (Cambridge: Tyndale House, 1991) 112-134.
— *First Century Christians in the Graeco-Roman World: Seek the Welfare of the City. Christians as Benefactors and Citizens* (Grand Rapids: Eerdmans, 1994).
— "Civil Litigation in Secular Corinth and the Church. The Forensic Background to 1 Corinthians 6:1-8" in *New Testament Studies* 37 (1991) 559-572; also in B.S. Rosner (ed.), *Understanding Paul's Ethics. Twentieth Century Approaches* (Grand Rapids: Eerdmans, 1995) 85-103.
— "The Achaean Federal Imperial Cult II: The Corinthian Church" in *Tyndale Bulletin* 46 (1995) 169-178.
— "Gluttony and Immorality at Elitist Banquets: The Background to 1 Corinthians 6:12-20" in *Jian Diao* 7 (1997) 77-90.
— *Philo and Paul Among the Sophists* (Cambridge: Cambridge University Press, 1997).
— "St Paul as a Critic of Roman Slavery in 1 Corinthians 7:21-23" in *Παυλεία* 4 (1998).
— *After Paul Left Corinth: The Influence of Secular Ethics and Social Change* (Grand Rapids: Eerdmans, 2001)
Wire, A. C., *The Corinthian Women Prophets: A Reconstruction Through Paul's Rhetoric* (Minneapolis: Fortress Press, 1990).
Witherington III, Ben, "Not So Idle Thoughts about EIDOLOTHUTON" in *Tyndale Bulletin* 44 (1993) 237-254.
— "Why Not Idol Meat? Is it What You Eat or Where You Eat it?" in *Biblical Review* 10 (3, 1994) 38-43, 54-55.
— *Conflict and Community in Corinth: a Socio-Rhetorical Commentary on 1 and 2 Corinthians* (Grand Rapids: Eerdmans 1995).
— *The Acts of the Apostles: A Socio-Rhetorical Commentary* (Michigan, Cambridge: Eerdmans, 1998).
Witt, Norman de, *St. Paul and Epicurus* (Minneapolis: University of Minneapolis Press, 1954).
Wolff, Christian, "Humility and Self-Denial in Jesus' Life and Message and in the Apostolic Existence of Paul" in A.J.M. Wedderburn (ed.), *Paul and Jesus. Collected Essays* (Sheffield: Academic Press, 1989) 145-160.
Wright, N.T., "Monotheism, Christology and Ethics: 1 Corinthians 8" in *The Climax of the Covenant in Christ and the Law in Pauline Theology* (Edinburgh: T and T Clark, 1991) 120-136.
Wuellner, W., "Greek Rhetoric and Pauline Argumentation" in E.R. Schoedel and R.L. Wilken (eds.), *Early Christian Literature and the Classical Intellectual Tradition: in honorem Robert M. Grant* (Paris: Beauchesne, 1979) 177-188.
— "Paul as Pastor: The Function of Rhetorical Questions in First Corinthians" in A.

Vanhoye (ed.), *L'Apotre Paul Personalite; Style Et Conception du Ministère*. BTL 73 (Leuven: Leuven University Press, 1986) 49-77.
— "Where Is Rhetorical Criticism Taking Us?" in *Catholic Biblical Review* 49 (1987) 448-63.
Yamsat, Pandang, "The Ekklesia as Partnership: Paul and Threats to Koinonia in 1 Corinthians." Unpublished PhD. Thesis (Sheffield University, December 1992).
Yeo, K.K., *Rhetorical Interaction in 1 Corinthians 8 and 10. A Formal Analysis with Preliminary Suggestions for a Chinese Cross-Cultural Hermeneutics* (Leiden: Brill, 1995).
Young, F.M. and Ford, D.F., *Meaning and Truth in Second Corinthians* (London: SPCK, 1987).
Zanker, P., "The Power of Images" in R.A. Horsley (ed.), *Paul. Empire. Religion and Power in Roman Imperial Society* (Pennsylvania: Trinity Press International, 1997) 72-86.
Zodhiates, S., *The Complete Word Study Dictionary New Testament* (Iowa: World Bible Publishers, 1992)

II. Literature Consulted for Chapter 5

A. Books

Aritonang, Jan S., *Mission Schools in Batak Land* (Indonesia) 1861-1940, ET by Robert R. Boehike (Leiden: E.J. Brill, 1994).
Gultom, Gomar, at.al., *Keyakinan dalam Pencobaan. Studi Kasus Gereja HKBP* (Jakarta: Pustaka Sopo Metmet, 1993).
Jones, Sydney, *Human Rights in Indonesia and East Timor: The Limits of Openness. Human Rights Asia* (New York, September 1994).
Hadikusuma, Hilman, *Anthropologi Agama* (Bandung: PT. Citra Aditya Bakti, 1992).
Nadeak, Moxa, et.al., (eds.) *Krisis HKBP: Ujian Bagi Iman dan Pengamalan Pancasila* (Biro Informasi HKBP, Oktober 1995).
Pedersen, Paul B., *Batak Blood and Protestant Soul: the Development of National Batak Churches in North Sumatra* (Michigan: Grand Rapids, 1970).
Siahaan, Hotman A., "Konflik HKBP di Pentas Politik Indonesia" in Einar M. Sitompul and Raini M.P. Hutabarat (eds), *Gereja di Pentas Politik. Belajar dari Kasus HKBP* (Jakarta: PT. Anem Kosong Anem, 1997) 1-40.
Simanjuntak, Bungaran A., "Konflik Status dan Kekuasaan Orang Batak Toba" Unpublished PhD. Dissertation (Gajah Mada University: Jogyakarta, 1 994).
Wirodono, Sunardian, *Gerakan Politik di Indonesia: Catatan 1994* (Jakarta: Puspa Swara 1994).

B. Primary Sources: Copies of Telegrams, Letters, Statements, Reports, Articles and News (see Appendixes).

Appendixes

Doc. No. Classification

Bibliography 261

01. Letter of the Chief of Indonesian Police dated 5 September 1990 to the Committee of the HKBP Synod, explaining the cancellation of its synod.
02. Letter of Dr S.M. Siahaan dated 16 January 1993 to the Executive Committee of the Community of Churches in Indonesia, asking the latter to review its letter of 28 December 1992 to the former.
03. Letter of Ephorus Nababan dated 21 September 1990 to the Chief of Indonesian Police, responding to the latter's letter dated on 5 September 1990.
04. Letter of M. Munawir Sjadzali, the Minister of Religion, dated 6 September 1990
05. Letter of General (retired) M. Panggabean dated 7 September 1990 to the leadership of the HKBP, asking the latter to convey his enclosed letter to the congregations. The enclosed letter explains the cancellation of the synod.
06. The Military Decree issued by Major General H.R. Pramono, dated 23 December 1992.
07. The Report of the Chairman of the HKBP Pastors' Meeting as printed in the SAI-HKBP *Immanuel* (1994) pp. 21-35.
08 Editorial of *The Jakarta Post,* 7 January 1993 entitled: "Of Church and state".
09 Daily News, *Kompas* 12 January 1993 entitled: "PTUN Medan Menunda SK Bakorstanasda dalam kasus HKBP."
10 *Idem.* doc. no. 02.
11 Circular letter of Dr S.M. Siahaan, the Acting Ephorus, dated 31 December 1992 to all members of the HKBP.
12 J.R. Hutauruk and N. Manurung, "HKBP di Indonesia (Suatu Upaya Meluruskan Informasi)" in the SAI-HKBP *Immanuel* 5 (1994) pp. 10-13; *Immanuel* 6 (1994) 7-10.
13 Correspondence between Clement John and Konrad Raiser of the WCC, dated 16 March 1995.
14 The Opening Address of the SAI-HKBP 52nd synod by Rev. Dr. P.W.T. Simanjuntak, as printed in the SAI-HKBP Immanuel 11 (1994) 70ff.
15 Letter of the Chief of Coordinating Agency of National Security and Defence dated 13 January to his subordinates, explaining the Military Decree issued on 23 December 1992.
16 The Weekly News of the AP-HKBP, *Warta HKBP* 18 (25 January 1993).
17 Letter of the Minister of Religion, Dr H. Tarmizi Taher, dated 7 May 1993 to the Chairman of the Community of Churches in Indonesia, stating that the leadership of Dr P.W.T. Simanjuntak and Dr S.M.Siahaan is recognized by the government.
18 Open Letter of the leaders of the GMKI, PIKI and GAMKI dated 25 October 1994, stating that there is no right for the government to grant legitimacy to the leadership of the church.
19 Letter of Jan Kawatu of the Ministry of Religion dated 3 February 1995 to the Central Coordinating Agency for the National Security and Defence, confirming the legitimacy of the leadership of Dr P.W.T. Simanjuntak.
20 Letter of Dr P.W.T. Simanjuntak to the president of Indonesia dated 1 February 1994 requesting an audience.
21 *The Jakarta Post* 23 March 1994, entitled "Conflict-ridden Batak Church suspends former bishop."
22 The Report of Commission I of the Indonesian People's House of Representatives, dated 7 June of its meeting with General Faisal Tanjung. See item 13.
23a The Jakarta Post 8 June 1994 entitled: "Govt has confusing stance on HKBP rift."

23b Daily News *Kompas*, 7 June 1994.
24 Letter of Ephorus Nababan dated 14 May 1994 requesting to meet General Faisal Tanjung.
25 Letter of Major General Hari Sabarno of the Armed Forces Headquarters dated 7 July 1994, informing Ephorus Nababan that the Chief of Indonesian Armed Forces is unable to meet him.
26 Telegram of the Chief of the Coordinating Agency of the National Security and Defence in Northern Sumatra, dated 10 August 1993 to his subordinates recognizing the leadership of Dr P.W.T. Simanjuntak.
27 Telegram of Colonel Edward Simanjuntak representing the Governor of North Sumatra dated 2 September 1993 to his subordinates, confirming the leadership of the SAI-HKBP faction.
28 Telegram of the North Sumatra Governor to his subordinates, dated 24 September 1993, forbidding anyone to represent the HKBP or to hold any worship in and outside the church building without the knowledge and consent of the SAI-HKBP leadership.
29 Letter of the head of Dolok Sanggul Sub-Regency dated 3 July 1995 to the heads of villagers under his jurisdiction, informing them that no business should be carried out with anyone in their offices without their recognizing the leadership of the SAI-HKBP faction.
30a-c Joint Statements of the Government Officials in Dairi Regency, and towns of Pematangsiantar and Bogor (West Java), forbidding Ephorus Nababan to conduct worship in their areas.
31 President Soeharto's Speech at the Darma Canti Night. Hari Raya Nyepi Caka 1914.
32 President Soeharto's Speech at the Maulid Remembrance of Prophet Muhammad on 28 August 1993.
33 Chapter 12 of the Book of Confession of the HKBP, on the government.
34 Magazine, *Forum Keadilan* 21 (4 February 1993), entitled: "Menggugat Bakorstanasda, Menangkap Pendeta."
35 Letter of Ephorus Nababan dated 8 February 1993 to President Soeharto, expecting that the extraordinary synod should not be allowed to take place.
36 Press Release of Ephorus Nababan and the head of the HKBP Information Bureau dated 10 February 1993, stating the illegality of the extraordinary synod to be held on 11-13 February 1993.
37a-f The Announcement of the HKBP Attorneys about the verdict of the State Administrative Court (PTUN) on the military decree, and its implications on the HKBP assets.
37g The PTUN verdict, dated 11 January 1993 on the suit made by Ephorus Nababan against Major General H.R. Pramono regarding the military decree issued by the latter on 23 December 1992, appointing Dr S.M. Siahaan as the Acting Ephorus of the HKBP.
38 Daily News *Kompas,* 12 January 1993, reporting on the court verdict.
39 Radiogramme of the Minister of Home Affairs, Rudini, dated 23 December 1992, commanding his subordinates to postpone any political and social congress or the like in February and March 1993 in order to make the People's Representatives Assembly successful.
40 Press Release of the Legal Aid Institution, Jakarta, on the Teror and Military Intervention in the HKBP crisis.

Bibliography

41 Magazine *Forum Keadilan* 21 (4 February 1993).
42 The Verdict of the PTUN Medan dated 06 February 1993, allowing Major General Pramono to implement the military decree which he had issued.
43 Jakarta Declaration, 10 June 1994, made by the pastors of the AP-HKBP faction.
44A-m Letters of Protests coming from Indonesian churches, mass organizations and Intellectuals, condemning the military decree.
45a Letter of Dr Gunnar Staalset, the General Secretary of the Lutheran World Federation to President Soeharto, dated 8 January 1993, questioning the military intervention in the HKBP internal affairs.
45b Circular letter of the General Secretary of the LWF to its members, national committees and members of the LWF council, opposing the military decree and acknowledging Ephorus Nababan as the legitimate leader of the HKBP.
46a-p Letters of National Council of Churches from Japan, Namibia, Ireland, Britain, India, Netherlands, Thailand, CCA, USA, Australia and Germany, rejecting the military decree, and acknowledging the leadership of Ephorus Nababan.
47 The Statement of the CCI Executive Committee, dated 4 January 1993, opposing the military decree.
48 Letters of the General Secretary of the CCI to Rev Dr S.M Siahaan, dated 28 December 1992, asking the latter to reject his appointment by the military decree, and threatening not to recognize his leadership should he accept it.
49 The Decision of the CCI Executive Committee dated 2-5 March, 1993.
50 Letter of the CCI Executive Committee to President Soeharto dated 10 February 1993, asking the latter to postpone the extraordinary synod.
51 The Weekly News of the HKBP Silindung District, "Na Lambok Malilung." No. 10 (June 1996).
52 The Report of the General Secretary of the CCI to the HKBP Ecumenical Partners (WCC, VEM, VELKD, CCA, LWF) presented at a meeting on 13-15 March 1995 in Geneva, entitled "To Proceed with the Efforts of the Reconciliation of HKBP."
53 Letter of Ephorus Nababan to the CCI Executive Committee, informing the plan of the Ministry of Religion to form a new church as a solution to the HKBP problem, and asking the CCI to prevent it from happening.
54 The Position Paper of the CCI on the HKBP problem.
55 Letter of Drs. Jan Kawatu of the Department of Religion to the CCI Executive Committee, dated 29 May 1995, asking the visit planned by the WCC to be postponed.
56 The Annual Report of Ephorus Dr P.W.T. Simanjuntak (1994-1996) presented to his faction synod 17-22 November 1996.
57 The Report on the 53th synod, 17-22 November 1996 written by the General Secretary of the SAI-HKBP faction, Dr S.M. Siahaan.
58 The Result of the Elders' National Meeting of the SAI-HKBP faction on 1-4 August 1996, presented at this faction's synod, 17-22 November 1996.
59 Explanation and Guidance given by Dr P.W.T. Simanjuntak at the SAI HKBP faction's extraordinary synod on 9-12 July 1998.
60 Daily News *Sinar Indonesia Baru,* 11 July 1998.
61 Daily News *Sinar Indonesia Baru,* 12 July 1998.
62 Daily News *Suara Pembaruan,* 18 November 1998.

Author Index

Abbott, F.F. and Johnson, A.C. 74n335, 149n183
Achtemeier Paul J. 83n382
Agrell, G. 88n405
Allison, D.C. 146
Andrews, Mary E. 13
Applebaum, S. 25n83
Arafat, K.W. 68n300
Aritonang, Jan S. 214n2
Auguet, R. 77ns352-53
Badian, E. 68n302
Baird, W. 5, 5n14, 53n245
Barclay, J.M.S. 58n265, 185n359
Barrett, C.K. 3n6, 11n27, 13, 23, 29, 34, 48n213, 85n389, 85n391, 86n392, 89n406, 90n412, 108n11, 110n24, 114, 116n47, 129n105, 130n113, 150, 151n189, 164n258, 186n362
Bartchy, S. Scott 37n150, 172n302, 175n315, 175n317
Barton, Stephen 110n29, 121
Baur, F.C. 12, 14, 22-23, 24n71, 29, 114, 153, 167n267, 167n270, 171, 176n319, 179, 181n340, 189n376
Best, E. 119-110
Black, D.A. 187, 188n374, 191n381
Blasi, A.J. 47
Blomberg, C. 129n106, 130n111, 145n159, 153n208, 187n372
Bookidis, N. 65
Borgen, Peder 16n26, 25n83
Bornkamm, G. 167n267, 167n268
Bradley, Keith 134, 136n135, 175n317, 175n318
Braudel, F. 53, 55
Braund, David C. 76n342
Breadslee, William A. 58n264
Brewer, D. Instone 137-38

Broneer, O. 64, 66n288, 193n385, 194n390
Broughton, T.R.S. 68n301
Bruce, F.F. 15n17, 22, 23n124, 34, 121n67, 148, 183n351
Brunt, John C. 17n28, 93n430, 213n9
Brunt, P.A. 71n317, 76n341, 132n116, 126n93
Byron, John 162n246
Cadbury, H. 66n290, 82n372
Campbell, J.P. 133n120, 134n127, 134n128
Carson, D. 168
Carter, Philippa 168
Carter, Timothy L. 14, 39, 155, 206
Castelli, E.A. 111n130
Catchpole, D. 14n11
Cha, Young-Gil 173n306
Chadwick, H. 109n13, 167, 178n324
Chapple, A.E. 13n4
Cheung, Alex T. 18, 19ns43-45
Chow, J.K 34n133, 35n138, 39, 43n181, 70n314, 75n338, 77ns350-51, 78n354, 80n369, 81, 114n36, 154n214, 155n217
Clarke, A.D. 39, 43, 111, 119
Clarke, G.W. 4n9
Conzelmann, H. 33, 85ns390-91, 116, 121n67, 122n74, 182n345, 185n356, 193n389
Corbier, M. 48n218
Crafton, Jeffrey A. 115
Crook, J.A. 45
Coye Still III, E 62n62, 95n437
Dahl, N.A. 5, 13
Daube, D. 159n234, 167n268, 179n332, 187n371
Davies, James A. 27
Davies, W.D. and Allison, D.C.

146n169
De Boer, Martinus 34n134
Deissmann, A. 39, 40
Delobel, J. 90n414
DeMaris, Richard E 35n136
Deming, Will 13n2
Denaux, A. 121n65
Dickson, John P. 156n222
Dixon, Suzanna 43n182, 44n189, 126n89
Dodd, C.H. 180n336, 184-85, 186n365
Doubschütz. E.40n171
Douglass, M. 155n218
Downing, F Gerald 53n247
Drane, J.W. 32n119
Duff, A.M. 173n308
Dumbrell, W.J. 122n76
Dungan, D.L. 86n86, 108n12, 120n59, 129n104, 130n104, 146, 149n179, 149n182, 179ns184-85, 152, 156n222, 159n234, 163
Dunn, J.D.G 5n14, 56ns258-59, 98, 111n31, 121n64
Ebner, M. 152
Ehrhard, A. 16n24, 62n273
Elliott, Neil 82n380
Ellison, H.L. 167n267, 180n337, 186n365
Engberg-Pedersen, T. 25n83, 42
Engels, D. 23n70, 36, 67, 94n432, 135, 135ns133-34
Fee, G.D. 3n2, 15-16, 17ns28-30, 24, 34, 42n179, 42ns89-90, 91n415, 105n1, 107n3, 108ns8-10, 109n15, 115, 116n45, 119n55, 121n64, 138n140, 148, 149n179, 180, 182n346, 185n356, 186-87, 190n398, 193
Ferguson, E. 78, 105-06n1
Filson F.V. 4, 4n8, 40n172
Finley, M.I. 38n152, 80n368, 126n88, 136
Fiore, B. 5

Fiorenza, S.E. 42n180
Fisk, Bruce N. 91, 118n52
Fitzgerald, John T. 165
Fjärstedt, B. 146
Foerster, W. 122
Forbes, Clarence A. 173n309
Fotopoulos, John 20, 21n56, 65n284
Frank, Richard I. 136n135, 43n183
Furnish, V.P. 64, 122n71, 186
Gager, John G. 40n170, 74n334, 78n358, 134n124, 174n312
Galinski, Karl 44n186
Gardner, Jane F. 73n326
Gardner, P.D. 53, 87n400, 107n4, 122n73, 108n10, 108n12, 116n48, 118n51, 119, 122, 124n81, 141n149, 142, 148n176, 151n195, 157n229, 158n232, 159n236, 161n239, 161n241, 164, 180n335, 182n347, 185n357, 187n372
Garnsey, P. 45n191, 48, 57n262, 79n364, 79n366, 124n84, 127n100,
Garrison, Roman 106n1
Garzetti, A. 126
Geagan, Daniel J. 69n305
Gelzer, M. 133n121
Gill, D.W.J. 39, 47, 66, 69, 73n329
Glad, Clarence E. 100n451, 157n228, 169-70, 184,
Glancy, J.A. 106n1, 176n320
Godet, F. 129n105, 138n140, 166n266
Goguel, M 85n387, 86n391
Goldstein, J. 26n85
Gooch, Peter D. 3, 17-21, 50-52, 93, 178, 202
Gooch, P.W. 178
Goodman, M. 124n82, 126n93
Gordon, J.C. 64n278, 76
Gordon, R. 76-77
Goulder, M.D. 13-14n9
Grant, F.C. 64
Grant, Robert M. 64-65
Grosheide, F.W. 99n449

Gultom, Gomar 223n35
Hadikusuma, Hilman 223n35
Hagge, H. 85n387
Hall, B. 99n449
Harding, Mark 194n390
Harrill, J.A. 174n314, 175n315, 176n320
Hartin, P.J. and Petzer, J.H. 209n5
Harvey, A.E. 147n169, 151n188
Harvey, Graham 25, 206
Hays, Richard B. 51n23390n412, 109n22, 185n358, 185, 187n372, 211n7
Hengel, M. 151n188, 153n209, 206
Héring, J. 85n388, 85n191, 121n69
Hock, R.F. 39, 78n359, 88n405, 108n12, 153-56, 162, 165n260, 170
Holladay, Carl R. 110n29
Hollander, Harm W. 137n138
Holmberg, B. 17, 40n172, 150n187
Hooker, Morna D. 103n454, 130n107, 141n150, 163n252
Hooleman, Joost 34n134
Hopkins, Keith 80n368
Horrell, D.G. 6, 11n26, 20, 24n77, 32n116, 39, 42-43, 42n179, 48, 59n266,73, 76, 79, 86, 89, 92, 96n442, 97n443, 98n445, 101n453, 107n2, 109n21, 116, 144-45, 146n169, 147n169, 148-49, 151ns194-95, 152n197, 154n215, 155-56, 159n234, 178, 188n375, 196
Horsley, R.A. 14, 28n92, 30, 31n105, 39n160, 53n244, 75, 78n356, 82n378, 82n380, 151, 121n67, 155, 206
Hurd, J.C. 3, 15-17, 19, 21, 85n391, 86n394, 107n3, 190, 202
Hutauruk J.R. and Manurung N. 219ns13-14, 232-34
Hyldahl, N. 5n14, 12n1, 22n65, 23n66, 114n37

Jeremias, J. 86n396
Jewett, A.R. 54ns250-51, 142n151
Jewett, R 52, 85n387
Jones, James L. 134
Jones, Sydney 226n54
Judge, E.A. 4n9, 37n150, 39, 40n172, 74, 126n94, 134n125, 173n307
Joubert, Stephen J. 47
Kaiser, Walter C. 137n139, 138, 138n140, 139n144
Käsemann, E. 14, 146, 161, 164
Kee, H.C. 177n323
Keifer, O. 44n187
Kelly, J.M. 45n191
Kennedy, Charles A. 66n288, 86n396
Kent, J.H. 68n304
Kim, Seyoon 148n175
Kling, C.F. 115n40, 130n108, 137n137
Klutz, Todd E. 33
Knox, W.L. 26n86
Koester, H. 33n122
Kraabel, A.T. 25n83
Kraemer, Ross Shephard 76n346
Kuck, David W. 13n3, 15n18
Lanci, John R. 124n85, 132n116, 144n155, 145n162
Laughery, G.J. 15n18
Lawson, W.H. 16n27, 26n86, 86n392, 90n412, 91n415, 91n417, 192n382, 193n389
Lee, Clarence L. 172n304
Lenski, R.C.H. 145n160, 186n365
Lentz, John Clayton Jr. 26n83, 26n85, 126n94, 127n97, 172n303
Lietzmann, H. 122n73
Lisle, Robert 64n280
Liftin, D. 39, 70
Lieu, Judith 94n433
Longenecker, R. 178
Louw, J.P and Nida, E.A. 121n62, 121n68
Lund, N.W. 179n334
Lüdemann, G. 23n70, 110

Lütgert, W. 12, 13n3
Lyttelton, M. and Forman, W. 50, 68n303, 74n336
Mack, Burton L. 110n28
McRay, J. 65n285
Magee, B.R. 59n267
Malherbe, A.J. 39n153, 40n172, 87n402, 108n10, 121n70, 122n74, 139n146, 161n240, 161, 170, 186n360, 190
Malina, B.J. 40n172
Manson, T.W. 13
Marshall, P. 3n7, 39, 58n263m 85n389, 116n46, 122n74, 123n80, 172n302, 154-55, 162-63, 168-69
Martin, D.B. 6, 9n24m 35n135, 39, 42n179, 45, 78n357, 87n401, 162n246, 170-71, 188
Martin, R.P. 4
Maxey, M. 132n115
Meeks, W.A. 6, 39, 40n172, 41n173, 53n244, 55n253, 60n269, 75n337, 79n367, 95n438, 96n439, 114n35
Meggitt, J.J. 11n27, 40n171, 42, 43n184, 45ns191-94, 46-50, 53n247, 79n367, 81n372, 90n412, 135ns131-32, 136
Meyer, H.A.E. 135n130, 151n195, 187n371
Milleker, E.J. 66n187
Mitchell, M.M. 4-5, 21ns57-58, 59, 60, 85n387, 86, 89n407, 95n436, 107n4, 109, 121, 179
Moffatt, J. 147
Momigliano, A. 73n327
Munck, J. 5, 6n17, 12n1, 22n65, 114n37
Murphy-O'Connor, J. 8n23, 13, 14n11, 65n285, 105-06n1, 115n41, 154n210
Morris, L.123n81, 159n235, 161n242, 187n372
Moulton, J.H. and Milligan, G. 121n67

Nadeak, Moxa 206, 217n7
Nakahashi, Osamu 90n412
Nasuti, Harry P. 139n145, 140n148
Neirynck, F. 146n165
Neller, K.V. 172, 180n335, 188
Newton, D. 59, 64n278, 64n280, 68n304, 88n404, 91, 95n435, 109n17, 123n86, 202-03, 211n7
Omanson, Roger L. 159n235
O'Rourke, J.J. 40n170, 172n304, 174n311, 174n313
Orr, D.G. 68n303
Oster, R.E. Jr. 70n313
Paige, T.P. 98n446
Parkins, Helen 5n16, 136n135
Pearce, S and Jones, S. 25n80, 26n84
Pearson, B.A. 14n13
Pedersen, Paul B. 214n2
Pfitzner, V.C. 193-95, 196n392
Pickett, Raymond 37n149, 39, 42n180, 54n248, 143n154
Pierce, C.A. 186n364
Pogoloff, S.M. 39, 154n213, 157.
Pomeroy, A.J. 79n367
Pomeroy, Sarah B. 44n189, 127n96
Price, S.R.F. 54n252, 74n332, 75n336, 82n378, 125n87
Price, S, 75 n. 336.
Prior, D. 128n101
Rainbow, Paul A. 27n88, 42n180, 48n213, 52n239, 65n256, 99n448, 120n57
Räisänen, H. 89n407
Ramsaran, Rollin A. 5n14, 99n449, 106n1
Ramsay, W and Lanciani, R. 132n117
Rauer, M. 54n251
Rawson, Beryl 44n189, 173n309
Rawson, B and Weaver P. 172n305
Read-Heimerdinger, J. 131n114
Rees, W. 66n290
Reitzenstein, R. 14, 122n73
Richardson, P. 88n403, 145n161, 155-56, 168, 178

Richardson, P and Gooch, P.W. 178n326
Richter, P.J. 38n152
Robertson, A and Plummer, A. 69n309, 107ns5-6, 108n7, 114, 115n38, 129n105, 130n108, 180n338, 188n373
Roebuck, C. 65n285
Roetzel, Calvin J. 90n410, 182n344
Romano, D.G. 67
Rose, F.S. 174n314
Rosner, Brian S. 38n152m 106n1
Ross, March Howard 212n8
Saller, R.P. 78n361, 133n118, 136n136
Salmon, E.T. 70ns316-17, 71, 73n330, 76n341, 76n345, 133n122
Sampley, J. Paul 153n206
Sanders, E.P. 179
Sanders, J.T. 24n75, 24n78
Savage, T.B. 81n372, 151n196, 152
Sawyer, W.T. 24, 54n252, 91
Schlatter, A. 13n3
Schlier, H. 187n369
Schmithals, W. 32, 6n17, 89
Schrage, W. 128
Schütz, J.H. 158-59, 177n322
Sellin, G. 34n134
Sherwin-White, A.N. 126, 133n119
Shilington, V. George 140n147
Shoe, L. 67n295
Siahaan, Hotman A. 215n3
Sibinga, J.S. 98n444
Simanjuntak, Bungaran A. 215n3
Sisson, Russell Barrett 85n387, 85n391, 109n14, 149n180, 187n367
Smith, D.E. 65n287
Smit, Joop F.M. 19n47, 20n56
Soden, F.H. Von 192n383
Songer, Harold S. 72n322
Spawforth, A.J.S. 67, 72-73, 75n340, 135
Spawforth, A and Carltledge, P 75n340.
Staumbaugh, J.E. 55n255
Still II, E.C. 62n272
Ste. Croix, B.E.M. De 75n338
Stone, M. 144n258
Stowers, Stanley K. 52n244, 106n1, 145n159, 72n322, 145n159, 153n208, 155n216
Stroud, Ronald S. 67n293, 69, 70n312
Sumney, Jerry L. 116n46, 193n384
Syme, Ronald 80n369
Tasker, R.V.G. 165
Taylor, Nicholas H. 54n249, 57n260, 130n112
Terry, Ralph Bruce 15n22, 60n270, 93n428, 93n429
Theissen, G. 6, 7, 11, 39-41, 42n179, 44n190, 45, 47-49, 50, 51n230, 67n298, 147, 151, 170, 188, 201, 206
Thielman, F. 24n71, 106n1, 128, 183, 187n365
Thiselton, A.C. 15, 34, 123
Thompkins, D.P. 135n133
Thrall, M. 186n364
Tomlin, Graham 15, 34n134, 35-36, 42n180, 169
Tomson, Peter J.26, 27n87, 28-29, 47, 52n238, 55n253, 57n261, 86n394, 90n411, 99n450, 144n156, 146n166, 180n333, 182ns341-42, 187n370
Trail, Ronald 121n63, 121n69
Trebilco, Paul R. 27n89
Treggiari, Susan 44n189, 174n310,
Tucker, T.G. 82n379
Tuckett, Christopher 13n9
Verbrugge, Verlyn D. 142n151
Vielhauer, P. 13
Volf, Judith M. Gundry 196
Stephen de Vos, Craig 43-44
Wallace-Hadrill, A. 79n364, 136n135
Walbank, Mary E. Hopkins 66
Walbank, M.H. 66n290

Watson, A. 63n276, 127n98
Watson, D.F. 100n451
Watson, F. 24
Weaver, P.R.C. 79n367, 80n368, 172n305, 173n309
Weber, M.. 136n135
Wedderburn, A.J.H. 34n133, 150n186
Weiss, J. 16n24, 85n388, 89n408, 179n329
Welborn, L.L. 4, 5n12
Wenham, D. 94n434, 149n179
West, A.B. 3, 76ns343-44, 77n350, 80n369
Westerholm, S. 183n349
Westermann, W.L. 172n302
White, Joel R. 35n136
Whittaker, C.W. 55n254, 62n274
Wiedemann, Thomas 133n118
Wiedemann, Thomas E.J. 78n362
Williams II, C.K. 66, 68n304, 132n116, 135n133
Willis, W. 9, 64n278, 85n387, 107n4, 108n8, 179n328
Willis, W.L. 51-52, 62n273, 66n289,87, 91n419
Wilson, A.N. 25n79, 33n121, 34n131
Wilson, Jack H. 34n131
Wilson R. Mcl. 433n121
Windisch, H. 151n195
Winter, Bruce W. 6n17, 8n23, 15n21, 38n152, 49n225, 67-69, 73n331, 79n365, 121ns70-71, 83-84, 106n1, 120n58, 120n60, 123-25, 135n133, 156, 165, 173n308, 174n314, 175n314, 176n319, 197, 200, 206
Wire, A.C. 34n134, 142n151
Wirodono, Sunardian 215n3
Witherington III, Ben 39, 42n179, 56n257, 65n285, 67n298, 80n371, 90, 115, 116n48, 121n70, 138n141, 154n216, 156n227, 170n296
Witt, Norman de 35
Wolff, Christian 150, 154n210
Wright, N.T. 25, 31-32, 109n23

Wuellner, W. 85n389, 86n396, 193n386
Yamsat, Pandang 3n2, 15n23, 21, 211n7
Yeo, K.K. 14, 27n88, 33n120, 47, 48n214, 51n232, 64n280, 85n391, 89n408, 211n7
Young, F.M. and Ford, D.F. 39n169
Zanker, P. 81ns375-76, 82n378
Zodhiates,S.123n7

Scripture Index

Numbers
18:8-31 *145*

Leviticus
16 *140n147*

Deuteronomy
25:4 *137-38,
   138n139,
   138n141*
32:17 *56n259*
32:21 *56n259*

Psalm
24 *99*
50:12 *99*
89:12 *99*

Matthew
10:8b *146n169*
10:9-10 *114*
10:10 *146*
10:10b *156*
10:11 *156*
10:40-2 *148*
22:21b *223*

Mark
3:31-35 *130n109*
6:10 *156*
9:41 *148*

Luke
9 *146n169*
10 *146n169*
10:5 *156*
10:7 *146*
10:7-8 *114, 155*

John
1:12 *122*

Acts
1:14 *130n109*
4:36 *131*
6:9 *26n83*
9:22 *131*
9:29 *26n83*
11:25 *131*
13:2 *131*
13:14 *131*
15 *23, 36, 131n114*
15:37-40 *131*
18:2-3 *189*
18:3 *189*
18:4 *144, 188-89*
18:6 *189*
18:7 *189*
18:8 *37n150*
18:12-17 *83*
18:13 *189*
18:18 *189*
20:33-34 *111*
20:34 *134, 140,190*
20: 33-35 *111,146,
   147n169*
20:34-35 *207*
21:17-26 *192*
23:16-17 *141*

Romans
1:21-23 *19*
2:15 *29*
2:22 *19*
3:27 *164*
9:3 *181*
14-15 *86n395*
16:1-2 *4*
16:23 *4,41,81n372,
   189*
16:24 *151*

1 Corinthians
1 *13*
1-4 *2,4,22,41-2,240*
1-7 *61n271*
1-10 *5n14*
1:1 *139-40*
1:5 *33*
1:1-6:11 *89*
1:10 *22,171,
   201,210,212*
1:10-12 *111*
1:10-17 *41*
1:10-18 *111*
1:10-4:21 *6n17,
   112,237*
1:11 *4, 20, 37, 94*
1:11-12 *19*
1:12 *4, 23-24, 114*
1:12-4:21 *4, 7,
   58n265,165,201*
1:13-18 *7*
1:14 *7, 189*
1:14-16 *20, 201*
1:16 *160*
1:17 *160*
1:17-3:16 *201*
1:18 *93, 119-20*
1:18-25 *41, 112*
1:22 *118n50,189*
1:23 *119,120,143*
1:23-24 *37*
1:26
   *10,11,40n171,42,
   46,137,190*
1:26-27 *47,190*
1:27 *187-88*
1:26-29
   10,11,37n150,40
1:27-28 *187,190*
1:29 *164n182*
1:30 *182*
1:31 *164*
2:1-5 *156*
2:2 *157*

2:3 *11,187-88,190*
2:3-4 *190*
3:1-3 *111n31*
3:4 *4,10,111*
3:5 *131n113*
3:5-4-5 *13*
3:6 *134,139-40*
3:6-9 *135*
3:10 *140*
3:18-19 *5*
3:22 *4,24*
4:1-5 *237*
4:3 *111*
4:3-4 *4,111*
4:4 *182n342*
4:6 *111,134*
4:6-7 *5*
4:6-8 *35*
4:7b *164*
4:8 *11,12n3,13,15,22,34-35,46*
4:10 *187-88,190*
4:10-13 *141*
4:10b *11*
4:11-12 *153*
4:12 *111,140-41, 143,157,189*
4:12a *140,190,207*
4:15 *140*
4:17 *38n151*
4:18-19 *4,116,201*
4:18-21 *111n131*
4:23 *157*
5 *42-43*
5:1 *20,44,61*
5:1-8 *60*
5:2c-5 *61n271*
5:3-5 *140*
5:6 *144*
5:6-8 *61n271*
5:9-10 *54n248*
5:9-13 *3,17n33,58,60,89*
5:10 *17n33,18n33*
5:11 *18n33*
5:12-13 *61*
5:13-19 *61*

5-6 *13n9*
5-7 *35*
5-14 *54*
5-16 *32*
6 *61,85,168*
6-10 *123n80*
6:1 *61n271*
6:2 *123*
6:1-11 *5,44*
6:2-3 *61n271*
6:3 *144*
6:4 *61n271*
6:6 *61n271*
6:9 *144*
6:9-11 *27, 38n151,43,53,58 n265,72*
6:9-13 *53*
6:11 *182n342*
6:12 *1*
6:12-20 *13n4,106n1,89 n403,106n1,124n 83,160,167-68,*
6:15 *144*
6:15-16 *62n372*
6:15b-16 *105n1*
6:16 *144*
6:18 *144, 182n342*
7 *59,61n271,64, 167,*
7:1 *58n265*
7:1-5 *70n313*
7:1-8:13 *89n408*
7:1-16:4 *201-02*
7:1-40 *15*
7:2 *61n271*
7:4 *123*
7:8 *130*
7:9 *61n271*
7:10-11 *146n165*
7:12-16 *58n265,61*
7:12-17 *54*
7:13-16 *38n151*
7:17-20 *37n151*
7:17-21 *172,175*
7:18 *182n382*
7:21 *37,172,175*

7:21-22 *173*
7:21-23 *37,105,165,173*
7:21b *174-75,176n320*
7:23 *172,175*
7:25 *94*
7:36 *61n271*
7:39-40 *140*
7:40 *130*
7-16 *5-7,58*
8 *52,85,90,92, 118n52,167-68*
8-9 *142n151*
8:1 *9,13n4,17,19, 21-22,27,32-33, 57,63,82,89,94 n431, 95-96,103, 145,192,202*
8:1-11:1 *2,5-6,8- 10, 11-12,18,21, 30,47,50,53,59- 61,61n271,84,88, 92,96,103,105,18 7,195,200,202,20 5,209-10,238*
8:1-3 *52, 111n31*
8:1-4 *31*
8:1-6 *98,103,193, 202*
8:1-7 *117*
8:1-13 *51,85,89-91, 93-94,104,204*
8:1-9:27 *92,95*
8:4 *17,19,30,33, 63,89,94,189*
8:4-5 *98,119*
8:4-6 *1,27,36,57, 94,103,187,210*
8:5 *56,72-73,125, 203*
8:4-13 *32*
8:4-18 *203*
8:6 *31n109,38n 151, 57,89,109, 203*
8:6-7 *38n151*
8:7 *3,10,19-20,22,*

24-27,32,38n151,
47, 50, 55-56,58n
264,63,94,100n
452, 186-87,203
8:7-12 11,188
8:7-13 16,19, 31,
90,93-94
8:8 1,17,47,57, 63n
277,94,98,103,11
7,119,202.210
8:9 8,19,57,105,
116-17,119-24,
128,143,169,186
8:9-10 11,94n431,
118
8:9-11 186-87
8:9-12 87n400,188,
203
8:9-13 1,9,37,60,86
n395,97,101-02,
104-05,109,117-
18,122n74,129,
147,176,187n365
8:9-9:18 121,123,
236
8:9-9:23 104,192-
93,196,199
8:9-9:27
93,95,97,99,104
8:10 17,19-20,32,
55-56,60,62-63,
70n313,75,82,90-
94,96,98,100n
452,117,120,139
n145,144,169
8:10-11 19n47
8:10-12 57n260,96,
187,196
8:10-13 104,169
8:10-10:22 101
8:11 32,60,96,119,
191
8:11-12 11,47,96,
120,191
8:11-13 60
8:12 130
8:13 19,86n395,
87n 400,96-

97,101, 160,186,
203
8-9 56,92
8 10 13n9,68n304
9 9,17,84,85n388,
85n391-92,86n
391,86n395-96,
88,92,85-86,101-
05,107,109,114-
15,118n52,122n
74,123n80,139n
146,154,156,158,
162,168,177,179,
181,183,196-98,
200,204-05,209,
212,214,237-38
9:1 17,86,105,140,
171
9:1a 105
9:1b-2 106
9:1-2 23,87n400,
116
9:1a-d 108
9:1b 108,111
9:1c 108
9:1c-d 113
9:1c+12a 113
9:1d 108
9:1-3 9,105,196,
203,237
9:1-14 162
9:1-18 85n387,89
9:1-27 46,97,106
9:2 9,108n10,153
9:1c-2 108
9:2b 108
9:2-3 116
9:3 1,3,9,86-87,
102,107-09,111,
115,152
9:4 123n80
9:4ff 87
9:4-5 129
9:4-6 105,122-23
9:4-8 128
9:4-10 129,139
9:4-11 107
9:4-12 117

9:4-12a 120,127-
28,197,236
9:4-13 150
9:4-14 143,238
9:4-18 23,105-
06,108,116-
18,120-21,121n
64,128,139n145,
157,238
9:4-27 197
9:5 24,111,123n80,
130-31,131n113
9:6 1131,207
9:7b-c 135
9:7-10 145
9:8 137
9:8-10 128
9:8-11 132,135
9:9 137n138
9:9a 137
9:9b-10 137
9:9-11 138
9:9-12 112
9:9-14 128
9:10 137
9:11 115,140,146,
47,152
9:11-12 139
9:12 105,117,122-
23
9:12a
113,116,123n80,
139-43,205
9:12a-b 106,123n
80,141,148
9:12b 102,106-07,
112,117-18,128,
140-41,143,148,
157-59,161,165,
177,190-91,197,
205,207-08,237
9:13 125,144-46,
165,
9:13-14 128,132,
143-44,146
9:14 110,112-13,
128,146n165+16
9,148,156-58,

197,204-05,209-10
9:14-18 *105,177, 209,237*
9:15 *102,105,117, 122-23,139n145, 159n235,177*
9:15a *113,133,137, 139,139n145,118 ,128,143,146,149 -50,159-60,*
9:15b *150,159-61, 206,238*
9:15b-17 *144*
9:15b-18 *144,149*
9:15c-d *161*
9:15-18 *104,117, 142-43,159,162, 197,205*
9:16a *161*
9:16b *161*
9:16c *161,177*
9:16-17 *161*
9:16-18 *102,156,162,197*
9:16-18a *163*
9:17 *161,162*
9:18 *107,115,105, 122,123n80,141, 143,163,196,198, 236*
9:18b *189*
9:19 *17,86,106, 120,122,123n80, 172,176,177,191*
9:19-23 *89,104-06, 109,123,140,166-68,170-71,175, 177-79,191,198-99,236,238*
9:20 *24,179,182n 382,184*
9:20a *171,179-81, 189*
9:20b *177,180-81, 183-84,189*
9:20b-21 *171*
9:20-21 *186,170,179,187*
9:20-22 *178*
9:20-22a *178-79,187n372,198*
9:20-22b *194*
9:21 *177,184,189-90*
9:22 *170,177*
9:22ff *130*
9:22a *11,170-71, 179,182n 383, 186-88,180*
9:22b *106,109,157, 169,177-78,187*
9:22b-23 *191*
9:23 *106,117,177, 196,194,238*
9:24 *86,194*
9:24a *193*
9:24-25 *195*
9:24-27 *89n409,97, 98n444,106,192-93,193n384,196, 199*
9:24-10:22 *89*
9:25 *194*
9:26 *195*
9:27 *97,104,106, 177,195*
9:29b-30 *100n451, 104,203*
10 *85,92,168*
10:1-4 *17,182n342*
10:1-10 *98*
10:1-14 *92,103*
10:1-20 *95*
10:1-22 *8-9,28,51, 56,60,89-90,92-95, 98,102, 104,193, 196,203-04,237*
10:1-11:1 *12,85*
10:6-12 *98*
10:8 *196*
10:13-14 *203*
10:14 *63n277,104, 139n145,187,203*
10:14-22 *31,85n 299,89-90,93*
10:15 *55,99*
10:15-22 *92*
10:15-19 *98*
10:16-22 *51*
10:18 *63n277,144*
10:19 *60,62n275, 63n277,82,104, 203*
10:19-20 *98,237*
10:20 *56,187*
10:20-22 *98-99*
10:20-23 *63n277*
10:21 *62,65n285*
10:21b *65n283*
10:21-22 *98*
10:21-23 *62*
10:23 *1,58,97,106n1, 117n49,105,124n8 3, 103,123n80,210*
10:23ff *13n4*
10:23-24 *17n33,237*
10:23-27 *99*
10:23-30 *94*
10:23-11:1 *8n23,89ns 408-09, 90,92,95, 99n449,204*
10:24 *82,104,117*
10:25 *7,29,62,99,102*
10:25-26 *60,104,203, 236*
10:25-27 *19,54n248, 99-100,117,248*
10:25-28 *29,90*
10:25-29 *24*
10:26 *57,99*
10:27 *19,29,82,99, 169*
10:27-28 *11,62,90*
10:27-29a *104,203*
10:27-29b *237*
10:28 *55,63,82*
10:28-29 *7,17n33*
10:28-29a *99,101-02, 117*
10:28b-29a *186-87*
10:29 *19,100,123n80, 203*
9:29b *123*

10:29-30 *204*
10:29b-30 *99-100,
  104,203*
10:30b *237*
10:31-11:1
  20,101,117,237
10:32 *24,37n151,
  102, 118,179,183*
11 *13n9*
11:1 *20,94,101,
  104, 111n30,119-
  20,140,160,164n
  202,237*
11:2-16 *5,38n151,
  70n313*
11:2-34 *61n271,89*
11:16 *111n31*
11:17-24 *37n150*
11:17-34 *5n17,6,41*
11:18 *6n17,94*
11:18a *4*
11:22 *11,38n152,
  79*
11:31 *21*
11:34b *38n151,94*
12:1 *22,27,58n265,
  72,94*
12:1-31a *19,89n
  408*
12:2 *19,38n151*
12:13 *37n151*
12:14-26 *70n313*
12:18 *42*
12:20-21 *18*
12:22 *42*
12:23a *42*
18:23b *42*
12:24 *42*
12:25 *94*
12:28 *42*
12:31b-13:13 *89n
  408*
12-14 *5,38,61n271,
  86,167*
13 *110n29*
12-15 *13n9*
14:1c-40 *89n408*
14:23 *38n151*

14:26 *117n49*
14:34-36 *38n151*
15 *34-35,61n271*
15:1 *113*
15:1-8 *130-31*
15:1-15 *89n409*
15:3 *113*
15:3-7 *113n32*
15:8 *113*
15:9 *113*
15:19 *141*
15:10-11 *160*
15:11 *113*
15:11b *207*
15:12 *5,20,38n151,
  42n180,113n32*
15:10 *141*
15:29 *5,35*
15:29-34 *124n83*
15:33-34 *38n151*
15:54-56 *182n382*
16:1 *94*
16:1-2 *142n151*
16:1-4 *61n271,142*
16:1-12 *89n408*
16:2 *37n150*
16:3f *111*
16:5-6 *107*
16:6 *207-08*
16:7 *38n151*
16:10 *6*
16:11b *207*
16:12 *4,61n271*
16:13-24 *89*
16:14 *6*
16:15 *37*
16:15-18 *4,6,61n
  271, 107,201,207*
16:17-18 *151,207*

2 Corinthians
1-9 *116*
1:1 *190*
1:1-2:13 *89*
1:15-2:2 *112*
2:14-6:13 *89n408*
2:17 *116n46*
3:1 *116n36*

4:3 *119-20*
5:12 *116n46*
6:14-7:1 *89n408*
6:16 *19*
7:2-4 *89*
7:5-9:15 *89*
8:1-5 *141*
8:2 *206*
8:5 *152*
8:13-14 *152*
10:1-13:13 *89*
10:7 *23*
10:12 *116n46*
10:18 *116n46*
10-12 *205*
10-13 *166*
11:4 *116n46*
11:7 *189*
11:7-10 *207*
11:7-11 *107,207*
11:7-15 *150n184*
11:8-9 *151*
11:9 *151*
11:10 *206*
11:12 *116n46*
11:12-13 *166n265*
11:13 *116n46,206*
11:20 *115*
11:22 *181*
11:23b *159n237*
11:23-29 *141*
11:27 *189*
12:11 *116n46*
12:11-13 *207*
12:14 *206*
12:16 *116,150n184*
12:16-18 *207*
12:17-18 *140*

Galatians
1:17,21 *131*
2:1 *131*
2:6 *130*
2:11ff *14*
2:13 *131*
1:17 *131*
1:21 *131*
2:1 *131*

2:12-15 *164*
2:13 *131*
4:8 *19*
6:12-15 *164*

Philippians
2 *190*
2:25-30 *151*
3:3 *164*
3:5 *151,181*
4:7 *157*
4:11-12 *141*
4:15f *151*
4:15-16 *107,207*
4:18 *107,207*

1 Thessalonians
1:9 *19*
2:5-10 *115*
2:9 *27,72,111,207*
4:11 *111*

2 Thessalonians
3:6-13 *111,158*
3:8-9 *207*

Paternoster Biblical Monographs
(All titles uniform with this volume)
Dates in bold are of projected publication

Joseph Abraham
Eve: Accused or Acquitted?
A Reconsideration of Feminist Readings of the Creation Narrative Texts in Genesis 1–3
Two contrary views dominate contemporary feminist biblical scholarship. One finds in the Bible an unequivocal equality between the sexes from the very creation of humanity, whilst the other sees the biblical text as irredeemably patriarchal and androcentric. Dr Abraham enters into dialogue with both camps as well as introducing his own method of approach. An invaluable tool for any one who is interested in this contemporary debate.
2002 / 0-85364-971-5 / xxiv + 272pp

Octavian D. Baban
Mimesis and Luke's on the Road Encounters in Luke-Acts
Luke's Theology of the Way and its Literary Representation
The book argues on theological and literary (mimetic) grounds that Luke's on-the-road encounters, especially those belonging to the post-Easter period, are part of his complex theology of the Way. Jesus' teaching and that of the apostles is presented by Luke as a challenging answer to the Hellenistic reader's thirst for adventure, good literature, and existential paradigms.
2005 */ 1-84227-253-5 / approx. 374pp*

Paul Barker
The Triumph of Grace in Deuteronomy
This book is a textual and theological analysis of the interaction between the sin and faithlessness of Israel and the grace of Yahweh in response, looking especially at Deuteronomy chapters 1–3, 8–10 and 29–30. The author argues that the grace of Yahweh is determinative for the ongoing relationship between Yahweh and Israel and that Deuteronomy anticipates and fully expects Israel to be faithless.
2004 / 1-84227-226-8 / xxii + 270pp

Jonathan F. Bayes
The Weakness of the Law
God's Law and the Christian in New Testament Perspective
A study of the four New Testament books which refer to the law as weak (Acts, Romans, Galatians, Hebrews) leads to a defence of the third use in the Reformed debate about the law in the life of the believer.
2000 / 0-85364-957-X / xii + 244pp

Mark Bonnington
The Antioch Episode of Galatians 2:11-14 in Historical and Cultural Context

The Galatians 2 'incident' in Antioch over table-fellowship suggests significant disagreement between the leading apostles. This book analyses the background to the disagreement by locating the incident within the dynamics of social interaction between Jews and Gentiles. It proposes a new way of understanding the relationship between the individuals and issues involved.

2005 / 1-84227-050-8 / approx. 350pp

David Bostock
A Portrayal of Trust
The Theme of Faith in the Hezekiah Narratives

This study provides detailed and sensitive readings of the Hezekiah narratives (2 Kings 18–20 and Isaiah 36–39) from a theological perspective. It concentrates on the theme of faith, using narrative criticism as its methodology. Attention is paid especially to setting, plot, point of view and characterization within the narratives. A largely positive portrayal of Hezekiah emerges that underlines the importance and relevance of scripture.

2005 / 1-84227-314-0 / approx. 300pp

Mark Bredin
Jesus, Revolutionary of Peace
A Non-violent Christology in the Book of Revelation

This book aims to demonstrate that the figure of Jesus in the Book of Revelation can best be understood as an active non-violent revolutionary.

2003 / 1-84227-153-9 / xviii + 262pp

Robinson Butarbutar
Paul and Conflict Resolution
An Exegetical Study of Paul's Apostolic Paradigm in 1 Corinthians 9

The author sees the apostolic paradigm in 1 Corinthians 9 as part of Paul's unified arguments in 1 Corinthians 8–10 in which he seeks to mediate in the dispute over the issue of food offered to idols. The book also sees its relevance for dispute-resolution today, taking the conflict within the author's church as an example.

2006 / 1-84227-315-9 / approx. 280pp

Daniel J-S Chae
Paul as Apostle to the Gentiles
His Apostolic Self-awareness and its Influence on the Soteriological Argument in Romans
Opposing 'the post-Holocaust interpretation of Romans', Daniel Chae competently demonstrates that Paul argues for the equality of Jew and Gentile in Romans. Chae's fresh exegetical interpretation is academically outstanding and spiritually encouraging.
1997 / 0-85364-829-8 / xiv + 378pp

Luke L. Cheung
The Genre, Composition and Hermeneutics of the Epistle of James
The present work examines the employment of the wisdom genre with a certain compositional structure and the interpretation of the law through the Jesus tradition of the double love command by the author of the Epistle of James to serve his purpose in promoting perfection and warning against doubleness among the eschatologically renewed people of God in the Diaspora.
2003 / 1-84227-062-1 / xvi + 372pp

Youngmo Cho
Spirit and Kingdom in the Writings of Luke and Paul
The relationship between Spirit and Kingdom is a relatively unexplored area in Lukan and Pauline studies. This book offers a fresh perspective of two biblical writers on the subject. It explores the difference between Luke's and Paul's understanding of the Spirit by examining the specific question of the relationship of the concept of the Spirit to the concept of the Kingdom of God in each writer.
2005 / 1-84227-316-7 / approx. 270pp

Andrew C. Clark
Parallel Lives
The Relation of Paul to the Apostles in the Lucan Perspective
This study of the Peter-Paul parallels in Acts argues that their purpose was to emphasize the themes of continuity in salvation history and the unity of the Jewish and Gentile missions. New light is shed on Luke's literary techniques, partly through a comparison with Plutarch.
2001 / 1-84227-035-4 / xviii + 386pp

Andrew D. Clarke
Secular and Christian Leadership in Corinth
A Socio-Historical and Exegetical Study of 1 Corinthians 1–6

This volume is an investigation into the leadership structures and dynamics of first-century Roman Corinth. These are compared with the practice of leadership in the Corinthian Christian community which are reflected in 1 Corinthians 1–6, and contrasted with Paul's own principles of Christian leadership.

2005 / 1-84227-229-2 / 200pp

Stephen Finamore
God, Order and Chaos
René Girard and the Apocalypse

Readers are often disturbed by the images of destruction in the book of Revelation and unsure why they are unleashed after the exaltation of Jesus. This book examines past approaches to these texts and uses René Girard's theories to revive some old ideas and propose some new ones.

2005 / 1-84227-197-0 / approx. 344pp

David G. Firth
Surrendering Retribution in the Psalms
Responses to Violence in the Individual Complaints

In *Surrendering Retribution in the Psalms*, David Firth examines the ways in which the book of Psalms inculcates a model response to violence through the repetition of standard patterns of prayer. Rather than seeking justification for retributive violence, Psalms encourages not only a surrender of the right of retribution to Yahweh, but also sets limits on the retribution that can be sought in imprecations. Arising initially from the author's experience in South Africa, the possibilities of this model to a particular context of violence is then briefly explored.

2005 / 1-84227-337-X / xviii + 154pp

Scott J. Hafemann
Suffering and Ministry in the Spirit
Paul's Defence of His Ministry in II Corinthians 2:14–3:3

Shedding new light on the way Paul defended his apostleship, the author offers a careful, detailed study of 2 Corinthians 2:14–3:3 linked with other key passages throughout 1 and 2 Corinthians. Demonstrating the unity and coherence of Paul's argument in this passage, the author shows that Paul's suffering served as the vehicle for revealing God's power and glory through the Spirit.

2000 / 0-85364-967-7 / xiv + 262pp

Scott J. Hafemann
Paul, Moses and the History of Israel
The Letter/Spirit Contrast and the Argument from Scripture in 2 Corinthians 3
An exegetical study of the call of Moses, the second giving of the Law (Exodus 32–34), the new covenant, and the prophetic understanding of the history of Israel in 2 Corinthians 3. Hafemann's work demonstrates Paul's contextual use of the Old Testament and the essential unity between the Law and the Gospel within the context of the distinctive ministries of Moses and Paul.
2005 / 1-84227-317-5 / xii + 498pp

Douglas S. McComiskey
Lukan Theology in the Light of the Gospel's Literary Structure
Luke's Gospel was purposefully written with theology embedded in its patterned literary structure. A critical analysis of this cyclical structure provides new windows into Luke's interpretation of the individual pericopes comprising the Gospel and illuminates several of his theological interests.
2004 / 1-84227-148-2 / xviii + 388pp

Stephen Motyer
Your Father the Devil?
A New Approach to John and 'The Jews'
Who are 'the Jews' in John's Gospel? Defending John against the charge of antisemitism, Motyer argues that, far from demonising the Jews, the Gospel seeks to present Jesus as 'Good News for Jews' in a late first century setting.
1997 / 0-85364-832-8 / xiv + 260pp

Esther Ng
Reconstructing Christian Origins?
The Feminist Theology of Elizabeth Schüssler Fiorenza: An Evaluation
In a detailed evaluation, the author challenges Elizabeth Schüssler Fiorenza's reconstruction of early Christian origins and her underlying presuppositions. The author also presents her own views on women's roles both then and now.
2002 / 1-84227-055-9 / xxiv + 468pp

July 2005

Robin Parry
Old Testament Story and Christian Ethics
The Rape of Dinah as a Case Study

What is the role of story in ethics and, more particularly, what is the role of Old Testament story in Christian ethics? This book, drawing on the work of contemporary philosophers, argues that narrative is crucial in the ethical shaping of people and, drawing on the work of contemporary Old Testament scholars, that story plays a key role in Old Testament ethics. Parry then argues that when situated in canonical context Old Testament stories can be reappropriated by Christian readers in their own ethical formation. The shocking story of the rape of Dinah and the massacre of the Shechemites provides a fascinating case study for exploring the parameters within which Christian ethical appropriations of Old Testament stories can live.

2004 / 1-84227-210-1 / xx + 350pp

Ian Paul
Power to See the World Anew
The Value of Paul Ricoeur's Hermeneutic of Metaphor in Interpreting the Symbolism of Revelation 12 and 13

This book is a study of the hermeneutics of metaphor of Paul Ricoeur, one of the most important writers on hermeneutics and metaphor of the last century. It sets out the key points of his theory, important criticisms of his work, and how his approach, modified in the light of these criticisms, offers a methodological framework for reading apocalyptic texts.

2006 / 1-84227-056-7 / approx. 350pp

Robert L. Plummer
Paul's Understanding of the Church's Mission
Did the Apostle Paul Expect the Early Christian Communities to Evangelize?

This book engages in a careful study of Paul's letters to determine if the apostle expected the communities to which he wrote to engage in missionary activity. It helpfully summarizes the discussion on this debated issue, judiciously handling contested texts, and provides a way forward in addressing this critical question. While admitting that Paul rarely explicitly commands the communities he founded to evangelize, Plummer amasses significant incidental data to provide a convincing case that Paul did indeed expect his churches to engage in mission activity. Throughout the study, Plummer progressively builds a theological basis for the church's mission that is both distinctively Pauline and compelling.

2006 / 1-84227-333-7 / approx. 324pp

David Powys
'Hell': A Hard Look at a Hard Question
The Fate of the Unrighteous in New Testament Thought
This comprehensive treatment seeks to unlock the original meaning of terms and phrases long thought to support the traditional doctrine of hell. It concludes that there is an alternative—one which is more biblical, and which can positively revive the rationale for Christian mission.
1997 / 0-85364-831-X / xxii + 478pp

Sorin Sabou
Between Horror and Hope
Paul's Metaphorical Language of Death in Romans 6.1-11
This book argues that Paul's metaphorical language of death in Romans 6.1-11 conveys two aspects: horror and hope. The 'horror' aspect is conveyed by the 'crucifixion' language, and the 'hope' aspect by 'burial' language. The life of the Christian believer is understood, as relationship with sin is concerned ('death to sin'), between these two realities: horror and hope.
2005 / 1-84227-322-1 / approx. 224pp

Rosalind Selby
The Comical Doctrine
The Epistemology of New Testament Hermeneutics
This book argues that the gospel breaks through postmodernity's critique of truth and the referential possibilities of textuality with its gift of grace. With a rigorous, philosophical challenge to modernist and postmodernist assumptions, Selby offers an alternative epistemology to all who would still read with faith *and* with academic credibility.
2005 / 1-84227-212-8 / approx. 350pp

Kiwoong Son
Zion Symbolism in Hebrews
Hebrews 12.18-24 as a Hermeneutical Key to the Epistle
This book challenges the general tendency of understanding the Epistle to the Hebrews against a Hellenistic background and suggests that the Epistle should be understood in the light of the Jewish apocalyptic tradition. The author especially argues for the importance of the theological symbolism of Sinai and Zion (Heb. 12:18-24) as it provides the Epistle's theological background as well as the rhetorical basis of the superiority motif of Jesus throughout the Epistle.
2005 / 1-84227-368-X / approx. 280pp

Kevin Walton
Thou Traveller Unknown
The Presence and Absence of God in the Jacob Narrative
The author offers a fresh reading of the story of Jacob in the book of Genesis through the paradox of divine presence and absence. The work also seeks to make a contribution to Pentateuchal studies by bringing together a close reading of the final text with historical critical insights, doing justice to the text's historical depth, final form and canonical status.
2003 / 1-84227-059-1 / xvi + 238pp

George M. Wieland
The Significance of Salvation
A Study of Salvation Language in the Pastoral Epistles
The language and ideas of salvation pervade the three Pastoral Epistles. This study offers a close examination of their soteriological statements. In all three letters the idea of salvation is found to play a vital paraenetic role, but each also exhibits distinctive soteriological emphases. The results challenge common assumptions about the Pastoral Epistles as a corpus.
2005 / 1-84227-257-8 / approx. 324pp

Alistair Wilson
When Will These Things Happen?
A Study of Jesus as Judge in Matthew 21–25
This study seeks to allow Matthew's carefully constructed presentation of Jesus to be given full weight in the modern evaluation of Jesus' eschatology. Careful analysis of the text of Matthew 21–25 reveals Jesus to be standing firmly in the Jewish prophetic and wisdom traditions as he proclaims and enacts imminent judgement on the Jewish authorities then boldly claims the central role in the final and universal judgement.
2004 / 1-84227-146-6 / xxii + 272pp

Lindsay Wilson
Joseph Wise and Otherwise
The Intersection of Covenant and Wisdom in Genesis 37–50
This book offers a careful literary reading of Genesis 37–50 that argues that the Joseph story contains both strong covenant themes and many wisdom-like elements. The connections between the two helps to explore how covenant and wisdom might intersect in an integrated biblical theology.
2004 / 1-84227-140-7 / xvi + 340pp

Stephen I. Wright
The Voice of Jesus
Studies in the Interpretation of Six Gospel Parables
This literary study considers how the 'voice' of Jesus has been heard in different periods of parable interpretation, and how the categories of figure and trope may help us towards a sensitive reading of the parables today.
2000 / 0-85364-975-8 / xiv + 280pp

Paternoster
9 Holdom Avenue,
Bletchley,
Milton Keynes MK1 1QR,
United Kingdom
Web: www.authenticmedia.co.uk/paternoster

Paternoster Theological Monographs

(All titles uniform with this volume)
Dates in bold are of projected publication

Emil Bartos
Deification in Eastern Orthodox Theology
An Evaluation and Critique of the Theology of Dumitru Staniloae
Bartos studies a fundamental yet neglected aspect of Orthodox theology: deification. By examining the doctrines of anthropology, christology, soteriology and ecclesiology as they relate to deification, he provides an important contribution to contemporary dialogue between Eastern and Western theologians.
1999 / 0-85364-956-1 / xii + 370pp

Graham Buxton
The Trinity, Creation and Pastoral Ministry
Imaging the Perichoretic God
In this book the author proposes a three-way conversation between theology, science and pastoral ministry. His approach draws on a Trinitarian understanding of God as a relational being of love, whose life 'spills over' into all created reality, human and non-human. By locating human meaning and purpose within God's 'creation-community' this book offers the possibility of a transforming engagement between those in pastoral ministry and the scientific community.
2005 / 1-84227-369-8 / approx. 380 pp

Iain D. Campbell
Fixing the Indemnity
The Life and Work of George Adam Smith
When Old Testament scholar George Adam Smith (1856–1942) delivered the Lyman Beecher lectures at Yale University in 1899, he confidently declared that 'modern criticism has won its war against traditional theories. It only remains to fix the amount of the indemnity.' In this biography, Iain D. Campbell assesses Smith's critical approach to the Old Testament and evaluates its consequences, showing that Smith's life and work still raises questions about the relationship between biblical scholarship and evangelical faith.
2004 / 1-84227-228-4 / xx + 256pp

Tim Chester
Mission and the Coming of God
Eschatology, the Trinity and Mission in the Theology of Jürgen Moltmann
This book explores the theology and missiology of the influential contemporary theologian, Jürgen Moltmann. It highlights the important contribution Moltmann has made while offering a critique of his thought from an evangelical perspective. In so doing, it touches on pertinent issues for evangelical missiology. The conclusion takes Calvin as a starting point, proposing 'an eschatology of the cross' which offers a critique of the over-realised eschatologies in liberation theology and certain forms of evangelicalism.
2006 / 1-84227-320-5 / approx. 224pp

Sylvia Wilkey Collinson
Making Disciples
The Significance of Jesus' Educational Strategy for Today's Church
This study examines the biblical practice of discipling, formulates a definition, and makes comparisons with modern models of education. A recommendation is made for greater attention to its practice today.
2004 / 1-84227-116-4 / xiv + 278pp

Darrell Cosden
A Theology of Work
Work and the New Creation
Through dialogue with Moltmann, Pope John Paul II and others, this book develops a genitive 'theology of work', presenting a theological definition of work and a model for a theological ethics of work that shows work's nature, value and meaning now and eschatologically. Work is shown to be a transformative activity consisting of three dynamically inter-related dimensions: the instrumental, relational and ontological.
2005 / 1-84227-332-9 / xvi + 208pp

Stephen M. Dunning
The Crisis and the Quest
A Kierkegaardian Reading of Charles Williams
Employing Kierkegaardian categories and analysis, this study investigates both the central crisis in Charles Williams's authorship between hermetism and Christianity (Kierkegaard's Religions A and B), and the quest to resolve this crisis, a quest that ultimately presses the bounds of orthodoxy.
2000 / 0-85364-985-5 / xxiv + 254pp

Keith Ferdinando
The Triumph of Christ in African Perspective
A Study of Demonology and Redemption in the African Context
The book explores the implications of the gospel for traditional African fears of occult aggression. It analyses such traditional approaches to suffering and biblical responses to fears of demonic evil, concluding with an evaluation of African beliefs from the perspective of the gospel.
1999 / 0-85364-830-1 / xviii + 450pp

Andrew Goddard
Living the Word, Resisting the World
The Life and Thought of Jacques Ellul
This work offers a definitive study of both the life and thought of the French Reformed thinker Jacques Ellul (1912-1994). It will prove an indispensable resource for those interested in this influential theologian and sociologist and for Christian ethics and political thought generally.
2002 / 1-84227-053-2 / xxiv + 378pp

David Hilborn
The Words of our Lips
Language-Use in Free Church Worship
Studies of liturgical language have tended to focus on the written canons of Roman Catholic and Anglican communities. By contrast, David Hilborn analyses the more extemporary approach of English Nonconformity. Drawing on recent developments in linguistic pragmatics, he explores similarities and differences between 'fixed' and 'free' worship, and argues for the interdependence of each.
2006 */ 0-85364-977-4 / approx. 350pp*

Roger Hitching
The Church and Deaf People
A Study of Identity, Communication and Relationships with Special Reference to the Ecclesiology of Jürgen Moltmann
In *The Church and Deaf People* Roger Hitching sensitively examines the history and present experience of deaf people and finds similarities between aspects of sign language and Moltmann's theological method that 'open up' new ways of understanding theological concepts.
2003 / 1-84227-222-5 / xxii + 236pp

John G. Kelly
One God, One People
The Differentiated Unity of the People of God in the Theology of Jürgen Moltmann

The author expounds and critiques Moltmann's doctrine of God and highlights the systematic connections between it and Moltmann's influential discussion of Israel. He then proposes a fresh approach to Jewish–Christian relations building on Moltmann's work using insights from Habermas and Rawls.

2005 / 0-85346-969-3 / approx. 350pp

Mark F.W. Lovatt
Confronting the Will-to-Power
A Reconsideration of the Theology of Reinhold Niebuhr

Confronting the Will-to-Power is an analysis of the theology of Reinhold Niebuhr, arguing that his work is an attempt to identify, and provide a practical theological answer to, the existence and nature of human evil.

2001 / 1-84227-054-0 / xviii + 216pp

Neil B. MacDonald
Karl Barth and the Strange New World within the Bible
Barth, Wittgenstein, and the Metadilemmas of the Enlightenment

Barth's discovery of the strange new world within the Bible is examined in the context of Kant, Hume, Overbeck, and, most importantly, Wittgenstein. MacDonald covers some fundamental issues in theology today: epistemology, the final form of the text and biblical truth-claims.

2000 / 0-85364-970-7 / xxvi + 374pp

Keith A. Mascord
Alvin Plantinga and Christian Apologetics

This book draws together the contributions of the philosopher Alvin Plantinga to the major contemporary challenges to Christian belief, highlighting in particular his ground-breaking work in epistemology and the problem of evil. Plantinga's theory that both theistic and Christian belief is warrantedly basic is explored and critiqued, and an assessment offered as to the significance of his work for apologetic theory and practice.

2005 / 1-84227-256-X / approx. 304pp

Gillian McCulloch
The Deconstruction of Dualism in Theology
With Reference to Ecofeminist Theology and New Age Spirituality
This book challenges eco-theological anti-dualism in Christian theology, arguing that dualism has a twofold function in Christian religious discourse. Firstly, it enables us to express the discontinuities and divisions that are part of the process of reality. Secondly, dualistic language allows us to express the mysteries of divine transcendence/immanence and the survival of the soul without collapsing into monism and materialism, both of which are problematic for Christian epistemology.
2002 / 1-84227-044-3 / xii + 282pp

Leslie McCurdy
Attributes and Atonement
The Holy Love of God in the Theology of P.T. Forsyth
Attributes and Atonement is an intriguing full-length study of P.T. Forsyth's doctrine of the cross as it relates particularly to God's holy love. It includes an unparalleled bibliography of both primary and secondary material relating to Forsyth.
1999 / 0-85364-833-6 / xiv + 328pp

Nozomu Miyahira
Towards a Theology of the Concord of God
A Japanese Perspective on the Trinity
This book introduces a new Japanese theology and a unique Trinitarian formula based on the Japanese intellectual climate: three betweennesses and one concord. It also presents a new interpretation of the Trinity, a co-subordinationism, which is in line with orthodox Trinitarianism; each single person of the Trinity is eternally and equally subordinate (or serviceable) to the other persons, so that they retain the mutual dynamic equality.
2000 / 0-85364-863-8 / xiv + 256pp

Eddy José Muskus
The Origins and Early Development of Liberation Theology in Latin America
With Particular Reference to Gustavo Gutiérrez
This work challenges the fundamental premise of Liberation Theology, 'opting for the poor', and its claim that Christ is found in them. It also argues that Liberation Theology emerged as a direct result of the failure of the Roman Catholic Church in Latin America.
2002 / 0-85364-974-X / xiv + 296pp

Jim Purves
The Triune God and the Charismatic Movement
A Critical Appraisal from a Scottish Perspective

All emotion and no theology? Or a fundamental challenge to reappraise and realign our trinitarian theology in the light of Christian experience? This study of charismatic renewal as it found expression within Scotland at the end of the twentieth century evaluates the use of Patristic, Reformed and contemporary models of the Trinity in explaining the workings of the Holy Spirit.

2004 / 1-84227-321-3 / xxiv + 246pp

Anna Robbins
Methods in the Madness
Diversity in Twentieth-Century Christian Social Ethics

The author compares the ethical methods of Walter Rauschenbusch, Reinhold Niebuhr and others. She argues that unless Christians are clear about the ways that theology and philosophy are expressed practically they may lose the ability to discuss social ethics across contexts, let alone reach effective agreements.

2004 / 1-84227-211-X / xx + 294pp

Ed Rybarczyk
Beyond Salvation
Eastern Orthodoxy and Classical Pentecostalism on Becoming Like Christ

At first glance eastern Orthodoxy and classical Pentecostalism seem quite distinct. This ground-breaking study shows they share much in common, especially as it concerns the experiential elements of following Christ. Both traditions assert that authentic Christianity transcends the wooden categories of modernism.

2004 / 1-84227-144-X / xii + 356pp

Signe Sandsmark
Is World View Neutral Education Possible and Desirable?
A Christian Response to Liberal Arguments
(Published jointly with The Stapleford Centre)

This book discusses reasons for belief in world view neutrality, and argues that 'neutral' education will have a hidden, but strong world view influence. It discusses the place for Christian education in the common school.

2000 / 0-85364-973-1 / xiv + 182pp

Hazel Sherman
Reading Zechariah
The Allegorical Tradition of Biblical Interpretation through the Commentary of Didymus the Blind and Theodore of Mopsuestia
A close reading of the commentary on Zechariah by Didymus the Blind alongside that of Theodore of Mopsuestia suggests that popular categorising of Antiochene and Alexandrian biblical exegesis as 'historical' or 'allegorical' is inadequate and misleading.
2005 / 1-84227-213-6 / approx. 280pp

Andrew Sloane
On Being a Christian in the Academy
Nicholas Wolterstorff and the Practice of Christian Scholarship
An exposition and critical appraisal of Nicholas Wolterstorff's epistemology in the light of the philosophy of science, and an application of his thought to the practice of Christian scholarship.
2003 / 1-84227-058-3 / xvi + 274pp

Damon W.K. So
Jesus' Revelation of His Father
A Narrative-Conceptual Study of the Trinity with Special Reference to Karl Barth
This book explores the trinitarian dynamics in the context of Jesus' revelation of his Father in his earthly ministry with references to key passages in Matthew's Gospel. It develops from the exegeses of these passages a non-linear concept of revelation which links Jesus' communion with his Father to his revelatory words and actions through a nuanced understanding of the Holy Spirit, with references to K. Barth, G.W.H. Lampe, J.D.G. Dunn and E. Irving.
2005 / 1-84227-323-X / approx. 380pp

Daniel Strange
The Possibility of Salvation Among the Unevangelised
An Analysis of Inclusivism in Recent Evangelical Theology
For evangelical theologians the 'fate of the unevangelised' impinges upon fundamental tenets of evangelical identity. The position known as 'inclusivism', defined by the belief that the unevangelised can be ontologically saved by Christ whilst being epistemologically unaware of him, has been defended most vigorously by the Canadian evangelical Clark H. Pinnock. Through a detailed analysis and critique of Pinnock's work, this book examines a cluster of issues surrounding the unevangelised and its implications for christology, soteriology and the doctrine of revelation.
2002 / 1-84227-047-8 / xviii + 362pp

Scott Swain
God According to the Gospel
Biblical Narrative and the Identity of God in the Theology of Robert W. Jenson
Robert W. Jenson is one of the leading voices in contemporary Trinitarian theology. His boldest contribution in this area concerns his use of biblical narrative both to ground and explicate the Christian doctrine of God. *God According to the Gospel* critically examines Jenson's proposal and suggests an alternative way of reading the biblical portrayal of the triune God.
2006 / 1-84227-258-6 / approx. 180pp

Justyn Terry
The Justifying Judgement of God
A Reassessment of the Place of Judgement in the Saving Work of Christ
The argument of this book is that judgement, understood as the whole process of bringing justice, is the primary metaphor of atonement, with others, such as victory, redemption and sacrifice, subordinate to it. Judgement also provides the proper context for understanding penal substitution and the call to repentance, baptism, eucharist and holiness.
2005 / 1-84227-370-1 / approx. 274 pp

Graham Tomlin
The Power of the Cross
Theology and the Death of Christ in Paul, Luther and Pascal
This book explores the theology of the cross in St Paul, Luther and Pascal. It offers new perspectives on the theology of each, and some implications for the nature of power, apologetics, theology and church life in a postmodern context.
1999 / 0-85364-984-7 / xiv + 344pp

Adonis Vidu
Postliberal Theological Method
A Critical Study
The postliberal theology of Hans Frei, George Lindbeck, Ronald Thiemann, John Milbank and others is one of the more influential contemporary options. This book focuses on several aspects pertaining to its theological method, specifically its understanding of background, hermeneutics, epistemic justification, ontology, the nature of doctrine and, finally, Christological method.
2005 / 1-84227-395-7 / approx. 324pp

Graham J. Watts
Revelation and the Spirit
A Comparative Study of the Relationship between the Doctrine of Revelation and Pneumatology in the Theology of Eberhard Jüngel and of Wolfhart Pannenberg

The relationship between revelation and pneumatology is relatively unexplored. This approach offers a fresh angle on two important twentieth century theologians and raises pneumatological questions which are theologically crucial and relevant to mission in a postmodern culture.

2005 / 1-84227-104-0 / xxii + 232pp

Nigel G. Wright
Disavowing Constantine
Mission, Church and the Social Order in the Theologies of John Howard Yoder and Jürgen Moltmann

This book is a timely restatement of a radical theology of church and state in the Anabaptist and Baptist tradition. Dr Wright constructs his argument in dialogue and debate with Yoder and Moltmann, major contributors to a free church perspective.

2000 / 0-85364-978-2 / xvi + 252pp

Paternoster
9 Holdom Avenue,
Bletchley,
Milton Keynes MK1 1QR,
United Kingdom
Web: www.authenticmedia.co.uk/paternoster

www.ingramcontent.com/pod-product-compliance
Lightning Source LLC
Chambersburg PA
CBHW070059020526
44112CB00034B/1649